# Consumer Culture and the Making of Modern Jewish Identity

Antisemitic stereotypes of Jews as capitalists have hindered research into the economic dimension of the Jewish past. The figure of the Jew as trader and financier dominated the nineteenth and twentieth centuries. But the economy has been central to Jewish life and the Jewish image in the world; Jews not only made money but also spent money. This book is the first to investigate the intersection between consumption, identity, and Jewish history in Europe. It aims to examine the role and place of consumption within Jewish society and the ways consumerism generated and reinforced Jewish notions of belonging from the end of the eighteenth century to the beginning of the new millennium. It shows how the advances of modernization and secularization in the modern period increased the importance of consumption in Jewish life, making it a significant factor in the process of redefining Jewish identity.

Gideon Reuveni is Reader in History and Director of the Centre for German-Jewish studies at the University of Sussex, UK. His central research and teaching interest is the cultural and social history of modern European and Jewish history.

# Consumer Culture and the Making of Modern Jewish Identity

GIDEON REUVENI

*University of Sussex, UK*

CAMBRIDGE
UNIVERSITY PRESS

# CAMBRIDGE
## UNIVERSITY PRESS

University Printing House, Cambridge CB2 8BS, United Kingdom

One Liberty Plaza, 20th Floor, New York, NY 10006, USA

477 Williamstown Road, Port Melbourne, VIC 3207, Australia

4843/24, 2nd Floor, Ansari Road, Daryaganj, Delhi – 110002, India

79 Anson Road, #06–04/06, Singapore 079906

Cambridge University Press is part of the University of Cambridge.

It furthers the University's mission by disseminating knowledge in the pursuit of education, learning, and research at the highest international levels of excellence.

www.cambridge.org
Information on this title: www.cambridge.org/9781107011304
DOI: 10.1017/9780511894893

© Gideon Reuveni 2017

First published 2017

Printed in the United States of America by Sheridan Books, Inc.

A catalogue record for this publication is available from the British Library.

ISBN 978-1-107-01130-4 Hardback
ISBN 978-1-107-64850-0 Paperback

# Contents

*List of Figures*                                                    *page* vii
*Preface*                                                                    ix
*Acknowledgments*                                                          xix

### PART I  NARRATIVES OF BELONGING

1   Producers, Consumers, Jews, and Antisemitism in German
    Historiography                                                          3
2   Ethnic Marketing and Consumer Ambivalence in Weimar
    Germany                                                                25
3   The Jewish Question and Changing Regimes of
    Consumption                                                            66
4   What Makes a Jew Happy? Longings, Belongings, and the
    Spirit of Modern Consumerism                                           82

### PART II  THE POLITICS OF JEWISH CONSUMPTION

5   Emancipation through Consumption                                      105
6   Boycott, Economic Rationality, and Jewish Consumers in
    Interwar Germany                                                      122
7   Advertising National Belonging                                        144
8   The Consumption of Jewish Politics                                    153

### PART III  HOMO JUDAICUS CONSUMENS

9   The Cost of Being Jewish                                              175
10  Place and Space of Jewish Consumption                                 190
11  The World of Jewish Goods                                             203

12    Spending Power and Its Discontents                          218
13    Beyond Consumerism: The Bridge, the Door,
      and the Cultural Economy Approach to Jewish History         234

*Index*                                                          251

# Figures

2.1   Mercedes-Benz advertisement                    *page* 31

2.2   Ad for Kosher Products at the Tietz Department Store
      in Berlin                                     34

2.3   Two Advertisement Stamps for Tomor Margarine with
      Painting by Moritz Daniel Oppenheim        35

2.4   The HAG Ad for the Jewish Press            38

2.5   "Antisemitic tendencies"                 41

2.6   Kunerol Ad for Kosher Margarine with Star of David     44

2.7   "No advert without the Mogen Dovid"          45

2.8   Two Examples of Advertising Material for the Convention
      of the German Innkeeper Association          46

2.9   Mystikum Products with Hexagram Logo        47

2.10  Example of the Visibility of the *Bulgaria's* Logo
      on the Streets of Dresden                 49

2.11  Advertising Poster for *Bulgaria* Cigarettes Featuring the
      Hamburg Sport Club Football Players (Hamburger SV)     51

2.12  A *Bulgaria* Cigarettes Advert from the *Völkischer
      Beobachter*, March 25, 1932                52

2.13  Advertisements Collage                   58

2.14  "A beautiful holiday brings pleasure and relaxation,"
      An Advertisement for the Flower Shop Hanisch in Leipzig   64

3.1   Mazola Oil                            73

6.1   "Correction"                        135

6.2   "Recommendable summer and bath resort"      137

7.1   Marok-Präparate Ad                 146

7.2   Ad for Stollwerck Chocolate. The Slogan Says: " 10 minutes
      rest – take Stollwerck gold out!"           147

7.3 Ad for Fry's Cocoa on the title page of "The Jewish Chronicle" Showing a Child Running with a Gun 148

7.4 Dr. Oetker's Call to German Housewives Not to Buy English Products 149

7.5 Palmin Margarine Advert Containing Explicit Racial References 151

8.1 An Advertisement Calling Readers of the *CV-Zeitung* to Obtain Boeson-Fruchtsaltz, before Coming to the *Centralverein* General Assembly 154

8.2 The Jewish Wine War: Palwin vs. Bozwin 159

8.3 Adverts for Phönix Life Insurance 168

9.1 An Advert of the Frankfurt Branch of the Carsch Department Store 176

12.1 Captain Webber's Organization Boycott Campaign Certificates 231

12.2 "Stop Persecution. Boycott German Goods. Buy British" 232

# Preface

"Three thousand ducats." With these words, a figure uniting all that seems repellent about Jews was presented on the world stage. Shylock, the money-hungry Christian-hating usurer of William Shakespeare's *The Merchant of Venice*, has contributed to the stigmatization of the Jews for centuries.[1] As Shakespeare was writing his play in the late sixteenth century, there were hardly any Jews remaining in England, much less Jewish moneylenders. But it was at this time that the old prejudice linking Jews and money began to receive new significance. Above all, it is in the confrontation between Shylock and Antonio, the actual merchant of Venice, that it becomes clear that it is not the traditional prohibition against money lending that is at issue. Instead, Shakespeare is dramatizing the conflict between two different economic systems.[2] Shylock's business practices differ sharply from Antonio's almost chivalric money dealings. Shylock, a product of a then new urban economic nexus, despises Antonio not only because he is a Christian but because "he lends out money gratis and brings down the rate of usance [. . .] in Venice."[3] Even so, Shylock still admits that "Antonio is a good man." There is no contradiction in this, and it is not to be understood as a moral double standard. In response to

---

[1] Dietrich Schwanitz, *Das Schylock Syndrom oder die Dramaturgie der Barbarei* (Frankfurt a.M: Eichborn, 1997).

[2] Bernard Grebanier, *The Truth about Shylock* (New York: Random Hause, 1962); Martin D. Yaffe, *Shylock and the Jewish Question* (Baltimore: The John Hopkins University Press, 1997); Benjamin Nelson, *The Idea of Usury. From Tribal Brotherhood to Universal Otherhood* (Chicago: The University of Chicago Press, 1969).

[3] All quotes are from William Shakespeare, The Merchant of Venice, available on Project Gutenberg www.gutenberg.org/cache/epub/2243/pg2243.html (February 11, 2017).

the question whether he heard any imputation to the contrary, Shylock explains: "Oh, no, no, no, no: my meaning in saying he is a good man is to have you understand me that he is sufficient." In the world of the financier Shylock, the terms "good" and "bad" are no longer understood as moral concepts; rather, they are used simply as economic categories. In this way, Shakespeare makes us aware of a developing confrontation of his period. The economy was rapidly evolving from a system dominated by barter into a currency-credit system. Shylock is the embodiment of a new value system and economic order that is subjugated to the ethos of individual investment for the sake of profit, which we commonly identify with modern capitalism.[4]

The image of the Jew as a capitalist or precapitalist prototype is deeply anchored in Western consciousness.[5] Both supporters and critics of the capitalist market economy, Jews and non-Jews, share this viewpoint. Even studies of the economic aspects of Jewish life, to a remarkable degree, find it difficult to shy away from the figure of the Jew as trader and financier. What is common to most of these discussions is that they conceive Jews first and foremost as moneymakers, overlooking the no less important dimension of Jews as money spenders.

This book developed from my uneven attempts to move away from this image of the capitalist (predominantly male) Jew and to call attention to the significance of spending – rather than gaining – in the process of redefining Jewishness in the modern period. Being Jewish has always been interconnected with consumption. Jewish dietary requirements, dress prescriptions, as well as the use of special objects for ritual purposes are just a few examples of how Judaism delineates consumer practices as markers of distinction. More often than not, Jewish rabbinical authorities have called upon Jews not to forgo their Jewishness when doing their shopping. Rules and regulations for buying and selling according to Jewish traditions have been prominent features in responsa and other rabbinic literature. Here we find questions regarding apposite Jewish lifestyle as well as the permissibility of specific products for Jewish use, for example, tomatoes or margarine, which were strictly forbidden for observant Jews until the start of the twentieth century. Rabbinic and community authorities urged Jews to display moderation on the marketplace, warning against the devastating implications of ostentatious consumption

---

[4] Joyce Appleby, *The Relentless Revolution: A History of Capitalism* (New York: W.W. Norton, 2010), 3–27.
[5] David Nirenberg, *Anti-Judaism: The Western Tradition* (New York: W.W. Norton, 2013).

for Jewish life. Some rabbis urged Jews to be more aware of the origin of the goods they purchased. Thus, for example, Samson Raphael Hirsch (1808–1888), one of the leading orthodox rabbinical authorities in nineteenth-century Germany, proclaimed in 1831 that Jews must not buy goods if their origin is unclear, because they might be stolen. That is why he recommended that Jews should not buy things from "a shepherd, a watchman, a man hired by the day or a craftsman, if it is usual for them to steal such things entrusted to their care."[6] Hirsch allowed the purchase of goods from women, servants, and children only if one could safely establish that they were the owners of the property.

Keeping a Jewish way of life has thus been not merely a matter of religious confession or a form of group or ethnic affiliation. It has also involved a distinctive relationship to various material objects. Such practices require a suitable and supportive infrastructure and commonly involve additional expense for those individuals who wish to live according to Jewish ways. But even for those Jews who don't actively practice religious Judaism, spending seems to have comprised a significant part of how their Jewishness was perceived and enacted.

By the turn of the twentieth century, the promotion of specific products to Jewish consumers had become an integral part of the marketing strategies of many Jewish and non-Jewish producers and retailers in Europe and across the Atlantic. Before the Great War, for example, one of the largest food manufacturers in Europe, which was owned by the Van den Berghs – a Jewish family from the Netherlands – mass-produced a kosher margarine called *Tomor* for consumers across Europe. Recognizing the special dietary requirements of Orthodox Jews, Van den Bergh promoted *Tomor* as a kosher substitute for butter to meet the needs of kosher households. At the same time, the brand sought to strengthen Jewish identity among what it considered as the growing number of assimilated Jews. Van den Bergh was not the only large-scale producer who acknowledged the existence of a Jewish market. In fact, all over Europe, Jewish and non-Jewish manufacturers produced special products for Jews. Well-known corporations such as Nestlé (Switzerland), Dr. Oetker (Germany), Kaffee Hag (Germany), J. S. Fry & Sons chocolate company (England), Jelen-Schicht soap manufacturer (Austrian/Czech), and Carmel wine (Palestine) launched special campaigns to attract Jewish consumers,

---

[6] Samson Raphael Hirsch, *Horev, oder Versuche über Iissroéls Pflichten in der Zerstreuung, zunächst für Iissroéls denkende Jünglinge und Jungfrauen* (Altona: Johann Friedrich Hammerich, 1837), 305–306.

presenting their goods as particularly suitable for Jewish households. This tendency was not confined to the realm of food consumption but entailed, for example, musical recordings and picture postcards featuring synagogues, historical sites, and rabbinical luminaries. Shipping companies such as Lloyd and Hamburg-Amerika-Linie, insurance businesses such as Allianz (Germany) and Phönix Life (Austria), and hotels and recreation resorts all over Europe advertised their services to Jewish consumers. By the early twentieth century, Jewish consumerism had become a crucial part of the Jewish experience, refashioning a Jewish sense of belonging in modern societies.

Only recently have scholars begun to acknowledge the crucial and neglected axis of consumption, identity, and Jewish history. Most notable are works by Andrew R. Heinze, Jenna Weissman Joselit, Marilyn Halter, and Elizabeth H. Pleckon on the role of consumption among Jewish immigrants in America.[7] These studies portray consumption as a crucial vehicle for the integration of Jewish newcomers, yet at the same time they also highlight the significance of consumption as an instrument to preserve and maintain a distinct Jewish sphere in America. Given the importance of consumption in the American way of life, these studies posit that Jews encountered modern consumer culture for the first time in the New World. As this study will demonstrate, this was far from being the case. Jews were already exposed to the new consumer culture in their European countries of origin to such an extent that part of the appeal of America was a result of consumer fantasies about a more comfortable and happy life that Jews already possessed before immigrating.

Leora Auslander's work on the aesthetics of everyday life among Jews in interwar Berlin and Paris is the most substantial published work on Jewish consumer culture in Europe.[8] By exploring lists of personal belongings that were put together by Nazi officials in the process of

---

[7] Andrew R. Heinze, *Adapting to Abundance: Jewish Immigrants, Mass Consumption, and the Search for American Identity* (New York: Columbia University Press, 1990); Jenna Weissman Joselit, *The Wonders of America: Reinventing Jewish Culture 1880–1950* (New York, 1994); Marilyn Halter, *Shopping for Identity: The Marketing of Ethnicity* (New York, 2000); Elizabeth Hafkin Pleck, *Celebrating the Family: Ethnicity, Consumer Culture, and Family Rituals* (Cambridge, MA: Harvard University Press, 2000).

[8] Leora Auslander, "'Jewish Taste'? Jews, and the Aesthetics of Everyday Life in Paris and Berlin, 1933–1942," in: Rudy Koshar (ed.), *Histories of Leisure* (Oxford: Berg, 2002), 299–331; ibid., "Beyond Words," *The American Historical Review* 110 (2005), 1015–1045; ibid., "Reading German Jewry through Vernacular Photography: From the Kaiserreich to the Third Reich," *Photography and Twentieth-Century German History* 48 (3) (2015), 300–334.

Aryanization, Auslander reconstructs the households of Jewish families in these cities. She finds sizeable differences between the households of Berlin Jews and Parisian Jews, suggesting that in matters of taste there was more in common between these Jews and their non-Jewish environment in each city than between the Jewish communities themselves. Her findings are extremely interesting as they demonstrate how embedded Jews were in their host societies, implying that we should reconsider recent trends in Jewish studies that conceptualize the Jewish past increasingly as a transnational history.

In recent years, we witness a growing interest of research in the involvement of Jews in consumer-oriented trades. Fascinating work on Jews and the department stores, the fashion industry, and retailing business have provided new and important insights on the place of Jews in the emergence of modern consumer culture in Europe and beyond since the mid-nineteenth century.[9] These works, to a large degree, are still preoccupied with Jews mainly as sellers of commodities rather than as consumers of goods. Auslander's pioneering work on Jewish taste in European society, notwithstanding, most research on Jewish consumption sidelines the multifaceted nature of consumption as social and cultural practice, and especially consumption as a means of establishing differences between individuals and groups. It is the purpose of this study to redress this imbalance by showing that consumption was used not only as a vehicle of integration but also as a way to mark out and maintain distinctions between Jews and other moderns. The thirteen chapters of this book will thus seek to demonstrate that it is this interplay between seemingly contradictory processes that determined and shaped the modern Jewish experience.

The work of Pierre Bourdieu provides a framework to conceptualize the cultural meaning of consumption without either collapsing consumer culture into an abstract process of homogenization or reducing it to a reflection of the preexisting social order.[10] The key term for understanding this

---

[9] Just to name here a few of the more recent studies: Paul Lerner, *The Consuming Temple: Jews, Department Stores and The Consumer Revolution in Germany* (Ithaca, NY: Cornell University Press, 2015); Gesa Kessemeier, *Ein Feentempel der Mode oder Eine vergessene Familie, ein ausgelöschter Ort: Die Familie Freudenberg und das Modehaus "Herrmann Gerson"* (Berlin: Hentrich & Hentrich, 2013); Christoph Kreutzmüller, *Final Sale in Berlin: The Destruction of Jewish Commercial Activity, 1930–1945* (New York: Berghahn, 2015).

[10] Pierre Bourdieu, *Distinction: A Social Critique of the Judgment of Taste* (Cambridge, MA: Harvard University Press, 1984).

social process is "distinction," a term that captures both the sense of classificatory schemes by which people distinguish between things and the use of these things and their meaning to achieve distinction within social relations. According to Bourdieu, this multifaceted process of classification does not simply imply difference, but is also used to establish hierarchy between groups, socioeconomic classes in particular. This book will seek to employ Bourdieu's approach to other groups as well and investigate how consumption helped to create and maintain multifaceted identities beyond the social hierarchy of the class society. It will thus underpin social agency, but will also explore Jewish consumer experiences using Jean Baudrillard's work on the blurring of the relationship between production and consumption in modern times. For Baudrillard, what distinguishes modern consumer capitalism is that it does not only produce goods but also engages in the production of consumers. This shift toward the production of consumers, according to Baudrillard, helped to create a new "postmodern" order in which social reality is no longer defined by either production or consumption, but by the simulation of both.[11] By focusing on the ways and forms in which a Jewish consumer market was identified and bolstered, the following study will seek to historicize Baudrillard's postulation.

The method of investigation employed in this book therefore has a dual function. It seeks, first, to examine how Jews were perceived and targeted as consumers. And, second, it investigates the role consumer culture played in Jewish life. The sources that will be used for this purpose are visual and printed representations, ranging from advertisements, material on marketing strategies by commercial companies, published scholarly work, as well as diaries, memories, and literary representations. This diverse body of sources was found in archival and special collections in a variety of locations in Germany, Israel, England, and the USA. The study itself is divided into three parts, each consisting of four chapters analyzing several distinct conceptual dimensions of the interplay between consumerism and the question of Jewish belonging. The main focus of this exploration will be Germany in the period between the two world wars. Yet, given the somewhat fragmentary state of the sources and the cultural approach to the topic, this investigation can only be partially confined in time and space. Depending on the topic studied, the discussion will at times branch out from the German interwar context in order to provide a more comprehensive picture of the role spending played in modern Jewish history.

---

[11] Jean Baudrillard, *In the Shadow of Silent Majority* (New York: Semiotex(e), 1983), 27.

The first part of the book will seek to explore how consumer culture could inspire new readings of the Jewish past. By juxtaposing the different narratives regarding Jews in pre-1933 Germany, Chapter 1 will show how a so-called consumerist perspective on the Jewish experience could move research beyond sterile binary divisions that tend to oscillate between approaches stressing inclusion of Jews and those highlighting their exclusion. Chapter 2 will explore products and services that were promoted to Jewish consumers. Examining the advertisements as well as other marketing strategies designed to allure Jewish consumers will serve as a backdrop for the discussion of the multifaceted relationship between processes of integration and practices that facilitated a sense of distinct Jewish sphere in the special period before the Nazi takeover. Moving from the Old Continent to Jewish communities that had emigrated from Europe to the United States, Chapter 3 will suggest that in different settings, particularly settler societies, consumer culture seems to occupy a more significant position in the social process than in societies that evolved based on the ethos of common origin. Underlining the examination of the Jewish experience in different regions of modernity is the question of whether Jews as individuals or as a community are able to integrate. Historically, the question of Jewish "compatibility" with modernity has given rise to a further, and no less fundamental, question regarding the "nature" of Jewish difference. An exploration of these questions will demonstrate that whereas historically Jews have struggled to combine their distinctiveness with the demand for political and social emancipation, since the Holocaust the very notion of Jewish difference, at least in the United States, has been undermined and as a result more than ever before Jews are preoccupied with the question of how to retain their identity. In this context, Israel seems to comprise a distinct regime of consumption. While initially consumption in the Jewish state served as an integral part of nation-building, in more recent times, consumerism has come to denote a longing to dissolve Israel's "special situation," and thus to become a society like all other (consumer) societies. It is an irony of history that while the Zionist topos of "normalization" is still prevalent in Israel today, it does not have the same political connotations as in the past, and is now overtly associated with consumer culture and the quest for a happy and comfortable life. The notion of happiness will be the topic of the final chapter of this section.

Indeed, consumption is not only about identity and the struggle to define and negotiate different notions of belonging. It also represents the wish to maximize pleasure and gain happiness. Chapter 4 will thus discuss different notions of Jewish happiness and will call attention to the much-neglected issue of Jewish economic sensibilities, especially as they pertain to questions of spending. After examining some of the major debates concerning the nature and place of happiness in Jewish traditional sources, this chapter will analyze conceptions of happiness using Jewish humor as its main source. This discussion will show that Jewish notions of happiness did not differ substantially from other meanings of happiness prevalent at the time. Yet, such similarities notwithstanding, it will be argued, a particularly "Jewish" pursuit of happiness can be identified. The quest for a more comfortable and pleasant life provided Jews simultaneously with a means of envisioning their cultural belonging and helped to maintain a sense of Jewish distinctiveness by appropriating a distinct ethos of spending as Jews.

The second part of the book will discuss the relationship between consumption and politics in the context of modern Jewish political movements. Starting at the end of the eighteenth century with debates over Jewish emancipation, the four chapters of this section will examine both the politicization of consumption and the commercialization of Jewish politics. Chapter 5 will explore the interaction between civil rights and consumption in the struggle for Jewish emancipation. This chapter will explore how the language of free enterprise and consumer choice was part of an effort to imagine and constitute a new phase in Jewish history epitomized by political recognition and social integration. The politicization of consumption as a result of nationalism and antisemitism in pre-Holocaust Europe will comprise the focus of the following two chapters.

In recent years, a number of innovative studies have been published on antisemitism and the marketplace. Most of this research deals with calls to boycott businesses owned by Jews as well as the official means by which Jewish organizations counter such efforts. Much less is known about how Jews as consumers reacted to Jewish exclusion in the marketplace. Chapter 6 will redress this imbalance by discussing the efforts to make Jews and other consumers more conscious of their purchasing power. This exploration will demonstrate how in the interwar period politics informed consumer choices, turning consumption into a highly charged activity. With Chapter 7 we will move away from antisemitism to a brief discussion of how, especially during the Great War, national sentiments became a powerful marketing device turning consumption to a new site of political mobilization. Exploring how Jewish political parties – particularly the Zionist movement – utilized consumption in order to promote their political agendas will comprise the focus of the final chapter of this section. Here we will see how politics became ever more commercialized. Looking at the Zionist political campaigns, we see that they were grounded in marketing principles such as the branding of political leaders and issues, targeted advertising, and staged media events. With its sophisticated marketing array, the Zionist movement sought to gain political as well as economic capital from the marketplace.

While the first two parts of the book mainly deal with the question of how Jews were conceived and targeted as a discrete group of consumers, the third and final section of the book will seek to explore Jewish perceptions of the question of spending and to give voice to the experiences of Jews as consumers. Based mainly on diaries, memories, and lists of household possessions, the four chapters of this section will deal with questions regarding the costs of being Jewish, the geography of Jewish spending, the world of Jewish goods, as well as the efforts to control and tame Jewish consumers. Gender played a crucial role in these discussions and will also comprise a central thread in the attempt to portray the *Homo Judaicus Consumens*, a term that draws on Joachim Prinz's idea of the strong interlinkedness between Jewishness and humanity in the modern age.[12] Exploring Jewish spending will thus demonstrate how consumer choices constitute a type of "cultural positioning" by which different goods and services took on a Jewish meaning. Taken together, these chapters demonstrate the close interaction between the idea of identity and modernity.

The final and concluding chapter of the book will move beyond consumerism to explore how a cultural economy approach to Jewish history could advance our understanding of the Jewish experience of modern times. Thus, instead of viewing the economy as an ontological (and preexisting) "other" to culture, this chapter will propose that economic activities be considered performative acts embedded within normative institutional frameworks and cultural practices. This approach maintains that the coherence of any economy as well its ability to function depends on the aptitude of people to interact with each other, to formulate values and norms, and to share symbolic representations. The potential of this so-called cultural economy approach to Jewish history will have become evident in previous sections of the book and will be demonstrated with

---

[12] Joachim Prinz, *The Dilemma of the Modern Jew* (Boston: Little, Brown and Company, 1962), 200–201.

further examples, proffering novel ways of integrating cultural history into economic history and vice versa.

It should be emphasized that there is nothing definitive in this study. My concerns here are to a large extent heuristic and my conclusions are still provisional. The book contains some obvious omissions, too. Above all, more should have been said on the actual spending habits of Jewish families in the prewar periods. Such information is available in household account books that could be found in different archives and in private possession. Collecting and processing such data is an important task that should be taken in a separate study. The question of how Jews responded to the promotional campaigns aimed at them is another topic that could only be partially addressed in this study, as well as the conspicuous involvement of pioneering Jews in the advertising industry.[13] The realm of Jewish consumer culture is so large and its history so little known that this book has done scarcely more than set out some preliminary markers that will hopefully facilitate the way for more detailed investigations of this important field of historical inquiry.

---

[13] For a recent stimulating study on the involvement of Jews in the American advertisement industry, see Kerri P. Steinberg, *Jewish Mad Men: Advertising and the Design of the American Jewish Experience* (New Brunswick, NJ: Rutgers University Press, 2015).

# Acknowledgments

It has taken quite some time for this book to emerge. As it was in the making in so many places across the globe for so long, I have accumulated considerable debts to a number of individuals and institutions that have helped shape my work along the way. I owe thanks not only for the support and kindness I have received over the years but also for the constancy and encouragement I needed to bring this research to fruition. Work on this book initially started when I was working with Michael Brenner, Nils Römer, and Anthony Kauders on a Jewish historiography project in Munich. I would like to thank Michael for inviting me to join the historiography project, which was an excellent starting point for me to think about Jews and consumer culture. Together with Nils Römer, I organized the first conference on Jews and consumption in 2006 in London. Over the years, Anthony Kauders read various sections of the book and I would like to thank him again for his invaluable support and wise advice. While still in Munich, I received a postdoc fellowship from the Rothschild Foundation Europe. This award allowed me to conduct the initial research on which the book is based.

At the beginning of 2007, I moved to Melbourne, Australia, with my family. At the University of Melbourne, I was fortunate enough to find myself in an environment that was both nurturing and supportive. In Melbourne, with Catherine Kovesi and Antonia Finnane I cofounded the *Cultural History of Economies Research Hub*, which became a meeting place for an interdisciplinary group of scholars who were interested in developing a cultural approach to the study of economies. I particularly benefited from my conversations with Antonia, Jackie Dickenson, Michael Hau, Helen Davies, and Ian Coller. The University of Melbourne also granted me an Early Career Research Award, with which I was able to travel to Israel and Germany to continue my research.

At the beginning of 2009, I was awarded a fellowship at the Herbert D. Katz Center for Advanced Judaic Studies, Philadelphia. This award provided me with the opportunity to work with a group of colleagues on different aspects of what one can broadly define as Jewish economic history. The three months I spent in Philadelphia boosted my research significantly. I would like to use this opportunity to thank David Ruderman for inviting me to the Katz Center. I can't name all the colleagues that assisted me during that year in Philadelphia, but would like to thank them all for discussing and sharing ideas with me. At the beginning of 2010, I was invited to the Kulturwissenschaftliches Kolleg, Konstanz as a visiting fellow and at the end of that year I became fellow at the Alfried Krupp Wissenschaftskolleg, Greifswald. Large sections of this book were written during my fellowships in these great institutions and the support I received was invaluable to the advance of my work.

Since September 2011, I have been working at the University of Sussex as director of the Centre for German-Jewish Studies. Here I have found a stimulating and hospitable environment that has helped me to bring this study to publication. I would like to thank all my colleagues at Sussex for their encouragement and support. I am in particular debt to Rachael Attwood (presently at the University of Westminster), Paul Betts (now in Oxford University), Saul Dubow (since the end of 2016 in Cambridge University), Daniel Kane, Claudia Siebrecht, Björn Siegel (now back in Hamburg), Kim Wünschmann, and above all Gerhard Wolf. I am also grateful to Diana Franklin and the members of the Centre for German-Jewish Studies London-based support group for their advice and encouragement.

Over the past few years, I have presented sections of this book in conferences and at talks in Australia, England, Germany, Israel, and the United States. On these occasions, I have been particularly privileged to meet and make friendships with colleagues whose work has had significant influence on my own. Leora Auslander, David Biale, Jacob Borut, John Efron, Sharon Gordon, Paul Lerner, Derek Penslar, Joachim Schlör, Sarah Stein, Sarah Wobick-Segev, and Carsten Wilke have all helped to shape and advance my own thinking on Jews and consumption. Alon Confino, Oded Heilbronner, and Moshe Zimmermann have nurtured this project over its long period of gestation. I am most grateful to Alon who put me in touch with Cambridge University Press. Leonore Maier and Aubrey Pomerance discussed ideas with me and helped me locate sources I needed for my research. Sarah Dry went over the text with the aim of making it more accessible to English readers. Michal Friedlander read the final draft and made valuable suggestions for revisions. At Cambridge University Press, I found an enduring and supportive team that eased the delivery of this book.

I am grateful to a number of presses for allowing me to make use of previously published material for this book. Chapter 1 is a revised and expanded version of "Productivist and Consumerist Narratives Regarding Jews in German History," in: Neil Gregor, Nils Roemer, and Mark Roseman (eds.), *German History from the Margins* (Bloomington: Indiana University Press, 2006), 165–185; Some sections of Chapter 2 were published as "Advertising, Jewish Ethnic Marketing, and Consumer Ambivalence in Weimar Germany," in: Gideon Reuveni and Nils Römer (eds.), *Longings and Jewish Belongings* (Leiden: Brill Publications, 2010), 113–137; and an earlier version of Chapter 13 was published as "The Bridge and the Door: On the Cultural Economy Approach to History," in: Dan Dinner, Gideon Reuveni, and Yfaat Weis (eds.), *Deutsche Zeiten: Geschichte Und Lebenswelt. Festschrift Zur Emeritierung Von Moshe Zimmermann* (Göttingen: Vandenhoeck & Ruprecht, 2012), 24–40.

My two sons Itamar and Yaron watched this study develop and grow over the years with admirable patience and understanding. Without their love, the book would have never been finished. Their digital skills also proved to be a valuable resource for me, particularly in the final stages of my work when I needed advice on how to prepare the images for publication. This book is dedicated to them with the hope that it will help to make them more conscious consumers and aware of their Jewish heritage.

# PART I

# NARRATIVES OF BELONGING

# Producers, Consumers, Jews, and Antisemitism in German Historiography

It is a truism that historians need sources for their research. A good historian, it is generally agreed even by those who emphasize the importance of models and theory, is one who allows her or himself to be guided by the records. Historians of nineteenth-century German antisemitism, for example, usually cite published reports of antisemitic behavior or utterances from the time. Given the importance of allowing documentary evidence to testify to the past, how should historians respond when the material they consult does not paint the expected picture? More specifically, how should they respond when they find an absence of evidence? Currently, what historians imagine the past to be is, perhaps understandably, to a great extent based on what is present in historical sources rather than on what is absent from these records. But too often historians remain complacent about or unaware of the meaning of such omissions and absences. To confront, to study and to theorize what is *not* recorded challenge basic rules of historical theory and methodology. It might also generate new ways of reading the past. This is particularly the case for Jewish histories, which run the risk of misinterpreting the experience of Jews in the past by relying only on Jewish materials.

One example of the pitfalls of Jewish history can be found in Shulamit Volkov's influential essay on antisemitism as a "cultural code."[1] According to Volkov, toward the end of the nineteenth century Germany underwent a process of cultural polarization defined by two opposing concepts

---

[1] Shulamit Volkov, "Antisemitism as a Cultural Code. Reflection on the History and Historiography of Antisemitism in Imperial Germany," *Leo Baeck Year Book* 23 (1978), 25–46.

toward Jews: antisemitism and emancipation. Professing antisemitism became a kind of a cultural code. It denoted membership in a cultural camp characterized by a radical antimodern mentality which rejected liberalism, capitalism, socialism, and democracy and called for the reestablishment of a National Community (*Volksgemeinschaft*). Volkov bases her argument on the published speech and writing of antisemites, as well as pleas in favor of Jewish emancipation. By portraying German society's relationship to Jews exclusively through documents that treat Jews as their main subject (either positively or negatively), Volkov generates a picture of straightforward binary opposition that in many ways reproduces the images of the sources she used. The question arises: was the Jewish theme really so central to life in Germany around the turn of the century? Can, and should, the Jews indeed be regarded as the touchstone of German society? If this were the case, we would expect to find the "Jewish theme" or at least anti-Jewish sentiments broadly expressed by members of the nationalistic, antimodern or anticapitalist camp. Yet, as the following will show, this kind of nexus cannot always be established. Jews were not always either included or excluded nor were they always treated, as we might expect based on hitherto research, within the broad framework of so-called reactionary modernism.[2]

## THE FIGHT AGAINST DIRT AND TRASH WRITINGS

The first example that I would like to examine here is the fight against so-called *Schund- und Schmutzschriften* (literally translatable as "Dirt and Trash writings"). An amazing number of works that fall under the heading of "the struggle against *Schund- und Schmutzschriften*" emanated from Germany between 1870 and 1933. The fight against so-called pulp and trash writings took place in newspapers, pamphlets, books, lectures, exhibitions, and special journals, in calls to boycott the shops where such documents were sold and in book burnings. The list of institutions and organizations that participated in this struggle is impressively long. Led by the Book Dealers' Association, it was joined by government and local authorities, churches, schools, political parties, libraries, and a variety of cultural and moral associations in more than thirty-three cities. Together,

[2] Jeffrey Herf, *Reactionary Modernism: Technology, Culture, and Politics in Weimar and the Third Reich* (Cambridge: Cambridge University Press, 1984).

they organized campaigns to wage war on pulp literature and promote so-called good literature.[3] Practically all of Germany's state and local archives have holdings documenting this struggle.

Today's observer may wonder at such intense preoccupation with the phenomenon of *Schund und Schmutz*, especially since there was never a commonly accepted definition of these two concepts. *Schund und Schmutz* was not to describe a particular sort of literary genre but instead to designate writings of reputedly low aesthetic and ethical value.[4] In other words, any publication could be, and clearly was, branded as *Schund und Schmutz*. Before World War I the novels of Karl May, for example, were labeled as "*Schund*" and their distribution attacked. Writings with socialistic touches or radical nationalistic literature were also often treated in the same way. This circumstance seems to explain the great variety of publications about the topic as well as the various types of *Schund und Schmutz* that they referred to.

A surprisingly broad coalition of people from all political and religious stripes viewed pulp literature as a social problem of the first order.[5] The vast amount of extant documentary material attests to how widespread were fears about the destructive influence of these works, referred to variously as pulp (*Schmutz*), trash (*Schund*), smut (*Unzucht*), and inferior (*untergeistige*) writings and kitsch. *Schund und Schmutz* writings became the scapegoat for all of society's social ills. Those educated men most actively engaged in fighting trash writings (*Schundkämpfer*) considered them a manifestation of a rival culture threatening to undermine the social order at whose head the educated male bourgeoisie had established itself. In particular pornography, homosexuality, internationalism and capitalism were viewed as diseases of society driving the popularity of *Schund und Schmutz* writings. At the same time, these alleged social ills were associated

---

[3] "Organisationen, Vereine etc. zur Bekämpfung der Schund- und Schmutzschriften" in: Geheimes Staatsarchiv Preußischer Kulturbesitz. Berlin, Rep 77 Tit 2772 Nr. 12.

[4] Wolfgang Kaschuba and Kaspar Maase (eds.), *Schund und Schönheit: Populäre Kultur um 1900* (Cologne: Böhlau Verlag 2001), and Mirjam Storim, *Ästhetik im Umbruch: Zur Funktion der "Rede über Kunst" um 1900 am Beispiel der Debatte um Schmutz und Schund* (Tübingen: Max Niemeyer Verlag, 2002).

[5] Georg Jäger, "Der Kampf gegen Schmutz- und Schund. Die Reaktion der Gebildeten auf die Unterhaltungsindustrie, *Archiv für Geschichte des Buchwesens* 31 (1988), 163–191; Detlev Peukert, Der Schund- und Schmutzkampf als "Sozialpolitik der Seele," in: *Das war ein Vorspiel nur ...* (Berlin: Akademie Verlag der Künste, 1983); Gideon Reuveni, "Der Aufstieg der Bürgerlichkeit und die bürgerliche Selbstauflösung. Die Bekämpfung der Schund- und Schmutzliteratur in Deutschland bis 1933 als Fallbeispiel, *Zeitschrift für Geschichtswissenschaft* 51 (2003), 131–144.

with Judaism and the Jews.[6] However, despite the prominence of Jews in the publishing world, an examination of the history of the war on *Schund und Schmutz* writings shows that it was not particularly marked by antisemitism. Even a magazine designed to wage war on trash, such as the *Hochwacht*, with its manifestly nationalist leanings, did not use antisemitic language or images in its struggle against pulp literature.[7] On the contrary, during the period prior to World War I, articles in the anti-trash struggle praised the cultural virtues of the Jews and their superior taste in reading. And both before and after the war, Jewish individuals and organizations played an active role in the struggle against *Schund und Schmutz* in the name of high culture and *Bildung*.[8] After 1918 the first official lists of pulp publications contained a number of works with a manifestly nationalistic and antisemitic character. These works, which fell into the category of patriotic trash literature (*patriotische Schundliteratur*), were banned from distribution by the 1926 Law for the Protection of Young People against Trash and Filth (referred to as "the Law").[9]

Despite the positive image enjoyed by the Jews in the context of the struggle against pulp writings, alongside efforts to repress works with a manifestly antisemitic character, it would be going too far to conclude that the struggle against pulp literature was used as a tool for combating antisemitism. At the end of 1928 for example, the Rhine-Westphalian Youth Welfare Department in Düsseldorf tried to ban an issue of the Nazi Party newspaper *Westdeutscher Beobachter* because of an article entitled "Sex Crime in the House of Tietz." The article described in great detail indecent sexual acts which a Jew was alleged to have perpetrated against a German girl at the department store owned by Leonhard Tietz, a Jew, in Cologne. The Düsseldorf Youth Welfare Department considered

[6] On these images of the Jew see for example Sander L. Gilman, *Smart Jews: The Construction of the Image of Jewish Superior Intelligence* (Lincoln: University of Nebraska Press, 1996); Michael Schmidt and Stefan Rohrbacher, *Judenbilder. Kulturgeschichte antijüdischer Mythen und antisemitischer Vorurteile* (Reinbek: Rowohlt, 1991); Julius H. Schoeps and Joachim Schlör (eds.), *Bilder der Judenfeindschaft* (Augsburg: Bechtermünz Verlag, 1999).

[7] On this magazine and its publisher Karl Brunner, who became famous after the War as the Weimar Republic film censor, see Paul Samuleit, "Aus der Geschichte des Kampfes gegen den Schund, in Samuleit Paul and Brunckhorst Hans, *Geschichte und Wege der Schundbekämpfung* (Berlin: Carl Heymanns Verlag, 1922), 3–22.

[8] Rudolf Schenda, *Die Lesestoffe der Kleinen Leute* (Munich: C.H. Beck, 1976), 172; Gabriele v. Glasenapp and Michael Nagel, *Das jüdische Jugendbuch* (Stuttgart: Verlag Metzler, 1996), 103.

[9] Margaret F. Stieg, "The 1926 German Law to Protect Youth against Trash and Filth: Moral Protectionism in a Democracy," *Central European History* 23 (1990), 22–56.

this article to be pornographic and harmful to young people, and demanded that distribution of the relevant issue of the newspaper be banned. After the application was rejected by the Berlin Examining Bureau for Trash and Filth on the grounds that banning the paper would constitute political censorship, the Chief Examining Bureau for Trash and Filth ruled that the need to protect young persons against corruption of their moral values outweighed the defense of the freedom of political expression. However, since the article was published in a daily newspaper the Bureau ruled that the risk of corrupting youth had passed and it no longer saw fit to ban the newspaper.[10]

### CONSUMER DISCOURSE VS. PRODUCER DISCOURSE

Antisemitism was viewed as a political outlook, not a social problem. Why, in the light of this state of affairs, did antisemitism as political ideology that provided a response to the "social question" not play a key role defining the struggle against pulp writings?[11] Undoubtedly many factors contributed to this situation. I would argue that a key element was the special nature of the struggle against pulp works: it was what may be called a "consumer discourse" rather than a "producer discourse." That is, it was a discourse dealing with consumption and the relationship between consumer and producer, rather than dealing with production or the character and the situation of the bourgeois classes. It should be emphasized that the two concepts of "consumer-discourse" and "producer-discourse" are not "two sides of the same coin" or "discourse" and "counter-discourse," as could be assumed from the two terms "consumer" vs. "producer." Instead, they are two types of discourse with different sorts of references and functions.

The "consumer-discourse" is concerned with the "masses," which as the main audience for commercialized culture are most exposed to supposedly detrimental or harmful influences. In many ways this discourse reflects the fears about a potential "dictatorship of the consumers":

---

[10] Archiv der Deutschen Bücherei Leipzig, 351/4/1, Protokolle der Oberprüfstelle für Schund- und Schmutzliteratur 1929, 13. See also Hans Wingender, *Erfahrungen im Kampf gegen Schund- und Schmutzschriften* (Düsseldorf: Published by the author, 1929), 50–54.

[11] On the "social question" and antisemitism: Moshe Zimmermann, "Die Judenfrage" als "die soziale Frage. Zu Kontinuität und Stellenwert des Antisemitismus vor und nach dem Nationalsozialismus," in *Faschismus und Faschismen im Vergleich* (Cologne: HS-Verlag, 1998), 149–163.

a situation in which consumers' tastes and demands would completely determine production and supply. One of the main features of this discourse is the implicit contrast between self-controlled bourgeois individuals on the one hand and the easily manipulated, undifferentiated masses on the other. Whoever belonged to these masses (mainly women, workers and youth) were seen by members of the bourgeoisie as "the other without" and were considered as a danger to the dominance of bourgeois values. In other words the "consumer-discourse" was used as a means to strengthen bourgeois self-definition.[12]

On the other hand, it is the producers who are at the center of the "producer discourse" which reflects the competition between and within the bourgeoisie. This type of discourse deals more with the division and conflicts among the middle classes, i.e. with what can be defined, from the point of view of this class, as "the other within." There is here a certain affinity between the so-called other without" and the "other within." Both others are frequently characterized by such perceived negative traits as femininity, materialism and imitation. Yet, while the "consumer-discourse " is defensive in attempting to preserve bourgeois values, the "producer-discourse" reflects schisms and frictions within the middle classes.

Bearing this proposed division between producer and consumer discourse in mind, let us return to our example and try to explain why antisemitism was not a defining feature of the anti-"dirt and trash" campaigns. The Jews, I would argue, were not considered members of the masses, and thus targets of commercialization, but instead were seen to belong to the producing classes, whose power was weakened in direct proportion to the growing power of the consumer masses.

The so-called capitalism debate is a further striking illustration of this state of affairs. While Jews played a central role in early discussions on the origins of capitalism, especially following Werner Sombart's notorious book *Juden und das Wirtschaftsleben* (1911), they were absent in discussions on the need to discipline consumers.[13] Even Sombart himself,

---

[12] For more on this notion see, for example: Martin Jay, "In the Empire of the Gaze: Foucault and the Denigration of Vision in Twentieth-century French Thought," in *Foucault: A Critical Reader* (ed.) David Counzens Hoy (New York: Basil Blackwell, 1986), 175–204.

[13] Werner Sombart, *Die Juden und das Wirtschaftsleben* (Leipzig: Duncker & Humblot, 1911). On the issue of disciplining consumption in Germany, see Warren G. Breckmann, "Disciplining Consumption: The Debate about Luxury in Wilhelmine Germany, 1890–1914," *Journal of Social History* 24 (1990/91), 485–505; Hartmut Berghoff (ed.), Konsumpolitik. Die Regulierung des privaten Verbrauchs im 20. *Jahrhundert*

writing on the problem of consumption, did not mention Jews, but focused exclusively on the role of women as initiators of consumer culture.[14]

## THE BOOK-SELLING CRISIS

The absence of Jews and Jewishness from certain type of discussions becomes even more evident in a comparison of parallel debates, for instance in the discussions on the situation of book reading after the Great War. As in many other areas of life, the book trade felt itself to be in crisis after the First World War. At the time, scholars considered the main reason for the so-called "book crisis" (*Buchkrise*) to be the great social changes in German society following the War, and the enduring economic instability and political crises of the period.[15] Hans Thomas, the editor of the German new right magazine, *Die Tat* ("The Deed"), summed up the situation in his characteristic style: "Your buying circles are changing. Readers' intellectual demands are dwindling. The scourge of proletarianization and vulgarization is spreading at the speed of light and supporting the tendency, already present, to a flattening and general leveling out."[16]

The core of this change was perceived as the "disintegration of the bourgeoisie" on the one hand and "the advent of mass society" on the other. Terms such as "*Vermassung*" (literally "massification"), "proletarianization," and "Americanization" were often used to describe the

(Göttingen: Vandenhoeck & Ruprecht, 1999). On Sombart and the Jews: Alfred Philipp, *Die Juden und das Wirtschaftsleben. Eine antikritisch bibliographische Studie zu Werner Sombart: Die Juden und das Wirtschaftsleben* (Strasburg: Heitz, 1929); Arthur Mitzman, *Sociology and Estrangement: Three Sociologists of Imperial Germany* (New Brunswick: Transaction Books, 1987); Toni Oelson, "The Place of the Jews in Economic History as viewed by German Scholars," *Leo Baeck Year Book* 7 (1962), 183–212; David S. Landes, "The Jewish Merchant. Typology and Stereotypology in Germany," *Leo Baeck Year Book* 19 (1974): 11–30; Paul R. Mendes-Flohr, "Werner Sombart's: The Jews and Modern Capitalism. An Analysis of its Ideological Premises," *Leo Baeck Year Book* 21 (1976), 87–107; Avraham Barkai, "Judentum, Juden und Kapitalismus; ökonomische Vorstellungen von Max Weber und Werner Sombart," *Menora* 5 (1994), 25–38. Jehuda Reinhartz, *Fatherland or Promised Land: The Dilemma of the German Jew 1893 – 1914* (Ann Arbor: The University of Michigan Press, 1975), 190–195.

[14] Werner Sombart, *Liebe, Luxus und Kapitalismus. Über die Entstehung der modernen Welt aus dem Geist der Verschwendung* (Berlin: Wagenbach, 1983), first published 1913.

[15] Gideon Reuveni, "The 'Crisis of the Book' and German Society after the First World War," *German History* 20 (2002), 438–461.

[16] Hans Thomas was the pen name of Hans Zehrer. Hans Thomas, "Das Chaos der Bücher," *Die Tat* 23 (1931), 647.

transition from a bourgeois society to a mass society. The growing popularity of new media such as film and radio and new leisure activities such as sport and dance were particularly seen as manifestations of the new mass society. When librarian Max Wieser even asked whether books still suited the modern mentality as a means of education, enlightenment and artistic expression he predicted that in the future, books would no longer play such a central role in society as they had in the past three hundred years.[17] In the eyes of contemporaries, the popularity of the new media – film, the gramophone and radio – meant the end of the monopoly of the written word as the repository of human knowledge and marked the transition from a culture in which the book was the main means of mediation between humans and their surroundings to a culture based on seeing and hearing.

In the Weimar period, this sort of cultural pessimism was not limited to political conservatives but characterized general attitudes to culture at the time. Right and left, men and women, Jews and Christians were united in the battle for the German book culture and in so doing they formed a joint culturally conservative front. "People practice sports, dance, spend their evening hours by the radio, in the cinema, and, outside working hours, everyone is so busy that nobody has time to read a book,"[18] the famous Jewish liberal publisher Samuel Fischer wrote in 1926. He claimed that the World War and the subsequent economic suffering had destroyed the bourgeois social fabric that had been the bedrock of German intellectual and cultural life.[19] He blamed the collapse of the bourgeois social

---

[17] Max Wieser, "Die geistige Krisis des Buches und die Volksbibliotheken," *Preußische Jahrbücher* 191 (1923), 184. For similar views, cf. Johannes Molzahn, "Nicht mehr Lesen! Sehen!" *Das Kunstblatt*, 12 (1928), 78–82; Hans Siemsen, "Bücherbesprechung," *Die Weltbühne* 21 (1923), 857–859; Siegfried Kracauer, "Die Photographie," in *Der verbotene Blick* (Leipzig: Reclam, 1992), 185–203.

[18] Samuel Fischer, "Bemerkungen zur Bücherkrise," Friedrich Pfäffin (ed.), *Der S. Fischer Verlag von der Gründung bis zur Rückkehr aus den Exil*, (Marbach: Ausstellungskatalog, 1985), 357–360, here 357.

[19] For a late formulation of the thesis of the collapse of the bourgeoisie, which is really a form of the theory of Germany's "special path" in history, cf., particularly, Hans Mommsen, "Die Auflösung des Bürgertums seit dem späten 19. Jahrhundert," Jürgen Kocka (ed.), *Bürger und Bürgerlichkeit im 19. Jahrhundert* (Göttingen: Vandenhoeck & Ruprecht, 1987), 288–315; Konrad H. Jarausch, "Die Krise des deutschen Bildungsbürgertums im ersten Drittel des 20. Jahrhunderts," Jürgen Kocka (ed.) *Bildungsbürgertum im 19. Jahrhundert. Politischer Einfluß und gesellschaftliche Formation* (Stuttgart: Klett Cotta, 1989), 180–206; Horst Möller, "Bürgertum und bürgerlich-liberale Bewegung nach 1918," Lothar Gall (ed.), *Bürgertum und bürgerlich-liberale Bewegung in Mitteleuropa seit dem 18. Jahrhundert* (Munich: Oldenbourg, 1997), 243–342.

associations, which had previously organized cultural and leisure activities and acted as a social glue, for bringing about the change in German society following the First World War. The loss of interest in reading was a clear reflection of these changes. Literary associations, readings, libraries and drama associations did more than merely disseminate culture: in fact, according to Fischer, they helped to create a special German form of shared culture (*Gemeinschaftsgefühl deutscher Kultur*).

The "Book crisis" was therefore primarily a book-*selling* crisis and mirrored the fear of publishers, booksellers and authors – the core of the male bourgeois educated classes – of the demise of "reading culture," which was regarded as a main component of bourgeois culture. With the decline of reading culture, these men feared that their social position was also at stake. The anxiety about the power of readers to determine the fate of a book reveals that the book crisis was, indeed, a feature of what I have termed "consumer discourse." Hence it is not surprising that Jewishness, despite the prominence of Jews in the German publishing world, was not a topic within this discourse. Even the *CV-Zeitung*, the official publication of *Centralverein deutscher Staatsbürger jüdischen Glaubens* (Central Association of German Citizens of Jewish Faith, hereafter *Centralverein*), which was extremely sensitive to any hint of antisemitism, did not mention it in its discussions of the German book crisis.[20]

### THE WAR ON ALCOHOL

A further example of the sometimes surprising absence of antisemitism or Jewish issues from contemporary debates in late nineteenth and early twentieth century Germany is the war on alcohol. Toward the end of the nineteenth century alcohol came to be widely recognized in Germany as a social problem. Military officials, churches, factory owners, and Social Democrats all viewed alcoholism as a sign of moral failure and even as a disease in itself. Antialcohol campaigners linked drinking to lost productivity and warned of the devastating influence on both the human body and on society as a whole. Studies of alcoholism confirmed these fears, presenting insobriety as responsible "for the degeneration of entire nations" and for "the deterioration of the race."[21] These studies reflected

---

[20] Hanns Martin Elster, "Wer liest noch Bücher? Eine Betrachtung über den Niedergang des deutschen Buches," CV-Zeitung (March 22, 1929), 141–142.

[21] On these studies in: Alfred Hegge, *Alkohol und bürgerliche Gesellschaft im 19. Jahrhundert* (Berlin: Colloquium Verlag, 1988) and Hasso Spode, *Die Macht der*

worries about the endurance of the German nation in an age of modernization and rapid industrialization. At the same time they also indicate the growing influence of science in the social domain and demonstrate how scientific language penetrated and shaped social discourse. Commentators often drew an analogy between the human body and society; both became pathological subjects of observation. Physicians played a central role in this development. As Abraham Baer noted in his extensive study on "alcoholism its divulgation and effects both on individuals and social organism" in 1878: "The medical practitioner is probably in the best position to observe alcoholism in the physical degeneration of the population; as lunatic asylums show the devastation of intellectual life, the workhouses, jails and prisons show in equally terrible dimensions the destruction inflicted by excess directly and indirectly on the moral fiber of human society."[22]

Abraham Adolf Baer, who worked as a medical adviser at the city jail of Plötzensee in Berlin, was a Jew from Posen.[23] His study on alcoholism rapidly came to be seen as the standard work and gave rise to the antialcoholism movement in Germany. One of the most important of the new organizations was the *Deutscher Verein gegen den Mißbrauch geistiger Getränke E.V.* (1883), which invited Baer to serve as its honorary chairman.

More interesting than the active involvement of Jews in the fight against alcohol is the position they held in the discourse against alcoholism. As in the case of *Schund- und Schmutzschriften*, Jews played a marginal role. Even in the discussions on the so-called *Alkoholkapital*, Jews did not receive special attention and were not treated distinctly. Visual representations of so-called "alcohol capitalists" were similarly not recognizable as Jews. The only known exception in which Jews were singled out in antialcohol discourse was the attempt within the Order of Good Templars

---

*Trunkenheit. Kultur- und Sozialgeschichte des Alkohols in Deutschland* (Opland: Laske and Budrich, 1993).

[22] "Wohl am meistens ist der Arzt in der Lage, den Alkoholismus in der physischen Degeneration der Bevölkerung zu beobachten; und wie in den Irrenanstalten die Verwüstungen des geistigen Lebens, so zeigen sich ihm in den Arbeits-, Gefangen- und Zuchthäuser in gleich erschreckender Weise die Zerstörungen, welche die Unmässigkeit mittelbar und unmittelbar dem sittlichen Leben der menschlichen Gesellschaft zufügt." Abraham Baer, *Der Alkoholismus: Seine Verbreitung und seine Wirkung auf den individuellen und sozialen Organismus sowie die Mittel, ihn zu bekämpfen* (Berlin: Hirschwald, 1878), iii.

[23] On Baer: Salomon Wininger, *Große Jüdische National-Bibliographie*, Vol 1 (Cernăuti: Buch und Druckerei Orient, 1925), 216–217.

in Austria, an organization dedicated to fighting alcoholism, to exclude Jews as well as other "non-Aryan" elements from the organization. The dispute between adversaries and supporters of the "Aryan paragraph" hindered the work of the Order and almost led to its disintegration. At the end Stephan Schöck, the leader of the antisemitic faction, was forced to leave the Order of Good Templars to found a new organization to fight alcoholism based on the principles of *völkisch* ideology.[24]

This incident remains at the margins of the German antialcohol movement, which did not harbor any special antisemitic tendencies even though the concepts of race and class were central to it. More frequent, in fact, are positive references to Jews as offering a role model for a "sober race." The equation of Jews with sobriety offered an opportunity to promote a positive image of Jews in the German society. In his widely circulated booklet *Wofür Kämpfen Wir?* (What are we fighting for?), Simon Katzenstein one of the central figures in the German Social Democratic Party's campaign against alcoholism, warned of the damages caused by alcoholism to the working classes.[25] He claimed that alcoholism was fostered by alcohol industry promotions to workers. "It is not true," he declared, "that alcoholism is caused only by adversity. Wide strata of workers who experience deep hardship and scarcity, such as women workers who worked as domestics, workers in the confection and textile industry or Jewish workers in Russia, are much less affected by alcoholism than other social groups."[26] Katzenstein did not explain, however, why these specific groups were particularly immune to alcohol abuse.

In his famous study on alcoholism, Abraham Baer conveys a similar attitude concerning the drinking habits of Jews. He lists a series of studies that demonstrated the special sobriety of Jews. He even presented the Jews as a kind of "universal representative of sobriety" who, although scattered in different climates and areas where all types of alcohol are available, continued their sober way of life. According to Baer, the reasons for this state of affairs lay in Jewish religious practices such as the celebration of Shabbat as a day of rest, as well as in the particular social and cultural disposition of Jews, i.e. in their inclination to avoid exhausting physical

---

[24] Johan Bergman, *Geschichte der Nüchterheitsbestrebungen* (Hamburg: Neulandverlag, 1925), 468.

[25] After the First World War Katzenstein became a member of the Weimar national assembly for the SPD. See: Joseph Walk, *Kurzbibliographie zur Geschichte der Juden 1918–1933* (Munich: K.G. Saur, 1988), 188.

[26] Simon Katzenstein, *Wofür Kämpfen Wir?* (Berlin: Deutscher Arbeiter-Abstinenten-Bund, 1909), 6.

professions and to cultivate strong family ties. According to Baer, the low rate of alcohol consumption among Jews explained why they tend to live longer than non-Jews and why their crime and suicide rates were lower.[27]

Some even considered drinking habits as a kind of criterion, or even a racial quality, that distinguished Jews from other people, especially those from northern and Eastern Europe. The Zionist sociologist Arthur Ruppin, for example, observed that while Christians prefer stimuli (*Reitzmittel*) such as alcohol which decreased alertness, Jews in contrast prefer those which increased awareness. "The Christian," he concluded, "seems to like the gloom (*Dämmerung*), while the Jew [prefers] the brightness (*Helle*)."[28] In light of such views, it is no surprise that alcohol consumption was regarded as a dangerous sign of assimilation and a threat to the endurance of the Jewish race.[29] As fascinating as such comments are, discussions about Jews were distinctly marginal to mainstream cultural anxiety about alcoholism, for the very reason that Jews were not considered part of the problem.

### ANIMAL PROTECTION

In contrast to the examples examined thus far, where there was a surprising lack of special attention paid to Jews, in other areas of social anxiety, Jews played a central role, even if their connection to the subject was tangential. An example is the discussion of animal protection in Germany.[30]

Reflecting a shift in the approach to nature that accompanied modernization, concern over the protection of animals emerged in the nineteenth century.[31] During this period many people moved from the countryside to the cities, leaving behind a centuries-old mode of living and working together with animals. As cities grew, this traditional appreciation of

---

[27] "Alkohol," *Der Israelit*, vol. 48, no. 15 (1907), 1–2. For more examples of this discussion see in, John M. Efron, *Medicine and the German Jews: A History* (New Haven: Yale University Press, 2001), 108–117.

[28] Arthur Ruppin, *Soziologie der Juden*, vol II. (Berlin: Jüdische Verlag, 1931), 100.

[29] For this kind of approach see for example the article "Abstinenz" written by the physician Aron Sandler in Ismar Elbogen and Georg Herlitz (eds.), *Jüdisches Lexikon*, vol. 1 (Berlin: Jüdischer Verlag, 1927), 55.

[30] I would like to thank John Efron for drawing my attention to this case.

[31] Miriam Zerbel, *Tierschutz im Kaiserreich. Eine Beitrag zur Geschichte des Vereinswesens* (Frankfurt a.M.: Peter Lang, 1993); Ute Hahn, "*Die Entwicklung des Tierschutzgedankens in Religion und Geistesgeschichte*" (Ph.D. diss., Tierärztliche Hochschule Hannover, 1980).

nature and of living together with animals contributed to a growing enthusiasm for house pets. Domestic animals symbolized a lost connection to life in the countryside and to nature itself. While in the countryside the human–animal relationship had been predominantly functional, in the industrial and technological world of the city it was based on sentiment and emotions. Eating an animal resident of the modern cities became a taboo; domestic animals were given names, and sometimes even received respectful burials. In short, animals were humanized, laying the foundation for the novel concept of animal rights. Not surprisingly, these animal rights activists made mainly ethical and moral arguments in their campaign to protect animals.[32] They stated, for instance, that cruelty toward animals encouraged human violence and even homicide. Teaching children to love animals (*Tierliebe*), they argued, was necessary to promote peaceful relations between human beings.[33]

Such pacifist ideals, endorsing tolerance among all people, were not always evident in the actions of the animal protection societies themselves. Since the mid-nineteenth century, such societies gained public attention mainly as a result of their vigorous struggle against the exploitation of animals for medical experiments and industrial use.[34] Celebrated composer Richard Wagner was also an enthusiastic supporter of the antivivisection movement. Wagner openly enunciated his support in an open letter of 1879 to Ernst von Weber, the founder of Dresden animal protection society in which he suggested measures such as breaking into laboratories where experiments on animals were conducted, as well as physical attacks on vivisectionists themselves.[35] Wagner not only condemned vivisectionists as enemies, but explicitly identified them with Jews. Jews were indeed among the group of specialists who conducted experiments on

---

[32] Orvar Löfgren, "Natur, Tier und Moral. Zur Entwicklung der bürgerlichen Naturauffassung," Utz Jeggle, Gottfried Korff, and Martin Scharfe (eds.), *Volkskultur in der Moderne. Probleme und Perspektiven empirischer Kulturforschung* (Reinbek: Rowohlt, 1986), 122–144.

[33] For an example of these arguments, see the programmatic writings of Eduard Bilz, *Der Zukunftsstaat. Staatseinrichtung im Jahr 2000* (Leipzig: Bilz Verlag, 1904); Ludwig Ankenbrand, *Tierschutz und moderne Weltanschauung* (Bamberg: Verlag und Druck der Handelsdruckerei, 1906).

[34] Hermann Stenz (ed.), *Die Vivisektion in ihrer wahren Gestalt. Unwiderlegliche Thatsachen aus der Fachlitteratur* (Berlin: Weltbund zur Bekämpfung d. Vivisektion, 1899); Hubert Brentschneider, *Der Streit um die Vivisektion im 19. Jahrhundert: Verlauf, Argumente und Ergebnisse* (Stuttgart: G. Fischer, 1962); Nicolaas Rupke (ed.), *Vivisection in Historical Perspective* (London: Croom Helm, 1987).

[35] Richard Wagner, "Offenes Schreiben an Ernst von Weber," *Gesammelte Schriften und Dichtungen* (Leipzig: G.W. Fritsch, 1888), 195–210.

animals, a fact which undoubtedly helped Wagner to establish this association. However, it was mainly the slaughter of animal by kosher butchers that reinforced the targeting of Jews as enemies of animals.

Jewish ritual slaughter, known as *shehitah*, was perceived as inhuman, cruel and torturous by animal rights campaigners. Already at their first conference in Gotha in 1879, animal protection societies in Germany decided that *shehitah* had to be stopped by legislative means. The campaigners based their charges of cruelty against *shehitah* on the observation that the cutting of an animal's throat leads to a torrential discharge of blood, followed immediately by several convulsive shudders by the beast. Animal protectionists saw this method of slaughter not only as cruel to the animal, but also as dangerous to the butcher. They dismissed all references to the ritual significance of this method of slaughter as "ridiculous and superstitious" and insisted that it should be forbidden.[36]

Switzerland was the first European country to adopt an anti-*shehitah* law in the mid nineteenth century.[37] Inspired by this success and despite numerous reports written by specialists that maintained that Jewish animal slaughter was no more inhumane or cruel than other methods of slaughter, animal welfarists in Germany launched an energetic and antisemitic propaganda campaign against *shehitah*, portraying the Jews both as enemies of animals and Germans alike.[38] Jews responded immediately to these attacks and sought to prevent an anti-*shehitah* legislation in Germany. Their polemic accentuated the importance of animal rights in Judaism and displayed Jewish ritual slaughter in a positive light. Ironically, as John Efron noted, all strands of German Jewry defended *shehitah*, though only a minority of them kept kosher.[39] According to Efron, this "united front" was a result of

---

[36] Quoted in: Miriam Zerbel, "Tierschutz und Antivivisektion," in *Handbuch der deutschen Reformbewegungen 1880–1933* (eds.), Diethart Krebs and Jürgen Reulecke (Berlin: Peter Hammer Verlag, 1998), 41.

[37] Pascal Krauthammer, "Das Schächtverbot in der Schweiz 1854 – 2000: Die Schächtfrage zwischen Tierschutz, Politik und Fremdenfeindlichkeit (Ph.D. diss., University of Zurich, 2000).

[38] On this see especially: Dorothee Brantz, "Stunning Bodies: Animal Slaughter, Judaism, and the Meaning of Humanity in Imperial Germany," *Central European History* 35 (2002), 167–194; and Robin Judd, "The Politics of Beef: Animal Advocacy and the Kosher Butchering Debates in Germany," *Jewish Social Studies* 10 (2003), 117–150; ibid., *Contested Rituals: Circumcision, Kosher Butchering, and Jewish Political Life in Germany 1843–1933* (Ithaca: Cornell University Press, 2007).

[39] Efron, *Medicine and the German Jews*, 206–222.

mounting antisemitism during the period. Indeed, it seems that the anti-*shehitah* campaign was not merely about animal slaughter but part of a larger antisemitic movement that had accelerated in late nineteenth-century Germany.[40]

Paul Förster, one of the leading figures of the anti-campaign in Germany was also an outspoken antisemite. Förster was a devoted animal welfarist, who edited the journal of the Dresden Animal Protection Society *Thier- und Menschenfreund* (Friend to Animals and Humans). He was also a well-known antisemite and one of the founders of the antisemitic party Deutsch-Soziale Partei "German social party" (as of 1894 Deutsch-Soziale Reformpartei), which he also represented in the German Reichstag.[41] Although all attempts to pass an anti-*Shehitah* legislation in the Reichstag failed, Förster and his party successfully introduced the so-called *Schächtfrage* ("slaughter question") onto the political agenda of their time. An anti-*shehitah* law in Germany came into force after the National Socialist Party assumed power. In August 1933, after passing the anti-*shehitah* legislation, Hermann Göring threatened to "commit to concentration camps those who still think they can continue to treat animals as inanimate property."[42]

Why did antisemitism play such a central role within the framework of animal protection, whereas antisemitism was marginal in the case of dirt and trash and antialcohol campaigns? I would argue that the key difference is animal protection debates were characterized by a "producer discourse" in which competition between different elements of the producers class (i.e. members of the bourgeoisie) was the primary source of anxiety. For example, along with Paul Forster's engagement with animal rights, he was also an adherent of naturopathy and a devoted vegetarian, both were considered part of the so called *Lebensreformbewegung*,

---

[40] Ibid. On this see also Reinhard Rürup, *Emanzipation und Antisemitismus. Studien zur "Judenfrage" der bürgerlichen Gesellschaft* (Göttingen: Vandenhoeck & Ruprecht, 1975).

[41] On this party: Dieter Fricke, "Deutsch-Soziale Reformpartei," in: Dieter Fricke(eds), *Lexikon zur Parteiengeschichte. Die bürgerlichen und kleinbürgerlichen Parteien und Verbände in Deutschland 1789–1945*, vol. II (Cologne: Pahl Rugenstein Verlag, 1984), 540–549; Stephan Ph. Wolf, Für Deutschtum, Thron und Altar. *Die Deutsch-Soziale Reformpartei in Baden, 1890–1907* (Karlsruhe: Heinz Wolf Fachverlag, 1995).

[42] Quoted in: Arnold Arluke and Boria Sax, "The Nazi Treatment of Animals and People," Lynda Birke and Ruth Hubbard (eds.), *Reinventing Biology: Respect for Life and the Creation of Knowledge*, (Bloomington: Indiana University Press, 1995), 228–260, here 244; also useful in this context is the website of the anti-vivisection group called "The Absurdity of Vivisection": http://vivisection-absurd.org.uk.

a movement dedicated to reforming bourgeois life in Germany.[43] Förster
was no exception here, but was a bona fide representative of those who
regarded themselves as *Freidenker* (freethinkers) and *Fortschrittskämpfer*
(fighters for progress). His involvement in attempts to reform bourgeois
life and his antisemitism thus present no contradiction. Far from it, antisemitism was widespread among different sections of this so-called reform
movement.[44] Indeed the discourses of the *Lebensreformbewegungen* seem
to support Volkov's claim that preindustrial romanticism, antimodern-
ism, anticapitalism and nationalism are all indicators of antisemitism.
Nevertheless, as I have argued above, what made these discourses more
likely to become antisemitic was not only the combination of these nos-
talgic impulses for a pre-modern past, but its nature as "producer discourse," reflecting anxieties mainly among educated middle-class men
of the rapid change driven by the bourgeois, which they associated with
the growing power of Jews. The debate over animal protection falls into
this pattern. In contrast to campaigners against alcohol and trash-and-dirt-
writings, animal protectionists were mainly concerned with the status of
the bourgeoisie in light of the rapid advance of modernity. They were much
less preoccupied with the threats to bourgeois society posed by the masses
with their growing purchasing power.

## THE STRUGGLE AGAINST THE DEPARTMENT STORES

An even more prominent example that confirms this pattern is the fight
against department stores. During the last third of the nineteenth century,
the department store came rapidly to occupy one of the pivotal positions
within the German distribution system.[45] The significance of the

---

[43] On this movement: Klaus Bergmann, *Agrarromantik und Großstadtfeindschaft*
(Meisenheim a. Glan: Hain, 1970); Wolfgang R. Krabbe, *Gesellschaftsveränderung
durch Lebensreform: Strukturmerkmale einer sozialreformerischen Bewegung in
Deutschland der Industrialisierungsperiode* (Göttingen: Vandenhoeck & Ruprecht,
1974); Andrew Lees, *Cities, Sin, and Social Reform in Imperial Germany* (Ann Arbor:
University of Michigan Press, 2002).

[44] According to Jürgen Reulecke antisemitism was actually the only common dominator of
this movement, which was very diverse and contained many different reform proposals.
This he claimed at a book presentation of: Diethart Krebs and Jürgen Reulecke (eds.),
*Handbuch der deutschen Reformbewegungen 1880–1933* (Berlin: Peter Hammer Verlag,
1998).

[45] The history of the department store in Germany has been an object of historical research
for some time. For an overview work see: Tim Coles, "Department Stores as retail
innovation in Germany: A Historical-Geographical perspective on the period
1870–1914," Geoffrey Crossick and Serge Jaumain (eds.), *Cathedrals of Consumption:*

department store was not only related to its revolutionary selling methods, but also to its active role in extending modern consumer culture. In this new culture, individuals and groups could find social definition through the act of buying. The key to the department store was display and quantity. By laying out consumer items in profuse displays, deliberately designed to lure shopper's eyes and stimulate their imagination, the department stores created what historian Rosalind Williams calls a "Dream World" of material luxury.[46] The department store was thus not merely a huge sales hall for an array of goods, but a place that transformed the act of buying into a "perceptual adventure," thereby changing consumption from an activity with a purpose to a purpose in and for itself.[47]

Given the rapid development of the department stores toward the end of nineteenth century Germany, it is no wonder that these "cathedrals of consumption," as contemporaries already referred to them, were at the center of public debate. Social critics of the time condemned department stores as avatars of materialism, accusing them of promoting moral turpitude. Thus the department stores were held responsible for encouraging criminal behavior, particularly among women from well-off strata. It was argued that the department stores operated as a retail version of a factory, displaying goods in a seductive way and hence taking advantage of – or indeed abusing – what was regarded as the easily influenced female psyche.[48]

*The European Department Store 1850–1939*, (Aldershot: Ashgate, 1999), 72–96; Klaus Strohmer, *Warenhäuser: Geschichte, Blüte und Untergang im Warenmeer* (Berlin: Klaus Wagenbach Verlag, 1980); Siegfried Gerlach, *Das Warenhaus in Deutschland: seine Entwicklung bis zum 1. Weltkrieg in historisch-geographischer Sicht* (Stuttgart: Steiner Verlag, 1988).

[46] Rosalind Williams, *Dream Worlds: Mass Consumption in Late 19th Century France* (Berkeley: University of California, 1982); see also Anne Friedberg, *Window Shopping: Cinema and the Postmodern* (Berkeley: University of California Press, 2000); Rachel Bowlby, *Just Looking: Consumer Culture in Dreiser, Gissing and Zola* (New York: Methuen, 1985).

[47] The term "perceptual adventure" was coined by Elizabeth and Stuart Ewen, *Channels of Desire: Mass Images and the Shaping of American Consciousness*, 2nd ed. (New York: McGraw-Hill, 1992), 45. On the special contribution of the department stores to the emergence of consumer culture see also: Susan Porter Benson, *Counter Cultures: Saleswoman, Managers, and Costumers in American Department Stores, 1890–1940*, (Urbana: University of Illinois Press, 1986), especially ch. 3; Rudi Learmans, "Learning to Consume: Early Department Stores and the Shaping of the Modern Consumer Culture (1860–1914)," *Theory, Culture and Society* 10 (1993), 79–102.

[48] On the phenomenon of shoplifting: Elaine S. Abelson, *When Ladies Go A-Thieving. Middle-Class Shoplifters in Victorian Department Stores* (New York: Oxford University

Small shopkeepers led the attacks against the department stores; they were most threatened by the emergence of this new form of retail enterprise.[49] Fearing that department stores would undermine their trade, these shopkeepers established special organizations to fight them. At first the institutionalized expression of shopkeepers' collective attempts to protect their economic position, these organizations rapidly became politicized, becoming an integral part of what contemporaries referred to as the political *Mittelstandsbewegung* (the political movement of the petit bourgeoisie). As members of a political movement the shopkeepers comprised a strong pressure group, hoping for a policy of "social protectionism" from the authorities. Their pleas for protection from the state against unfair competition were effective and in the period before the First World War, they successfully lobbied for legislation that levied special taxes on department stores.[50] These limited successes, notes the historian Robert Gellately, "operated as a kind of safety-valve which helped to reduce or neutralize inner social tension of the Wilhelmian society."[51]

The hostility towards the department stores revealed the difficulties of the shopkeepers and of the *Mittelstand* as such to grasp, let alone master, the upheavals and challenges of modernity. Fears for their economic well-being merged with antimodernization, antisocialism and antisemitic sentiments, comprising what historian Philip Nord calls "the politics of resentments."[52] Jews played a key role in this context. They became the major target group in the attacks on department stores, turning antisemitism into a kind of integrating ideology of the *Mittelstandsbewegung*, culminating in a view that associated the "social question" with the

Press, 1989); Patricia O'Brien, "The Kleptomania Diagnosis: Bourgeois Women and Theft in Late Nineteenth-Century France," *Journal of Social History* (1983), 65–77; Uwe Spiekermann, "Theft and Thieves in German Department Stores 1895 – 1930: A Discourse on Morality, Crime and Gender," Geoffrey Crossick and Serge Jaumain (eds.), *Cathedrals of Consumption: The European Department Store 1850–1939*, (Aldershot: Ashgate, 1999), pp. 135–160.

49  Robert Gellately, "An der Schwelle der Moderne: Warenhäuser und ihre Feinde in Deutschland," Peter Alter (ed.), *Im Banne der Metropolen. Berlin und London in den zwanziger Jahren*, (Göttingen: Vandenhoeck & Ruprecht, 1993), 131–156.

50  Uwe Siekermann, *Warenhaussteuer in Deutschland: Mittelstandsbewegung, Kapitalismus und Rechtsstaat im Späten Kaiserreich* (Frankfurt a.M., Peter Lang, 1994).

51  Robert Gellately, *The Politics of Economic Despair: Shopkeepers and German Politics 1890–1914* (London: Sega, 1974), 214.

52  Philip G. Nord, *Paris Shopkeepers and the Politics of Resentments* (Princeton: Princeton University Press, 1986); cf. also Heinrich August Winkler, *Zwischen Marx und Monopol: Der deutsche Mittelstand vom Kaiserreich zur Bundesrepublik Deutschland* (Frankfurt a.M.: Fischer, 1991).

"Jewish question." The slogan *"Die sociale Frage ist wesentlich die Judenfrage"* (the social question is essentially the Jewish question) gained rapid popularity among the lower middle classes denoting the emergence of a new kind of antisemitism.[53] The fact that the owners of many department stores were indeed Jewish furthered the acceptance of this bigotry. Jews were viewed as *Grosskapitalisten* (big capitalists) who lived in a grand fashion at the expense of the nation as a whole.[54]

With the foundation of the Weimar Republic, the national assembly abolished all laws against the department stores, which, despite economic instability, entered into a period of growth and expansion. This commercial success did little to increase the social popularity of the department stores.[55] Hyperinflation and mass unemployment further intensified popular resentment against the department stores and attacks against the stores grew in step with increasing assaults against Jews.[56] Panic was the word used by contemporaries to describe the reaction of the *Mittelstand*.[57] The Nazis were quick to capitalize on this anxiety. All kinds of Nazi organizations were mobilized for this cause, turning the field of consumption into a combat zone against what were perceived as largely Jewish department stores. Thus for example, the leader of National Socialist Women's Organization declared in May 1929 to a mass meeting in Munich: "When a Jewish palace, one department

---

[53] On modern Antisemitism see for example: Rürup, *Emanzipation und Antisemitismus. Studien zur "Judenfrage" der bürgerlichen Gesellschaft*; Jacob Katz, *From Prejudice to Destruction: Anti-Semitism, 1700–1933* (Cambridge MA: Harvard University Press, 1980); Moshe Zimmermann, *Wilhelm Marr: The Patriarch of Antisemitism* (New York: Oxford University Press, 1986); Shulamit Volkov, "Zur sozialen und politischen Funktion des Antisemitismus: Handwerker im später 19. Jahrhundert," in *Antisemitismus als kultureller Code* (Munich: C.H. Beck, 2000), 37–53.

[54] For a comprehensive discussion of the Jewish association of the department stores, see, Paul Lerner, *The Consuming Temple: Jews, Department Stores and The Consumer Revolution in Germany* (Ithaca: Cornell University Press, 2015).

[55] Werner Rubens, *"Der Kampf des Spezialgeschäftes gegen das Warenhaus (mit besonderer Berücksichtigung der Zeit von 1918 bis 1929),"* (Ph.D. diss., University of Cologne, 1929).

[56] On violence against Jewish department stores in this period see Simone Ladwig-Winters, *Wertheim – ein Warenhausunternehmen und seine Eigentümer: Ein Beispiel der Entwicklung der Berliner Warenhäuser bis zur 'Arisierung'* (Münster: LIT, 1996). On antisemitism during the Weimar period: Anthony Kauders, *German Politics and the Jews: Düsseldorf and Nuremberg 1910 – 1933* (Oxford: Clarendon Press, 1996); Dirk Walter, *Antisemitische Kriminalität und Gewalt: Judenfeindschaft in der Weimarer Republik* (Bonn: Dietz, 1999); Cornelia Hecht, *Deutsche Juden und Antisemitismus in der Weimarer Republik* (Bonn: Dietz, 2003).

[57] Theodor Geiger, "Die Panik im Mittelstand," *Die Arbeit* 7 (1930), 637–654; and August Winkler, *Zwischen Marx und Monopol*, 38–51.

store after the other, can be built, we women must bear the responsibility. It is through the hands of the woman that the earnings of the man flow back into the economy, and only she possesses the weapon against the Jew."[58]

Boycott actions against department stores at the end of the 1920s do not seem to have achieved their objectives. Despite the rousing invective, the lower middle class was not eager to renounce the consumer pleasures offered by department stores and they continued to visit them.[59] Nevertheless such calls for boycotts represent a further indication of the centrality of the Jew in what I initially defined as a "producer discourse." That is, in an age in which bourgeois culture developed into something purchasable, as Michael Miller has noted in his work on the Bon Marché, the department stores as the principle medium of consumption became the arbiter of bourgeois identity.[60] In this sense the fight against the department stores was also a struggle for bourgeois identity and it revealed the schisms and frictions within these classes, singling out Jews as a dangerously powerful force.

### BEYOND BINARISM

As we have seen, the role and significance of antisemitism as a cultural code was variable. Jews were neither included nor excluded all of the time. In significant discourses they did not figure at all. This discovery comes as something of a surprise, indicating a discrepancy between the actual situation of Jews within German society and our historiographical assumptions about how they were treated and perceived. Indeed, one can trace areas of social discourse completely lacking antisemitism, despite the fact that they contained aspects of pre-industrial nostalgia and anti-capitalism commonly associated with hostility toward Jews. In this sense the absence of the "Jew" as a topic from specific discourses is as striking as his presence in others. The specific cases I have described in this chapter provide a robust challenge to that historiographical approach

---

[58]  Quoted in: Heinrich Uhlig, *Die Warenhäuser im Dritten Reich* (Cologne: Westdeutscher Verlag, 1956), 36.

[59]  Only after assuming power did the Nazis initiate a process of Aryanization, in which Jews were systematically removed from all positions in the department stores. On this see Uhlig, *Die Warenhäuser,* as well as Robert Gellately, "German Shopkeepers and the Rise of National Socialism," *The Wiener Library Bulletin* 28 (1975), 31–40.

[60]  Michael B. Miller, *The Bon Marché: Bourgeois Culture and the Department Store, 1869–1920* (Princeton: Princeton University Press, 1981), 185.

which conceptualizes antisemitism mainly within the broad framework of so-called "reactionary modernism."[61]

Why then do Jews figure in some discourses and not others? This chapter has tentatively suggested that the answer to this question lies in different modes of discourse, referred to here as "consumer discourse" and "producer discourse". Examination of these discourses shows a clear split. In the "consumer discourses" I have discussed, such as the struggle against pulp writings, and alcohol and the so-called "book crisis," anti-semitism played a minor role. In "producer discourses," on the other hand, surrounding the fight for animal rights, and the struggle against department stores, antisemitism was far more central. This model of explanation recognizes not only the importance of context to matters of antisemitism but also the potential for very different attitudes towards Jews to exist simultaneously. It reveals the complexity of social reality and the difficulty, especially for contemporaries, of interpreting it. Jews found themselves in a world in which antisemitism, at least in the period before the Nazis assumed power, played an equivocal role. In a sense, this claim seems to reinforce Hannah Arendt's observation that German society did not confine individual Jews to assuming a specific "Jewish identity," but posited them in a kind of a twilight zone, rendering them with "an empty sense of being different."[62] This notion of the in-between situation of the Jews also calls into mind Georg Simmel's analysis of the stranger.[63] In Simmel's terminology, the stranger is not just the wanderer who comes today and leaves tomorrow, having no specific structural position within a group. On the contrary, he is an element of the group itself, although never fully part of it. According to this view, the stranger belongs to what Simmel classifies as the "inner enemy." Nevertheless, being a stranger is for Simmel a positive attribute, as "it is a specific form of interaction." Moreover in Simmel's view, not being "bound by commitments which could prejudice his perception, understanding, and evaluation of the given" makes the stranger an ideal intermediary in the traffic of goods as well as in the traffic of ideas. According to Simmel, the prototype of the stranger is the merchant and the classical example is the Jews.[64] By treating

---

[61] Herf, *Reactionary Modernism*.

[62] Hannah Arendt, "Privileged Jews," *Jewish Social Studies* 8 (1946), 3–30, here 30.

[63] All quotations are from Georg Simmel, *The Sociology of Georg Simmel*, trans. by Kurt Wolff (New York: Free Press, 1950), 402–408.

[64] On Simmel's attitude towards the Jews: Amos Morris-Reich, "The Beautiful Jew is a Moneylender: Money and Individuality in Simmel's Rehabilitation of the 'Jew'," *Theory Culture & Society* 20 (2004), 127–142.

the stranger as a sociological phenomenon Simmel provides an analysis that goes beyond the old binary oppositions of colonizers versus colonized or oppressors and oppressed. In this respect he reveals the ambivalent ontological situation of the Jew as at once included and excluded from society.

Historians of German Jewish relations have often oversimplified this picture, ignoring ambiguities that call into question conventional notions about the place of Jews in German history.[65] Given what happened in Germany after 1933, it is understandable that historians have tended to concentrate more on what could be referred as the "producer" narrative at the expense of the "consumer" perspective of this history. An attempt to generate a so-called "consumer" narrative of Jewish German history could deepen our understanding of the multifaceted interrelationships between Jews and other Germans and move research beyond sterile binary approaches which stress either inclusion or exclusion. In the following chapters, I take a first step in the direction of such a consumer-oriented approach.

---

[65] On this see also: Moshe Zimmermann, "Jewish History and Jewish Historiography – A Challenge to Contemporary German Historiography," *Leo Baeck Institute Year Book* 35 (1990), 35–52 and Samuel Moyn, "German Jewry and the Question of Identity: Historiography and Theory," *Leo Baeck Institute Year Book* 41 (1996), 291–308.

## 2

# Ethnic Marketing and Consumer Ambivalence
# in Weimar Germany

Modern shopping spaces are arenas for goods and services from around the world, making shopping perhaps the most profound and tangible experience of present-day multiculturalism. The cultural diversity of the marketplace is perhaps best represented by the food industry. In order to open up new markets for their products, food manufacturers and suppliers have targeted new consumers beyond those who are the traditional consumers of their foodstuffs. It is no surprise, then, that present-day shoppers "act as skilled navigators who frequently engage in cultural swapping to sample the many tastes, themes and sounds of different cultures."[1]

The emergence of a marketing regime that advances cultural differences by simulating the diverse needs of different consumer groups, while making this allegedly distinct demand available to a wider consumer market, conforms to observations regarding the changing relationship between production and consumption. Today, many social critics observe, capital does not only have to produce goods assuming that consumption will run by itself, "it is [also] necessary to produce consumers ... [and] demand."[2] According to this approach, the breakdown of the seemingly logical relationship between production and consumption is an upshot of the overproduction of meaning, creating a new order "which is no longer that of either

---

[1] Ahmad Jamal, "Marketing in a Multicultural World: The Interplay of Marketing, Ethnicity and Consumption," *European Journal of Marketing*, 37 (11/12) (2003), 1599. Cf. also on this: Costa Janeen Arnold and Gary J. Bamossy (eds.), *Marketing in a Multicultural World: Ethnicity, Nationalism, and Cultural Identity* (Thousand Oaks, CA: Sage, 1995).
[2] Jean Baudrillard, *In the Shadow of Silent Majority* (New York: Semiotex(e), 1983), 27.

production, or consumption, but that of the simulation of both."[3] This shift towards the production of demand represents for many contemporary social critics the beginning of a new so-called post or late modern era in which "the principle of simulation, and not of reality ... regulates social life."[4]

It is, however, questionable whether such a strict distinction between production and consumption ever existed. Critics of consumer capitalism sometimes write about consumption from a declinist perspective, as if there existed an earlier state in which utility and need, rather than the mere communication of meaning, defined our relationship to objects.[5] From a historical point of view, the relationship between production and consumption, or between economy and culture for that matter, is much more complex and manifold than sometimes suggested by thinkers of such prominence as Theodor Adorno, Hannah Arendt, and Pierre Bourdieu. Indeed, in such a declinist vein, Zygmunt Bauman recently claimed that consumerism creates a new "liquid" society, hollowing out a shared public domain, transcending territorial identities, and eroding more solid identities based on work and locality.[6]

In attempting to sort out the complex relationship between producers and consumers, the question of how and who determines supply is key. While producers typically display themselves as powerless to the changing demands of consumers, they also seek whenever possible to stimulate consumption by enhancing the symbolic value of their products. The introduction of marketing campaigns promoting special products and services for Jews at the beginning of the twentieth century is a good example of such a producer-led change in consumption. In this chapter I will explore the central unit of expression of this marketing campaign – the advertisement. An analysis of these marketing campaigns reveals that consumer culture not only provided a new arena in which to reimagine the

---

[3] Ibid. 89, as well as in his "Simulacra and Simulations," in: *Selected Writings*, trans. Mark Poster (Stanford: Stanford University Press, 1988), 166–184.

[4] Jean Baudrillard, "Symbolic Exchange and Death," in: *Selected Writings*, trans. Mark Poster (Stanford: Stanford University Press, 1988), 120. On this see also: Michael Featherstone, *Consumer Culture and Postmodernism* (London: Sage, 1991).

[5] Daniel Miller, "Consumption as the Vanguard of History: A Polemic by Way of an Introduction," in: *Acknowledging Consumption* (London: Routledge, 1995), 26.

[6] In the last few years we have witnessed a wave of new work trying to conceptualize the relations between culture and economy. A prominent example is Paul du Gay and Michael Pryke (eds.), *Cultural Economy: Cultural Analysis and Commercial Life* (London: Sage, 2006). More on this see in Chapter 13.

position of Jewish consumers in the broader culture but also helped define ways in which Jews were expected to practice their Jewishness.

The discussion will be broken into three sections. First, I will address the question of Jews as consumers to suggest that the so-called renaissance of Jewish life after the Great War was, among other things, a product of the developing consumer culture at that time. The following section will draw on the advertisement sections of Jewish newspapers to examine how the creation of Jewish consumers, as targets of those ads, fostered a feeling of belonging to a wider (non-Jewish) community. This discussion will further suggest that while approaching consumers as Jews promoted a Jewish self-understanding, it also generated confused and ambivalent feelings among Jewish consumers who now had to consolidate different notions of belonging. The concluding section of this discussion will examine the process by which advertisers rendered their products "Jewish" in order to appeal to the allegedly special needs and demands of Jewish consumers. By focusing on advertisements for kosher food as well as on the special promotion campaigns prior to Jewish holidays, this section will further explore the notion of consumer ambivalence.[7] It will propose that the introduction of "Jewish" products to the marketplace cannot be conceptualized merely as an upshot of the emergence of new regimes of consumer culture that acknowledged and facilitated Jewish distinctiveness.[8] In the period before 1933, consolidating a Jewish culture of origin was a highly charged matter as Jews were continuously confronted with questions about belonging. Thus, it seems that at the beginning of the last century ethnic-niche marketing fostered feelings of ambivalence among Jewish consumers, rendering them, as Arendt noted, with "an empty sense of being different."[9]

## ACKNOWLEDGING THE JEWISH CONSUMER

Historians generally agree that Germany's Jews rapidly joined the bourgeoisie in the nineteenth century out of a desire to integrate into German society, suggesting an alleged proclivity between Jewish traditions and bourgeois values. Rather than resulting in a loss of Jewish identity, some

---

[7] On the notion of consumer ambivalence see: Cele Otnes, Tina M. Lowrey and L.J. Shrum, "Toward an Understanding of Consumer Ambivalence," *The Journal of Consumer Research* 24 (1997), 80–93.

[8] Alon Confino and Rudi Koshar, "Regimes of Consumer Culture: New Narratives in Twentieth-Century German History," *German History* 19 (2) (2001), 135–161.

[9] Hannah Arendt, "Privileged Jews," *Jewish Social Studies* 8 (1946), 30.

historians maintain, this process led in fact to the reconsolidation of a Jewish minority as a discrete sociocultural group that, while having become modernized, was still quintessentially Jewish.[10] In this context, consumption was conceptualized in the framework of the bourgeoisie society mainly as a venue of acculturation. Jews took a conspicuous interest in the consumption of high culture, which suggested that they should be considered as a bourgeois group that was simultaneously modern and Jewish.[11] According to this approach, the embracing of the bourgeois lifestyle should no longer be considered as a group of processes that led to the dissolution of a Jewish sphere, but as a way in which mutually nurturing components created a distinctive Jewish identity that defined itself in societal and cultural terms, not only in religious or ethnic terms.

In *The Renaissance of Jewish Culture in Weimar Germany*, one example of such a culturally directed examination, Michael Brenner suggests that Jewish identity in this period was based more on culture than on religion. Brenner argues that the "Jewish renaissance in literature, art, music, and scholarship was no return to traditional Judaism but an attempt to integrate selected aspects of this tradition into the framework of a modern secular culture."[12] The rediscovery of Jewish life and the search for Jewish community, or *Gemeinschaft*, after World War I is displayed here as an answer to the dilemmas of a modern Judaism that was torn between the norms of the majority society and a determination to express cultural distinctiveness. Brenner's study of Weimar Jewry is a good example of the prevailing approach that treats Jews not as objects but as subjects of their history. In his account, Jews are active and conscious participants in the refashioning of Jewish life. Brenner eloquently describes the shift from the so-called non-Jewish German Jew who strove to blend into the majority society to the "authentic" Jewish Jew who struggled to secure Jewish survival in the modern world.

---

[10] Shulamit Volkov, *The Magic Circle: Germans, Jews and Antisemites [in Hebrew]* (Tel Aviv: Am Oved, 2002), 189.

[11] Marion Kaplan, *The Making of the Jewish Middle Class: Women, Family, and Identity in Imperial Germany* (New York: Oxford University Press, 1991). For a general discussion of civil society and German Jews see: Till van Rahden, "Jews and the Ambivalence of Civil Society in Germany, 1800–1933: Assessments and Reassessments," *Journal of Modern History* 77 (2005), 1024–1047.

[12] Michael Brenner, *The Renaissance of Jewish Culture in Weimar Germany* (New Haven: Yale University press, 1996), 21.

While acknowledging the issue of Jewish agency, however, it is important to be aware of social processes that go beyond the process of emancipation, the influence of antisemitism, or the search for Jewish authenticity. Thus, I propose to consider more carefully developments that could have facilitated cultural diversity, specifically in the evolution of a new consumer culture in Europe. Consumer culture did not act solely to foster a sense of separate Jewish identity, nor did it simply facilitate Jewish belonging to a larger culture of consumption. Paradoxically, it did both. As a social arrangement in which structures of meaning and feeling were organized primarily around the act of purchase, consumer culture contributed immensely to the process of standardizing and homogenizing society.[13] At the same time, it allowed individuals and groups to distinguish themselves through the act of buying. Studying the dynamic of consumer cultures in relation to Jewish history reveals how minorities are simultaneously able to maintain a separate identity through consumption while, as consumers, coming to feel a sense of belonging to the majority culture surrounding them.

Examining advertisements, a central pillar of the emerging consumer culture, in the Jewish press of the Weimar period illustrates this development. As we shall see, both Jewish and non-Jewish advertisers saw Jews as a well-defined target group for products and services. Advertising and marketing campaigns, thereby, encouraged and maintained a Jewish distinctive sphere. As the following discussion will also show, Jews were considered a middle-class group and an affluent section of the general consuming public. In these terms, they were an integral part of the bourgeoisie. The primary factor that differentiated them from other consumer groups was their religious affiliation, not their lifestyle, class, or any putatively conspicuous consumption. In other words, from the viewpoint of the consumer culture, religion and to some extent ethnicity were central to shaping Jewish distinctiveness in the modern era.

## CONSUMER AMBIVALENCE

Reading the advertising sections of the press during the Weimar period gives an impression of economic vibrancy and prosperity, not of the actual scarcity and adversity of the time. This split between the virtual world of advertisements and the difficult reality of everyday life in Weimar Germany

---

[13] For this notion of consumption, see Victoria de Grazia's introduction in Victoria de Grazia and Ellen Furlough (eds.), *The Sex of Things: Gender and Consumption in Historical Perspective* (Berkeley: University of California Press, 1996).

is an integral feature of the period. Rather than diminishing the importance of advertising as a historical source, it increases it. While the prosperity presented in the advertising section was unattainable for many, advertising was not merely deceptive or escapist. Instead, advertising from this period contains what scholars call "displaced meaning."[14] It is through advertisements that we can learn about the values, images, and expectations of contemporaries. The advertising sections of the Jewish press were no different. There, too, a plethora of products and services were offered, though it is doubtful whether their Jewish target population, even if considered affluent, could actually have afforded them. The image of the Jews as an affluent group is central here because it obviously influenced the nature of the products and services advertised in the Jewish press. Indeed, the advertising pages in Jewish newspapers contain numerous advertisements for luxurious products such as cars, pianos, life insurance, holiday resorts, and even detective services: all considered to be part of a modern bourgeois lifestyle. However, that lifestyle was not considered only a Jewish one. Such advertisements did not appear solely in the Jewish press, and the majority did not target the Jewish public specifically. Advertisements that did appear in Jewish newspapers were generally anodyne and could have been published in almost any newspaper. Neutral phrases such as "For those with refined taste" (*Für Feinschmecker*) or "Those who know buy" (*Kenner kaufen*) invoked a sense of high quality among the consumer public and aimed to generate a feeling of belonging to a group defined by a refined taste and lifestyle, not necessarily by gender, social status, ethnic origin, or religion. It was, above all, the desire to appeal to as many consumers as possible that determined the kinds of images and language advertisers used.

Yet the fact that these advertisements appeared in Jewish newspapers is significant. The editorial sections of Jewish newspapers, especially during the Weimar years, were preoccupied with the subject of Jewish exclusion.[15] Thus the use of these surfaces for commercial advertisements could be

---

[14] On the notion of displacing meaning see: Grant McCracken, *Culture and Consumption: New Approaches to the Symbolic Character of Consumer Goods and Activities* (Bloomington: Indiana University Press, 1990), 104–117.

[15] On the growing antisemitism during that time period, see: Dirk Walter, *Antisemitische Kriminalität und Gewalt: Judenfeindschaft in der Weimarer Republik* (Bonn: Dietz, 1999); Cornelia Hecht, *Deutsche Juden und Antisemitismus in der Weimarer Republik* (Bonn: Dietz, 2003); Nicola Wenge, *Integration und Ausgrenzung in der städtischen Gesellschaft. Eine jüdisch-nichtjüdische Beziehungsgeschichte Kölns 1918–1933* (Mainz: Philipp von Zabern Verlag, 2005).

FIGURE 2.1 Mercedes-Benz advertisement
From: *Jüdisches Wochenblatt* vol. 4, no. 43 (November 1927), 365.

interpreted as an acknowledgment of a distinct Jewish space suggesting a regime of identities in which Jews were introduced to a variety of lifestyles and cultural affiliations that seemed to complement each other rather than contest existing notions of Jewishness. An advertisement from 1927 will illustrate this point.

In this advertisement for Mercedes-Benz, the company's logo appears next to a line of Mercedes cars being driven across Germany, which is presented with its pre–World War I borders. Displaying the car as modern and dynamic, this advertisement also evokes nationalistic sentiments, suggesting that driving a Mercedes-Benz will help restore Germany's sense of unity and lost pride. It appeared in a Jewish newspaper beside an ad for kosher margarine and lessons for New Hebrew. Referring simultaneously to Jewish religious requirements, new notions of Jewish culture of origins as represented in New Hebrew, and German nationalistic sentiments as well as general notions of modernity, this single page of advertising demonstrates how Jews were embraced as German consumers and, conversely, how they could develop a sense of belonging to a wider consumer community as Jews. Given the images of inclusion suggested by these advertisements, the persistent airing of anxieties about exclusion on the editorial pages of the same newspaper becomes puzzling. This same tension emerges in German Jewish historiographies that oscillate between presenting narratives of Jewish inclusion and exclusion.

Setting aside the question of whether Jews were in fact more included or excluded, the very presence of this binary opposition, and the fact that contemporaries conceptualized their realities in such terms, highlights what is perhaps the most profound Jewish experience of modernity: Jews felt that they were held in a state of suspension between acceptance and rejection. Given the significance of this experience of ambivalence, we should not be tempted to consider the tension between the editorial pages and the advertisement section merely as a reflection of the contrast between discrimination and integration. The interplay between inclusion and exclusion is central for any examination of the Jewish middle-class experience.[16] The advertisement sections as well should be read in these terms, suggesting that the experience of ambivalence informed how Jews felt and presumably even behaved as consumers. Thus, the advertisement page discussed above suggests that Jewish consumers experienced multiple emotional states as they were confronted with seemingly different and at times even contrasting cultural affiliations promoted by these advertisements. This experience of consumer ambivalence becomes even more evident when Jews were specifically targeted as a discrete consumer group.

### ADVERTISING JEWISH

Both the products and services themselves and the way they were marketed to the Jewish people reveal the tendency of the consumer culture to standardize the marketplace and the inclusion of the Jews into the majority society as consumers. This process, as Leora Auslander has suggested, might explain the absence of a distinctive Jewish taste.[17] Nonetheless, numerous advertisements consciously targeted a Jewish consumer public, nurturing what seems to be a distinct Jewish identity. Advertisements of that kind may be grouped into two main categories: (1) advertisements for products and services that were aimed solely at the Jewish consumer public and (2) advertisements for mainstream products and services that were promoted to accord with the specific needs of the Jewish public, or at least attract their attention. Among the first type were religious articles, Haggadoth, matzoth, Hanukkah

---

[16]  van Rahden, "Jews and the Ambivalence," 1033.
[17]  Leora Auslander, "'Jewish Taste?' Jews and the Aesthetics of Everyday Life in Paris and Berlin, 1920–1942," in Rudy Koshar (ed.), *Histories of Leisure* (Oxford: Berg, 2002), 299–318.

candles, and so forth. The second type of advertising presented a broader and far more diverse range of products and services.

First and foremost in the second category were products certified as kosher and therefore suitable for Jewish consumption. The words "kosher" or "kosher for Passover," generally written in Hebrew, graphically distinguish Jewish newspaper advertising pages from those in general newspapers. Every Jewish newspaper of the period contained advertisements for kosher bakeries, for butchers using kosher slaughter methods, and for chain stores, such as the famed Herman Tietz department stores, which had special kosher sections. The name of the rabbi who had granted the *hechsher* (kosher certificate) often appeared beside the word "kosher," although this information (vital for observant Jews) did not feature prominently in all of the advertisements (see Figure 2.2).

In this context, it is worth devoting some time to the role of food advertisements specifically aimed at Jewish consumers. More than any other product, these nurtured an essentialist approach to Jewish identity that considered the Jews, despite their international dispersion, as a unified group with a coherent identity.

Margarine is the most prominent of the industrially manufactured foods that was marketed as kosher. The first margarine was patented in France in 1869. It was developed as a cheap alternative to butter, suitable for use by the armed forces and the lower classes. Initially produced using a mixture of vegetable and nonkosher animal fat, rabbis warned against the new product, describing margarine as a "fake butter" that is strictly forbidden for Jewish use.[18] The first certified kosher pure vegetarian margarine, named "Tomor," appeared in 1904. It was produced by Van den Bergh, a Dutch corporation. Van den Bergh's founder was a Dutch industrialist, Simon Van den Bergh (1819–1907), who was also an observant Jew. The origin of the name Tomor is unclear, but it may reasonably be assumed that, like many other brands of vegetarian margarine introduced prior to the world war, such as Palmin and Palmona, the name "Tomor" hinted at margarine's derivation from

---

[18] Michael Cahn, *Butter Verfälschung: Eine Warnung für jeden jüdischen Haushalt* (Frankfurt a.M.: J. Kauffmann, 1891). I am grateful to Dov Weinstein who made me aware of the rich literature dealing with the margarine question.

From this literature we learn that while it was forbidden to consume margarine, Jews were allowed to trade with it.

Aktiengesellschaft für

# Rituelle
# Bedarfsartikel

unter Aufsicht des Rabbinats
der Kaschruth-Kommission der
jüdischen Gemeinde in Berlin

in den Warenhäusern

# Hermann Tietz
Leipziger Strasse        Alexanderplatz

## IV. STOCK:

# Alle Koscher-
# Lebensmittel

Fleisch / Geflügel / Wurst / Kolonial-
waren / Pflanzenfette / Weine / Liköre

FIGURE 2.2  Ad for Kosher Products at the Tietz Department Store in Berlin
From: CV-Zeitung (May 7, 1926), 268.

coconut, which grows on the tree called *Palm* in German and *tomer* in
Yiddish.[19]

---

[19] See the first ads for "Tomor," in: *Ost und West*, vol. 6 (7) (1906), 511; *as well as in Ost
und West* 7 (3) (1907), 216. It should be also noted that despite its name, Tomor was
made out of almond milk rather than coconut.

FIGURE 2.3 Two Advertisement Stamps for Tomor Margarine with Painting by Moritz Daniel Oppenheim
From: The author's private collection.

The name "Tomor" gave a hint of exoticism to margarine and signaled the product's target population – the Jewish consumer population. The Van den Bergh brothers, who managed the corporation in the early twentieth century, were well aware of the special challenges of keeping kosher and of kosher margarine's economic potential among Jewish consumers in Central Europe. Accordingly, Tomor margarine's marketing campaign highlighted the Jewish way of life, illustrating advertisements, calendars, postcards, and other promotional materials with paintings by the famous German Jewish painter Moritz Daniel Oppenheim (1799–1892).[20]

Marketing campaigns depicting margarine as a part of traditional Jewish family life were intended to promote the sense of Jewishness among its consumers. A Jewish cookbook and various pamphlets clarifying Jewish religious law were also used to encourage sales of Tomor

---

[20] Wolfgang Krebs, *Tomor eine Koschere Margarine vom Niederrhein und ihre religiöse Werbung* (Kleve: Verlag für Kultur und Technik, 2002). On Moritz Daniel Oppenheim see: Ezra Mendelsohn, *Painting a People: Maurycy Gottlieb and Jewish Art* (Hanover: University Press of New England, 2002).

margarine. The key message was that kosher margarine simplified the preparation and expanded the range of Jewish kosher meals. Since margarine was manufactured from vegetable oil, it could be used in cooking both meat and dairy dishes. It also allowed Jewish cooks to broaden their range by introducing new recipes previously prohibited by the laws of kashrut. Margarine did not only enrich and improve Jewish cuisine, suggested these advertisements: it could also help protect the Jewish way of life from assimilation by making it easier to keep kosher.[21]

When butter became a luxury during the 1920s, competition between margarine manufacturers for the growing consumer market intensified, to the benefit of the relatively small segment of Jewish consumers. Local producers of kosher margarine were found in almost every major German city.[22] One of Van den Bergh's main rivals in the area of kosher margarine was the *Westdeutsche Nahrungsmittelwerke mbH* corporation, founded in 1907 in Duisburg. A kosher margarine called "Hadassah" was one of the first brands produced by the corporation before the Great War.[23] In the 1920s, it began marketing other kosher brands under the supervision of Dr. Josef Carlebach, an orthodox rabbi from Hamburg. Some of the company's brand names were Hebrew or Yiddish derivations, such as *Matana, Temimo,* and *Azuma.* Unlike Van den Bergh, the owners of *Westdeutsche Nahrungsmittelwerke* were not Jews, and their interest in kosher margarine was purely commercial.

Margarine was not the only product that revealed the economic potential of the Jewish consumption market. Other products that were marketed specifically to the Jewish public by awarding them kashrut certification include cleaning liquids, such as Solerine metal polish, toothpaste, and soap.

Still more common were kosher coffee and kosher chocolate, including the brands *Feodora* and *Stollwerck*, the latter striving to become a model German company under National Socialism.[24] Both brands are still sold in German stores today. We will return to the discussion of chocolate and other comfort foods in later sections of this book.

---

[21] See, for example, marketing material for the 25th anniversary publication that could be found in the *Israelitischer Kalender, September 1928 to October 1929* (Frankfurt a.M.: Verlag von M. Lehrberger & Co., 1928).

[22] For instance, "Ruth" and "Debora" were manufactured in the city of Frankfurt or "Makabi," while "Chinom" and "Schomen" were labels marketed in Hamburg.

[23] On this corporation see: Stadtarchiv Duisburg, Bestand 63–28.

[24] Sacha Widdig, *Stollwerck: Schokolade aus Köln* (Erfurt: Sutton Verlag, 2013); Tanja Junggeburth, *Stollwerck 1839–1932. Unternehmerfamilie und Familienunternehmen* (Stuttgart: Franz Steiner Verlag, 2014); Gerald D. Feldman, "Thunder from Arosa: Karl Kimmich and the Reconstruction of the Stollwerck Company 1930–1932," *Business and Economic History: Journal of the Business History Conference* 26 (2) (1997), 686–695.

HAG Coffee is an even more fascinating example of a product that received kashrut certification to comply with the Jewish public's needs – it, too, is still marketed worldwide as a brand of decaffeinated coffee. HAG Coffee's sales promotion system was renowned for its innovation and originality. It was first marketed prior to the Great War as a modern, healthy brand aimed at the broadest consumer group possible. Inevitably, the company's sophisticated marketing staff discovered the Jewish consumer market and targeted it with kosher coffee. One can safely assume that this recognition of the importance of Jewish customers occurred at the same time as when HAG Coffee was planning to penetrate the American market, before World War I. In a letter sent in 1914 by HAG Coffee's charismatic founder Ludwig Roselius (1874–1943) to the company's sales manager, Roselius asks him not to overlook the fact that New York is "the world's largest Jewish city." "The German experience," he wrote, "has taught us that the Jews recognize the benefits of decaffeinated coffee long before others, and just as they set the tone in matters like going to the theatre and travelling to leisure resorts or spas, they will be the first to try decaffeinated coffee in America."[25] In Germany, a special advertising campaign for HAG Coffee was aimed at the Jewish public ahead of the Passover holiday, and it apparently derived from the company's competition with Korinthen, a rival decaffeinated coffee that, unlike HAG, was produced from grains and was thus not kosher for Passover. According to the company's in-house newspaper, *HAG-Post*, HAG advertised its "Coffee for Passover" in special advertisements placed in a range of Jewish newspapers every year.[26]

The attention devoted to the Jewish public by HAG Coffee's marketing team is particularly interesting in view of the much debated figure of Ludwig Roselius, the dynamic founder and manager of HAG Coffee. Formally, the company strove to maintain neutrality in all religious and political matters. Responding to a Jewish client who threatened to sever his business relationship with HAG after hearing that the company and its manager supported Hitler, HAG Coffee denied having any formal as well as informal ties with the Nazi movement or to any other political party. Depicting such allegations as rumors spread by malevolent parties, the letter goes on to mention recent Nazi press attacks against HAG kosher coffee as evidence of its distance from National Socialism. This response

[25] A letter from Ludwig Roselius to Otto Haupt, 18.3.1914, in: HAG Archiv Böttcherstrasse Bremen, Kleine Archiv-Mappen.

[26] These papers are: *CV-Zeitung*, Berlin; *Der Israelit*, Hamburg; *Israelitische Wochenschrift*, Hamburg; *Das jüdische Familienblatt*, Frankfurt a.M. [assumingly the *Israelitisches Familienblatt*]. This list is taken from: HAG-POST, no. 3 (April 1, 1927), 7, and HAG-POST, no. 4 (March 1, 1928), 8.

FIGURE 2.4   The HAG Ad for the Jewish Press
Here from: The *Israelit* no. 14 (April 7, 1927), 15.

was published in the company's internal newspaper *HAG-Post* in May 1932. The company's sales representatives were specifically instructed to enclose this letter in their everyday business portfolio and to regard it as the official and binding position of HAG Coffee declaring, "anyone who drinks coffee HAG is dear and important to us. Which political affiliation or creed he is, is for us completely irrelevant."[27]

There were, however, good reasons to question the political leanings of HAG's director, Ludwig Roselius. Renowned both as a smart business-man who transformed HAG into a worldwide brand and as an art collector and philanthropist, Roselius in fact had close links with the German right wing.[28] Two people in particular influenced Roselius and his endeavors: the composer Richard Wagner, whom Roselius greatly admired, and Houston Stewart Chamberlain, one of the founding fathers of racial antisemitism in Germany, with whom Roselius corresponded regularly. With the Nazi rise to power, Roselius became an ardent supporter of the new regime and, on his death in 1943, was laid to rest in a state ceremony in his hometown of Bremen.[29] How could a man who belonged to such antisemitic right-wing circles market his company's flagship product with

[27] "Jeder, der Kaffee HAG trinkt, ist uns lieb und wert. Welcher politischen Einstellung oder welchen Glaubens er ist, ist uns dabei vollkommen gleichgültig." In: HAG-POST, no. 12 (May 28, 1932), 2.

[28] Dieter Pfliegensdörfer, *Ludwig Roselius ... wie ihn keiner kennt* (Bremen: Universität Bremen, 1987); Arn Strohmeyer, Parsifal in Bremen. Richard Wagner, *Ludwig Roselius und die Bötterstrasse* (Weimar: VDG, 2002); Nicola Vetter and Ludwig Roselius, *Ein Pionier der deutsche Öffentlichkeitsarbeit* (Bremen: H.M. Hauschikd, 2002).

[29] In an open letter to the HAG companies' workers, entitled Kaffee Hag:
*Ein Herz schlägt für die Reichskanzlei* (HAG Coffee: A heart beats for the Chancellor of

Hebrew lettering attesting to its kosher status? It is difficult to propose a conclusive answer with the few sources available. Perhaps Roselius is an example of a non-antisemitic right-wing German. A more reasonable explanation is that, as a businessman, Roselius did his utmost to achieve the highest profits for his company, in whatever situation, applying any methods.[30] At any rate, HAG's kosher coffee demonstrates that producers and advertisers were well aware of the varied needs of their customers and tailored their marketing accordingly.

BEYOND KOSHER

Kosher was just one signifier of a growing marketing regime that identified Jews as a discrete group of consumers. Publishers also reached out to Jewish consumers. Both Jewish and non-Jewish publishers produced books, periodicals, art illustrations, greetings cards, and calendars explicitly intended for Jewish buyers. Jewish music was also produced and marketed specifically for Jewish consumers. During the years of the Weimar Republic, almost all leading record companies in Germany produced Jewish music.[31]

In the advertising pages of Jewish newspapers, we can also find advertisements for cooking stoves specially adapted to the needs of the traditional Jewish kitchen. Detergent, shaving cream, soap, and toothpaste were other products overtly marketed for Jewish consumers. Even the *Leo-Werke* (Leo Works), one of Europe's largest toothpaste manufacturers in the interwar period, made efforts to secure the Jewish market for its toothpaste *Chlorodonts-Zahnpasta*. Under the title "Clarification to all the rigorously devout Israelites!" (*Zur Aufklärung aller gläubigen streng Israeliten!*), the Leo Factory published a statement in *Der Israelit*, the official journal of the Orthodox movement in Germany, dispelling rumors that pork fat was used to make the company's toothpaste. According to this statement, these malicious rumors were spread by a competitor. The Chlorodont toothpaste, it was further asserted, was

the Reich), Roselius expressed his ardent support to the new regime shortly after the Nazi takeover. The letter is available at www.salmoxisbote.de/Bote18/Roselius.htm.

[30] As late as mid-1932 HAG still maintained that Roselius kepts himself aloof from political matters, suggesting that only on rare occasions he gave voice to his views and that was always on economic and related forging policy issues. See in HAG-POST, no. 12 (May 28, 1932).

[31] Fritz Scherbel, "Wiedergabe durch jüdisches Synagogale Musik und ihre Schallplatte," *Jahrbuch für gross Berlin* (1930), 66–72; Hermann Schildberger, "Die Schallplatte im Dienst des Jüdischen Gottesdienstes," *Jahrbuch für gross Berlin* (1931), 65–72.

"manufactured under strict scientific supervision using only vegetable fat so that observant Jews could use it without worry." While announcing that its flagship product was suitable for Jewish use, the Leo Factory also advertised in the Nazi press, in addition to zealously targeting Jewish consumers in Eastern Europe as we learn from Chlorodont advertisements in the Yiddish press of the period. Such adverts could be found in Jewish newspapers in Eastern Europe long after it became illicit to advertise German products to Jews in the Third Reich.

Back in Germany, even in times of rising antisemitism before 1933, some non-Jewish-owned companies made great effort to address and secure Jewish consumers. A salient case is the chocolate manufacturer Erich Hamann from Wilhelmsdorf in Berlin. As late as 1930, when the Nazi party became the leading force in German politics, the Erich Hamann Company placed an advert in several leading Jewish newspapers with nationwide circulation that refuted rumors suggesting the company or its employees were antisemitic. As with Chlorodont the Hamann announcement accused competitors of spreading this malicious rumor, and, as in the case of HAG Coffee, it explicitly stated that Hamann Chocolatier (which still operates in Berlin today) opposed such views and wished to continue to serve Jewish costumers (Figure 2.5).

This marketing regime was not limited to consumer goods but also included different types of services. Thus, for example, the German shipping company *Hamburg-Amerika Linie* (HAPAG) regularly advertised in Jewish newspapers, noting that it provided kosher food on some of its ships.[32] HAPAG's main rival, North German Lloyd (*Norddeutscher Lloyd*) provided kosher meals to all its America destinations, indicating in its ads that its *streng ritual Küche* (strict ritual kitchen) was under the supervision of the rabbinate of the city of Bremen. It is likely that such services were directed toward Jewish immigrants from Eastern Europe who passed through Germany on their journey to the New World. The North German Lloyd also advertised that on request passengers could get kosher meals on journeys to most of its other destinations as well. It is, however, not clear as to what extent Jewish passengers made use of the kosher options offered to them by the shipping companies. In fact, contemporary reports frequently cite the lack of kosher food on the ships. Interestingly the

[32] HAPAG was run until 1918 by Albert Ballin, who was known as one of the people closest to Kaiser Wilhelm II. On Ballin, Eberhard Straub, *Albert Ballin. Der Reeder des Kaiser* (Berlin: Siedler, 2001); Susanne Wiborg, *Albert Ballin* (Hamburg: Ellert & Richter Verlag, 2000).

Wir haben festsiellen müssen, dass über uns und unsere Firma verleumderische Behauptungen im Umlauf sind, als seien bei uns an irgendeiner Stelle

# antisemitische Tendenzen

sei es offen, sei es versteckt, vorhanden. Es handelt sich um Machenschaften unlauterer Konkurrenz! Niemand steht bei uns antisemitischen Bestrebungen oder gar Parteien nahe! Niemals sind von oder bei uns solche Bestrebungen unterstützt oder auch nur geduldet worden. Das Gegenteil ist richtig, sowohl nach geschäftlicher wie nach privater Richtung hin.

Wir wären aufrichtig dankbar, wenn uns, um sie gerichtlich verfolgen zu können, die Urheber oder Verbreiter solcher Verleumdungen **namhaft** gemacht werden würden.

*Erich Haman*

**Bittere Schokoladen**

Kurfürstendamm 26a    Brandenburgische Str. 17
Leipziger Str. 82    Unter den Linden 14
Potsdamer Str. 22    Teplitzer Str. 40
Pariser Str. 28/29.

FIGURE 2.5 "Antisemitic tendencies" Advertisement of the chocolate manufacturing company Erich Haman, Berlin, denying allegations of antisemitic tendencies of the firm or any of its employees
Here from: *CV-Zeitung* 5 (November 28, 1930), 620.

blame for the absence of kosher food was directed to Jewish passengers who failed to show an interest in maintaining dietary restrictions, rather than to the shipping companies themselves.[33] Despite such

---

[33] See, for example, the reports of the *Verein zur Förderung rituale Speisehäuser* here published in: *Deutsch Israelitische Zeitung: Organ für die Gesamtinteressen des Judenthums*, 48 (1931), 7.

complications, shipping companies continued to advertise kosher services in the Jewish press.

A handful of overtly Jewish or Hebrew brand names existed in the marketplace alongside the mainstream products and services, mentioned above, that also targeted Jewish consumers. In addition to kosher margarines, some of which were given Hebrew names, other products, such as the butter, under the brand of *Gan Eden* (Paradise), vitamins branded as *Hermon*, or Malkah Cigarettes were further examples of the use of Hebrew most likely with the intent to appeal to Jewish consumers. In the book trade, the use of Hebrew names was even more pronounced. Publishing houses like *Jüdische Verlag, Hermon, Eshkol*, or the famous Jewish bookstore *Kedem* in Berlin are a few of the well-documented examples of this specialist trend in Jewish publishing.[34]

## THE STAR OF DAVID: A JEWISH LOGO?

Another fascinating and even less known aspect of this history of the Jewish ambivalence on the marketplace is the use of the Jewish Star (or Shield) of David either for promotion of specific products or as a company trademark. According to Gershom Scholem the Star of David is not an ancient Jewish emblem. The use of the six-pointed star as a Jewish symbol, he claims, dates to the nineteenth century when Jews looked for a striking and simple symbol that would "represent" Judaism just as the cross hallmarked Christianity. This inclination led to the ascendancy of the *Magen David* (Shield of David) in official use, on ritual objects, and in many other ways.[35] Thus, for example, in 1822 it was used on the Rothschild family coat of arms when they

---

[34] The *Adressbuch für den jüdischen Buchhandel* (Berlin: Jalkut, 1927) listed over 450 bookstores and publishers specializing on the Jewish market. The city of Frankfurt alone, which had a Jewish population of around 29,000 in 1925, had sixteen self-proclaimed Jewish bookshops. See Ernst Fischer and Stephan Füsse (eds.), *Historische Kommission Des: Geschichte des Deutschen Buchhandels Im 19. und 20. Jahrhundert*, vol. 2 (Berlin: Walter de Gruyter, 2012), 393–397; see also Volker Dahm, *Das jüdische Buch im Dritten Reich* (Munich: C.H. Beck, 1993); Katrin Diehl, *Die jüdische Presse im Dritten Reich Zwischen Selbstbehauptung und Fremdbestimmung* (Berlin: de Gruyter, 1997); Herbert Freeden, *Die jüdische Presse im Dritten Reich* (Berlin: Jüdischer Verlag, 1987).

[35] Gershom Scholem, *Das Davidschild – Geschichte eines Symbols* (Frankfurt a.M.: Jüdischer Verlag, 2010); Max Grunwald, "Ein altes Symbol in neuer Beleuchtung," *Jahrbuch für jüdische Geschichte und Literatur* 4 (1901), 119–131; Johanna Michaelis, "Das Davidsschild," *Der Morgen* 10 (2) (1934), 80–86; M. Gaster, "The MAgen David," *Rimon*, no. 3 (1923), 28–30; Georg Eisner, *Vom Hexagramm zum*

were raised to the nobility by the Austrian emperor, and from 1840 Heinrich Heine signed his correspondence from Paris in the *Augsburger Allgemeine Zeitung* with a *Magen David* instead of his name, indicating his Jewish origin in spite of his conversion. At the end of the nineteenth century the Zionist movement adopted the Shield of David as its insignia, and eventually the state of Israel made it official by putting it on its flag.[36] According to Scholem, it is precisely because of the equivocal history of the six-pointed star as a Jewish symbol that the first Zionist Congress of 1897 chose it as the pictogram for the new movement of national aspirations. On the one hand, Scholem explains, during the nineteenth century, the Star of David was widely diffused. Because it was found, for example, on many new synagogues and Jewish cemeteries, and on the stationery of many charitable organizations, it was easily recognizable. On the other hand, in the eyes of contemporaries it did not evoke explicit religious connotations. This lack of religious association, Scholem postulated, became its virtue. "The symbol did not arouse memories of the past: it could be filled with hope for the future."[37]

Even so, as late as 1917 the Hungarian rabbi Dr. Béla Vajda could still claim that the Star of David was just one of several Jewish symbols and could not be considered as the exclusive emblem of Jewry.[38] During World War I, military officials on both sides of the frontline started using the Star of David to mark the gravestones of the Jewish fallen soldiers. As a result, the six-pointed star had become an exclusively Jewish symbol by the war's end. The six-pointed star remained clearly associated with Jews through the 1920s and was reinforced by National Socialist iconography that used the symbol to mark Jewishness, eventually forcing Jews to wear the *Judenstern* (Jewish star, or yellow badge) in order to designate and degrade them.[39]

*Davidstern: Sein Weg zum Symbol der Juden*, web version available at www.eisner-georg .ch/Andere/Davidstern/Davidstern.pdf.

[36] Don Andelman and Lea Shamgar-Handelman, "Shaping Time: The Choice of the National Emblem of Israel," in: Emiko Ohnuki-Tierney (ed.), *Culture Through Time: Anthropological Approaches* (New Haven: Stanford University Press, 1990), 193–229.

[37] Gershom Scholem, "The Curious History of the Six Pointed Star; How the 'Magen David' Became the Jewish Symbol," *Commentary* 8 (1949), 251.

[38] Béla Vadja, "Menora, Davidschild und Salomos Siegel," *Mitteilungen der Gesellschaft für jüdische Volkskunde* 20 (3/4) (1917), 42.

[39] For an interesting apologetic reaction for this identification, see two articles that were published under the title "Davidsschild und Hakenkreuz" (*Shield of David and the Swastika*) *in the Montatsschrift für Geschichte und Wissenschaft des Judentums* 66 (1922), 1–11.

**Streng rituell...**

wird Kunerol erzeugt, in modernen, appe-
titlich reinen Anlagen, die vom Publikum
jederzeit besichtigt werden können.
Kunerol ist garantiert reines, 100%iges
Pflanzenfett. Seine besonderen Vorzüge
sind: Großer Nährwert, leichte Verdau-
lichkeit und lange Haltbarkeit.

Kunerol wird unter ständiger
Aufsicht des Herrn Bezirks-
rabbiners S. Ehrenfeld zu
Mattersburg hergestellt.

**KUNEROL**
**100% REINES KOKOSNUSSFETT**

FIGURE 2.6  Kunerol Ad for Kosher Margarine with Star of David
From: *Die Stimme: Jüdische Zeitung* (April 7, 1932), 3.

Even without National Socialism, it is clear from the evidence at hand that the hexagram was widely used to designate and address Jewish consumers. More often than not, Jewish butchers and other food manufacturers used the Star of David to identify special services on the marketplace. Some advertisers seem to have put the six-pointed star on their adverts for no obvious reason except to "out" themselves as Jewish or simply to lure Jewish consumers, most colorfully Siegmund Breitbart, a vaudeville strongman and Jewish folklore hero, who used it as his insignia.

Advertisements for rubber goods, medical equipment, and margarine all featured the Star. Thus, for example, the Austrian *Kunerol Werke*, one of the Europe's foremost margarine manufactures, designed a whole series of adverts for its kosher margarine in which the Star of David loomed behind an orthodox Jew blessing the wine.

The use of the six-pointed star increased during the early 1930s and became even more frequent after the Nazis came to power in January 1933. This might explain why, by July 1933, one shrewd printing company in Berlin already offered Shield of David plates (*Klischees*) proclaiming "no advert without the Mogen Dovid" (Figure 2.7).

To what extent did the Jewish association with the hexagram influence how it was used and perceived beyond the Jewish context? Since the late

FIGURE 2.7 "No advert without the Mogen Dovid."
From: *Frankfurter Israelitische Gemeindeblatt* vol. 11, no. 11 (1933), 303.

Middle Ages, the hexagram had often been used in Central Europe as a symbol to indicate establishments offering food and drink to passersby. Before 1933 the symbol adorned the marketing materials, including advertising stamps and badges, for gatherings of gastronomy associations in Germany and Switzerland (Figure 2.8).

In southern Germany, in particular, the Star was used as a trademark for brewery guilds. Several breweries, like Würzburg Hofbräu (founded 1643) and Maisel beer, another South German brewery that was founded in 1887, used the *Brauerstern* (brewery star) as their logo, and it remains so today.[40] Porcelain manufacturers from all over Europe also used the

---

[40] Matthias Trum, "Historische Darstellungen, Zunftzeichen und Symbole des Brauer- und Mälzerhandwerks," Technical University Munich, MA thesis (2008) available at www.brauerstern.de/index.html.

FIGURE 2.8 Advertising Material for the Convention of the German Innkeeper Association
From: The author's private collection (left) and Museum im Schloss Neu-Augustusburg, Weißenfels (right).

six-pointed star as backstamps for their products.[41] At the beginning of the twentieth century, a growing number of companies and commercial organizations adopted the hexagram as their logo. It could be seen on advertisements for diverse goods and services from fabric to steel.

Many of these companies were not Jewish-owned, and their use of the six-pointed star was not intended to evoke any Jewish associations. However, given the growing identification of the hexagram as a Jewish emblem, it is difficult not to question the commercial use of the symbol, especially in cases of businesses owned by Jews. A case in point is Ludwig Scherk, who founded in 1906 a perfumery in Berlin. Scherk Company first produced face powders and then moved onto perfume, becoming a prominent cosmetic maker after the Great War with branches in Berlin, New York, and Vienna. Since 1910 the company's flagship brand

[41]   W. Burton and R. L. Hobson, *Handbook of Marks on Pottery and Porcelain* (London: Macmillan and Co., 1909); Ludwig Danckert, *Directory of European Porcelain* (London: NAG Press, 2004).

FIGURE 2.9   Page from the Scherk company product catalog with Mystikum Hexagram Logo, 1920/1926 (Inv. nr. 2009/239)
Courtesy of the Jewish Museum Berlin with permission of Irene Alice Scherk.

had comprised a series of cosmetic products marketed under the name Mystikum and featuring a six-pointed star as its logo.

Some argue that the use of the symbol was an allusion to Ludwig Shrek's Jewish heritage. There is, however, little evidence to support this claim.[42] For one thing, Scherk and his family were not observant Jews. Fritz Scherk, one of Ludwig and Alice's two sons, depicted his parents as "wholeheartedly freethinkers" (*vollkommene Freidenker*) who did not change their ways even when his pious grandparents moved to live with them in Berlin, at times to the overt discontent of the latter.[43] And still, when reflecting on the immediate postwar situation in 1919, Ludwig Scherk depicts with great apprehension the "flagrant (*Schsmlos*), scurrilous (*niederträchtiger*) Jewish hatred" of the time. His wife Alice recalled

[42]   In fact, it is more likely that the use of the hexagram as logo for Mystikum is more connected to its history as a symbol of alchemy. But also for this there is no evidence.
[43]   Scherk Tagebuch Dairy entry from June 1 to 21, 1919 (Jewish Museum Berlin).

a few months later how with the progression of the war the situation "for us Jews" became ever more difficult due to growing antisemitism.[44] From the family logbook we learn that like other families of similar social standing, the Scherks led a typical bourgeois lifestyle and while consciously Jewish, their Jewishness seemed to consist mostly in loose sentiments of affiliation to a religious minority group – a sense of belonging that became ever more palpable as antisemitism increased. With this in mind, it seems that even if initially Ludwig Scherk did not intend to invoke any Jewish sentiments with the Mystikum six-pointed star logo, it could very well be the case that his Jewishness helped to establish such a connotation.

An even more intriguing example is the Bulgaria cigarette factory in Dresden, which was the capital of German cigarette industry at the beginning of the twentieth century. After purchasing the cigarette factory "Bera" in 1925, the tobacconist Salomon Krenter introduced to the market, *Bulgaria*, his own cigarette label.[45] Krenter's idea was to produce a high-quality cigarette at a lower price by using only premium tobacco imported from Bulgaria (thus the name).[46] As a trademark for the new brand, Krenter chose Ilse Lagerfeld's six-pointed star design in the colors of the Bulgarian flag – white, green, and red – to which she added the blue color, creating a powerful logo that over the years appeared in differed variations, many of which incorporated the Jewish Star of David.

It is highly unlikely that Krenter and Lagerfeld were unaware of the Jewish connotation of the six-pointed star they registered as the trademark in February 1926. According to one interpretation, since the star symbol was also known as the "Seal of Solomon," it implied that the cigarette manufacturer guaranteed his product with all the authority of the biblical King Solomon.[47] Such speculations notwithstanding, Lagerfeld created an imposing design that became the centerpiece of a promotional campaign

---

[44]  Ibid., entries September 9, 1919, and June 6, 1920.

[45]  Volker Ilgen, "Bulgaria," *Trödler- und Sammler Journal*, no. 5 (2005), 168–175; Eric Lindner, "Jüdische Unternehmer in der Dresdner Zigarettenindustrie," *Dresdner Hefte* 24 (1) (1996), 73–57; HStADD, 11045 Amtsgericht Dresden, 1355, Bl. 17654.

[46]  Hans Tischert, *Stätten deutscher Arbeit* (Berlin: Europa-Pressedienst, 1930), 123–130. It should be further noted that *Bulgaria* was not the first label to make reference to the Bulgarian origins of its tobacco by using the colors of the Bulgarian flag. It was also not uncommon to use names of states or cities from the Balkans for cigarette brand names. On such and other examples, see Dirk Schindelbeck, Christoph Alten, Gerulf Hitt, Stefan Knopf and Sandra Schürmann, *Zigarettenfronten. Die politischen Kulturen des Rauchens in der Zeit des Ersten Weltkriegs* (Marburg: Jonas Verlag, 2014); more generally on the tobacco industry in Bulgaria, Mary C. Neuburger, *Balkan Smoke: Tobacco and the Making of Modern Bulgaria* (Ithaca: Cornell University Press, 2013).

[47]  Ilgen, "Bulgaria," 168.

FIGURE 2.10 An example of the Visibility of the *Bulgaria's* Logo: a billboard on a house in Dresden with Bulgaria ad (photograph Max Nowak) Courtesy of the Sächsische Landesbibliothek-Staats-und Universitätsbibliothek Dresden/Deutsche Fotothek.

for the new cigarette brand.[48] At the end of the 1920s, the *Bulgaria* logo was highly visible on a range of marketing materials, including cigarette packs, advertisements, the company's letterhead, billboards (including the company's building itself), and even children's toys. The company's name and logo even adorned the first ball-shaped house in the world, built in Dresden in 1928.[49]

Despite its successful launch, the brand could not save Krenter's company. The difficult economic situation and the harsh competition of the time forced Krenter to surrender his control over the company in order to save the brand. In 1928 the Reemtsma Company from Hamburg, which at that time already controlled around 20 percent of the German cigarette market, took over *Bulgaria*. Reemtsma's interest in the new brand must

---

[48] Not much is known about Ilse Lagerfeld except that since 1929 she was a member of the German advertising association (Deutschen Reklame-Verbands) and the aunt, by marriage, of the famous fashion designer Karl Lagerfeld. See information in the archive of the Museum of Labor (Museum der Arbeit) Hamburg, available at http://46.163.108.17/zeig .FAU?sid=953C3EB511&dm=1&ind=4&ipos=Lagerfeld%2C+Ilse.

[49] The Dresden ball-house did not survive the war, but images of it with the *Bulgaria* name and logo are available on the Internet.

have been substantial. Not as with many of their other acquisitions, the *Bulgaria* label remained to a large extent unaffected. Krenter was kept as managing director for two more years, while Ilse Lagerfeld continued to design *Bulgaria* products well into the 1930s. In fact, the whole arrangement was supposed to remain secret, among other reasons, because Reemtsma had come under attack for antitrust violations.[50]

While this consultation helped the *Bulgaria* cigarette to maintain its distinct identity, the Reemtsma takeover offered new marketing opportunities. As a result, *Bulgaria* became one of the leading brands of low-priced cigarettes in Germany. Beyond the backing of a major cooperation, the introduction of a new type of sport cigarettes helped *Bulgaria* to establish its leading position on the German cigarette market.

On the eve of 1933, the six-pointed star logo adorned major sport competitions sponsored by *Bulgaria*; it featured on collectible sport card albums produced by the company, as well as on advertisements in local and national newspapers, including the Jewish as well as the Nazi press.

The *Bulgaria*'s Star of David soon came to the attention of certain members of the National Socialist party, and they were not pleased by what they saw. After spotting a series of large *Bulgaria* ads in the official Nazi party publication *Völkischer Beobachter* (*VB*), the Saxony Nazi party press officer wrote a fuming letter to the publisher, expressing deep dismay at the unambiguous use of the *Judenstern* (see Figure 2.12). He was equally offended by founder Phillipp F. Reemtsma's vindications of his company's expansion policies.[51]

It is not clear what sparked more outrage: Reemtsma's response or the fact that the *VB* had allowed him to voice his position in the principal party newspaper. To be sure, there was more at stake here than just a protest against the commercial use of an alleged Jewish symbol. The accusation that Reemtsma produced "Jewish cigarettes" reflected a deeper National Socialist resentment of big business in general.[52] National Socialist

[50] Erik Lindner, *Die Reemtsmas: Geschichte einer deutschen Unternehmerfamilie* (Munich: Piper, 2008), 46–49.

[51] "Ein Nachwort zum Prozess Reemtsma gegen Levita," *Völkischer Beobachter* (January 6/7, 1932).

[52] Tino Jacobs, *Rauch und Macht: Das Unternehmen Reemtsma 1920 bis 1961* (Göttingen: Wallstein, 2008); Waltraud Sennebogen, *Zwischen Kommerz und Ideologie: Berührungspunkte von Wirtschaftswerbung und Propaganda im Nationalsozialismus* (Munich: Meidenbauer, 2008); Michael Werner, *Stiftungsstadt und Bürgertum: Hamburgs Stiftungskultur vom Kaiserreich bis Nationalsozialismus* (Munich: Oldenbourg Verlag, 2011), 415; Christoph Maria Merki, "Die nationalsozialistische Tabakpolitik," *Vierteljahrshefte für Zeitgeschichte* 46 (1) (1998), 19–42; Robert Proctor, *The Nazi War on Cancer* (Princeton: Princeton University Press, 1999), 234–236.

FIGURE 2.11 Advertising Poster for *Bulgaria* Cigarettes Featuring the Hamburg Sport Club Football Players (Hamburger SV), from the beginning of the 1930s.[53] Courtesy of the Museum der Arbeit Stiftung Historische Museen Hamburg.

---

[53] According to Werner Skrentny, an expert on HSV history, the player with the ball is Walter Risse (1893–1969), later member of the SA. Behind him on the left is Hans Rave (1903–1977), and on the right Asbjörn Halvorsen (1898–1955), a Norwegian international, who was imprisoned by the Germans and was in concentration camps

FIGURE 2.12  An example of a *Bulgaria* Cigarette Advert from the *Völkischer Beobachter* celebrating the origins of the brand's tobacco. This specific advert from March 25, 1932, featured two prominent – one modern, the other historical – buildings in the city of Dresden proclaiming "as a badge of distinction the people of Bulgaria were given the title 'the Germans of the Balkans.' This indicates that these brave people confront the challenges of modern civilization with infinite resilience."
From: `Völkischer Beobachter*, March 25, 1932.

spokesmen blamed Reemtsma, and its success in swallowing up competitors, for the economic plight of many small businesses. Especially among the ranks of the *Sturmabteilung* (SA), the notorious Nazi party assault division, Reemtsma products stirred much hostility.[54] In its search for new fiscal resources, the SA sought to produce its own cigarette brand. Manufactured by a small cigarette factory in Dresden, the storm trooper cigarettes provided handsome revenue for the SA and helped to raise its profile. With slogans like *"Gegen Trust und Konzern"* (against Trust and Corporate), the new brand sought to portray itself as David fighting the Goliaths of large industry. Other small cigarette manufacturers targeted Nazi smokers, urging the party followers "smoke only your own brands."[55]

At the beginning of the 1930s the Nazi attacks on the cigarette empire from Hamburg increased. Beyond calls to boycott the company's products, in a number of places retailers of Reemtsma brands were beaten,

---

from August 5, 1942, until his liberation in April 11, 1945. Risse, Rave, and Halvorsen were members of the Hamburger SV team, which won the German championship 1927/1928 in the final 5:2 against Hertha BSC Berlin. It is not clear whether *Bulgaria* sponsored the HSV team or simply used these images to promote its products without the team or the players' consent. Since German football was at the time officially amateur, legally *Bulgaria* could have done so. An e-mail from Werner Skrentny to the author (October 17, 2014).

[54]  Henry Ashby Turner, *German Big Business and the Rise of Hitler* (New York: Oxford University Press, 1985), 267–270.

[55]  Thomas D. Gran, *Stormtroopers and Crisis in the Nazi Movement: Activism, Ideology and Dissolution* (London: Routledge, 2004), 87–119.

and their display windows were smashed. The Bulgaria brand in Dresden, in particular, was subject to severe attacks, as local SA groups persistently harassed Bulgaria cigarette smokers and even threatened to personally harm key members of the company. In March 1932, Phillip F. Reemtsma warned Harry Carl Schnur, manager of the Bulgaria factory, that the Nazis were planning to attack him. With the help of Reemtsma, Schnur and his family managed to escape to the Netherlands, eventually moving to England and finally to the United States, where Schnur assumed an academic career as a Latin professor.[56] With the meteoric success of the National Socialist party in elections in the early 1930s, the situation for the Reemtsma Corporation became even more alarming. Preparing for the possibility of a Nazi government in Germany, Phillipp F. Reemtsma took a direct approach. As early as 1932, he started conversing with a number of prominent Nazi officials, including Hermann Göring, ultimately managing to negotiate an arrangement that secured the firm its dominant position in the German cigarette market following a Nazi takeover.

Still more pertinent for our purposes here is how the head of the Franz Eher Verlag, Max Amann, responded to furor over publication of the *Bulgaria* cigarette ads in the leading Nazi newspaper. Amann acknowledged the great similarities between the *Bulgaria* star and the Jewish Star of David. Yet he rejected the suggestion that because of this resemblance, Nazi publications should ban the *Bulgaria* cigarette advertisements. Many German companies, Amann argued, used the six-pointed star in modified forms as a trademark. He added that the five-pointed star, a principal communist symbol, was also a common emblem used for commercial purposes. Does this mean, he asked rhetorically, that Nazi newspapers are obliged to proscribe all advertisements with the five-star logo just because of the similarity with the communist emblem? Amann cited the Munich Pschorr brewery as an example of a "pure" German company with an alleged Soviet/Jewish-star-like logo. He then concluded that since many German firms that used the logo were important sources of revenue to the Nazi movement,

---

[56] On this incident see Lindner, *Reemtsmas*, 9. Harry Carl Schnur was the son of David Schnur, a well-known tobacconist, and a prominent member of the Reemtsma company's board of directors. For brief biographical information see "Schnur, David (1882–1948), Industrieller," *Österreichisches Biographisches Lexikon und biographische Dokumentation*, vol. 10 (Vienna: Verlag der Österreichischen Akademie der Wissenschaften, 1994), 419; as well as Harry Carl Schnur, *Vallum Berolinense – Ein Exilberliner erlebt den Mauerbau* (Berlin: Abgeordnetenhaus Berlin, 2011), 6–21.

continuing to ban such advertisements would do the party more harm than good.[57]

It is no coincidence that Amann, who was born and based in Munich, made reference in his response to the six-pointed star logo of a South German brewery. As indicated above, the hexagram was a traditional mark of breweries and inns in these parts of Germany. The pressure to eliminate the use of the so-called *Brauerstern* was so great that even *Der Stürmer* came out in support of the age-old tradition. This most virulently antisemitic of all Nazi newspapers, on which pages the six-pointed star was frequently seen as an epitome of all things Jewish, intervened on behalf the South German hostelry industry. Under the heading "The Six-Pointed Star: What Many Do Not Know," the notorious weekly denied any direct connection between the two stars. The hexagram is an old German hostelry insignia, explained the weekly, and it should not be mistaken for the *Judenstern*. "That the Jews chose the six-pointed star as the symbol of their blood-tainted race," the Stürmer proclaimed, "should not mean than the owner of a wine bar and brasserie will be deemed Jewish by this ambiguous sign."[58]

Despite such attempts to complicate and diversify the potential meanings of the hexagram, it remained strongly associated with Jews and gradually disappeared from the non-Jewish marketplace. By the mid-1930s the Reemtsma Company had decided to relinquish its provocative *Bulgaria* cigarette logo, first by changing it to an eight-pointed star and finally by replacing it with the crown of the Bulgarian king. The *Bulgaria* brand had acquired permission to use the Bulgarian king's arms for one of its products in 1927, but only after making it the brand main logo under National Socialism was the company nominated as an official cigarette supplier of the Bulgarian court.[59] This did not seem to have much impact on the fiscal situation of the brand. Fewer than 10 years after *Bulgaria* cigarettes were depicted "as one of the most interesting businesses in the German economy," a financial inspection of the Reemtsma Company

---

[57] The letter is cited in Lindner, *Reemtsmas*, 78–79. On other similar complaints some of which reached the Reich USCHLA, the national party court in Munich, see Gran, *Stormtroopers and Crisis*, 110–119.

[58] "Dass die Juden diesen sechstern als Zeichen ihrer blut verdorbene Rasse sich erwählten, darf nicht dazu verleiten dass die Gessinnung des Inhabers einer Wein oder Bierstube nach diese mehrdeutigen Zeichen beurteilt wird." In: "Der Sechsstern: Was viele nicht wissen," *Der Stürmer* 13 (32) (September 1935).

[59] For this correspondence and the official Bulgarian certificate Museum der Arbeit, Hamburg Archive Inventory-No: MA.A 2005/064.178, and MA.A 2005/064.179.

indicated that the Dresden brand did not make much profit under National Socialism.[60] In August 1939 just a couple of weeks before the beginning of World War II, the *Bulgaria* cigarette factory was officially shut down. Thanks to its striking Star of David–like logo, the products would become desirable collectors' items.

Following World War II, in a period when most western societies made antisemitism a marginalized "politically incorrect" position, the commercial use of the Star of David dwindled. Today it is a potent symbol of Jewishness. In fact, the six-pointed configuration became such a charged symbol that when the sports giant Nike released its special 2014 football World Cup commercial campaign, which told the story of an evil plot to drain life out the world game with a team of clones, some Jewish groups accused the multinational corporation of antisemitism. What prompted this allegation was not only the depiction of dark-haired clone players with big noses, but the logo of the heartless team that resembled the Star of David. Eventually, even the Anti-Defamation League intervened, dismissing the accusation on the basis that "just because it appears to look like the Star of David, it does not mean it is."[61]

### CREATING A JEWISH MARKETPLACE

Returning to the early twentieth century, the question remains: why, in a period of growing antisemitism, were Jews targeted as a discrete consumer group, especially one that was identified largely according to its religious needs? This targeting occurred despite the fact that the number of observant Jews, and the significance of religion in Jewish life more generally, was declining. The answer lies in the dynamics of the consumer culture of the Weimar period. I suggest that the economic hardship and political instability in the years following the Great War actually enhanced rather than undermined consumer culture.[62] Advertisers were compelled more than ever to identify new markets in order to stimulate consumption. It is against this broader backdrop of opportunistic marking that the

---

[60] Tischert, *Stätten deutscher Arbeit*, 130; Ilgel, Bulgaria, 175; as well as in Sächsisches Staatsarchiv/Hauptstaatsarchiv Dresden: 11773 Fa. Jasmatzi AG, Dresden, Nr. 162 Revisionsberichte u.a. Bulgaria (1936–1938).

[61] Cited in Ilan Ben Zion, "ADL rejects anti-Semitism in Nike ad," *The Times of Israel* (September 30, 2014), available at www.timesofisrael.com/adl-rejects-anti-semitism-in-nike-ad/.

[62] I elaborated on this notion of the close interplay between economic adversity and consumer culture in Gideon Reuveni, *Reading Germany*: Literature and Consumer Culture in Germnay Before 1933 (New York: Berghahn, 2006), especially in chapters three and four.

targeting of Jewish consumers is best understood. The fact that Jews were a small, and possibly declining minority, did not undermine this marketing strategy.[63] It is also likely that stereotypes of Jewish affluence persisted despite the economic hardships they faced.

It would be a mistake to regard Jews in this context as being passively subjected to external market driving forces. As I've demonstrated in this chapter, Jews participated actively both as the producers of advertising and as consumers of it. As Deshpande and Stayman write, "minority group consumers, awareness of minority status simultaneously breeds a heightened self-awareness of group or ethnic identity."[64] The Jews of Germany were certainly well aware of their minority status in German society before 1933, and unavoidably so thereafter. Hence, contrary to historian Till van Rahden's suggestion that we should "eliminate the still prevalent distinction between majority and minority cultures,"[65] it seems to me that only by acknowledging the minority/majority distinction, even if it is "merely" a subjective perception, can we start appreciating the complexity of the interplay between different notions of belonging. The claim for the right to be different is in this sense informed by the interaction between a minority status and what well may be a subjective perception of a majority culture. In this spirit I would like to briefly consider the Jewish press and its efforts to create a Jewish marketplace by cultivating a distinct sense of Jewish consumer consciousness.

Jewish newspapers actively sought advertisers for their pages. By calling upon their readers to choose Jewish products and services, these periodicals sought to make their readers more conscious about their shopping. Some newspapers introduced a coupon system, which also helped show shop owners how effective it was to advertise in the Jewish press. Others, like *Der Israelit*, the official publication of the orthodox movement, initiated special competitions, with readers asked to choose the most effective and aesthetically appealing advertisers in the newspaper.[66] Even more creative was *Monatsschrift*, the monthly

---

[63] On this see: Alfred Marcus, *Die wirtschaftliche Krise des deutschen Juden, eine soziologische Untersuchung* (Berlin: G. Stilke, 1931); Jacob Lestschinsky, *Das wirtschaftliche Schicksal des deutschen Judentums: Aufstieg, Wandlung, Krise, Ausblick* (Berlin: Zentralwohlfahrtsstelle der Deutschen Juden, 1932).

[64] Rohit Deshpande and Douglas M. Stayman, "A Tale of two Cities: Distinctiveness theory and Advertising Effectiveness," *Journal of Marketing Research*, 31 (1994), 62

[65] van Rahden, "Jews and the Ambivalence," 1042.

[66] "Preis-Susschreibung," *Der Israeli* (December 6, 1928), 21.

magazine of the B'nai B'rith order in Berlin. Thus, for example, under the heading "Open Your Eyes!" the B'nai B'rith monthly printed a picture of a building in Berlin that was retouched so that the billboard that usually adorned its facade was removed. The readers were then asked to identify which business advertised on that building. It was further indicated that this company frequently advertised over the pages of the B'nai B'rith journal.[67] More than eight hundred people provided correct answers to the challenge, identifying the billboard of Stadtküche Kraft, a wine and luxury food business, on an office building in Tauentzienstraße 3, a major shopping street in the western inner city of Berlin – an area where many middle-class Jewish families resided. A year later the journal went a step further, this time creating a whole-page collage of faintly manipulated adverts that appeared in the monthly. Readers were now asked to list all these businesses (Figure 2.13).

The results of this competition were advertised on May 1928. This time nearly two thousand postcards were sent to the B'nai B'rith publisher. Of these, 1,421 had provided a complete and correct list of all the advertisers in the collage. Ninety-two of the answers were written in the form of a poem. One of the verses printed in the journal was that of a certain Max Blum in which he playfully described the B'nai B'rith marketing exercise as a fabulous idea, benefiting advertisers, the publisher, and the fraternity.[68]

The B'nai B'rith order also published a special member's register, sponsored by advertising from businesses that were "thoroughly familiar," and in agreement with the order mission statement, and could be trusted with the sensitive contents of the address book.[69] Evidence from the 1920s suggests that the personal information of Jewish community members was in fact sold for commercial purposes.[70]

All Jewish newspapers worked hard to lure potential advertisers. The newspaper of the Jewish community in Frankfurt, for example, placed whole-page adverts proclaiming that "announcements in the (Frankfurt) *Gemeindeblatt* will be read by thousands!" and would help

---

[67] "Augen auf! Preisausschreiben! 23 Preise für gute Beobachter," *Monatsschrift der Berliner Logen U.O.B.B.* 6 (10) (January 1927), 206. The results of the competion were made public in the following issue of February 1927, 230.

[68] "Die idee ist wirklich köstlich; die Reklame wunderbar; für die Inseraten alle, für Verlag und Brüderschar," in: Max Blum, "Zum Preisauschreibung!" *Monatsschrift der Berliner Logen U.O.B.B.* 8 (2) (May 1928), 102.

[69] "Adressbuch der Berliner Logen U.O.B.B," *Monatsschrift der Berliner Logen U.O.B.B.* 8 (3) (June 1928), 117.

[70] "Warnung," *Gemeindeblatt der Israelitischen Religionsgemeinde Dresden* 3 (6) (October 1927), 14.

FIGURE 2.13  Advertisements Collage
From: *The Monatsschrift der Berliner Logen U.O.B.B.* vol. 7, no. 12 (March 1928), 230.

failing business to gain new customers and successful ones to thrive. Another interesting example is the advertising agency Jac. Strenlicht, which designed a series of adverts for the Dresden *Gemeindeblatt*. One featured a shut door, with the question "who comes through locked doors?" The answer was the newspaper itself, which penetrated the front door of every consumer, unlike sales representatives who might never manage to speak to an occupant. According to this logic, advertisements in the *Gemeindeblatt* benefited from the fact that each member of the Jewish community received a copy of the monthly delivered to his or her home free of charge, thus making the newspaper an important intermediary between Jewish consumers and the marketplace.

Some newspapers took a more forthright approach, targeting businesses and Jewish community leaders directly in order to promote their advertising spaces. A case in point is the official publication of the *Centralverein* (Central Association of German Citizens of Jewish Faith). Following the collapse of the German Empire, the *Centralverein*, switching from monthly to weekly publication, changed its name accordingly, from *Im deutschen Reich* (in the German Empire) to *CV-Zeitung*. This reform involved extra costs, which the *Centralverein* hoped to recover through advertising revenue. The *Centralverein* hired the advertising agency Rudolf Mosse, perhaps the most prominent advertisement business in prewar Europe, with branches in over 15 German cities and across Europe. In a memorandum sent to all directors of the association's local branches, the *Centralverein* explained that Jewish purchasing power would surely make the new weekly an attractive venue for advertisers. Wishing to take no chances, the *Centralverein* called upon all members of its executive board to use personal business connections to promote advertising in the association's new publication.[71] In May 1923, for instance, a *Centralverein* representative managed to meet George Tietz, owner of one of the largest department stores in Berlin, to try and persuade him to advertise in the *CV-Zeitung*.[72] After briefly hearing the appeal, Tietz referred the *Centralverein* representative to the office of Herr Adler, head of Tietz marketing operations, who reported that the Tietz Company just agreed to purchase advertising space in the new Jewish weekly. That said, Adler made it clear that like Georg Tietz he would not allow private concerns to interfere with business interests. From the point of view of the Tietz department store, Adler asserted, there is no reason to advertise in a weekly newspaper that gets in the hands of only a small fraction of consumers in Berlin. Yet on a personal

[71] Letter signed by Ludwig Holländer, "An die Landesverbände und Syndici des Centralverein!" (March 1922), in: The Central Archives for the History of the Jewish People (hereafter, CAHJP), CVA, record no. HM2/8733, fr. 0947.

[72] On the Tietz family and their department stores see Georg Tietz, *Herman Tietz: Geschichte einer Familie und ihre Warenhäuser* (Sttutgart: Deutsche Verlag-Anstalt, 1965).

basis Adler offered assistance to the newly founded weekly, strongly advising the *Centralverein* to concentrate its efforts in securing advertisements for brand-named products that were not time- or place sensitive. Such products – including cigarettes, chocolates, cosmetics, fashion goods, automobile companies, and insurance – Adler explained, are more suitable for a national weekly newspaper with a relatively small print run.[73] Most German newspapers at the time, even the big dailies, were essentially regional and did not have nationwide readership. Given the dispersal of Jews, the German Jewish press developed local community newspapers but also a number of publications with a countrywide outreach such as the liberal *CV-Zeitung*, the Zionist weekly *Jüdische Rundschau*, or the Orthodox *Der Israelit*, just to name here a few prominent examples. Such newspapers were not considered appropriate publications for advertisements from local businesses. Even big department stores, such as the Berlin Hermann Tietz, were reluctant to advertise in such outlets. Nevertheless, it is clear from the announcement section of the *CV-Zeitung* that Tiez continued advertising in the weekly throughout the 1920s.

The tension between the local and the national was not the only challenge Jewish newspapers like the *CV-Zeitung* faced.[74] The Jewish press landscape of the prewar period reflected the deep schisms within German Jewry. When the *Centralverein* debated how it should retitle its new publication, one of the leading options was *Deutschtum und Judentum* (Germanness and Jewishness). Advocates of this heading claimed that it best epitomized what the *Centralverein* stood for, and that it made a clear statement against Zionism.[75] Eventually "Germanness and Jewishness" became the weekly's subtitle. It was decided to remove the term "Jewish" from the publication's main heading because of concerns that no Christians would purchase a newspaper with the word "Jewish" in its title. To make the new weekly even more "familiar" for a broader readership, the *CV-Zeitung* adopted the layout of the *Berliner Tageblatt*,

---

[73] "Bericht über eine Unterredung mit Herrn Georg Tietz bzw. Herren Adler Fa. Hermann Tietz," CAHJP), CVA, record no. HM2/8733, fr. 0981.

[74] For some Jewish periodicals that addressed the Jewish world, the challenge was even broader. The Hebrew weekly *Haolam* (the World), the central organ of the World Zionist Organization, underscored the extent of its global reach, depicting itself as particularly suitable for brands that wish to cross national borders. See the editorial, "'*Haolam*' and advertising for Jewish organizations," *Haolam* (1931), 31.

[75] CAHJP, CVA, record no. HM2/8733, fr. 0411. For a discussion of the relationship between these two terms, Christoph Schulte (ed.), *Deutschtum und Judentum: Ein Disput unter Juden aus Deutschland* (Stuttgart: Reclam, 1993).

a popular daily newspaper that was issued by Rudolf Mosse publishing house.

The success of the Jewish press also brought harsher competition between Jewish publications for advertising revenue. In their contract with the Mosse advertising agency, for example, the *Centralverein* prohibited Mosse from representing any other Jewish newspaper. The rivalry was not constrained to newspapers representing competing worldviews. In 1928 the Jewish community in Berlin, the largest in Germany, assigned Leo Winz, the former editor of the Jewish magazine *Ost und West*, to professionalize its community newspaper. Winz completely transformed the Berlin *Gemeindeblatt*, modernizing its appearance and transforming it into a voluminous illustrated magazine with ample advertising possibilities. Within a short period of time the Berlin *Gemeindeblatt* experienced a significant boost to its print run, growing from 58,000 copies of each edition sold in 1928 to 87,000 copies in 1931. Winz' advertising strategies were so successful that the Berlin *Gemeindeblatt* no longer relied upon community subsidies.[76]

At the beginning of 1929 Winz approached the *Centralverein* to offer his advertising expertise to the *CV-Zeitung*. He suggested that if the *CV-Zeitung* merged its advertising section with that of the Berlin *Gemeindeblatt* it would put an end to the pointless and "mutually interfering" (*gegenseitig störende*) competition between the two, in which, he found it important to add, the *Centralverein* was the losing party. According to Winz such a merger would significantly enhance the appeal of both newspapers to potential advertisers by achieving a combined circulation of 130,000 copies.[77] It is unclear whether the *Centralverein* seriously considered working with Winz, who was an avowed culture Zionist, but it used his proposition to negotiate an improved agreement with the Mosse agency that year.

The world economic crisis at the end of the 1920s and escalating unemployment in Germany made the Jewish press more dependent than ever on advertising revenues with concomitant pressure on advertising sections to continue to provide much needed income. At the same time, cash-poor advertisers were much more careful about where they promoted their products and services. The Rudolf Mosse agency, for

---

[76] Brenner, *Renaissance of Jewish Culture*, 55–56. On Winz and his work for the Ost West see David A. Brenner, *Marketing Identities: The Invention of Jewish Ethnicity in "Ost und West"* (Detroit: Wayne State University Press, 1998).

[77] CAHJP, CVA, record no. HM2/8733, fr. 0863–0865.

example, warned the *Centralverein* that it was losing some of its customers due to the high advertising rates in the *CV-Zeitung*.[78] Given the
growing difficulty in securing commercial advertisers, Jewish newspapers
started developing their "small ads" section in which individuals were
given the opportunity to buy and sell goods. To launch their small ads
section, the Mosse agency offered special vouchers providing a 20 percent
discount on private announcements in the *CV-Zeitung*. These "small ads"
played an even more important role in local Jewish newspapers, helping to
forge a distinctly Jewish marketplace.

Jewish periodicals also sent promotional letters to Jewish community
leaders asking them to urge their members to advertise in Jewish newspapers. Like the Berlin *Gemeindeblatt*, other Jewish periodicals sought to
modernize and make their publications even more attractive for commercial advertisers. To create new marketing opportunities for the struggling
Jewish newspaper business, they published special sections on popular
topics such as theater, modern art, film, and sport, as well as articles aimed
at women and youth. More than any other focus, however, it was the
Jewish holy days, with their elaborate meals and gift-giving, that became
the centerpiece of a marketing regime designed for Jewish consumers.

### RELIGIOUS MARKETING

In the early twentieth century, the Jewish high holidays underwent
a transformation from being strictly religious occasions to becoming
family-oriented celebrations marked with festive meals and gift-giving.
This change occurred in step with the so-called domestication of the
Christmas holiday. Both Christian and Jewish shifts were a result of
increasing modernization and embourgeoisement, which dated to the
nineteenth century and was characterized by the novel separation of
public and private domains, of the home from the outside world that we
take for granted today.[79] As a consequence, the family became not only
the cornerstone of bourgeois life but also the principal arena for religious

---

[78] Ibid., fr. 0698–0703.

[79] On this process in the Jewish context and especially how it affected Jewish women see:
Kaplan, *The Making of the Jewish Middle Class*; Elizabeth H. Pleck, *Celebrating the Family.
Ethnicity, Consumer Culture, and Family Rituals* (Cambridge: Harvard University Press,
2000). On the process of commercialization within Christianity, see: Rondney Clapp (ed.),
*The Consuming Passion: Christianity & the Consumer Culture* (Downers Grove: Inter-
Varsity Press, 1998); Robert Laurence Moore, *Selling God: American Religion in the
Marketplace of Culture* (New York: Oxford university Press, 1994).

life and practice. Perhaps the most definitive expression of the "domestication of religion" was the process by which the religious context was commercialized. Two main components were the focus of this process in the Jewish sphere – the holiday meal and the gift.

While the domestication and commercialization of religion affected both Jews and Christians alike, for Jews the family had always been important in maintaining a Jewish way of life, a feature I will discuss in more detail in the final sections of this book. For advertisers seeking to court customers, the Jewish holidays presented an opportunity for marketing products to enhance Jewish homes and family life during these important events.[80] The principal focus of these marketing campaigns was the holidays of Rosh Hashanah, Purim, Passover, and Chanukah, with special emphasis on food products that could be served at holiday meals. Fish, geese and ducks, wine, and especially baked goods and confectionery helped to endow each holiday with a distinctive character. Flowers also contributed to a special holiday atmosphere, claimed advertisers. Using the slogan "a beautiful holiday brings pleasure and relaxation" (*Ein schönes Fest bringt Ihnen Genuß und Erholung*), a Leipzig flower shop promoted the idea that flowers could transform the home into a scented, colorful place and imbue the holiday with its special atmosphere (Figure 2.14).

A comparative study of preholiday advertisements in Jewish and Christian newspapers shows that the menu of the Jewish holiday meal and the special touches that were supposed to endow the home with a celebratory atmosphere and make the holiday "a sentimental event" did not differ significantly from Christian holiday customs.[81] This similarity is borne out by the language used in the advertisements. Particularly in the case of parallel holidays celebrated by both faiths, such as Easter and Passover, similar phrases are used to appeal to both Jews and Christians. Advertisers referred to Passover with the Hebrew word *Pessach* but used the German term for Easter, *Ostern*. This usage apparently did not confuse readers about whether Passover was in fact a Jewish holiday. Paradoxically, it appears that non-Jewish businesses were more comfortable using the Hebrew term in their adverts, as in the cases of

---

[80] Alain Finkielkraut even went so far as to suggest that "in Christian society, the Jewish family and Jewish nation are two indistinguishable structures: leaving one in any way means deserting the other." In: Ibid., *The Imaginary Jew* (Lincoln: University of Nebraska Press, 1994), 105.

[81] Kaplan, *The Making of the Jewish Middle Class.*

**Ein schönes Fest** *bringt Ihnen Genuß und Erholung*

wenn Sie Ihr Heim aufnahmefähig machen für die Feierstimmung, die der Frühling mit seinem jungen Grün und dem Blütenzauber den Pessachtagen verleiht. Schon einige Blumen, ein kleines, geschmackvolles Arrangement oder eine trauliche Ecke mit blühenden und Blattpflanzen beleben Ihr Heim und erfreuen Ihr Gemüt mit Duft und Farbenspiel. HANISCH's gärtnerische Spezialitäten vom einfachen Strauß bis zu den sinnigsten Dekorationen genießen Weltruf. HANISCH's preiswerte und gediegene Festgeschenke verbürgen Qualität und erregen überall Freude und Bewunderung. Dies gilt besonders für meine als Festgruß sehr begehrte

Zum Postversand **echte Rosenthalvase, neueste Form**, mit Füßchen, mit Frühlingsblumen gefüllt, oder gepflanzter Glücksklee im Ziertopf m. Untersetzer, mit Frühlingsblumen garniert, inkl. Porto und Verpackung zu . . . . . . . . . . . . . . . . . . . . . . RM 2.50

Jeder andere Blumenschmuck, auch für den verfeinerten Geschmack, wird auf Wunsch jederzeit zu ebenso volkstümlichen Preisen zusammengestellt. Meine hervorragende Stadt- und Versandorganisation gewährleistet pünktliche und tadellose Zustellung, innerhalb Leipzig frei Haus. — Besuchen Sie auch die in allen meinen Geschäften neueröffnete **Kakteenschau**, Sie werden wie immer zuvorkommend bedient und fachmännisch beraten. **Kaufen Sie deshalb in meinen altrenommierten Geschäften!**

**J. C. Hanisch, Leipzig**  Grimmaische Straße 29  /  Hauptbahnhof-West
Petersstraße 44  /  Sammelnummer 701 56

Wegen des starken Andrangs zu den Feiertagen erbitte ich Ihre rechtzeitige Bestellung

FIGURE 2.14 "A beautiful holiday brings pleasure and relaxation" – An Advertisement for the Flower Shop Hanisch in Leipzig
From: *Gemeindeblatt der israelitischen Religiongemeinde zu Leipzig* (March 27, 1931), 6.

HAG Coffee (see Figure 2.4) or the Miller optical chain store in Frankfurt, whose advertisements featured the word "*Pessach*" as well.

The second issue on which holiday advertisements focused was the gift.[82] Here we find advertisements phrased in general terms, such as "A camera is an appropriate gift for the holiday" (*Für Festage als passende Gabe ein Photo Apparat*), or advertisements relating to a specific holiday, such as the one inserted by the famous bookshop "Kedem" in Berlin – "Give books as a Purim present!" (*Schenkt Bücher zu Purim!*). In the run-up to Chanukah, a holiday for which gift-giving became increasingly important during this period, we find numerous advertisements for *Chanuka-Geschenke* (Chanokah presents) in the Jewish press. Interestingly, the advertisements do not provide much information about the identity of the gift-giver or its recipient. The focus of these advertising campaigns was the gift itself, which was promoted as a holiday present because of its sentimental, educational, or practical value. Records and musical instruments, toys, household appliances, books, and even life insurance were just a few of the products proposed as holiday gifts in the Jewish press.

[82] For a general survey on the different interpretations of the gift see: Aafke E. Komter (ed.), *The Gift: An Interdisciplinary Perspective* (Amsterdam: Amsterdam University Press, 1996).

The products and services marketed to Jews as Chanukah presents were similarly marketed to Christians as Christmas presents. The gifts themselves carried no specific religious or cultural connotations. Nonetheless, by promoting certain goods as gifts suitable for specifically Jewish holidays, advertisers helped to create and reinforce a special sense of Jewishness based on religious sentiments and a feeling of common cultural origins.

In this way, I would argue that consumer culture has played a much greater role in forming and promoting notions of Jewishness than previously thought. Exploring advertisements for different products and services in the Jewish press reveals a multifaceted development in which advertisers recognized Jews as a distinct group of consumers. By stimulating Jewish consumption, consumer culture seemed to facilitate a new regime of identities in which multiple coexisting culture affiliations are supposed to inform consumer behavior. Conversely, this marketing regime promoted diverse notions of Jewishness, which spanned religion, nationality, ethnicity, family, and the individual itself. In the period before the Nazi takeover, in particular, this development seemed to facilitate a strong sense of consumer ambivalence in which Jews were confronted with different notions regarding their belonging. To what extent this kind of niche marketing to ethnic groups was limited to the Jews and whether, if at all, non-Jewish consumers participated in it, or were even aware of it, are important questions that await further research.

Some scholars of the Jewish experience have argued that by concentrating in particular economic sectors, the Jews protected themselves from the loss of a collective identity. With the development of consumer capitalism, Jews could potentially bulwark their collective identity by spending as well as by earning money. If the experience of being Jewish in this period was indeed shaped by consumption, how did this development affect understanding of the so-called Jewish question?

# 3

# The Jewish Question and Changing Regimes
# of Consumption

The study of Jewish consumption seeks to investigate a crucial and neglected axis of consumption, identity, and Jewish history. It aims to examine the role and place of consumption within Jewish society and the ways consumerism generated and reinforced Jewish notions of belonging in modern times. By assuming a "consumerist" approach to Jewish history, this research strives to move beyond the common binary divisions in the history of Jews that tend to oscillate between approaches stressing the inclusion of Jews and those that highlight their exclusion. It suggests that as consumers Jews were able to develop a self-understanding based on heterogeneous elements taken from a diversity of cultural representations and practices facilitating a feeling of belonging to a wider consumer community, yet still retaining a clear sense of Jewish distinctiveness.

This chapter will deal with different aspects and advance varied arguments on the topic at hand. I will, for instance, suggest that in different settings, for example, in settler societies, such as in the Americas and Australia, consumer culture seems to occupy a more significant position in the social process as a vehicle for promoting social integration in societies that evolved based on the idea of origin. As a "society of strangers," to use Georg Simmel's terminology, whose members have distant origins and distinct cultural backgrounds, people in settler societies seem to be bound by their desires and common future aspirations rather than by taboos or obligations to a real or imagined primordial community. According to this approach, consumer capitalism traditionally served a more important role in generating a communal national identity in a place like the United States than it would in European countries. To extend the argument, such consumerist cultures as the United States

66

would also be more appreciative of traditional Jewish activities around buying and selling than would production-oriented European countries. Israel occupies a middle ground between the production-oriented approaches of European countries and the consumerist orientation of settler societies. It is, on the one hand, a society constructed out of immigrants. On the other hand, the idea of "belonging" in Israel is based on a strong sense of a common (Jewish) descent. I will briefly deal with the Israeli context toward the end of this chapter. The main focus of the following pages will be on the changing meanings and functions of consumption within the specific setting of American Jewry in the twentieth century.

I begin this chapter with a question that has shaped the modern Jewish experience since the end of the eighteenth century – the so-called Jewish Question. In different times and places we find various formulations of this question. At its core, however, the "Jewish question" is whether Jews, as individuals or as a community, are able to integrate into a modern, predominantly non-Jewish society. Historically, questioning of the compatibility of Jews with modernity has given rise to a further, and no less fundamental, question regarding the "nature" of Jewish difference. While Jews and non-Jews have developed various understandings of what constitutes Jewish difference, the question of how Jewishness relates to modernity is central. Certain Jews have sought to reform Judaism, thereby making it more "compatible" with modern life. Others have turned to politics, reaffirming Jewish difference and rendering it a prerequisite for their integration into society. A third path, taken by millions of Jews, is migration. Hoping to find a better life, over three million Jews left Europe between the beginning of the nineteenth century and World War I. About 85 percent of them headed to the United States.[1]

The experience of Jewish consumers in American culture is well documented, and this chapter draws upon an established body of research.[2]

---

[1] Hasia Diner, *A New Promised Land: A History of Jews in America* (Oxford: Oxford University Press, 2003).

[2] See, for example, Andrew R. Heinze, *Adapting to Abundance: Jewish Immigrants, Mass Consumption, and the Search for American Identity* (New York: Columbia University Press, 1990); Marilyn Halter, *Shopping for Identity: The Marketing of Ethnicity* (New York: Schocken Books, 2000); Elizabeth Hafkin Pleck, *Celebrating the Family: Ethnicity, Consumer Culture, and Family Rituals* (Cambridge, MA: Harvard University press, 2000); Jenna Weissman Joselit, *A Perfect Fit: Clothes, Character, and the Promise of America* (New York: Henry Holt and Company, 2001); Ibid. and Susan L. Braunstein (ed.), *Getting Comfortable in New York: The American Jewish Home, 1880–1950* (New York: The Jewish Museum, 1990).

This history reveals how the changing regimes of consumer culture turned the so-called Jewish Question on its head. While in the past, Jews struggled to negotiate their difference in order to promote integration, since the Holocaust the very notion of Jewish difference in America has been questioned, and Jews more than ever before are preoccupied with the question of how to reinstall and preserve their distinctiveness.

Consumer culture, I argue, facilitates both processes of the making and the blurring of differences. As a social arrangement in which structures of meaning and feeling are organized primarily around the act of purchase, consumer culture endorses processes of standardization rendering a sense of homogeneity and social cohesion. At the same time, however, consumption also allows individuals and groups to design distinct social definitions through the act of buying. Studying the changing nature and dynamic of consumer cultures in the context of Jewish history thus reveals this multifaceted process by which minorities are able to maintain a separate identity through consumption while, as consumers, to feel integrated in their surrounding societies.

### LONGING FOR BELONGING

Demographically speaking, the story of American Jewry is one of spectacular rise. When the Declaration of Independence was signed on July 4, 1776, about two and a half thousand Jews lived in America. During the nineteenth century their numbers rose steadily. By the turn of the century over one million Jews lived in the United States, and just before 1933, that number had grown to approximately 4.5 million, with most Jewish Americans living in New York.[3] Where did these Jews come from and why?

There were two major waves of Jewish immigration to the United States. The first took place in the middle of the nineteenth century, as vast numbers of immigrants from central and northern Europe arrived in America, seeking a new life. Most of the Jews immigrating to America at this time came, like other immigrants, in search of economic opportunity. Increasing numbers of anti-Jewish policies in the wake of the Napoleonic era, and a sense of dismay after the failure of the liberal revolutions of 1848, further motivated Jewish immigrants. It was during a second wave of immigration, between

---

[3] Sidney Goldstein, "Jews in the United State: Perspective from Demography," in: Joseph B. Gittler (ed.), *Jewish Life in the United States: Perspectives from Social Sciences* (New York: New York University Press, 1981), 31–102; Hasia Diner, *The Jews of the United States, 1654 to 2000* (Berkeley: University of California Press, 2006), 71–112.

1881 and 1924, when the infamous Immigration Act of that year virtually halted immigration that the majority of Jews arrived in the United States. Most of these second-wave newcomers were Yiddish speakers, escaping persecution and stifling economic conditions in Eastern Europe. Notwithstanding significant social and cultural tensions between different groups of Jewish immigrants, they had much in common, including their reasons for leaving Europe, their largely successful integration into American culture, and the forms of Judaism they came to practice.[4]

The perception of America as a utopian place of emancipation and material prosperity helped create a collective identity for American Jews.[5] Although the reality of life in the United States did not always match the utopian fantasies of the *goldene Medinah* ("land of Gold" or "golden land"), Jews perhaps more than any other group embraced the idea of the American Dream and in fact played an active role in shaping and propagating the notion of America as the Promised Land.[6] A telling example is Israel Zangwill's celebrated play *The Melting Pot*, the hit of New York's 1908 theatrical season.[7]

The play depicts the life of a Russian-Jewish musician – David Quixano – who arrives in America in the wake of the 1903 Kishinev pogrom, during which his entire family was killed. In America, David writes a great symphony called "The Crucible," expressing his hope for a society free of ethnic division and hatred and falls in love with Vera, a beautiful Russian (and Christian) immigrant. The climax of the play comes when David meets Vera's father who turns out to be the Russian officer responsible for the annihilation of his family. Vera's father admits his guilt, the symphony is performed to accolades, and David and Vera live happily ever after, or, at least, agree to wed and kiss as the curtain falls.

---

[4] Lloyd P. Gartner, "Immigration and the Formation of American Jewry, 1840–1925," in: Marshal Sklare (ed.), *The Jew in American Society* (New York: Behrman House, 1974), 31–50.

[5] Ben Halpern, "America is Different," in: Marshall Sklare (ed.), *The Jew in American Society* (New York: Behrman House, 1974), 67–90; Rael Meyerowitz, *Transferring to America: Jewish Interpretations of American Dreams* (Albany, NY: State University of New York Press, 1995).

[6] Eli Lederhendler, *Jewish Responses to Modernity: New Voices in America and Eastern Europe* (New York: New York University Press, 1994), 104–139.

[7] Israel Zangwill, *The Melting Pot* (New York: The American Jewish Book Company, 1921), available at www.gutenberg.org/files/23893/23893-h/23893-h.htm. The following section owns much of its insights to David Biale, "The Melting Pot and Beyond: Jews and the Politics of American Identity," in: David Biale, Michael Galchinsky and Susannah Heschel (eds.), *Insider/outsider: American Jews and Multiculturalism* (Berkeley: University of California Press, 1998), 17–34.

As much as Zangwill's play extols America as a place of reconciliation, it also reflects a deep-seated tension between its assimilationist message and explicitly Jewish content. Zangwill's own position in this matter is ambivalent. On the one hand, he claims that Jews are "the toughest of all white elements that have been poured into the American crucible."[8] On the other hand, he suggests that Jews are not just any group of immigrants, but the quintessential Americans.

Despite the soaring rhetoric of the theater, in reality it was very unlikely in the early twentieth century that any immigrant group would abandon its ethnic distinctiveness, whether it wanted to or not. Nor did the idea of a radical melting pot find much support among the key figures of the Jewish community. Jewish social thinkers like Horace Kallen instead argued for a more malleable concept of what it meant to be American, a so-called democracy of Nationalism or cultural pluralism that would acknowledge difference.[9] Thinkers like Kallen could draw on the work of John Dewey, one of America's most influential philosophers of the last century, in portraying America as a "complex and compound" nation. "Such terms as Irish-American or Hebrew-American or German-American are false terms," wrote Dewey,

because they seem to assume something which is already in existence called America, to which the other factors may be externally hitched on. The fact is, the genuine American, the typical American, is himself a hyphenated character. This does not mean that he is part of America and some foreign ingredient is then added. It means that … he is international and interracial in his make-up. He is not American plus Pole or German. But the American is himself Pole-German-English-Spanish-Italian-Greek-Irish-Scandinivian-Bohemian-Jew-and so on.[10]

This vision of a hyphenated American, it should be noted, is purely European: people of African, Asian, or South American origin are granted no place in it. For Jews, being identified as white Europeans reinforced the positive image of America as an "enlightened" and receptive place even as it implied a deeper level of racism directed toward Americans of non-European origin. This vision of an enlightened America was opposed to

---

[8] Ibid., "Afterword," 204.
[9] See, for example, his 1915 essay "Democracy Versus the Melting-Pot: A Study of American Nationality," reprinted in Horace M. Kallen, *Culture and Democracy in the United States* (New Brunswick: Transaction Publishers, 1998, org. 1924), 59–118.
[10] John Dewey, "Nationalizing Education," in: Jo Ann Boydston (ed.), *The Middle Works, 1899–1924* (Carbondale, IL: Southern Illinois University Press, 2008), 205.

the negative image of the bigoted and discriminatory Old World. To be sure, Jews faced discrimination in America as well. In the years leading up to World War II, antisemitism was on the rise in the United States. Yet Jews of European origin could pass as white, while blacks could not. This very basic observation provides an important insight into the nature of American racism and helps us to better understand the different trajectories of these groups in the twentieth century.[11]

Jews were given the opportunity to realize the American Dream of social mobility and economic progress. Their ambitions were largely fulfilled as the number of white-collar workers expanded. Whereas in 1900 approximately 60 percent of American Jews held blue-collar jobs, by 1930 only 30 percent did manual work.[12] An integral part of this process of embourgeoisement was the creation of a Jewish consumer market, which served both to Americanize the Jewish newcomers and to enact their Jewishness.

The historical significance of consumerism in America is well-documented. Scholars have even argued that for Americans spending became a form of citizenship, an important ritual of national identity.[13] At the same time that consuming allowed individuals to feel part of a collective nation, it also enabled ethnic groups to maintain separate identities. As in the metaphor of the melting pot, consumption offered a compelling way for Jews, as well as other white European minorities, to realize their desires for full citizenship without completely assimilating. As Andrew Heinze postulated in his seminal book *Adapting to Abundance*, being American meant having things, and Jews more than any other groups of newcomers embraced this culture of Americanization through consumption.[14] I will now examine a few examples of this phenomenon in the interwar period.

---

[11] Eric Goldstein, *The Price of Whiteness: Jews, Race, and American Identity* (Princeton: Princeton University Press, 2006); Karen Brodkin, *How Jews Became White Folks and What that Says About Race in America* (New Brunswick: Rutgers University Press, 2000); Cheryl Greenberg, "Pluralism and Its Discontents: The Case of Blacks and Jews," David Biale, Michael Galchinsky and Susannah Heschel (eds.), *Insider/outsider: American Jews and Multiculturalism* (Berkeley: University of California Press, 1998), 55–88.

[12] Beth S. Wenge, *New York Jews and the Great Depression: Uncertain Promise* (Syracuse: Syracuse University Press, 1999), 15.

[13] See, for example, Daniel Horowitz, *The Morality of Spending. Attitudes Towards the Consumer Society in America* (Baltimore: John Hopkins University Press, 1985); Lizabeth Cohen, *A Consumer's Republic: The Politics of Mass Consumption in Postwar America* (New York: Vintage Books, 2004).

[14] Heinze, *Adapting to Abundance*.

## INTEGRATION WITHOUT ASSIMILATION

Advertising offers a clear example of how American consumer culture adapted to the diverse and changing needs of different consumer groups. Advertisements of major American companies appeared more frequently in the Yiddish press than in the foreign-language newspapers of other immigrant groups, suggesting that these companies quickly identified Jews as a strong prospective market for national brands.

Seeking to expand the market for its baby food, the Borden Company, a well-known American manufacturer of food and beverage products, took exceptional measures to court Jewish customers. The company set up a special department to provide free advice on baby nutrition. In an advertisement for the department, it invited Jewish mothers to use this service, promising that inquiries in Yiddish would receive a prompt reply. Another compelling example of how advertising translated commodities considered American – in this case, the donut – into a Jewish context by targeting Jewish women is the advertisement in Figure 3.1 for Mazola oil.

Another such ad features the renowned Jewish baseball player Andy Cohen. Cohen came to play for the New York Giants in 1926, partly to draw Jewish fans who would otherwise be inclined to support the New York Yankees. During Cohen's successful 1928 season, vendors responded to his popularity by selling "Ice Cream Cohens" at the Polo Grounds' concession stands.[15]

Advertisements were not the only method used to address Jewish consumers. In 1921, Gold Medal Flour published a Jewish cookbook. This collection of recipes for soups, poultry, fish, eggs, cakes, condiments, and ice cream, all written in Yiddish, was the result of a contest that promised Jewish housewives who entered the possibility of $500 in prize money and publication of the winning recipes.[16]

An even more intriguing example of such marketing ploys is the Maxwell House Coffee Haggadah, first published in the early 1930s when Maxwell attempted to make coffee drinking a new Passover tradition. More than fifty million copies of this Hebrew-English Haggadah have been printed, making it the most widely used Haggadah in the world.

---

[15] Tilden Edelstein, "Cohen at the Bat," *Commentary* 76 (5) (1983), available at www .commentarymagazine.com/article/cohen-at-the-bat/.
[16] Jenna Weissman Joselit, *The Wonders of America* (New York: Hill and Wang, 1994), 190; Barbara Kirshenblatt-Gimblett, "Kitchen Judaism," in: Susan L. Braunstein and Jenna Weissman Joselit (eds.), *Getting Comfortable in New York* (Bloomington: Indiana University Press, 1991), 75–105.

FIGURE 3.1 The ad states: "American bagels – doughnuts – fried in Mazola Oil have wonderful taste" and then calling Jewish housewives' attention to the fact that since Mazola is made from pure vegetable oil it can replace animal fat and thus help to Americanize the Jewish kitchen and to diversify Jewish cooking. The ad also contains a recipe for donuts
From: *The Jewish Morning Journal* (December 30, 1920).

Jews were not passive recipients of this marketing effort. As elsewhere, Jews in America were disproportionately active in business, from clothing, furniture, and real estate sales to movie production. The populous Jewish neighborhoods of New York City were dense with retail stores of all types during the heyday of immigration in the late nineteenth and early twentieth centuries. Street markets even sold specialized luxury items such as fur coats, overtly targeting Jewish consumers. Moreover, as in Europe, Jewish newspapers in America sought to make their readers into consumers. Even the leading Jewish socialist newspaper *Forverts* (Forward) actively encouraged consumption by promoting the newspaper as a space for advertising. By playing up the purchasing power of its readers, the newspaper tried to persuade manufacturers and advertisers that advertising in the *Forverts* would pay off in increased sales. In a special illustrated brochure, the Yiddish daily asserted, "there is nothing strange, mysterious or secret about the Jewish field. It is just like any other portion of the great American market of which it is an integral part. Good merchandising principles are just as sound when applied on the East Side or Bronx as in Portland or Sacramento."[17] The newspaper also offered expert advice for advertisers wishing to familiarize themselves with the Jewish market. Other marketing and advertising agencies offered similar services, the most well known of which was the Joseph Jacobs Organization. Founded in 1919, the company still offers its services under the slogan "when it comes to the Jewish market ... we know what to say."[18] These agencies helped manufacturers adopt and develop special marketing strategies aimed at Jewish consumers, as was the case of the Maxwell House Haggadah – an idea that was developed by the Joseph Jacobs advertising agency.

This highly sophisticated and well-designed marketing regime reflected a unique American Jewish lifestyle derived, as Jenna Weissman Joselit notes, "from American notions of consumerism, gender, privacy, and personal happiness as well as from Jewish notions of tradition, ritual, memory, and continuity."[19] Most scholars agree that the experience of consumer culture in the early twentieth century had a profound impact on American Jews, creating a distinct American Jewish way of life.

## COMMODIFYING JEWISHNESS

Following World War II, American consumption experienced an unprecedented boom, making it the hallmark of what some thinkers have called "post," "late," or even "liquid" modernity; the latter is a concept

---

[17] Quoted in: Joselit, *The Wonders of America*, 145.

[18] Kerri P. Steinberg, *Jewish Mad Men: Advertising and the Design of the American Jewish Experience* (New Brunswick, NJ: Rutgers University Press, 2015); Daniel Pope and William Toll, "We Tried Harder: Jews in American Advertising," *American Jewish History* 72 (1) (1982), 26–51. Today the company has changed the slogan to "When it comes to the Jewish Market ... we discovered it." See www.josephjacobsadvertising.com/.

[19] Joselit, *The Wonders of America*, 4.

developed by Zygmunt Bauman to denote the shift from the period of "solid" modernity that preceded it. According to Bauman, the postwar consumer society is "a society of credit cards, not savings books. It is a 'now' society. A wanting society, not a waiting society."[20] Although the idea of such a straightforward temporal disjuncture is problematic, it is clear that consumer culture has undergone major changes since World War II. Foremost among these changes was the emergence of new marketing techniques that both promoted cultural differences by addressing the needs of different consumer groups and helped to create a homogeneous set of national consumers with equal access to diverse products.

As described in Chapter 2, ethnic niche marketing originated in the beginning of the twentieth century. The rapid growth of certified kosher products is a good example of how this multicultural marketing regime worked. During the prewar years, economic interests were identified with groups defined by a set of distinct religious and cultural needs. In the decades since World War II, and particularly since the beginning of the new millennium, boundaries between distinct ethnic groups have begun to break down. The contemporary marketing of kosher foods to non-Jews is one result.

According to some estimates, the kosher market grew from being $35 billion industry in 1994 to being worth $65 billion in 10 years, with more than 90,000 certified kosher products on sale in the United States in 2005.[21] Indeed, it is becoming difficult not to buy kosher products these days. According to one consumer survey from 2003, 28 percent of Americans said they have knowingly bought a kosher product; only 8 percent of those did so for religious reasons. Promoting his new namesake brand of lactose-free kosher cheesecake, comedian Jackie Mason suggested that the kosher food success story is connected to the growing awareness of the food we eat. "Gentiles," he drolly claimed, "have finally learned that Jews make food with no junk, dirt, or garbage."[22]

Although there is no guarantee that kosher supervision makes products any more hygienic or wholesome, the word has become another marketing term that appears on labels, along with "organic," "all natural," "no

---

[20] Peter Beilharz (ed.), *The Bauman Reader* (Malden, MA: Wiley-Blackwell, 2001), 321.

[21] Vicky Hallett, "Bring Home the Kosher Bacon," *US News & World Report*, (February 11, 2003), available at www.usnews.com/usnews/culture/articles/031110/10 kosher.div.htm.

[22] Ibid. On this see also Seth Wolitz, *The Renaissance in Kosher Cuisine: From Ethnicity to Universality* (Jerusalem: Institute of the World Jewish Congress, 1999).

preservatives," and "gluten-free."[23] To be sure, merging the notions of "Jewish" with "kosher" sets up inaccurate expectations about people and food, often with misleading, even if delicious, results. In some sense, kosher food is no more "Jewish" than vegetarian food is Buddhist. The assumed connection between health and kosher may be a myth, but as many marketing experts now proclaim, it is a myth that leads to sales.[24]

By introducing so-called ethnic or multicultural products into a wider, undefined consumer market, food manufacturers and wholesale suppliers have sought to make commodities available to consumers beyond the specific group or cultural circle with whom these products were normally associated. An illuminating case in point is the slogan "You Don't Have to Be Jewish to Love Levy's Rye Bread," an award-winning advertising campaign from the early 1960s that introduced Jewish ethnicity into mainstream marketing.[25] Another fascinating example for the crossing of Jewish culture to the non-Jewish market is the Bar/Bat Mitzvah. According to journalist Elizabeth Bernstein, upscale non-Jewish kids in present-day America are envious of the lavish parties their Jewish classmates are throwing. The result is that some parents are giving them catered thirteenth birthday parties with DJs and dancers that bear a striking resemblance to contemporary Jewish celebrations.[26]

Commodifying Jewish culture and packaging it as a tempting possibility for non-Jews is then part of a new regime of consumption in which identities are fixed and become accessible to "outsiders." The transformation of Jewishness into something both indelible and consumable also applied to American Jews, giving rise to what we now may well call "google Judaism." For the "google Jew," or perhaps "Jewgle," Jewishness is

---

[23] Halter, *Shopping for Identity*, 111–117, as well as Frederick Kaufman, "The Secret Ingredient: Keeping the World Kosher," *Harper Magazine* (January 2005), 75–81.

[24] On this see: Mintel Kosher Foods Market report from 2003, available at www .marketresearch.com/product/display.asp?productid=862026&xs=r#pagetop; and the website "Kosherization of the World," available at www.molokane.org/molokan/Dog ma/Kosherization_World.html#1.

[25] It should be here noted that the sixties with the civil rights movement and other social introspection were a crucial period for the development of the concept of ethnicity and ethnic identity in America. See, for example, Todd Gitlin, *The Sixties Years of Hope, Days of Rage* (New York: Bantam Book, 1987); for the Jewish context see, for example, Eli Lederhendler, *Jewish Immigrants and American Capitalism, 1880–1920: From Caste to Class* (New York: Cambridge University Press, 2009); Ibid. (ed.), *Ethnicity and Beyond: Theories and Dilemmas of Jewish Group Demarcation* (New York: Oxford University Press, 2011).

[26] Elizabeth Bernstein, "You Don't Have to Be Jewish to Want a Bar Mitzvah," *The Wall Street Journal January* 243 (9) (2004), 1–8.

not so much about faith, a regimen of distinctive ritual practices, or even a sense of common descent, but a matter of choice, a personal orientation that corresponds individual taste and emotional sentiment. The new American "Jewgle" does not only browse through the mall of different traditions and notions of Judaism, "bookmarking" his or her own self-styled idea of "being Jewish," but also engages in cultural swapping in order to sample the many lifestyles, tastes, themes, and sounds of other cultures as well.

The overlapping of Jewish and consumer cultures poses no less challenging questions in Europe, where in recent years Jewish culture has gained unprecedented popularity, becoming entrenched in non-Jewish politics of remembrance and questions about cultural pluralism and European identities.[27] Jewish festivals, concerts, films, museums, historical restorations, publications, lectures, and readings, as well as restaurants cater to largely non-Jewish consumers. The Jewish Museum in Berlin, for example, attracted over a quarter of a million visitors even before the installation of its permanent exhibition was complete.[28] Ritual objects like menorahs feature as centerpieces of Jewish museums in Europe, many of which are under private, non-Jewish administration. These institutions cater to a diverse group of European non-Jewish and Jewish consumers, and their goods from Star of David–shaped pretzels to clothing, books, and artifacts fill the shopping bags of tourists from around the world. For a non-Jewish public looking to come to terms with the past, this form of consumable Jewishness is enticingly accessible. Yet, as some commentators argue, the creation of this "virtual" state of Jewishness is problematic because it is fixed on what is conceived of as an extinct Jewish culture, ignoring the evolving Jewish life in Europe today.[29]

---

[27] This section is firmly based on the introduction to Gideon Reuveni and Nils H. Roemer (eds.), *Longing, Belonging, and the Making of Jewish Consumer Culture* (Leiden: Brill Publications, 2006), 18.

[28] Jack Zipes, "The Contemporary German Fascination for Things Jewish: Toward a Minor Jewish Culture," in: Sander L. Gilman and Karen Remmler (eds.), *Re-emerging Jewish Culture in Germany: Life and Literature since 1989* (New York: New York University Press, 1994), 15–45.

[29] Ruth Ellen Gruber, *Virtually Jewish Reinventing Jewish Culture in Europe* (Berkeley: University of California Press, 2002); Jeffrey M. Peck, *Being Jewish in the New Germany* (New Brunswick: Rutgers University Press, 2006).

## BEYOND AMBIVALENCE

Coming back to the question with which we opened this chapter, it seems that this so-called marketplace multiculturalism has turned the "Jewish question" on its head. Whereas until the mid-twentieth century, in America, as elsewhere, Jews were constantly questioned about the nature of their difference, in post-Holocaust America the very idea of Jewish difference is contested. Surely, American Jews are today white, dominant, middle-class "insiders," much more than members of the marginalized "outsider" groups of American society. Although most American Jews do not see themselves as privileged or even as simply "white people," the overwhelming majority of them feel at home in the United States and regard it as their *Heimat*. Some observers today even wonder whether Jews are not getting too comfortable in America alluding to the challenges this development poses to "Jewish identity."[30] The blurring of boundaries between Jewish and American consumer cultures also significantly alters the meaning of consumer goods. Perhaps the most prominent example of such a trajectory is the bagel, no doubt the most quintessential Jewish food in America.[31]

According to filmmaker Tiffany Shlain, what makes the bagel so fundamentally Jewish is not merely just its origins, but even more so its shape, which is defined by an outside rather than an inside, epitomizing the Jewish experience as the quintessential outsiders in western society.[32] After reading a report about the popularity of the bagel in the United States, the late commentator Leonard Fine dryly asserted, "it is not the Jews who are assimilating into America; it is America that is assimilating into the Jews."[33] Yet, as David Biale recently noted, the assimilation of the bagel into the mainstream, and its mixing with other foods such as bacon, also had a price. It undermined the bagel's distinct origin as a Jewish

---

[30] See, for example, Alan M. Dershowitz, *The Vanishing American Jew: In Search of Jewish Identity for the Next Century* (New York: Touchstone 1998); Riv-Ellen Perll, "The (Un) Importance of Jewish Difference," *Mosaic* (November 17, 2014), available at http://mos aicmagazine.com/response/2014/11/the-unimportance-of-jewish-difference/. For a broader overview, Jonathan Sarna, *American Judaism: A History* (New Haven: Yale University Press, 2004), 209–239; Eli Lederhandler, *New York Jews and the Decline of Urban Ethnicity, 1950–1970* (Syracuse: Syracuse University Press, 2001).

[31] For an illuminating history of the bagel see Maria Balinska, *The Bagel: The Surprising History of a Modest Bread* (New Haven: Yale University Press, 2008).

[32] See Tiffany Shlain film, *The Tribe* (2005), available at http://tribethefilm.com/.

[33] Quoted in Halter, *Shopping for Identity*, 198. There is evidence suggesting that the Matzos that Jews eat during the Passover holiday is making a similar way into mainstream taste as many European and American supermarkets sell kosher Matzos all year long.

product.[34] Interestingly, the most profound illustration of how the bagel lost its Jewishness took place in the mid-1990s when the roll-with-the-hole finally made Aliyah and arrived in the Jewish State.

The word "bagel" is of course no stranger than Modern Hebrew. Until not so long ago most Israelis typically associated the bagel כַּעַך (Keach) with either a rock-hard biscuit ring called bagalech (pretzels); a large, soft, and sweet Arabic loaf (*Bagale Aravi*); an in-between version called the *Bagale Yerushalmi*; or the dachshund. So it came to pass that just as the Jewish ring-shaped roll started bagelizing America, in Israel the American Bagel came to be understood as no more than another American fast-food product that hit Israel's shores during the 1990s.[35] With this observation in mind we finally strike the troublesome question of the relationship between different regions of Jewish consumption as well as the nature and role of consumer culture in the Jewish state.

As elsewhere, consumption in Israel has multiple meanings. A salient expression of this ambiguity is the approach of the Zionist movement toward modern consumer culture. As we will see in later sections of this study, most Zionist thinkers associated consumption with femininity and Diaspora Jews, regarding it as an impediment for the "normalization" of Jewish society and even as a threat to Jewish endurance as a whole. To be sure, the call to "normalize" Jewish life was not exclusively Zionist. It constituted a central thread in discussions of the "Jewish question" since the end of the eighteenth century. For Zionism, at least, "normalization" meant not only the return to the land of Israel but the inversion of the occupational pyramid of Jews, so that its base would consist of "healthy" agricultural and manual laborers instead of what the socialist Zionist Ber Borochov called the "luft" economics of Diaspora Jews.[36] It also underscored Jewish (national) distinctiveness instigating the Jews' *Eigen-Sinn* as a prerequisite for Jewish integration among the family of nations. Even a pragmatic politician like Chaim Weizmann, who eventually became the state of Israel's first president, proclaimed in a speech from

---

[34] David Biale, "Jewish Consumer Culture in Historical and Contemporary Perspective," in: Gideon Reuveni and Nils H. Roemer (eds.), *Longing, Belonging, and the Making of Jewish Consumer Culture* (Leiden: Brill Publications, 2006), 36.

[35] Maoz Azaryahu, "McIsrael? On the Americanization of Israel," *Israel Studies* 5 (1) (2000), 41–64.

[36] Ber Borochov, "The Economic Development of the Jewish People," available at www .angelfire.com/il2/borochov/eco.html. For more general discussion of the Zionist view see Mitchell B. Hart, *Social Science and the Politics of Modern Jewish Identity* (Stanford: Stanford University Press, 2000).

1935, "the content of Zionism is changing all values according to which Jews lived under the pressure of foreign cultures."[37] For him, as for most other Zionist leaders, Zionism was not merely about colonizing a "new world" but about making a homecoming to an old one. The attempt to reconstitute an independent and self-sustaining Hebrew culture was thus perceived as an act of emancipation by which Jewish people should become a nation "like all other nations."

While denouncing consumption as an activity that undermines Jewish resilience, like other political movements of its time, the Zionist movement too had to reconcile its utopian ideals with the pragmatic needs of a political organization operating in a consumer-oriented society.[38] Early on the Zionist movement utilized cutting-edge marketing practices to promote its message, to raise funds, and to reinforce national consolidation. The Zionist ambivalence toward consumption is indicative of the complex and often strained relations between nationalism and consumerism. At times the two seem to mutually reinforce each other, while on other occasions they appear to undermine one another. Yet, while consumer culture in most postwar western societies operated in a cultural environment that strove to surpass nationalist tensions, Israel still faces significant challenges to national consolidation, not to mention the difficulty of operating in a constant state of war.

In Israel, daily life is lived in the contrast between the morality of consumption, which fulfills a longing to maximize pleasure, and the ethics of a warrior society dedicated to the experience of pain. It is not surprising that under such circumstances sites of consumption do not simply represent a "dream world" of affluence and material comfort. Indeed, as the Israeli sociologist Nathan Sznaider cogently observes, for many Israelis consumption stands for "order and regularity rather than abandon."[39] According to Sznaider, "Malls and streets full of boutiques represent the yearning for a rational bourgeois way of life, a nostalgia for a world not yet gained. It is a dream of quiet pleasures, of sitting in a cafe and bathing in the sun without fearing that a bomb will end it all."[40] In contrast to the American Jewish

---

[37] Quoted in Azaryahu, "McIsrael," 47.

[38] For similar dilemmas see Margaret Mary Finnegan, *Selling Suffrage: Consumer Culture and Votes for Women* (New York: Columbia University Press, 1999).

[39] Nathan Sznaider, "Consumerism as a Civilizing Process: Israel and Judaism in the Second Age of Modernity," *International Journal of Politics, Culture and Society* 14 (2) (2000), 311.

[40] Ibid., 312. For similar views see Uri Ram, "Citizens, Consumers and Believers: The Israeli Public Sphere between Capitalism and Fundamentalism," *Israel Studies* 3 (1) (1998),

context in which consumption seems to spur Jewish distinctiveness, and the European context that fixed Jewish virtual difference, in Israel consumer culture denotes a longing to dissolve the nation's upheavals, and to be like all other consumer societies. It is an irony of history that while the Zionist topos of "normalization" is still prevalent in Israel today, it does not have the same political connotations as in the past and is now clearly associated with consumer culture and a deep longing for a secure and more comfortable life. As we shall see in the next chapter, this demand has deeper roots in Jewish experience and culture.

24–44. For a broader discussion of Israel as a consumer society see Yoram S. Carmeli and Kalman Applbaum (eds.), *Consumption and Market Society in Israel* (Oxford: Berg Publishers, 2004); Orit Rozin, *The Rise of the Individual: A Challenge to Collectivism* (Boston: Brandies University Press, 2011).

# 4

## What Makes a Jew Happy? Longings, Belongings, and the Spirit of Modern Consumerism

What is happiness? Efforts to answer this question and to understand human happiness have absorbed a great deal of thought throughout the ages. In different periods and places, we find various understandings of what happiness is and how to attain it.[1] For Aristotle, for instance, genuine happiness lies in action guided by the intellect and by reason that leads to virtue, since this alone provides true value and not just amusement. Aristotle thus holds that contemplation is the highest form of moral activity because it is continuous, pleasant, self-sufficient, and complete. Christian theologians, such as Augustine, argued that it is only in the love of God that we find permanent and enduring happiness without the fear of loss that erodes our happiness.[2] Modern philosophers, mainly from the utilitarian school of thought, associated happiness with pleasure and the absence of pain. For John Stuart Mill, the two elements that constitute happiness are tranquility and excitement. In contrast to some continental philosophers of his time, who did not ascribe to happiness any special role in their system of ethics, Mill regarded happiness as the highest normative principle, arguing "actions are right in proportion as they tend to promote happiness; wrong as they tend to produce the reverse of happiness."[3]

---

[1] For a historical account of these different conceptualizations: Ignacio L. Götz, *Conceptions of Happiness* (Lanham, MD: University Press of America, 1995); Nicholas White, *A Brief History of Happiness* (Oxford: Blackwell, 2006); Darrin M. Mcmahon, *Happiness: A History* (New York: Atlantic Monthly Press, 2006).

[2] Martin Prozesky, *Religion and Ultimate Well-Being: An Explanatory Theory* (London: Macmillan, 1984).

[3] John Stuart Mill, *Utilitarianism* (London: Parker, Son, and Bourn, 1863), 9–10.

Today the topic of happiness is a popular one for empirical research in the social sciences. Sociologists, psychologists, and especially economists study with great interest the various sources of happiness and its multifaceted effects. Much effort is devoted to attempts to generate scales to measure levels of happiness. Special journals such as the *Journal for Happiness Research* or the online World Database of Happiness provide detailed information on past and current trends in happiness research.[4] Unlike scholars in earlier times, today's happiness researchers shun straightforward definitions of happiness and avoid giving sure prescriptions on how to attain it. They allow for broader concepts of happiness, by referring to happiness as "subjective well-being," "contentment," or "satisfaction from life-as-a-whole."

The shift away from an objective and prescriptive notion of happiness to a subjective view of well-being is connected to the long-term cultural and social changes that we commonly denominate with the term "modernity."[5] The subjective notion of happiness reflects the idea that happiness cannot be taken for granted as an outcome of remote, general, and unchangeable causes but rather can be achieved by changing the social order and assuming a certain lifestyle.[6] It was the work of the Enlightenment that turned the pursuit of happiness into a natural right held by each individual. Even the German philosopher Immanuel Kant who did not regard happiness as a moral end in itself eventfully recognized the significance of happiness as an utmost purpose of all rational beings.[7] Ultimately, the political, social, and economical arrangements of modern society are to a large extent designed to maximize both human progress and, above all, personal happiness.[8] In this sense the pursuit of happiness is quintessential to modernity.

---

[4] On this, for example, Richard A. Easterlin, *Happiness in Economics* (Cheltenham: Edward Elgar Publ., 2002); Bruno S. Frey and Alois Stutzer, *Happiness and Economics: How the Economy and Institutions Affect Well-Being* (Princeton: Princeton University Press, 2002); the World Database of Happiness, available at http://worlddatabaseofhappiness.eur.nl.

[5] J.S. Coleman, *Foundations of Social Theory* (Cambridge, MA: Harvard University Press, 1990); J.K. Galbraith, *The Culture of Contentment* (Boston: Houghton Mifflin Co., 1992).

[6] Albert O. Hirschman, *Rival Views of Market Society* (Cambridge MA: Harvard University Press, 1992), 105.

[7] Emanuel Kant, *Practical Philosophy* (Cambridge: Cambridge University Press, 1996), 68. On Kant's concept of happiness, Paul Guyer, *Kant on Freedom, Law, and Happiness* (New York: Cambridge University Press, 2000); Beatrix Himmelmann, *Kants Begriff des Glücks* (Berlin: de Gruyter, 2003).

[8] Robert E. Lane, *The Market Experience* (Cambridge: Cambridge University Press, 1991), 423–548.

The consumer market is perhaps one of the most prominent places in which the modern notion of individual happiness is played out. It presents a plethora of goods and services that are supposed to provide consumers with a veritable paradise of comfort and pleasure. Advertising and marketing play a crucial role in this process. They place the consumer at the heart of a market economy by portraying human contentment in the association between people and products.[9]

Many historians trace the origins of modern consumerism to the Romantic movement, with its emphasis on heroic individualism and self-creation. In this interpretation, consumption stems from a Romantic ethic in which the individual is bound to realize himself or herself in the experience of novelty and gratification that he or she attains at the marketplace.[10] According to this approach, the logic of the modern pursuit of happiness lies in the notion that there is always something else worth pursuing; the quest for that next something and its realization are perceived as a source of happiness.[11]

Notwithstanding these diverse and at times convoluted understandings of the concept of well-being, happiness is still considered to be a vital incentive for human action and is highly valued. This is especially true in the cultural settings of the modern West where individuals are expected to make choices to maximize their happiness rather than fulfill the obligations of traditional social frameworks.[12] In this chapter, I wish to explore this notion of happiness in the context of Jewish culture in Europe. By examining the "longings" of Jews as they pertain to their belongings, I will try to distinguish a Jewish notion of well-being and juxtapose it with other "general" concepts of happiness. This exploration will further advance our discussion of the multifaceted interplay between processes of cultural homogenization and ways in which minorities generate and sustain exclusive group identity in the modern age.

The following discussion will open with a short overview of some of the debates concerning the nature and place of happiness in Jewish traditional sources. After examining the Jewish intellectual discourse on happiness,

---

[9] William Leiss, Stephen Kline and Sut Jhally, *Social Communication in Advertising: Persons, Products, and Images of Well-Being* (Toronto: Methuen, 1986).

[10] Colin Campbell, *The Romantic Ethic and the Spirit of Modern Consumerism* (Oxford: Basil Blackwell, 1987).

[11] Robert E. Lane, *The Market Experience: George Katona, Psychological Economics* (New York: Elsevier, 1975).

[12] For a general discussion see Coleman, *Foundations of Social Theory*; Galbraith, *The Culture of Contentment*.

the discussion will explore notions of happiness using sources of a more everyday nature – Jewish humor. This examination will show that both intellectual and more everyday interpretations of "Jewish" happiness did not differ substantially from other concepts of happiness common to their time. Instead, the pursuit of happiness enabled Jews to imagine cultural belonging, though, as we will see below, in some cases it also contributed to a sense of Jewish distinctiveness.

## CONCEPTS OF JEWISH HAPPINESS

It is a commonly held belief that happiness is not a significant topic in traditional Judaism. This view is based on three presuppositions concerning the nature of Judaism and Jewish history.[13] First, since the history of the Jews is replete with persecution, bloodshed, and suffering, it is more common to conceive of Jewish history as a story about the struggle for survival under difficult conditions – as a history of suffering – rather than to associate it with the pursuit of happiness. Second, there seems to be a discrepancy between the collective terms through which traditional Judaism understands itself and the pursuit of happiness as an individual endeavor. Third, and perhaps most relevant to our discussion here, in the cultural setting of modern consumer capitalism where the pursuit of happiness is to a large extent determined by the possession and use of material goods and services, living a Jewish life appeared irrelevant if not an obstacle to the attainment of material happiness.

The following pages will argue to the contrary. This of course is not an entirely original endeavor. In her comprehensive study of the concept of happiness in premodern Judaism, Hava Tirosh-Samuelson has already pointed to the significance of happiness in traditional Jewish thought. She did not only reconstruct the ways some prominent Jewish thinkers dealt with the question of happiness but also presented happiness as an interpretive category for the study of Judaism. According to Tirosh-Samuelson, "Judaism understood itself as the best path to happy life." The belief that Judaism was the sole path to human well-being, she propounded, is "one of the major reasons for the survival of Jewish life."[14] It was this conviction in the ability of Judaism to provide

---

[13] The following section draws on the work of Hava Tirosh-Samuelson, *Happiness in Premodern Judaism: Virtue, Knowledge, and Well-Being* (Cincinnati: Hebrew Union College Press, 2003).

[14] Tirosh-Samuelson, *Happiness in Premodern Judaism*, 439.

happiness that empowered Jews, building resilience to uphold their distinctiveness.

What then constitutes happiness according to traditional Jewish thought? Tirosh-Samuelson maintains that in traditional Judaism, happiness was not equated with the possession of material goods, wealth, power, or fame.[15] It was not conceived of as a subjective feeling of satisfaction manifested in a short period of time, but rather as an objective state of affairs in which a person successfully organizes all activities into a meaningful pattern for the duration of his or her life. In concrete terms this meant that in order to be happy, "Jews had to live in accordance with Torah and become wise."[16] The core of this concept of happiness lies then in the identification of Torah, which is equated with wisdom or, as Tirosh-Samuelson puts it, in the "demanding that Jews pursue wisdom as part of their loyalty to God."[17]

This antimaterialistic concept of happiness that places learning at its hub is not confined to the premodern period. In more recent periods as well it remains a prevailing approach to the question of happiness among pious Jews. Thus, for example, the influential Orthodox rabbi Eliyahu Eliezer Dessler (1892–1953) proclaimed in his *Michtav Meeliyahu* (a letter from Eliyahu), "there is no happiness in the world of material things; there is only happiness in spiritual concerns. The one who enjoys a rich spiritual life is happy. There is no other kind of happiness in existence."[18]

This concept of happiness is doubtless part of the efforts to shield Judaism from the misgivings of modernity and ensure the continuation of traditional Jewish ways. Interestingly there are some indications that this objectivist approach to happiness, which places learning and the pursuit of wisdom at its core, facilitated the Jewish reception of certain modern ideas, such as the German Enlightenment notion of *Bildung* as well as the rigid division between material and spiritual culture. The attack of Rabbi Samson Raphael Hirsch (1808–1888) against the prevailing utilitarian understanding of happiness of his time is a salient manifestation of this affinity between traditional Judaism and a certain vision of modernity. In *The Nineteen Letters on Judaism*, Hirsch berates the fictitious addressee of the treatise, Benjamin, by saying: "It was but natural that you found your Judaism in contradiction to your own conception of the purpose of human existence, inasmuch as your conception was one which Judaism rejects and against whose baser tendencies, the desire for pleasure and the deification

---

[15] Ibid., 439.    [16] Ibid., 5.    [17] Ibid., 440.
[18] Eliyahu E. Dessler, *Strive for Truth. Michtav Me-Eliyahu* (Jerusalem: Feldheim Publishers, 1988), 29.

of material wealth, it wages unceasing warfare."[19] Yet this criticism was not intended to alienate Judaism from modernity. On the contrary, according to Hirsch, Jewish religion and progress are built on the very same foundations – education and culture. To emphasize this, Hirsch adopted the proverb יפה תלמוד תורה עם דרך ארץ ("An excellent thing is the study of the Torah combined with the ways of the world," Ethics of the Fathers 2.2) as the motto for his movement.[20]

Research has already given considerable attention to these genuine or alleged overlaps between Judaism and modernity.[21] For our discussion I would like to draw attention to a different aspect of this story. Because traditional Judaism excluded women from the world of letters, the achievement of genuine happiness through the learning of the Torah was available only to men. From this perspective, discussions of the nature of happiness within Judaism are also those about the nature of Judaism itself. The following passage provides a particularly illuminating illustration of this struggle to establish cultural hegemony based on an ascetic male concept of happiness:

As the world becomes ever more sophisticated, the destruction becomes ever greater; evil ways become good in men's eyes. They make them into laws and morals, and they pass them on from father to son. Every peculiar thing in the world seems reasonable to them, the proper approach – of making do with little – they consider peculiar; the refraining from luxuries, they see a failure to fulfill one's duty, and everyone copies whatever his fellow man does. One who enjoys only as much as he needs of this world is called lazy, and one who refrains from acquiring more possessions than necessary is considered weak and pitiful. One who chases after luxuries is thought industrious, however, and by their material possessions, they glorify themselves and think themselves great. They make their stomachs into god; their clothing into their *Torah*, and the improvement of their homes, their morality.[22]

---

[19] Samson Raphael Hirsch, *The Nineteen Letters on Judaism* (Jerusalem: Feldheim Publishers, 1969), 93.

[20] Samson Raphael Hirsch, "Religion Allied to Progress," in: *Judaism Eternal: Selected Essays from the Writings of Samson Raphael Hirsch* (London: The Soncino Press, 1956), 224–244, here 236. On Hirsch and his movement, Mordechai Breuer, *Modernity within Tradition: The Social History of Orthodox Jewry in Imperial Germany* (New York: Columbia University Press, 1992).

[21] On this, for example, Bryan Cheyette and Laura Marcus (ed.), *Modernity, Culture and "the Jew"* (Cambridge: Polity Press, 1998); Shulamit Volkov, *Germans, Jews, and Antisemites: Trials in Emancipation* (Cambridge: Cambridge University Press, 2006).

[22] Quoted in: Alexander Aryeh Mandelbaum, *Simchah – The Spark of Life: A Comprehensive Exploration of the Virtue of Simchah, "Jewish Happiness" and How to Attain It* (Jerusalem: Feldheim Publishers, 1995), 97–98.

These lines were originally written in Arabic by Rabbi Bahya ibn Paquda in his eleventh-century *Chovot Halevavot* (Duties of the Heart), probably one of the most popular ethical books in the modern Jewish world. Still available on Amazon, this book reflects a type of cultural pessimism more familiar to us from recent times. Calling modern man *Homo Consumens*, sociologist Erich Fromm, for example, referred to modern times as the "beginning of a period in which man ceases to be human and becomes transformed into an unthinking and unfeeling machine ... [who has] no aim except producing and consuming more and more."[23] In the same manner, Hannah Arendt claimed that in modern market society "the ultimate standard of measurement is not utility and usage at all, but 'happiness,' that is, the amount of pain and pleasure experienced in the production or in the consumption of things."[24]

While Fromm, Arendt, and many other critics of modern society, Jews and non-Jews alike, refer to the shortcomings of modernity in universal terms, similar arguments were utilized as part of an ongoing effort to generate and uphold an exclusive sense of Jewish belonging. In both cases happiness was identified with a set of so-called high culture values and distanced from what was considered to be an inferior, namely, material popular culture. This type of cultural criticism in the Jewish setting merits further discussion elsewhere. Here, I wish to point out that the hierarchical separation between a putatively homogeneous and lasting spiritual culture, and a fragmentary, fleeting material culture, not only reflected the fears and doubts of those groups of mainly male Jewish thinkers who struggled to organize and tame Jewish society but also underlined how important the pursuit of material happiness was becoming in Jewish society. Interestingly, this notion of the centrality of material prosperity in Jewish life also draws on biblical perceptions of happiness. For the people of ancient Israel, happiness was not only associated with knowing God's favor but also with the acknowledgment of worldly pleasures that in an uncertain world are quick to be denied.[25] The worldly pleasures of affluence, family life, fertility, longevity, and peace shaped a more common notion of happiness, sometimes lamented Jewish community leaders and intellectuals advocating a spiritual approach. Or, as Michael Wex has

---

[23] Erich Fromm, *The Revolution of Hope* (New York: Rinehart, 1968), 1, 28, and 38. On this see also Wolfgang Schmidbauer, *Homo Consumens: Der Kult des Überflusses* (Stuttgart: Deutsche Verlag-Anstalt, 1972).

[24] Hannah Arendt, *The Human Condition* (Chicago: University of Chicago Press, 1958), 309.

[25] Mcmahon, *Happiness*, 80.

recently phrased it, "the idea that suffering is good for the Jews seemed to have been embraced by everyone except the Jews who did the suffering."[26]

## SOURCES OF HAPPINESS

Although not as systematic and easy to obtain as the texts exulting the notion of spiritual happiness, we briefly discussed above, a substantial and diverse body of sources can be used to explore what seemed to be a more common and widespread notion of "material happiness" in Jewish society. Here, I would like to discuss just one of these sources – Jewish humor.

By the end of the nineteenth century, humor had become a subject of serious academic research. Perhaps the most notable and influential attempt to conceptualize humor is to be found in Sigmund Freud's 1905 study *Jokes and Their Relations to the Unconscious*. According to Freud, humor is a means to obtain pleasure. The pleasure of humor, Freud explained, "comes about … at the cost of a release of affect that does not occur: It arises from *an economy in the expenditure of affect*" (emphasis in original).[27] Seeing humor as a mental performance representing a method of regaining unfulfilled pleasures led Freud to the conclusion that we need humor "to make us feel happy in our life."[28] This conception of humor had an immense influence on Jewish humor research for two main reasons. First, Freud incorporated in his seminal analysis many examples of what he referred to as "Jewish jokes." Second, since Jewish humor owes a great debt to Jewish suffering, Freud's insights into the physiological significance of humor as a coping mechanism and a device to gain pleasure provided a readymade framework for Jewish humor research.[29] Consequently, Jewish humor offered not only a way to transcend persecution, rejection, and despair but also a way to express the

---

[26] Michael Wex, *Born to Kvetch: Yiddish Language and Culture in All of Its Moods* (New York: St. Martin Press, 2005), 145.

[27] Sigmund Freud, *Jokes and Their Relations to the Unconscious* (London: The Hogarth Press, 1960), 228–229.

[28] Ibid., 236.

[29] Stanley J. Schater, *Laugh for God's Sake: Where Jewish Humor and Jewish Ethics Meet* (Jerey City: Ktav Publishing, 2008); Ruth R. Wisse, *Some Serious Thoughts about Jewish Humor* (New York: Leo Baeck Institute, 2001); Arthur Asa Berger, *The Genius of the Jewish Joke* (Northvale: Jason Aronson, 1997); Elliott Oring, *The Jokes of Sigmund Freud: A Study in Humor and Jewish Identity* (Northvale, NJ: Jason Aronson, 1997). For criticism of this concept of Jewish Humor see Dan Ben-Amos, "The 'Myth' of Jewish Humor," *Western Folklore* 32 (1973), 112–131.

Jewish resilience, optimism, and zest for living. In this respect, the notion of a distinctive Jewish humor facilitated the presentation of the Jews as a modern, cultivated, self-determining, and happy people.[30] Not surprisingly, most scholarship on Jewish humor was produced by a relatively small group of educated, mainly, men living outside the confines of the traditional Jewish community. These intellectuals conducted research on what they termed "Jewish humor" as part of their attempt to explore and retrieve Jewish authenticity.[31] In this sense the concept of Jewish humor reflects a longing for a more genuine and comprehensive Jewish life.

This approach to humor accompanied a conception of modernity as a threat to Jewish endurance. Yet, unlike the criticism of modernity put forward, for example, by Orthodox Jews who sought to protect Jewish life by promoting learning and abstinence, in seeking to restore and maintain Jewish life these critics of modernity validated nearly all things considered "Jewish." The very notion of Jewish humor hence appears to stem from the conceptualization of the Jewish people as a distinct social group, which consists of complex networks of multiple interrelationships and affiliations.

What then can we learn from Jewish humor about happiness? In order to answer this question we need to adopt a more sociocultural approach to humor, an approach that considers humor as a social phenomenon, an index and reflection of social attitudes through which we can grasp culturally shaped ways of thinking and feeling.[32] Seeing humor as a link between human expectations and social experience will thus provide a framework to investigate what really matters in society and culture. Let us turn to examine a few examples and see if we can answer the question posed at the outset of this discussion – what makes a Jew happy?

---

[30] On this see, for example, Avner Ziv (ed.), *National Styles Humor* (New York: Greenwood Press, 1988); Chris Powell and George E. Paton (eds.), *Humor and Society: Resistance and Control* (London: Macmillan, 1988); Sig Altman, *The Comic Image of the Jew: Explorations of a Pop Culture Phenomenon* (Rutherford: Fairleigh Dickinson University Press, 1971). For a general discussion on humor and ethnicity see: Christy Davies, *Ethnic Humor around the World. A Comparative Analysis* (Bloomington: Indiana University Press, 1990).

[31] Interestingly there is evidence in rabbinical sources suggesting that the Rabbis were not particularly well disposed toward humor. This, however, does not deny the existence of humor in Jewish tradition. On this, for example, Avner Ziv (ed.), *Jewish Humor* (London: Transaction Publishers, 1997).

[32] On this see especially Mary Douglas, "Jokes," in: ibid., *Implicit Meanings: Essays in Anthropology* (London: Routledge & Kegan Paul, 1975), 90–114. For a different approach to humor research, Arthur Asa Berger, *Blind Men and Elephants: Perspectives on Humor* (New Brunswick: Transaction Publishers, 1995).

## JOKES AND THEIR RELATIONS TO (JEWISH) HAPPINESS

Happiness, as we have seen, is an elusive and subjective concept. Hence any attempt to analyze Jewish happiness will not only be partial and inconclusive but also highly contentious. Nevertheless, I will risk such an attempt and suggest that what makes Jews happy, typically but certainly not exclusively, is money. A Yiddish folk saying puts it like this: "What are the three things hardest for man to bear? Heart disease, stomach troubles, and worst of all – an empty purse."[33]

Money is a serious thing and commonly is not a subject to ridicule. Yet Jewish humor is loaded with images and references to money. Let us take the following story as an example:

The teacher in a Polish public school asked the pupils to write a brief composition on the subject. "What I Would Do with Fifty Thousand Dollars?"

About half an hour later all the pupils handed in their work with the exception of Joseph Shereshevsky, whose paper was blank.

"You didn't do anything!" commented the teacher.
"But this represents my answer to your question,"
said the pupil, "If I had fifty thousand dollars
I would just do nothing."

A somewhat different example can be found in the following story:

At the funeral of the richest man in town a great many mourners turned out to pay their last respects to the dead. Among the multitude was a stranger who heaved deep sighs as he followed the hearse. "Are you a close relation to the deceased?" someone asked him empathically.

"I'm of no relation at all!" he replied.
"Then why do you weep?"
"That is why."

These stories, which appear in different versions in many Jewish humor anthologies, illustrate the special place ascribed to money in Jewish popular culture. They challenge classification and hierarchy, yet they affirm the power of money. Affluence is depicted here as a state that lies beyond daily worries and the struggle for survival; it is imagined as a kind of heaven of self-fulfillment and material happiness. To be sure, Jewish humor does not idealize poverty, and as the folklorist Nathan Ausubel noted, "if the rich don't enjoy their pleasures, and if money can't buy happiness, neither is poverty the virtue it is credited to

---

[33] Nathan Ausubel (ed.), *A Treasury of Jewish Humor* (New York: Doubleday, 1951), 287.

be."[34] In one of his stories on which *Fiddler on the Roof* is based, Sholem Aleichem provides his own interpretation of this dismissive approach to poverty, proclaiming, "God hates a pauper, and the proof is that if God loved the pauper, the pauper wouldn't be poor."[35] This negative approach to poverty and pauperism is also apparent in the Yiddish language, which, as Michael Wex observed, has developed an unusual extensive vocabulary of poverty, want, and stymied desire.[36] According to Wex the emergence of this lexis reflects what he denotes as a "culture of *Kvetch*," in which *Kvetching* (complaining) is made a way of knowing and a means of apprehension that sees the world through cataract-colored glasses.[37] On a more basic level, this preoccupation with pauperism in Jewish popular culture provides a further indication that up until National Socialism, poverty was the main threat that Jews had to deal with in the modern world, even greater than antisemitism or assimilation.[38]

The most prominent and popular figure of Jewish humor representing this special preoccupation with money is the *schnorrer*. The *schnorrer* is often portrayed as a Jewish beggar with chutzpah, who shows resourcefulness in getting money from others as though it is his right to receive it.[39] At times the *schnorrer* is represented as a poor Jew with a unique interpretation of middle-class values, as, for example, in Israel Zangwill's play *The King of Schnorrers*.[40] For Menasseh Bueno Barzillia Azevedo da Costa, Zangwill's Sephardic *schnorrer*, schnorring is not merely looked upon as a means for making a living; he regards it as a calling that precludes him from doing any other type of work. Thus, when Yankele ben Yitzchok, the young East European *schnorrer*, hesitantly expresses his desire to marry Menasseh's daughter, the "king of the schnorrers" embraces him and declares that as a responsible father he will never consider resting his daughter's future happiness on such an uncertain basis as work. He then explains to Yankele that schnorring "is the only occupation that is regular all year round. Everything else may fail – the

---

[34] Ibid.   [35] Quoted in Wex, *Born to Kvetch*, 146.   [36] Ibid., 141.   [37] Ibid., 2.

[38] For an elaborate discussion of the discourse on Jewish pauperism see Derek Penslar, *Shylock's Children: Economics and Jewish Identity in Modern Times* (Berkeley: University of California Press, 2001).

[39] Nathan Ausubel (ed.), *A Treasury of Jewish Folklore* (New York: Crown Publishers, 1948), 267–268; Arthur Asa Berger, *The Genius of the Jewish Humor* (Northvale, NJ: Jason Aronson Inc., 1993), 104–108.

[40] Israel Zangwill, *The King of Schnorrers* (New York: Dover Publications, 1965).

greatest commercial houses may totter to the ground ... the Schnorrer,"
Menasseh concludes, "is always secure."[41]

On other occasions the *schnorrer*'s chutzpah is so overwhelming that it
seems to represent a different set of values than those generally accepted
by the rest of the community. The following story illustrates this:

For several years two brothers had presented themselves at the home of Rothschild
once a month and each had been given 100 Marks. Then, one died, so the survivor
made the usual call alone.

The keeper of the Rothschild funds handed him the usual 100 Marks. "But
you've made a mistake!" the schnorrer protested. "I should get 200 Marks, 100
for my brother."

"No," said the treasurer, "your brother is dead. This is your hundred."
"What do you mean?" The schnorrer drew himself up indignantly.
"Am I my brother's heir ... or is Rothschild?"

The climax of the *schnorrer* jokes is no doubt the moment of confrontation between the beneficiary and his benefactor. The *schnorrer* shows no
respect for his sponsor, and he doesn't appear to acknowledge his depen-
dency. In this sense, there is something almost heroic about the way the
*schnorrer* confronts the well-offs. A short example will suffice to illustrate
this point:

The schnorrer begged the Baron for some money for a journey to Ostend; his
doctor had recommended sea-bathing for his troubles. The Baron thought Ostend
was a particularly expensive resort; a cheaper one would do equally well.
The schnorrer, however, rejected the proposal with the words: "Herr Baron,
I consider nothing too expensive for my health."

According to Freud, the notion that the *schnorrer* treats his sponsor's
money as his own is based on a Jewish tradition in which the rich are
obliged by law to give alms and should even be grateful for this opportunity for beneficence. Thus for Freud the *schnorrer* jokes represent
a conflict between middle-class and religious attitudes toward charity.
"There is really no advantage in being a rich man if one is a Jew," Freud
noted, "other people's misery makes it impossible to enjoy one's own
happiness."[42] For Freud, so it seemed, this observation is no longer a joke
but a pitiful reality.

Reading the *schnorrer* as a form of rebellion against the irrationality of
traditional Jewish social values is just one way of interpreting this figure.
On a different level, *schnorrer* jokes can be seen to do exactly the opposite,

---

[41] Ibid., 46.     [42] Freud, *Jokes and Their Relations to the Unconscious*, 113.

namely, to mock excessive deference to the world of work, duty, and money. This criticism displays especially the rich as a group of people robbed of the possibility of human joy and freedom. The numerous tales about the Baron Rothschild, who allegedly once said, "It isn't enough for you to love money, it's also necessary that money should love you," illustrate the second kind of interpretation. "What then does Baron Rothschild do that we poor Jews don't?" a poor Jew asks in one of the many Rothschild folktales, and the answer follows, "Good God, he has nothing to do all day long! His servants do everything for him. They help him put on his clothes so that he doesn't even have to put his hand in cold water. He's got so many suits of cloths and changes of underwear that he is kept busy dressing all the time. He pulls on and pulls off, pulls on and pulls off. Why, it's enough to drive a person crazy."

The Rothschild tales as well as the *schnorrer* stories may be considered part of a genre that the humor researcher Christie Davies refers to as "jokes from the iron cage." These jokes, Davies observes, emerged in the modern industrial age as one more tool for forcing individuals to confirm with the so-called rational demands of modern organizations and society, while they function as a device protesting against the constraints of the iron cage.[43]

Jewish humor seems to reproduce this pattern. But whether it affirms or undermines the logic of the iron cage, Jewish humor does not ignore the power of money. There is, of course, nothing uniquely Jewish about the idea that humor reflects the desire for social mobility or that money and humor go together. The fact that a joke works, as Mary Douglas has noted, "only when it mirrors social form"[44] is probably why Jews and non-Jews can equally appreciate the *schnorrer* jokes. Still both the *schnorrer* and Rothschild are Jewish figures, and in this sense they also represent a particularly Jewish situation and for that matter even a particularly Jewish approach to money.

According to historian Yitzhak (Ignaz) Schipper, Jews were forced early on to acknowledge the magical power of money. Money, he contended, "afforded [the Jewish people] respect and prestige; money was their only defense amidst economically predatory peoples. It was a salvation and a balm; only money could make the oppressor mild."[45]

---

[43] Christie Davies, *Jokes and Their Relations to Society* (Berlin: Mouton de Gruyter, 1998), 65 and 71.

[44] Douglas, "Jokes," 106.

[45] Ignaz Schipper, "Anfänge des Kapitalismus bei den abendländischen Juden im frühen Mittelalter," *Zeitschrift für Volkswirtschaft, Sozialpolitik und Verwaltung* 15 (1906), 564.

For Heinrich Graetz (1817–1891), probably the most prominent Jewish historian of the nineteenth century, the accumulation of wealth by Jews represents nothing less than evidence for the working of the hand of God and the balanced justice of history. "Is it not wonderful," he asked rhetorically in his "Letters to an English Lady" from 1883, "that the great power of capital is in the hands of the Jews?"[46] Hence, for Graetz, Schipper, and many other Jews of the pre–World War II period, the accumulation of wealth was associated with Jewish interest and self-assertion, and it was conceived of as an embodiment of Jewish empowerment.

Yet money was not merely important as a source of Jewish power and resistance. For Sholem Aleichem Kasrilovka *melamed* (religious teacher), for example, becoming rich meant a life with "no worrying about making a living, about getting money to provide for Sabbath."[47] The *melamed* even goes so far to imply that if only he had as much money as Rothschild, he would be even wealthier as he could always teach on the side. As the richest man in the world the Kasrilovka *melamed* envisions not only how he will benefit his family and fellow Jews but also how with the power of money he will end all wars and create a world without envy and animosity. In such a world, Sholom Aleichem speculates, there will be no weapons and troops; no thunder and shouting; no rivalries and hostility; and as a result no Turks, Englishmen, Frenchmen, Gypsies, and, *oy vey*, no Jews too.[48] Finally, he even considers abolishing money altogether and creating a world where "there would be no work for the tempter, and lust itself would cease to be!" "But that's all very well," the *melamed* reflects, suddenly becoming sober as he realizes that if it comes to that, he still needs money to keep the Sabbath.[49] Sholem Aleichem's *melamed* does not appear to acknowledge any benefit for him as a Jew from the abolishment of money. He doesn't regard it as an option that could resolve his basic existential problem: how to provide for the Sabbath, suggesting that a world without money does not offer any obvious advantages for him as a Jew.

The significance of this story thus lies exactly in the correspondence between money's purchasing power and the Sabbath, in the positive relationship between worldly pleasures and religious life. Rejoicing in the Sabbath (*Oneg Shabbat*) is not perceived or performed as an

---

[46] Heinrich Greartz, *Briefwechsel einer englische Dame* (Stuttgart: Levy & Müller, 1883), 31.
[47] Sholom Aleikhem, *The Bewitched Tailor* (Moscow: Foreign Languages Publishing House, 1950), 113.
[48] Ibid., 116.    [49] Ibid., 117.

exclusively spiritual affair; it also involves festivity and worldly traits such as a banquet with special food, nice tableware, and elegant clothing, all of which require money as well as a certain level of infrastructure to provide the necessary goods and services. The concept of *Oneg Shabbat* thus draws on a vision of the good and happy life that conforms to the spirit of modern consumerism, yet adapts it to a special Jewish setting.

\* \* \*

# PART II

# THE POLITICS OF JEWISH CONSUMPTION

In her 1958 work *The Human Condition*, Hannah Arendt addressed the challenge of reasserting a positive vision to political action following the devastations of World War II. Motivated by the experience of the Nazi horrors as well as the persistent threat of a new war, Arendt hoped to identify a novel political framework that could sustain the principles of free citizenship even in times of conflict and war.[1] At the heart of her analysis Arendt placed a distinction between two modes of human activity: the *vita activa* and the *vita contemplativa*. To the former category Arendt assigned labor, work, and action; to the latter she assigned thinking, willing, and judging. With this division in hand, Arendt critiqued the long-standing tradition in western culture of subordinating the world of human action, the *vita activa*, to the life of contemplation, or *vita contemplativa*.

According to Arendt, the fundamental human condition is not merely determined by the consciousness of being-in-the-world, as advocated by her protégé Martin Heidegger, but by the awareness of being in-the-world -with-others. All human activities, Arendt writes, "are conditioned by the fact that men live together."[2] From this insight Arendt develops her argument on the centrality of political action within the realm of human activities. For Arendt, politics encompasses not only power and its mobilization but also active participation in public life. Her concept of citizenship accentuates the significance of civic engagement and collective

---

[1] Hanna Fenichel Pitkin, *The Attack of the Blob: Hannah Arendt's Concept of the Social* (Chicago: Chicago University Press, 1998), 112.
[2] Hannah Arendt, *The Human Condition* (Chicago: University of Chicago Press, 1998), 22.

deliberation.[3] Within this framework, Arendt also emphasizes the importance of material objects. Since "human existence is conditioned existence," she writes, "it would be impossible without things, and things
would be a heap of unrelated articles, a 'non-world', if they were not
conditioners of human existence."[4] For Arendt, then, the things of the
world have the function of stabilizing human life. The objectivity of things
means that despite the ever-changing nature of human beings, we can
retrieve our sameness, that is our identity, by being related to the same
chair and the same table. In other words, "against the subjectivity of men
stands the objectivity of the men-made world ... a world between men and
nature ... Without a world between men and nature, there is eternal
movement, but no objectivity."[5]

Despite her emphasis on the psychological and social function of
objects, Arendt does not locate the practice of acquiring goods – that is,
consumption – within either the *vita activa* or the *vita contemplativa*.
According to Arendt, the practice of spending money defies both these
modes of activity. Like many other thinkers of her time, Arendt considered politics and consumption two fundamentally different realms and
saw the latter as a quintessentially apolitical endeavor that undermined
critical thinking. She used binary terms – autonomy/heteronomy, public/
private, necessity/surplus, use/waste, and active/passive – to describe the
contrast between the realms and considered their interplay a kind of zero-
sum game. More of one, she believed, inevitably meant less of the other.

What is particularly intriguing about Arendt's approach to consumption is how it corresponds to her views on Jews and politics. In a well-
known interview with the German journalist Günter Gaus from 1964, she
made a clear distinction between community membership based on
a notion of common origin and shared fate, and one based on mutual
interest. According to Arendt, politics can be performed only within the
latter community of interest. The Jews, whom she describes as "a classical
example of worldless people," are, in her view, an example of the former:
a community of common descent that is withdrawn from the world. For
Arendt this form of community tends to generate what she calls "humanity in form of fraternity," which, as she noted in a speech on the occasion

---

[3] On this see also Hannah Arendt, *The Promise of Politics* (New York: Schocken books,
2005). For a comparative discussion of Arendt's concept of citizenship see Margaret
R. Somers, *Genealogies of Citizenships: Market, Statelessness, and the Right to Have
Rights* (Cambridge: Cambridge University Press, 2008).
[4] Arendt, *The Human Condition*, 9.    [5] Ibid., 137.

of receiving the prestigious Lessing Prize from the city of Hamburg in 1959, "invariably appears historically among persecuted peoples and enslaved groups."[6] Since this form of "humanity of the insulted and injured" applies mainly to those belonging to the mistreated groups, an inevitable result of this state of affairs, Arendt argues, is that this type of community manifests little sense of responsibility toward the world.[7] When specifically asked by Günter Gaus whether Jews are thus apolitical people, Arendt cautiously replied that although Jewish communities were to a certain extent political, and the Jewish religion a national religion, "the concept of the political" does not fully apply to the Jewish people, at least not until the foundation of the State of Israel.[8]

The exemption of Jews as a group from the "political" might be connected to Arendt's rejection of the primacy of a life of contemplation, which she associates with Judaism. Yet for Arendt it is not the "human condition" but rather the "Jewish condition" of victimization and exclusion from the world of political realities that accounts for the creation of the passive, worldless, and thus nonpolitical Jew. Intriguingly, and despite Arendt's skepticism regarding the idea of a Jewish polity, her approach here corresponds to prevailing Jewish nationalist interpretations dating the onset of modern Jewish political life to the formation of Jewish mass political movements at the end of the nineteenth century.[9] Like many other commentators of her time, Arendt drew a connection between the allegedly nonpolitical Jewish individual and the pariah status of Jews as a religious, social, and economic ostracized group. It is in this context that the link between Jews and consumption becomes legible. Arendt depicts both in a similar manner. Moreover, she links Jews with the emergence of the modern, passive, and worldless consumer society. In *The Origins of Totalitarianism* she noted "that Jews were unable or unwilling to develop along industrial capitalist lines, so that the net result of their activities was scattered, inefficient organization of consumption without an adequate

---

[6] Hannah Arendt, "On Humanity in Dark Times: Thoughts about Lessing," in: *Men in Dark Times* (San Diego: Harvest Book, 1968), 13.

[7] Ibid., 16–17.

[8] Hannah Arendt, "What Remains? The Language Remains: A Conversation with Günter Gaus," in: *Essays on Understanding, 1935–1954* (New York: Harcourt Brace & Company, 1994), 17.

[9] Even the great Jewish historian Salo Wietmar Baron in his seminal study "The Jewish Community" has described Jewish traditional social life as "a sort of little state, inter-territorial and non-political, but nonetheless quasi-totalitarian." Salo W. Baron, *The Jewish Community*, vol. 1 (Philadelphia: Jewish Publication Society, 1942), 208.

system of production."[10] In a similar vein she has written in another essay that "the fateful role of supplying usurious capital, which served consumption, but had only destructive influence on production," deprived the capacity of Jews to comprehend, let alone act, politically.[11] The Jews, she argued, "without knowledge of or interest in power, never thought of exercising more than mild pressure for minor purposes of self-defense."[12] In an essay from 1946 on what she refers to as "privileged Jews," Arendt went so far as to argue that those wealthy Jews, who were in the position of influence, consciously chose not to get involved in power politics. In her view the "privileged Jews" were more concerned with preserving their own riches and special status within and outside the Jewish community, so that their main political goals never went beyond the politics of survival.[13] "Almost across the board," she proclaimed, "Jewish politics, to the extent that it exists at all, is run by people who have likewise grown up – without ever growing powerful! – worshiping power and opportunistic success."[14] It is interesting to note that almost 100 years before Arendt wrote these words, the Anglo-Jewish writer and philanthropist Charlotte Montefiore gave voice to similar concerns regarding the relation between Jews and power. In her "Few Words to the Jews," from 1855, Montefiore observed, "as long as we [Jews] are in the city, trading, buying, and selling we have great power, but there our power ceases."[15]

Arendt's view on the concentration of Jews in consumer-oriented professions neatly corresponds to her position on so-called Jewish passivity, and the failure of Jews to act politically. This approach is confirmed by Arendt's more fundamental observations regarding the blurring of boundaries between the private and public realms as a result of triumph of the social over the political in modern times. Arendt even identifies a link between the rise of modern antisemitism and the emergence of a modern consumer society in which the capacity to resist and to act politically is eroded by conformism. Arendt depicts the modern social realm as a space of "mere togetherness," characterized by exchange and decay, futility,

---

[10] Hannah Arendt, *The Origins of Totalitarianism* (Cleveland: World Publ. Co., 1962), 29.

[11] Hannah Arendt, "Antisemitism," in: Jerome Kohn and Ron Feldman (eds.), *Jewish Writings* (New York: Schocken Books, 2007), 74.

[12] Arendt, *The Origins of Totalitarianism*), 37.

[13] Hannah Arendt, "Privileged Jews," *Jewish Social Studies* 8 (1946), 3–30. For some reason this article was not included in the collection of Arendt's Jewish writings.

[14] Arendt, *Jewish Writings*, 242. See also Cahnman, which cites research on minority group politics that indicates that there is some kind of pattern here.

[15] Charlotte Montefiore, *A Few Words to the Jews* (London: John Chapman, 1855), 36.

and speechlessness, which is akin to the "worldless" of the Jewish people.[16]

Despite these similarities, researchers have not paid much attention to the overlaps between Arendt's conceptualization of the social, her approach to consumerism, and her critical reading of the Jewish experience. To be sure, Arendt's concept of the nonpolitical Jew has not found much agreement among scholars of Jewish history. Identifying many forms of political engagement among Jews, most scholars today reject both Arendt's approach and Zionist interpretations that link the birth of Jewish political life to the idea of Jewish sovereignty. A growing body of research finds evidence of a Jewish political existence in all periods and places of Jewish history.[17] Daniel J. Elazar, one of the pioneering scholars working on the topic, argues that Jews have developed a distinguished political tradition in different historical settings and amid varied political institutions. According to him, this tradition was fostered by the concept of covenant, which diffused power into different spheres of Jewish communal life.[18] In a similar vein, David Biale claimed in his seminal *Power and Powerlessness in Jewish History* that power consists in the ability to maintain a collective way of life, as well as to manage one's communal affairs. Diaspora Jewry, he argues, possessed such power in many historical periods. For historian Zvi Gitelman, what is common to all Jewish political traditions from antiquity to the present is a quest for utopia, "that is a search to improve the world, for *tikun olam.*"[19] These claims are strikingly opposed to Arendt's views on Jewish political aloofness.

While the liaison between Jews and politics underwent significant change during the last decades of the twentieth century, the dichotomist approach to politics and consumption as two separate if not antithetical realms, as exemplified by Arendt's work, went through a careful revision

---

[16] Trevor Norris, "Hannah Arendt and Jean Baudrillard: Pedagogy in the Consumer Society," *Studies in Philosophy and Education* 25 (2006), 465. Further on this issue: Phillip Hansen, *Hannah Arendt: Politics, History, and Citizenship* (Cambridge: Polity Press, 1993), 137–142.

[17] For some examples of this new approach to Jewish politics see: Ruth R. Wisse, *Jews and Power* (New York: Schocken Books, 2007); Michael Walzer, Menachem Lorberbaum and Noam J. Zohar (eds.), *The Jewish Political Tradition*, 2 vols. (New Haven: Yale University Press, 2000/2003); David Biale, *Power & Powerlessness in Jewish History* (New York: Schocken, 1986).

[18] Daniel J. Elazar, "Covenant as the Basis of Jewish Political Tradition," in: *Kinship & Consent: The Jewish Political Tradition and Its Contemporary Uses* (New Brunswick, NJ: Transaction Publishers, 1997), 21–58.

[19] Zvi Gitelman (ed.), *The Quest for Utopia: Jewish Political Ideas and Institutions through the Ages* (Armonk: M.E. Sharpe, 1992), X.

as well. Since the end of World War II, the complex relationship between politics and consumption has captured the attention of scholars, politicians, and policymakers. Today it almost goes without saying that politics and consumption are closely intertwined. This shift reflects major political and cultural as well as academic reorientations. Awareness of the political significance and relevance of consumption increased with the rise of neoliberalism, the crisis of older producer-oriented politics, and, finally, the collapse of communism in Eastern Europe. In the academic world, the so-called cultural turn, with its emphasis on agency and meaning, provoked new readings of the concept of power, accentuating the complexity of social and political realities as well as their interrelationships. According to this approach, consumption did not merely "penetrate" and reconfigure existing social conditions in order to reinforce certain power relations, as suggested by Arendt and other social critics of her generation.[20] Instead, social relations themselves are seen as political activities that "emanate through the work of consumer choice."[21] Thus the human field is now conceptualized as a complex ensemble of social, economic, political, and cultural practices in which the consumer is no longer considered merely a passive entity subjected to overwhelming forces, but an active participant in the process of constructing the social matrix. The ambivalence toward consumption revealed by these differing approaches – it is alternatively viewed as an instrument of agency and emancipation and of subjection and conformity – is precisely what makes it a politically relevant activity. A similar observation can be made on the significance of the political for our understanding of Jewish history as well.

Focusing on the first third of the twentieth century, the following chapters will explore the relationship between consumption and politics in the context of modern Jewish history. The discussion will be broken into four main sections, each of which explores a different aspect of consumption as a political site. Chapter 5 calls for attention to the interface between the idea of civil rights and consumption. It suggests that while those fighting for Jewish emancipation tended to view the free market economy as offering the hope of civil liberties and recognition,

---

[20] On this see, for example, Daniel Horowitz, *The Morality of Spending. Attitudes towards the Consumer Society in America* (Baltimore: John Hopkins University Press, 1985).

[21] Evan Watkins, *Everyday Exchanges: Marketwork and Capitalism Common Sense* (Stanford: Stanford University Press, 1998), 18.

this approach was also based on a strong sense of what we today call consumer citizenship.[22]

Chapter 6 explores how politics figured and shaped consumer habits. A major part of this discussion will deal with antisemitism in the marketplace. Rather than dealing with the well-studied calls to boycott Jewish-owned businesses, this chapter will concentrate on how Jews as consumers reacted to antisemitism in the marketplace. Special attention will be given here to the so-called Jewish "buycott": active attempts to alert Jewish consumers to the antisemitic tendencies of certain companies and to organize Jews to buy designated products and services. This chapter will demonstrate how politics rendered consumption a highly charged activity and a site for political enactment.

Chapters 7 and 8 examine the processes by which consumption became a new resource for political mobilization. Focusing on the Zionist movement, Chapter 8 demonstrates not only how political propaganda applied marketing principles in the branding of political leaders, making targeted political advertisements and following market segmentation strategies, but also how closely entangled it was with commercial interests. Put together these chapters will reveal the close interplay between politics and consumption in the Jewish context.

---

[22] On the notion of the consumer citizen in the German context different articles in: Geoff Eley and Jan Palmowski (eds.), *Citizenship and National Identity in Twentieth-Century Germany* (Stanford: Stanford University Press, 2008).

# 5

# Emancipation through Consumption

Contemporary scholars use concepts such as political consumerism and consumer citizenship to highlight the significance of consumption as an activity and as a site of political action.[1] As exemplified by Lizabeth Cohen's work on the emergence of the Consumers' Republic in the United States, this approach represents an epochal claim about the changing relationship between state, society, and consumption following World War II. According to Cohen, in the second half of the twentieth century, policy makers, business and labor leaders, and many ordinary Americans formed a unique alliance in the United States. Together, she argues, these groups sought to reconstruct the nation's economy and reaffirm its democratic values by promoting the expansion of mass consumption.[2] Victoria de Grazia develops a similar argument for postwar Europe. In her study *Irresistible Empire: America's Advance through*

---

[1] The literature on these issues is constantly growing. I will therefore mention only a few titles that I found useful for my work: Martin Daunton and Matthew Hilton (eds.), *The Politics of Consumption: Material Culture and Citizenship in Europe and America* (Oxford: Berg, 2001); Michele Micheletti, *Political Virtue and Shopping: Individuals, Consumerism, and Collective Action* (New York: Palgrave Macmillan, 2003); Jörn Lamla and Sighard Neckel (eds.), *Politisierter Konsum – konsumierte Politik* (Wiesbaden: Verlag für Sozialwissenschaften, 2006); Dhavan V. Shah, "Lewis Friedland," in: Douglas M. McLeod and Michelle R. Nelson (eds.), *The Politics of Consumption – The Consumption of Politics [special issue of the Annals of the American Academy of Political and Social Science, v. 611]* (Los Angeles: Sage Publications, 2007); Kate Soper and Frank Trentmann (eds.), *Citizenship and Consumption* (New York: Palgrave Macmillan, 2008). See also the special issue of *Journal of Consumer Culture*, vol. 7 (2) (2007).

[2] Lizabeth Cohen, *A Consumers' Republic: The Politics of Mass Consumption in Postwar America* (New York: Vintage Books, 2004).

*Twentieth Century Europe* she suggests that the struggle between American free market ideology and the planned economy of the Soviet Union gave way to a new European regime in which mass consumption was mainly conceived as a political matter involving rights and democracy.[3] Thus the so-called Consumers' Republic epitomizes a state in which not only national interest became bound up with mass consumption but so did the very notion of citizenship. As Cohen cogently observes, the postwar era witnessed the triumph of the "ideal of the customer as citizen who simultaneously fulfilled personal desire and civic obligation by consuming."[4] Still, the history of what Cohen, de Grazia, and others identify as consumer citizenship is based on a century-long trend of entwining these notions and making them central to the guiding principle of a market-oriented society in which the members of modern states are expected to realize personal desire and civic obligation by, among other things, consuming.

This chapter will explore the interface between these ideas in the context of the struggle for Jewish emancipation. Focusing on Moses Mendelssohn's economic views and the debate about Jewish compatibility with modernity, the following pages will seek to demonstrate how the use of the language of free enterprise and consumer choice was part of an effort to imagine and constitute a new phase in Jewish history epitomized by political recognition and social integration.[5] This reading of the struggle for Jewish emancipation is inspired by Pierre Bourdieu's observation that "the emergence of the economic field marks the appearance of a universe in which social agents can admit to themselves and admit publicly that they have interests, ... a universe in which they can not only do business, but also admit to themselves that they are there to do business, that is, to conduct themselves in a self-interested manner."[6] In the Jewish case, the notion of interest appears almost interchangeable with the concept of rights, making the association between the free market

---

[3] Victoria De Grazia, *Irresistible Empire: America's Advance through Twentieth-Century Europe* (Cambridge, MA: Harvard University Press, 2005).

[4] Lizabeth Cohen, "Citizens and Consumers in the US in the Century of Mass Consumption," in: Martin Daunton and Matthew Hilton (eds.), *The Politics of Consumption: Material Culture and Citizenship in Europe and America* (Oxford: Berg, 2001), 214.

[5] Victor Karady, *The Jews of Europe in the Modern Era* (Budapest: Central European University Press, 2004), 26.

[6] Pierre Bourdieu, *Practical Reason: On the Theory of Action* (Stanford: Stanford Univesity Press, 1994), 105–106.

and the idea of citizenship one of the hallmarks of the struggle for Jewish emancipation.[7]

## THE MARKETPLACE BETWEEN CIVILITY AND CIVIL SOCIETY

Historians trace the emergence of the market, or the "economy," as a discrete category in public discourse to the development of new concepts on human conduct and the foundations of the social body that evolved in a particular time and place – eighteenth-century Europe. Thus, for example, Albert Hirschman's seminal discussion of the opposition between the passion and the interest reveals how political thinkers of the early modern period sought to restrain what they considered to be the overwhelming power of sovereigns, in both domestic and international matters, through the expansion of the market.[8] By the mid-eighteenth century, Hirschman notes, "it became the conventional wisdom ... that commerce was a civilizing agent of considerable power and range."[9]

According to this reading the language of free enterprise and consumer goods was designed to promote civility and facilitate the idea of participation and free citizenship. Even the stock exchange was seen as "a place more venerable than many courts of justice, where the representatives of all nations meet for the benefit of mankind."[10] Voltaire in his *Letters Concerning the English Nation* famously noted that on the trading floor "the Jew, the Mahometan, and the Christian transact together, as though they all professed the same religion, and give the name of infidel to none but bankrupts."[11] Notwithstanding his otherwise hostile views toward Jews, Voltaire concludes his comments on the Royal Exchange in London

---

[7] Uriel Tal, "German-Jewish Social Thought in the Mid-Nineteenth Century," in: Werner E. Mosse (ed.), *Revolution and Evolution 1848 in German-Jewish History* (Tübingen: J.C.B Mohr, 1981), 299–328.

[8] Albert Hirschman, *The Passion and the Interest: Political Arguments for Capitalism before Its Triumph* (Princeton: Princeton University Press, 1977). Further on this see also Joyce Appleby, *Economic Thought and Ideology in Seventeenth Century England* (Princeton: Princeton University Press, 1978).

[9] Albert Hirschman, *Rival Views of the Market Society and Other Recent Essays* (Cambridge, MA: Harvard University Press, 1986), 107; see also David Graeber, *Debt: The First 5,000 Years* (New York: Melville House, 2003), 165–210.

[10] Voltaire, Letters Concerning the English Nation, first published in 1731, available at www2.hn.psu.edu/faculty/jmanis/voltaire/letters-on-england.pdf, 24.

[11] Ibid. On Voltaire and antisemitism see Arthur Hertzberg, *The French Enlightenment and the Jews* (New York: Columbia University Press, 1990). For a more nuanced reading of Voltaire's views on Jews, see Harvey Chisick, "Ethics and History in Voltaire's Attitudes toward the Jews," *Eighteenth-Century Studies*, 35 (4) (2002), 577–600.

by stating that "if one religion only were allowed in England, the Government would very possibly become arbitrary; if there were but two, the people would cut one another's throats; but as there are such a multitude, they all live happy and in peace."[12]

Central to the development of such views was the concept of interest, a concept that became more closely associated with that of material prosperity and the augmentation of fortune as the nineteenth century approached. As demonstrated, for example, in Jeremy Bentham's 1787 treatise entitled *Defence of Usury*, this change did not escape the observant eyes of contemporaries who explained it as a symptom of the growing number of people with access to wealth.[13] According to historian Benjamin Nelson, the institutionalization of the credit system epitomized a movement from a social order that was based on the notion of exclusive fraternalism to the impartial social relationships of modern industrial society – a development he felicitously depicts as a shift "from tribal brotherhood to universal otherhood."[14]

THINKING ABOUT JEWS IN ECONOMIC TERMS

The image of the Jews is overloaded with tropes and motifs taken from the sphere of economics, and for good reason. In premodern Europe, Jews were bound into the estate system as a quasi-independent guild of commercial people, so that their economic transactions were closely associated with their identity as Jews, as was their trustworthiness as business partners in general. Knowing that both their right of residency and their well-being were contingent on their economic utility, European Jews adopted, and at times even promoted, modes of thinking about Jews in economic terms. Indeed, Jewish discourse, especially of the mercantilist age, was thick with economic tropes.[15] A revealing example is Menasseh

---

[12] Voltaire, Letters Concerning the English Nation.

[13] Bentham's *Defence of Usury* is available at www.econlib.org/library/Bentham/bnthUs .html. More generally on his attitude to Jews, see Lea Campos Boralevi, "Jeremy Bentham and the Jews," *European Judaism: A Journal for the New Europe* 13 (1) (Autumn, 1979), 22–28.

[14] Benjamin N. Nelson, *The Idea of Usury: From Tribal Brotherhood to Universal Otherhood* (Princeton: Princeton University Press, 1949).

[15] For a comprehensive and stimulating discussion of the Jewish economic discourse see: Jonathan Karp, *The Politics of Jewish Commerce: Economic Ideology and Emancipation in Europe, 1638–1848* (Cambridge: Cambridge University Press, 2008). On Jews and mercantilism: Jonathan Israel, *European Jewry in the Age of Mercantilism, 1550–1750*, 3rd ed. (London: Littman Library of Jewish Civilization, 1998).

Ben Israel's famous letter to Oliver Crowell written in 1655, in which he pleaded for Jewish resettlement in England. Jews had been expelled from the British Isles in 1290. Ben Israel's petition for the readmission of Jews was based to a large extent on economic thinking in terms of profit and utility. Ben Israel promoted the Jews as proficient and innovative merchants who would advance the national economy. What distinguished Jewish business practices, Ben Israel claimed, was that the Jews remained economically active long after their non-Jewish counterparts had settled down and realized their working capital in ownership of real estate. Prosperous Jewish merchants, he proclaimed, would not cease to develop their businesses and would thus continue to benefit the economy of the state over a longer period than would their non-Jewish contenders.[16] Ben Israel was not the first to overtly praise the Jews' economic merits. In an appeal to the authorities of the city of Venice in the year 1638, Rabbi Simone Luzzatto argued for the Jewish right of residency by exalting the extraordinary capability of the Jews for commerce, declaring that "wherever Jews have settled, business and commerce have flourished."[17] Yet, unlike Ben Israel who argued for the readmission of Jews to England, Luzzatto pleaded on behalf of Venetian Jewry to prevent their expulsion.

Luzzatto's appeal was written while Venice was declining in importance as a port. The discourse is based on the observation that the Venetian-Christian middle class shunned commercial activity, leaving

---

[16] Lucien Wolf (ed.), *Menasseh Ben Israel's Mission to Oliver Cromwell: Being a Reprint of the Pamphlets Published by Menasseh Ben Israel to Promote the Re-admission of the Jews to England 1649–1656* (London: Macmillan, 1901); also available at www.judaica-frankfurt.de/content/titleinfo/675126. On Ben Israel and his appeal see: Ismar Schorsch, "From Messianism to Realpolitik: Menasseh ben Israel and the Readmission of the Jews to England," *Proceedings of the American Academy for Jewish Research* 45 (1978), 187–208; Yosef Kaplan, Henry Méchoulan and Richard Henry Popkin (eds.), *Menasseh Ben Israel and his World* (Leiden: Brill Publications, 1989); João Ricardo Faria, "The Readmission of the Jews to England: The Mercantilist View," *European Journal of the History of Economic Thought* 6 (4) (1999), 513–522.

[17] Benjamin Ravid, *Economics and Toleration in Seventeenth Century Venice: The Background and Context of the Discorso of Simone Luzzatto* (Jerusalem: American Academy for Jewish Research, 1978), 66. On the connection between the two addresses see also Benjamin Ravid, "How profitable the nation of the Jews are: The 'Humble Addresses' of Menasseh ben Israel and the 'Discorso' of Simone Luzzatto," in: Jehuda Reinharz and Daniel Swetschinski (eds.), *Mystics, Philosophers and Politicians: Essays in Jewish Intellectual History in Honor of Alexander Altmann* (Durham: Duke University Press, 1982), 159–180.

this area of economic life to foreigners. Based on this view, Luzzatto sought to convince the Venetian authorities that it was in the city's interest to foster local Jewish merchants rather than allowing foreign merchant groups to settle in Venice. Luzzatto not only questioned the loyalty of such groups of foreigners but also warned that since these merchants were rooted in the places of their origin, and their interests were purely financial, they were likely to evade local taxation and to return to their home countries, taking their capital with them to the detriment of Venice.[18]

Despite the differences between their appeals, both Luzzatto and Ben Israel depict Jews as the embodiment of modern *homo economicus*. By boosting the Jews' economic utility they aim not only to protect Jewish interest but also to endorse the so-called *doux-commerce* thesis, according to which there is a positive link between commercial activity and civil society, and commerce is perceived as a powerful vehicle of civilization.[19] It thus appears that in the age of mercantilism, Jewish economic sensitivities were characterized by a strong ethos of utility, a positive attitude to trade, and a favorable view of the free market economy.[20]

Not only Jews highlighted the "Jewish contribution" to economic progression. In the context of the debates regarding readmission of Jews to England, Sir Josiah Child commented as follows: "subtiller the Jews are, and the more Trades they pry into while they live here, the more they are like to increase Trade, and the more they do that, the better it is for the Kingdom in general, though the worse for the English merchant."[21] The French thinker Charles de Montesquieu, who avowed as a general rule that "wherever the ways on men are gentle there is commerce; and wherever there is commerce, there the ways of men are gentle," gave Jews credit for creating this civilizing form of modern commerce.[22] In a chapter in *The Spirit of the Laws* (first published in 1748) entitled "How Commerce Broke through the Barbarism of Europe," Montesquieu proclaims: "the Jews invented letters of exchange; commerce, by this method,

---

[18] Isaac E. Barzilay, "John Toland's borrowings from Simone Luzzatto: Luzzatto's 'Discourse on the Jews of Venice' (1638), the major source of Toland's writing on the naturalization of the Jews in GB and Ireland (1714)," *Jewish Social Studies* 31 (1969), 78.

[19] On this see also Hirschman, *The Passion and the Interest*, 67–114.

[20] Derek J. Penslar, *Shylock's Children: Economics and Jewish Identity in Modern Europe* (Berkeley: University of California Press, 2001), 66.

[21] Quoted in Israel, *European Jewry in the Age of Mercantilism*, 160. See also David S. Katz, *Philo-Semitism and the Readmission of the Jews to England, 1603–1655* (Oxford: Clarendon Press, 1982).

[22] Cited in Hirschman, *The Passion and the Interest*, 60.

became capable of eluding violence, and of maintaining everywhere its ground; the richest merchant having none but invisible effects, which he could convey imperceptibly wherever he pleased."[23] And the English poet and essayist Joseph Addison famously characterized the Jews as "pegs and nails in a great building, which, though they are but little valued in themselves, are absolutely necessary to keep the whole frame together."[24]

Toward the end of the eighteenth century, both the general approach to trade and attitudes toward Jews and their position in the social and economic fabric began to change. While in the early modern period the association of Jews with commerce facilitated a positive image of Jewish economic qualities, from the end of the eighteenth century onward the depiction of Jews as backward, unproductive, and a group immersed in stiff religious tradition became more prevalent. Jonathan Karp has indicated that "this shift in the perception of Jews was directly linked to changing economic doctrines in the period of the Enlightenment, which clearly reflected, if not informed, a revision of the approach toward the Jews."[25] The irony of this new "modern" consciousness is that despite the triumph of capitalism, with which Jews were so closely associated in modern times, a recognition of Jewish backwardness seemed to replace the earlier perception of the Jews as a progressive people and indeed modernizers. These conflicting depictions of the Jewish economic makeup and the interplay between Jews and modernity became the focus of a new discourse on Jews and Jewishness since the Enlightenment.[26]

The nineteenth century was haunted by the discussion about the nature of Jewish difference and the question of whether Jews were able to integrate and become "useful" members of modern society. Internalizing the supposition that Jews had to transform themselves to become compatible with modern life, calls to reform the Jewish way of life were voiced from both within and without Jewish circles. Evaluations of the economic position of the Jews, together with different schemes for regenerating Jewish society, were debated vehemently.

---

[23] Charles de Montesquieu, *The Spirit of the Laws*, available at http://etext.virginia.edu/toc/modeng/public/MonLaws.html. For further discussion see Arnold Ages, "Montesquieu and the Jews," *Romanische Forschungen* 81 (1/2) (1969), 214–219.

[24] Joseph Addison, *Spectator*, no. 495 (September 27, 1712), 202.

[25] Jonathan Karp, "Can Economic History Date the Inception of Jewish Modernity?" in: Gideon Reuveni and Sarah Wobick-Segev (eds.), *The Economy in Jewish History: New Perspectives on the Interrelationship between Ethnicity and Economic Life* (New York: Berghahn Books, 2010), 23–42.

[26] For an insightful and comprehensive discussion see mainly the first and fourth chapters of Penslar, *Shylock's Children*.

## MOSES MENDELSSOHN AND THE IDEA OF MARKETPLACE
## CITIZENSHIP

Christian Wilhelm Dohm's treatise *Über die bürgerliche Verbesserung der Juden* (On the Civic Improvement of the Jews), published in 1781, is perhaps the best-known example of these discussions.[27] According to Dohm, Jews could be tolerated only after going through a form of economic or social conversion, in the course of which they were supposed to move away from commerce and take up more physical and thus "productive" occupations in the crafts and agriculture. About a century after Dohm first introduced his plan for a radical restructuring of Jewish economic makeup, the Zionist movement proposed a similar "normalization" of Jewish life – a process that, among other things, aimed to invert the occupational pyramid of Jews so that its base would consist of "healthy" agricultural and manual labor instead of what the socialist Zionist Ber Borochov, for example, called the "*luft* economics" of Diaspora Jews.[28] Not all Jews or non-Jews shared this view regarding the supremacy of production over commerce or for that matter linked the process of emancipation with the reform of Jewish economic life. Perhaps the most prominent representative of this latter approach is the prominent German-Jewish philosopher Moses Mendelssohn.

It is in the context of the debate over Dohm's stipulations for the "amelioration" of the civil state of the Jews that we learn about Mendelssohn's economic views.[29] In his preface to the German translation of Manasseh Ben Israel *Vindiciae Judaeorum*, Mendelssohn notes,

---

[27] For a general overview of the debates see, for example, Robert Liberles, "From Toleration to *Verbesserung*: German and English Debates on the Jews in the Eighteenth Century," *Central European History*, 22 (1) (1989), 37–48; Jonathan M. Hess, *Germans, Jews and the Claims of Modernity* (New Haven: Yale University Press, 2002); Carol Iancu, "The Emancipation and Assimilation of the Jews in the Political Discourse Regarding the Granting of Citizenship to the French Jews during the French Revolution," *Studia Judaica*, 18 (2010), 89–115.

[28] Ber Borochov, "The Economic Development of the Jewish People," available at www.angelfire.com/il2/borochov/eco.html. On Borochov's economic thinking see Jerry Z. Muller, *Capitalism and the Jews* (Princeton: Princeton University Press, 2010), 189–218. For more general discussion of the Zionist view see Mitchell B. Hart, *Social Science and the Politics of Modern Jewish Identity* (Stanford: Stanford University Press, 2000). On the notion of the Luftmensch see Nicolas Berg, *Luftmenschen: Zur Geschichte einer Metapher* (Göttingen: Vandenhoeck & Ruprecht, 2008).

[29] See also David Friedländer, *Briefe über die Moral des Handels, voran ein Gewissensfall im Handel, nebst einem Schreiben v. Mendelssohn* (Berlin, 1817), also available at www.judaica-frankfurt.de/content/titleinfo/424142.

in some modern publications, there is an echo of the objection: "the Jews are an unproductive people; they neither till the ground, cultivate the arts, nor exercise mechanical trades ... but only carry and transport the raw or wrought commodities of various countries from one to another. They are, therefore, mere consumers, who cannot but be a tax upon the producers."[30]

Mendelssohn discards this view outright. He claims that there is nothing innately debasing about the nature of Jewish traditional occupations.[31] On the contrary, Mendelssohn saw the Jewish concentration in commerce as particularly useful for both state and society. This perspective was based on Mendelssohn's fundamental rejection of what eventually became a prevailing distinction in modern times between "productive" and "unproductive" labor.[32] According to the philosopher, by mediating between producers and consumers, merchants perform a crucial social and economic function. As middlemen, they supply consumers with goods and thus not only provide an important service for manufacturer and customer alike but also stimulate production by expanding the market. In Mendelssohn's words, through the middleman, "commodities become more useful, more in demand, and also cheaper."[33] In this sense, the brokers are as "productive" as the producers. To illustrate his point Mendelssohn asks his reader to "imagine a workman who is obliged to go himself to the agriculturist for the raw material, and also to take it himself to the warehouse-man in a manufactured state" and to compare him to "a workman" who works with an intermediate dealer.[34] The latter system is depicted not only as more efficient, promoting "real industry," but also as enabling a better and happier life "without extraordinary exertion of strength" for both producer and consumer.[35] This positive view of commerce rests upon Mendelssohn's approach to the distinction between "doing" (*Tun*) and "making" (*Machen*) as two corresponding aspects of productivity. "Not he alone who labors with his hands," he proclaimed, "but, generally, whoever does, promotes, occasions, or facilitates anything that may tend to the benefit or comfort of his fellow-creatures, deserves to be called producer."[36]

---

[30] Moses Mendelssohn, *Jerusalem: A Treatise on Ecclesiastical Authority and Judaism*, vol. I (London: Longman, 1838), 94.
[31] This section is based on Karp, *The Politics of Jewish Commerce*, 122–134.
[32] For a brief overview on the history of this distinction, which came to play a central role in Marxist thought, see Denis Patrick O'Brien, *The Classical Economists Revisited* (Princeton: Princeton University Press, 2004), 274–282.
[33] Mendelssohn, *Jerusalem*, 96.    [34] Ibid., 97.    [35] Ibid.    [36] Ibid., 95.

Mendelssohn's approach is further grounded in his thinking about the reciprocity between the state and the market economy. Unlike the philosophers of the mercantile age such as Montesquieu, who commended commerce primarily as an agent of civilization, Mendelssohn also accentuated the positive correlation between economic expansion and civic freedom. In citing Holland as a model of a commercial society, he sought to illuminate how the combination of economic and political freedom facilitated prosperity. A thriving economy such as that of the Netherlands, he argued, could only arise when allowed to develop freely. That is why Mendelssohn called upon governments

to abolish monopolies, exclusive and privileged rights; to accord equal rights and freedom to the smallest jobber and the largest commercial firm; in a word, to promote competition of every kind between middlemen; to encourage rivalry between them so that the price of things finds its equilibrium ... [allowing] every consumer ... to benefit without excessive effort, from the industry of others.[37]

According to Jonathan Karp, what appears here as a state-of the-art political economy is firmly based on Mendelssohn's response to the thinkers of the Scottish Enlightenment, foremost among them Adam Smith.[38] Yet, while Karp underscores Adam Smith's influence on Mendelssohn's reprimand of the productive/nonproductive distinction, I would like to draw attention to another component of Smith's thinking that I believe had a profound impact on Mendelssohn's deliberations.

Challenging both older mercantile as well as more recent physiocratic economic doctrines, Smith sees the significance of consumption as the powerhouse of modern economy, displaying it as a positive force that stokes production and increases the wealth and well-being of the nation. "Consumption is the sole end and purpose of all production," Smith affirmed in *The Wealth of Nations*.[39] For Smith "this maxim is so perfectly self-evident, that it would be absurd to attempt to prove it."[40] It is with this declaration, Martin Daunton and Matthew Hilton contend that the consuming individual began to shape the market, and ultimately the modern liberal state.[41]

Conflating the notion of citizenship with the capacity to act as free independent consumers and producers seems to also underline Mendelssohn's approach. Following Smith, Mendelssohn argues that "the

---

[37] Cited in Karp, *The Politics of Jewish Commerce*, 127.     [38] Ibid.
[39] Adam Smith, *An Inquiry into the Nature and Causes of the Wealth of Nations*, available at www2.hn.psu.edu/faculty/jmanis/adam-smith/wealth-nations.pdf, 537.
[40] Ibid., 538.     [41] Daunton and Hilton, *Politics of Consumption*, 9.

largest and most valuable portion of the state consists of mere consumers."[42] The well-being of a state, he insists, as well as of every individual in it, "requires many things [*Dinge*] both sensual and intellectual, many goods [*Güter*] both material and spiritual; and he who, more or less directly or indirectly, contributes towards them, cannot be called mere consumer; he does not eat his bread for nothing; he produces something in return."[43]

Mendelssohn hence rejects the notion of the passive useless consumer. For him consumption is an activity integral to the social process comprised of exchange and the ability to use different types of goods.[44] In his study *On Religious Power and Judaism* he blatantly affirms that "the authority [*Befugnis*] – i.e. the moral ability [*das sittliche Vermögen*] – to use things [*Dinge*] as a means for promoting one's happiness is called a right," and it is this right that "constitutes man's natural freedom."[45] What I find most fascinating about Mendelssohn's approach is not only how he amalgamates the language of objects (*Dinge, Güter, Vermögen*) with the language of morals but also the strong connection he establishes between the two and the notion of happiness – an association that constitutes one of the hallmarks of the spirit of modern consumerism.[46]

Mendelssohn's recognition of the significance of consumption was essential to his identification of economic competition as a positive social force that promoted both individual rights and social and political tolerance. "Only through competition and rivalry," he wrote in his response to Dohm, "through unlimited freedom and equality of rights among all buyers and sellers – be they of whichever estate, appearance, or religion

---

[42] Mendelssohn, *Jerusalem*, 99–100. Compare this with Smith, *Wealth of Nations*, 70.

[43] Ibid., 96.

[44] He qualifies this approach by stating "This ability is called 'moral' if it is consistent with the laws of wisdom and goodness. And the things [*Dinge*] that can be used in this way are called *goods* [*Güter*]. So man has a right to certain goods, i.e. certain means of happiness, so long as this right doesn't contradict the laws of wisdom and goodness." From Moses Mendelssohn, *Jerusalem: Or on Religious Power and Judaism*, online version available at www.earlymoderntexts.com/pdf/mendjeru.pdf.

[45] A modified translation from ibid., 9 and 13.

[46] Again, it is interesting to point to the influence of Adam Smith, who wrote in the *Wealth of Nations*, 70,

No society can surely be flourishing and happy, of which the far greater part of the members are poor and miserable. It is but equity, besides, that they who feed, clothe, and lodge the whole body of the people, should have such a share of the produce of their own labour as to be themselves tolerably well fed, clothed, and lodged.

More broadly on the spirit of consumerism: Colin Campbell, *The Romantic Ethic and the Spirit of Modern Consumerism* (London: Blackwell, 1987).

they may – only through these invaluable advantages do all things acquire their value."[47] To be sure, Mendelssohn was well aware that some people, Jews included, might seek to gain inappropriate benefits or even abuse the open marketplace. He was also mindful of the accusations against the alleged unscrupulous Jewish trade methods. "These are great evils," Mendelssohn noted, "which crush the producer's industry and the consumer's enterprise, and which should be counteracted by laws and by the police regulations."[48] In other words, Mendelssohn did not think that the struggle against commercial malpractices should in any way undermine the idea of a free marketplace economy. Far from it, he believed that only free competition and economic rivalry could ensure people's trust in the marketplace. Writing on the eve of the modern age, Mendelssohn depicted the prohibitions, monopolies, and economic restrictions of his day as the main aggravators of commercial ill practices. In so doing he established a strong reciprocity between the idea of a *Rechtsstaat* (rule of law) and the free market economy. According to him, only in a free state can competition serve to regulate social relations and work for the benefit of both consumers and producers.

A similar view was propagated by the Hamburg lawyer and politician Gabriel Riesser (1806–1863), one of the most prominent advocates of Jewish emancipation in Germany at the beginning of the nineteenth century.[49] Arguing "from a purely legal standpoint, from simple principles of national economy that look toward general utility," Riesser challenged those who condemned the economic position of Jews as an impediment for emancipation.[50] In his 1831 "Defense of the Civil Equality of the Jews" Riesser demonstrated how such views were advanced precisely by those who hoped to gain an advantage by excluding the Jews from competition.[51] Drawing on the work of Ignaz von Rudhart,

---

[47] This translation is cited in: David Sorkin, *Moses Mendelssohn and the Religious Enlightenment* (Berkeley: University of California Press, 1996), 114.

[48] Ibid., 98.

[49] Moshe Rinnot, "Gabriel Riesser: Fighter for Jewish Emancipation," *Leo Beack Institute Yearbook* 7 (1962), 11–38.

[50] Gabriel Riesser, Vertheidigung der bürgerlichen Gleichstellung der Juden gegen die Entwürfe des Herrn Dr. H. E.G. Paulus, *Den gesetzgebenden Versammlungen Deutschlands gewidmet* (Altona: Johann Friedrich Hammerich, 1831), 118. The translation is based on "Excerpts from the Pamphlet by Gabriel Riesser proposing the Emancipation of the Jews (1831)," available at the German History in Documents and Images, http://german historydocs.ghidc.org/sub_document.cfm?document_id=341&language=english.

[51] Ibid.

a Bavarian scholar and civil servant, to support his claim about the economic usefulness of Jewish hawkers, Riesser seemed to corroborate Mendelssohn's proclamation that even "the pettiest trafficking Jew is not a mere consumer, but a useful inhabitant (citizen, I must say), of the state – a real producer."[52] It thus appears that Riesser like Mendelssohn before him equated civil rights with consumer choices, suggesting that economic and civic freedom are inextricably linked.

As noted at the outset of this chapter, the association between rights and goods became more prevalent in the second half of the twentieth century. To be sure, mass consumption is a product of late nineteenth- and early twentieth-century urbanization, rising living standards and the developments of new technologies that significantly improved the production, dissemination, and accessibility to goods for all members of society. But despite the emergence of a new consumer culture, there are no major signs indicating that the notion of the marketplace as the key site of consumption influenced the social and economic thinking of the period. Very little is written on consumption in these formative years.[53] This is most definitely the case in the relevant Jewish discourse. Although as we have seen, the principle of consumer sovereignty formed an integral part of Mendelssohn's idea of citizenship; later Jewish thinkers did not attach the same significance to consumption in the context of the struggle for emancipation. Given Jewish clustering in consumer-oriented professions, it is, however, difficult not to discern a link between what seems to be a Jewish commitment to a laissez faire economy and the spirit of modern consumerism.

### THE MARKETPLACE AND JEWISH AFFIRMATION

During the second half of the nineteenth century, German Jewish periodicals such as *Die Neuzeit* in Vienna and the *German Allgemeine Zeitung des Judentums* openly propagated a free market economy as inherently valuable and as a basis for Jewish integration. It was claimed that Jews,

---

[52] Mendelssohn, *Jerusalem*, 99. Riesser mainly cites Ignaz von Rudhart, *Über den Zustand des Königreichs Baiern nach amtlichen Quellen* (Stuttgart: J. G. Cotta, 1827), 63–89.

[53] Donald Winch, "The Problematic Status of the Consumer in Orthodox Economic Thought," in Frank Trentmann (ed.), *The Making of the Consumer: Knowledge, Power and Identity in the Modern World* (Oxford: Berg Publishers, 2006), 31–51, here 43; Jean-Christophe Agnew, "'Coming up for Air' Consumer Culture in Historical Perspective," in: John Brewer and Roy Porter (eds.), *Consumption and the World of Goods* (New York: Psychology Press, 1993), 19–39.

who for centuries had been forced into commerce, finally found themselves in an advantageous position in a world that was becoming increasingly commercialized.[54] Ludwig Philippson (1811–1889), rabbi of
Magdeburg and chief editor of the *Allgemeine Zeitung des Judentums*,
saw the marketplace, and especially industrial development, as a pathway
for emancipation following the dismal 1848 revolutions.[55] Plans such as
those of the Jewish relief organization *Alliance Israélite Universelle* to
establish an agricultural colony in Palestine in order to "reawaken the
taste for work in a nation so long disinherited" were sharply rebuked by
him and others as erroneous and a total waste of money.[56]

Philippson's denunciation of schemes to reform the Jewish economic
makeup was based on his reading of Mosaic social legislation as an
endorsement of occupational freedom and modern ideas about the free
market. In an article published under the title "The Industrial Mission of
the Jew," Philippson ascribed the great contribution and social mission of
the Jews to their role as initiators of the modern banking system, without
which the modern state and industry could not have developed.[57] In the
last section of his article he further explained that the Middle Ages was
characterized by exclusionary practices. Religion, nationality, origin, status, vocation – everything was exclusionary, rendering a shredded society
with Jews on the bottom rung. According to Philippson, the marginal
position of Jews in premodern times rendered them natural critics of the
medieval social system. Naturally, and subsequently, Jews were thus seen
as disposed to advocate human rights, individual liberty, and civil society,

---

[54] On this approach see, for example, *Allgemeine Zeitung des Judentums* (February 21,
1853), 103–104; (December 16, 1862), 738–740 (January 15, 1867), 42–44.

[55] *Allgemeine Zeitung des Judentums* (January 2, 1856), 43.

[56] Ibid. (February 2, 1869), 92. The newspaper continued to maintain this position into the
twentieth century. For example, in an editorial from May 29, 1908, it was argued that "a
minority like us" could not afford to have a large proletariat and that Jews should
concentrate on free professions in order to sustain their existence as a group. For an
interesting discussion of the Jews as commercial people see also Sigmund Mayer, "Die
Juden als Handelsvolk in der Geschichte," in: *Ein jüdischer Kaufmann 1831–1911.*
*Lebenserinnerungen* (Leipzig: Verlag von Duncker und Humblot, 1911), 360–400;
Max Eschlbacher, "Wirtschaftsgeschichte der Jude," *Im deutschen Reich* 10 (1909),
551–557.

[57] Ludwig Philippson, "The industrial Mission of the Jew," *Allgemeine Zeitung des
Judentums* (July 23, 1861), 423–425 (July 30, 1861), 439–442 and (August 6, 1861),
457–459. For an elaborate discussion of Philippson's position see Penslar, *Shylock's
Children*, 146–148. On Jews and banking: Gideon Reuveni, "Geldverleiher,
Großunternehmer und Angestellte: Jüdische Bankiers – Ein Überblick," in:
Beate Borowka-Clausberg (ed.), *Salomon Heine in Hamburg-Geschäft und Gemeinsinn*
(Göttingen: Wallstein, 2013), 120–131.

all of which Philippson hoped would be achieved by the development of a modern industrial state and a free market economy.

In another article initially published in a general business journal, Philippson rhetorically asked whether the merchant class was inclined to be more liberal in its political convictions. Since commercial business is cosmopolitan in its nature, Philippson argued, and since the merchant has to get his goods from all regions and countries, he has no prejudice against nations and classes. "Since [the merchant] has to seek the best sources and distribution channels for his goods, he knows neither friend nor foe."[58] Philippson, like Mendelssohn, considered economic competition a constructive mechanism for invigorating business and regulating social relations. According to this view, the only enemies of the businessmen are obstacles to movement, monopolies, and special privileges constraining free trade. A free economy, Philippson argued, could flourish only under a liberal and nonbigoted political system and vice versa.[59]

With this approach, Philippson continues a premodern tradition of seeing the merchant as more receptive and enlightened than the craftsman or farmer, with the difference that a demand for political rights is now attached to this claim. In a Jewish framework, this meant that Philippson recognized that competition could only serve the interest of a minority group specializing in commerce, if it was a constituent part of a transparent and stable regime embedded in state structures that provided protection and a guarantee that free enterprise would not conflict with collective wants only inadequately registered by market signals.[60]

At the end of the nineteenth century, the belief in the laissez faire economy as a positive force regulating society also informed the work of liberal Jewish organizations such as the Central Association of German Citizens of the Jewish Faith (*Centralverein*), which was founded in 1893

---

[58] *Allgemeine Zeitung des Judentums* (December 16, 1862), 738.

[59] Philippson, "The Industrial Mission of the Jew" (August 6, 1861), 458. Philippson develops this idea in his "Das Judentum im Staat und in der Gesellschaft," *Allgemeine Zeitung des Judentums* (September 14, 1869), 735–740; (September 21, 1869), 758–762. For a general discussion of the political orientation of German Jews in the nineteenth century, Jacob Toury, *Die politischen Orientierungen der Juden in Deutschland: von Jena bis Weimar* (Tübingen: Mohr & Siebeck, 1966); For the antisemitic critique of capitalism Matthew Lange, *Antisemitic Elements in the Critique of Capitalism in German Culture: 1850–1933* (Bern: Peter Lang Verlag, 2007).

[60] More broadly on this point see Frank Tentmann, "National Identity and Consumer Politics: Free Trade and Tariff Reform," in Patrick O'Brien and Donald Winch (eds.), *The Political Economy of British Historical Experience, 1688–1914* (Oxford: Oxford University Press, 2002), 215–242.

to represent Jewish interests and to combat antisemitism.[61] One of the underlining premises of the fight against antisemitism was that "the Jewish question is not simply a religious or racial matter, but a question of economic rivalry."[62] In the postemancipation period the *Centralverein* gave voice to the position that legal protection and political rights alone could not guarantee Jewish endurance.[63] As Derek Penslar insightfully notes, a prevalent view, at least among members of the *Centralverein*, was that Jewish "prosperity and viability, now depended on the fortunes of economic liberalism."[64] This approach becomes even more prevalent in the context of the struggle against the economic boycott of Jews, particularly in the period after World War I.

Well aware of the potential peril of the racialization of the marketplace, fears of economic strangulation through boycott preoccupied the Jewish discourse much more than agitation for social segregation. In the words of Alfred Wiener, who anticipated in an article from mid-1932, "should The Reich come, then farewell to Justice and prosperity, farewell to public spiritedness and free enterprise."[65] In a similar vein the German-Jewish historian Raphael Straus noted, "should it ever be the case [that] the state divests itself of this protection, the Jews will be completely lost."[66] For German Jews, at least, the association between free enterprise and citizenship was finally shattered with the rise of

---

[61] Avraham Barkai, *"Wehr dich!": der Centralverein deutscher Staatsbürger jüdischen Glaubens (C.V.) 1893–1938* (Munich: Becks Verlag, 2002).

[62] "Die Judenfrage ist keine Religions, keine Rassensfrage, sondern eine Frage der wirtschaftlichen Kunkurrenz," in: Alphonse Levy, "Die Erziehung zur produktiven Arbeit," *Im deutschen Reich* no. 2 (1895), 59.

[63] For the *Centralverein* position see, for example, Eugen Fuchs, "Die Bestrebungen und Ziele der Centralverein," *Im deutschen Reich*, 1 (4) (1895), 145–161; Ludwig Holländer, *Die sozialen Voraussetzungen der antisemitischen Bewegung in Deutschland: Vortrag gehalten im Central-Verein deutscher Staatsbürger jüdischen Glaubens* (Berlin: Levy, 1910).

[64] Penslar, *Shylock's Children*, 150. The most outspoken representative of this view in the postwar World War II period was the American Jewish historian Ellis Rivkin. In his *radical new interpretation of modern Jewish history*, he went so far as to argue that "capitalism and capitalism alone emancipated the Jews." Ellis Rivkin, *The Shaping of Jewish History: A Radical New interpretation* (New York: Scribners, 1971), 159.

[65] Alfred Wiener, "Programmerfüllung oder Agitation: Was würde eine Hitler-Merheit tun?" *CV-Zeitung* (June 24, 1932), 261. The translation is here based on Donald L. Niewyk, *The Jews in Weimar Germany* (New Brunswick: Transaction Publishers, 2001), 83.

[66] Raphael Straus, *Die Juden in Wirtschaft und Gesellschaft* (Frankfurt a.M: Europäische Verlagsanstalt, 1964), 120.

National Socialism. By making the calls to boycott Jews an official state policy, it became apparent that the marketplace was not inherently a cultivating force promoting rights and tolerance but could just as easily turn into a locus of exclusion and persecution. These economic boycotts are the topic of the next chapter.

# 6

## Boycott, Economic Rationality, and Jewish Consumers in Interwar Germany

In recent years scholars have published a number of innovative studies on antisemitism and the marketplace.[1] Much of this work emphasizes the link between the rise of the modern market economy and an increasingly negative view of the voracious Jewish capitalist as a decisive force in modern life. These scholars argue that, in addition to anxiety about the shift to an increasingly capitalist society, fear of rampant competition and envy of the business success of Jews help to explain why Jews became a vulnerable and unpopular group in modern societies. Studies of attempts to boycott Jewish-owned businesses have identified these episodes that are perhaps the most salient and tangible expressions of anti-Jewish resentments in the marketplace. Much less is known about how Jewish consumers themselves reacted to Jewish economic exclusion. The very idea of boycotting Jews was informed by the notion of Jewish domination and the supposedly overwhelming power of Jews as moneymakers, or capitalists, in

---

[1] Derek Penslar, *Shylock's Children: Economics and Jewish Identity in Modern Europe* (Berkeley: University of California Press, 2001); Jerry Muller, *Capitalism and the Jews* (Princeton: Princeton University Press, 2010); Gideon Reuveni and Sarah Wobick-Segev (eds.), *The Economy in Jewish History: New Perspectives on the Interrelationship between Ethnicity and Economic Life* (New York: Berghahn Books, 2010); Hannah Ahlheim, *"Deutsche, kauft nicht bei Juden!" Antisemitismus und politischer Boykott in Deutschland 1924 bis 1935* (Göttingen: Wallestein Verlag, 2011); Christoph Kreutzmüller, *Ausverkauf. Die Vernichtung der jüdischen Gewerbetätigkeit in Berlin 1930–1945* (Berlin: Metropol Verlag, 2012); Stefanie Fischer, *Ökonomisches Vertrauen und antisemitische Gewalt: Jüdische Viehhändler in Mittelfranken, 1919–1939* (Göttingen: Wallstein, 2014).

modern society.[2] Yet consumption remains an overlooked category in these analyses. The widespread use of slogans such as "don't buy from Jews," "buy your Christmas presents only in Christian shops," or "each to his own," already widely circulated in Central and Eastern Europe during the nineteenth century, conveys the significance of consumption for understanding the Jewish experience of the marketplace.

The aim of this chapter is to scrutinize the miscellaneous attempts to exclude Jews from the marketplace from a consumerist point of view. The following pages will demonstrate how consumption became a highly charged political activity and a key site for both the formation of and resistance to the process of politicization of Jewish difference at the beginning of the twentieth century. This investigation will further show how the tendency of the modern marketplace to both address and promote distinct identities among consumers made it an arena in which the question of belonging became a contentious issue. With the rise of National Socialism, the marketplace was further transformed into a site of segregation reflecting a new social order, one in which economic rationality was based on the notion of racial supremacy rather than mere profitability. This development shattered a widespread supposition among Jews and other Europeans about the marketplace as an inherently cultivating force operating, as Adam Smith hoped, according to an "invisible and rational hand."[3] Studying different forms of economic boycott as well as ways by which Jewish organizations countered such attacks demonstrates the subtle tension between the view of the marketplace as a site of civilization, the use of consumption to reaffirm agency, and the reality that in the interwar period economic interest fostered Jewish exclusion.

---

[2] David Nirenberg, *Anti-Judaism: The Western Tradition* (New York: W.W. Norton, 2013), 423–472; Marvin Perry and Frederick M. Schweitze, *Antisemitism: Myth and Hate from Antiquity to the Present* (New York: Palgrave, 2002), 119–174; Aly Götz, *Warum die Deutschen? Warum die Juden? Gleichheit, Neid und Rassenhass 1800–1933* (Frankfurt a.M.: S. Fischer Verlag, 2011), 70–109; Shulamit Volkov, "Antisemitism as a Cultural Code: Reflections on the History and Historiography of Antisemitism in Imperial Germany," *Leo Baeck Institute Yearbook* 23 (1978), 25–46.

[3] Quoted in Maurice Godelier, *Rationality and Irrationality in Economics* (New York: Monthly Review Press, 1972), 49. On the Jewish perception of the marketplace see Gideon Reuveni, "Emancipation through Consumption: Moses Mendelssohn and the Idea of Marketplace Citizenship," *Leo Baeck Institute Yearbook* 59 (2014), 1–16.

## THE COLD POGROM

Calls to boycott Jews, or the "cold pogrom," have a long history that predates National Socialism by more than four decades.[4] In the late nineteenth century, German courts were called to deal with the attempts to boycott Jewish-owned businesses. In 1897, the Zionist Viennese weekly *Die Welt* reported about six Jewish businessmen from the city of Munich who sued the nationalistic newspaper *Deutsches Volksblatt* for distributing leaflets urging consumers not to buy from Jews.[5] At the end of 1898 *Die Welt* revealed that two hundred thousand copies of a similar pamphlet calling upon Christians not to do their shopping in Jewish outlets were circulated in the city of Berlin alone.[6] By 1900 the newspaper referred to boycotts of Jewish business as a popular sport (*Lieblingssport*), especially before Christmas.[7]

Jews were boycotted in three different ways: Jewish-owned businesses were targeted for avoidance; Jewish consumers were refused service; and Jewish employees were excluded from working. The scope and effectiveness of each type of these boycotts in Germany in the period before the rise of National Socialism remains a subject of debate among scholars.[8] Some argue that the calls to boycott Jews seriously threatened Jewish life, while others claim that at least until the beginning of the 1930s this form of anti-Jewish agitation remained a marginal phenomenon with neither wide support nor even a positive image, especially in larger urban centers. However, what I would like to argue here is that the marketplace boycotts

---

[4] Miriam Beard, "Anti-Semitism – Product of Economic Myth," in: Isacque Graeber (ed.), *Jews in a Gentile World* (Westport: Greenwood Press, 1942), 362–401; Pawel Korzec, "Boycott, Anti-Jewish," in: Michael Berenbaum and Fred Skolnik (eds.), *Encyclopedia Judaica*, vol. 4 (Detroit: MacMillan Reference USA, 2007), 109–110; Henry Wasserman and Eckhart G. Franz "'Kauft nicht bei Juden!' Der politische Antisemitismus des späten 19. Jahrhunderts in Darmstadt," in: *Juden als Darmstädter Bürger* (Darmstadt: E. Roether, 1984), 121–134; and, more recently, Ahlheim, *"Deutsche, kauft nicht bei Juden!"*; ibid., "Establishing Antisemitic Stereotypes: Social and Economic Segregation of Jews by means of Political Boycott in Germany," *Leo Baeck Institute Yearbook* 55 (2010), 149–173.
[5] Anonymous, "Antisemitischer Boycott," *Die Welt* 1 (17) (1897), 8.
[6] Anonymous, "Boykottierung," *Die Welt* 2 (48) (1898), 10.
[7] Adam, "Der Boycott der Juden," *Die Welt* 3 (49) (1899), 4.
[8] For this discussion and for further literature see Cornelia Hecht, *Deutsche Juden und Antisemitismus in der Weimarer Republik* (Bonn: Dietz, 2003), 332–344; Nicola Wenge, *Integration und Ausgrenzung in der städtischen Gesellschaft: Eine jüdisch-nichtjüdische Beziehungsgeschichte Kölns 1918–1933* (Mainz: Verlag Phillip von Zabern, 2005), 297–301, 336–357; Anthony Kauders, *German Politics and the Jews: Düsseldorf and Nuremberg 1910–1933* (Oxford: Clarendon Press, 1996).

designate a conceptual change toward consumers, turning them into political agents, and to shopping, making it into a highly charged political act.

The two initial types of boycott mentioned above – those targeting Jewish businesses and Jewish consumers – were primarily consumer boycotts in which the relations between rights and desires, the status of consumers, and the cultural and political meaning of consumption played a central role.[9] The language of court cases from the time reveals how these episodes unfolded in a consumerist context. During the years of the Weimar Republic, German courts frequently arbitrated attempts to boycott Jews, with hundreds of trials taking place in the 1920s.[10] These proceedings reveal a tension between different types of individual rights: the right to free expression of opinion as opposed to the right of privacy, and the idea of citizenship as an expression of the right to belong to the nation. As a rule, statements such as "don't buy from Jews," or for that matter "don't buy from antisemites" and "avoid doing business with Protestants," were protected under article 118 of the Weimar Constitution that guaranteed freedom of speech to every German citizen.[11] Only in cases in which the court could establish tangible distress or damage to other rights of individual consumers or businesses were such appeals considered illegal.

For example, in 1931 the National Socialist newspaper *Coburger Nationalzeitung* in Bavaria announced an essay competition asking its readers to report on their experiences of the perils of buying from and selling to Jews.[12] Based on this evidence the newspaper proclaimed that shopping in Jewish stores "contaminates German goods" and should be considered "treachery to the German struggle for freedom."[13] Discussing

---

[9] Lisa A. Neilson, "Boycott or Buycott? Understanding Political Consumerism," *Journal of Consumer Behaviour* 9 (3) (2010), 214–227; Monroe Friedman, *Consumer Boycotts: Effecting Change through the Marketplace and the Media* (New York: Routledge, 1999), ch. 9.

[10] On these boycott trials and for the main contemporary legal literature on the subject see Donald L. Niewyk, "Jews and the Courts in Weimar Germany," *Jewish Social Studies* 37 (2) (1975), 99–113; Sibylle Morgenthaler, "Countering the Pre-1933 Nazi Boycott against the Jews," *Leo Baeck Institute Yearbook* 36 (1991), 127–149; Ahlheim, *"Deutsche, kauft nicht bei Juden!"*

[11] Christoph Gusy, *Die Weimarer Reichsverfassung* (Tübingen: Mohr Siebeck, 1997).

[12] "Die Nachteile irgendwelchen geschäftlichen Verkehrs mit Juden im Kauf bei Juden, als auch im Verkauf an Juden sowohl für die Allgemeinheit wie auch für den einzelnen an Hand von Selbsterlebnissen oder bei anderen beobachteten, kurz gefaßt Beispielen darzustellen und zu beweisen." Reported in: "Landesgericht Koburg verbietet Boykott-Preisausschreibung," *CV-Zeitung* 11 (March 13, 1931), 121.

[13] Ibid.

the lawsuits filed by some Jewish businessmen against the newspaper, the provincial high court condemned this boycott attempt "because it refuses German citizens the right to exist in the economic sector for no other reason than their affiliation to the Jewish race."[14]

In another case, the court of the city of Jena found it reprehensible when threats were made to publicly name customers of a Jewish-owned department store, because "under the law every individual is free to buy wherever he likes. Whether he buys from department stores or from other shops is entirely his own business."[15] But not all court cases were settled with a verdict against the boycott. Some courts considered the calls to boycott Jewish businesses a form of legitimate political opinion with no confirmable influence on consumer behavior.[16] Whether the boycotts were defended or declared illegal by the courts, the concept of rights and the issue of consumer choice played a central role in these discussions.

Even the Nazi party, who comprised the powerhouse of the boycott movement during the Weimar years, appropriated the vocabulary of the free market and consumer agency when advocating its politics of Jewish exclusion. For the Nazis, boycotting Jews constituted a legitimate measure of self-defense, aimed at protecting consumer interests. At least formally, the calls to boycott Jews sought to redress the alleged imbalance of Jewish economic supremacy by facilitating "fair" competition in the market-place. An example of this can be found in the following rhyme that contemporary observers report was sung enthusiastically by groups of German nationalists: "It is not right if you buy from a Yid/ for the Jews it is never too bad/ but your country's businessmen/ they are pushed to the verge of ruin."[17]

Promoting economic boycott accentuated the idea of consumer responsibility by transforming consumer choice into a form of political action.

---

[14] Cited in Hans Lazarus, "Neue Rechtssprechungen zur Boykottfrage," *CV-Zeitung* (January 29, 1932), 39–40. The translation is based on Morgenthaler, "Countering the Pre-1933," 143.

[15] Cited in *CV-Zeitung* (August 19, 1932), 351. The translation is based on Morgenthaler, "Countering the Pre-1933 Nazi Boycott," 144.

[16] For a detailed critical discussion of such a case see Rudolf Callmann, *Zur Boykottfrage. Ein Gutachten* (Berlin: Philo Verlag, 1931).

[17] "Kaufst Du beim Jud, das ist nicht recht/ Dem Juden geht es niemals schlecht/ Doch deines Landes Kaufmannsstand/ Der wandelt an Verderbens Rand," cited in Fritz Marburg, *Der Antisemitismus in der Deutschen Republik* (Vienna: Kommissions-Verlag Josef Brenner, 1931), 55. Apparently there were other versions of this chant in circulation. The *CV-Zeitung* of May 6, 1930, cites the following version of this rhyme: "Kauf nicht beim Jud, das ist nicht recht, der Jud ist Deutschland Henkersknecht. Unterstützt den deutschen Gewerbestand, dann bleibt Eure Geld in Deutscher Hand."

This action was framed in personal terms. The calls to boycott Jews often employed the direct second person *Du* (you) form, rather than the polite and somewhat impartial third person *Sie*, underlining the personal agency and autonomy of consumers.[18] This approach, firmly embedded in the promotional culture of the period, gave rise to a commercial-style politics that embraced the language of modern consumerism. The Nazis even offered incentives such as cash bonuses, gift hampers, and sweepstakes to encourage consumers to avoid doing business with Jews.[19]

The Nazi appeal to the shoppers was explicitly gendered. In many of their publications, the Nazis exclusively addressed women, urging them to support German businessmen by shopping only in non-Jewish stores. Transforming household shopping responsibilities into an ideology of consumer rights and obligations, the Nazis sought to politicize women's consumer consciousness. At the same time, this simplistic distinction between a feminine consumer and a masculine producer prompted further antisemitic fantasies about relations between putatively dominant Jewish businessmen and submissive female customers. It is little wonder, then, that Nazi propagandists sought to empower women by emphasizing the economic and political significance of their consumption. A salient expression of this propensity can be found in the publications of the *Kampfgemeinschaft gegen Warenhaus und Konsumverein* (Association for the Struggle against the Department Store and the Consumer Cooperative), a National Socialist organization founded in Munich in 1930 to represent what the Nazis considered to be German middle-class interests.[20] The association considered women "the soul of the middle class" (*die Seele des Mittelstandes*) and launched a campaign to instill an awareness of the politics of consumption among German housewives.[21] Using the *Du* second-person form of address, the association urged German women not to buy from Jews: "Gerade an

---

[18] Moritz Föllmer, "Was Nazism Collectivistic? Redefining the Individual in Berlin, 1930–1945," *Journal of Modern History* 82 (1) (2010), 61–100.

[19] Ahlheim, "*Deutsche, kauft nicht bei Juden!*", as well as in Kreutzmüller, *Ausverkauf*. More generally on commercial culture under National Socialism see, Jonathan S. Wiesen, *Creating the Nazi Marketplace: Commerce and Consumption in the Third Reich* (New York: Cambridge University Press, 2010); Pamela E. Swett, *Selling under the Swastika: Advertising and Commercial Culture in Nazi Germany* (Stanford: Stanford University Press, 2013).

[20] On this organization see, for example, Mathias Rösch, *Die Münchner NSDAP 1925–1933: Eine Untersuchung zur inneren Struktur der NSDAP in der Weimarer Republik* (Munich: Oldenbourg, 2002), 285–286 and 334–339; Detlef Mühlberger, *Hitler's Voice: Organisation and Development of the Nazi Party* (Bern: Peter Lang Verlag, 2004), 194.

[21] Rösch, *Die Münchner NSDAP*, 335.

*Dich* wenden wir uns! Für *Dich* ist dieses Blatt geschrieben! *Du* sollst es beherzigen, denn durch *Deine* Hände geht der größte Teil des deutschen Volks-Einkommens" (We turn to *you* with good reason! This gazette is written for *you*! *You* should take into account that it is *you* who manages the largest portion of the German people's income).

In addition to urging shoppers not to purchase from Jewish businesses, the Nazis threatened to publish the names of those who shopped from Jewish outlets, hence making public what was otherwise considered to be a private matter and a nonpolitical choice.[22] Slogans such as "you impair your reputation if you buy in Jewish businesses!" (*Sie schaden ihrem Gute Ruf, wenn Sie in jüdischen Geschäften kaufen!*) or "anyone who buys from Jews is a traitor to the people" (*Wer beim Juden kauft, ist ein Volksverräter*) reveal how politicized the matter of consumer choice and belonging had become, although there is no indication, however, that such lists were ever published during the Weimar years.[23]

During the Third Reich, the *Centralverein* received many reports of threats, especially in small places, to expose the identity of shoppers who patronized Jewish business. One such report reveals that in the town of Goldap in July 1935, local Nazi officials took photos of people entering a Jewish-owned business and threatened female customers with the loss of their husbands' jobs if they continued shopping there.[24] The Nazis even organized public gatherings under headings such as "tell me from whom you buy, and I'll tell you who you are" (*Sag mir, bei wem du kaufst, und ich sage dir, wer Du bist*) to denounce those alleged *Spießer* (*petite bourgeoisie*), *Mucker* (moaner), and *Nörgler* (nagger) consumers, who, despite National Socialism, still bought from Jews.[25] These are just two examples of the many ways in which Jews were economically persecuted under National Socialism.[26] At the same time, they provide evidence that during

[22] Morgenthaler, "Countering the Pre-1933 Nazi Boycott," 133.

[23] For these and other examples see Marburg, *Der Antisemitismus in der Deutschen Republik.*

[24] This report is from the *Centralverein* archive (CVA) that was uncovered in Moscow after the collapse of the Soviet Union. For this study I used the microfilm copy of the archive that is available at the Central Archive of the Jewish People (hereafter: CAHJP) in Jerusalem. All references from this archive will cite the original record number as well as the number of the microfilm frame. "Der Firma Schiftan, Goldap," CAHJP, CVA, record no. HM2/8783, fr. 2057.

[25] CAHJP, CVA, record no. HM2/8778, fr.1765.

[26] For a more detailed discussion on the economic persecution of Jews during the 1930s in Avraham Barkai, *From Boycott to Annihilation: The Economic Struggle of German Jews, 1933–1942* (Hanover: Brandies University Press, 1989).

this time consumers continued to patronize Jewish-owned businesses, even in the provincial locations considered strongholds of Nazi power. Indeed, the Nazis initiated a set of special surveys to determine why "Germans," women in particular, persisted in shopping in Jewish-owned stores.[27] The fact that in the 1920s consumers could be "outed" as antisocial, subversive to the state, or simply as Jewish, suggests that the act of buying by then had ceased to be understood as a private matter and was already regarded as a political act with strong racial ramifications.

### PRECARIOUS PLEASURES

The third pillar of the boycott strategy against the Jews was to attempt to ban them as consumers. In the mid-1920s, the slogan "Don't sell to Jews!" (*Verkauft nicht an Juden!*) appeared. According to contemporary observers, the difficulty of persuading shoppers to shun Jewish-owned businesses during the economic upheavals of the postwar period prompted the call instead to boycott Jews as consumers.[28] Perhaps the best-known example of this practice is the case of holiday trips to resorts, hotels, and spas.

At the beginning of the twentieth century, taking a break from everyday life in order to revitalize the body and enliven the mind began to be understood as a natural right, owed to every working individual in exchange for his labor. The idea of a vacation reflected new notions of the good life that combined material prosperity, education, and health.[29] Despite the significance of the *idea* of the vacation, up to the start of the Great War, holiday-making was still a privilege almost entirely restricted to the fairly well-to-do. In prewar Germany, for instance, just 11 percent of the general population could afford to take a yearly vacation.[30] So, although vacationing was becoming increasingly important and widespread, it was not yet, in this period, a mass phenomenon. But it is precisely because it remained a privileged activity that the vacation in this period is such a revealing social

[27] Heinrich Uhlig, *Die Warenhäuser im Dritten Reich* (Cologne: Westdeutscher Verlag, 1957), 138.

[28] Georg Baum, "Der völkische Boykott und seine Rechtslagen," *CV-Zeitung* 5 (13) (1925), 221.

[29] On the history of tourism in central Europe see, for example, Hasso Spode, *TraumZeitReise: Geschichte und Philosophie des Tourismus* (Wiesbaden: VS Verlag für Sozialwissenschaften, 2009); Rüdiger Hachtmann, *Tourismus-Geschichte* (Göttingen: Vandenhoeck & Ruprecht, 2007).

[30] Christine Keitz, *Reisen als Leitbild. Die Entstehung des modernen Massentourismus in Deutschland* (Munich: dtv, 1997), 52.

mechanism. Beyond the quest for a change of atmosphere and recreation, the holiday was also a time for socializing, networking, and display. Visiting the great centers of European civilization or spending time closer to "nature" in a spa and a resort became a status symbol through which, to use Pierre Bourdieu's terminology, economic capital was utilized to gain social and cultural capital, and vice versa. Given this conjunction, it is not surprising that even the etiquette guides of the period started warning against mixing business and pleasure when traveling for a holiday. In addition, the emerging tourist centers were renowned as marriage markets for the well-to-do of European societies.[31]

Like other city dwellers, Jews were keen to take time off from their daily lives in the growing conurbations. In Germany, Jews comprised around 1 percent of the general population. Yet, at the beginning of the twentieth century, their number among the vacationists was disproportionally higher.[32] As a recently emancipated minority group that dwelled mostly in cities, Jews were keen to translate their relative economic success into social capital. Their quest for social consolidation and a getaway was cannily nurtured by the burgeoning tourist industry that identified Jews as a distinct group of consumers particularly suggestible to the idea of a vacation. Luring Jewish holidaymakers by offering kosher food or the opportunity to celebrate Jewish life cycle events such as weddings and bar mitzvahs, the growing tourist industry promoted holiday spots as sites of emancipation without complete assimilation. For the Jewish middle classes, going on holiday offered a chance not only to regenerate body and mind but to display economic power and, most importantly, to attain social recognition.[33] Their diaries and correspondence reveal the social imperatives – and opportunities – of such vacations as well as the more

---

[31] See, for example, Sholem Aleichem's satirical novel *Marienbad*, which tells the story of wealthy Jewish women from Warsaw who hope to marry off their daughters while vacationing in the famous spa town at this time. Sholem Aleichem, *Marienbad*, translated by Aliza Shevrin (New York: G.P. Putnam Sons, 1982, first published as a book form in 1917). For a more general overview of Jewish travel literature see Leah V. Garrett, *Journeys beyond the Pale: Yiddish Travel Writing in the Modern World* (Madison: University of Wisconsin Press, 2003).

[32] On Jewish tourism see Michael Brenner, "Zwischen Marienbad und Norderney: Der Kurort als 'Jewish Space'," *Jüdische Almanach* (2001), 119–137; Robert Kriechbaumer (ed.), *Der Geschmack der Vergänglichkeit. Jüdische Sommerfrische in Salzburg* (Wien: Bölau, 2002); Miriam Trindel-Zadoff, *Nächstes Jahr in Marienbad Gegenwelten jüdischer Kulturen der Moderne* (Göttingen: Vandenhoeck & Ruprecht, 2007).

[33] Marion A. Kaplan, *The Making of the Jewish Middle Class: Women, Family, and Identity in Imperial Germany* (New York: Oxford University Press, 1991), 119–126.

personal relaxation that was to be had. One had to "be seen," noted businessman Isidor Hirschfeld in the diary of his holiday on the North Sea island of Helgoland in 1894.[34]

The special social function of the vacation for Jews provides at least a partial explanation for why the holiday resort became a site of Jewish exclusion, even though Jews were not the only group for whom the so-called *Modebädern* (fashionable resort) was a means of gaining social capital.[35] In Germany, at least, the identification of Jewish parvenus with the new resorts was explicit. Asserting that it was "not a luxury resort, [and was] free of Jews" (*Kein Luxusbad, Judenfrei*), a resort on the small island Hiddensee in the Baltic Sea distanced itself from the negative image of a Jewish consumer interested only in luxury.[36] The image of the Jewish social climber was coupled with other fears about "inappropriate and vulgar" Jewish behavior. In an 1882 letter to his wife, the popular German novelist Theodor Fontane described the Jews he met during his holiday on the North Sea island of Norderney as "cheeky," and "obtrusive" and having "ugly crook faces."[37] As this language makes clear, for some, Jews were not welcome in such exclusive locales as holiday resorts.[38]

Political beliefs, social bigotries, and economic interests contributed to patterns of Jewish consumption to varying degrees. In the case of both Jewish and antisemitic businesses we might expect group solidarity as well as political outlook to overcome economic interests. But what about the

---

[34] He also adds in passing that on the occasion perhaps "a girl with money will fall in love with us." Quoted in: Monika Richarz, *Jüdisches Leben in Deutschland. Selbstzeugnisse zur Sozialgeschichte im Kaiserreich* (Stuttgart: Deutsche Verlags-Anstalt, 1979), 248.

[35] Traveling to the so-called *Modebädern* was also conceived in terms of conspicuous consumption, a concept coined by Thorstein Veblen to depict the behavioral characteristic of the *nouveau riche* and was, at least in Germany, explicitly associated with Jews. Thorstein Veblen, *Theory of the Leisure Class: An Economic Study in the Evolution of Institutions* (New York: Macmillan, 1899). On the Jewish context see David Brenner, "Out of the Ghetto and into the Tiergarten: Redefining the Jewish Parvenu and His Origins in Ost und West," *German Quarterly* 66 (2) (1993), 176–194.

[36] CAHJP, CVA, record no. HM2\8760. This case is also mentioned in Frank Bajohr, *"Unser Hotel ist Judenfrei." Bäder-Antisemitismus im 19. und 20. Jahrhundert* (Frankfurt am M.: Fischer Taschenbuch, 2003), 35.

[37] Quoted in Bajohr, *"Unser Hotel ist Judenfrei,"* 30.

[38] For a broader exploration of the connection between language and violence in the German Jewish context see Thomas Pegelow Kaplan, *The Language of Nazi Genocide: Linguistic Violence and the Struggle of Germans of Jewish Ancestry* (Cambridge: Cambridge University Press, 2009); more generally on language and power Pierre Bourdieu, *Language & Symbolic Power* (Cambridge, MA: Harvard University Press, 1991).

majority of businesses, which operated according to free market forces? Restaurants, hotels, and resorts had to be attentive to the changing demands of their customers in order to stay afloat. Aiming to secure a solid pool of regular clients, these consumer-oriented tourist businesses were intent on addressing specific target groups with their marketing materials. This consumer-oriented attentiveness makes the marketplace a sensitive seismograph of social change and cultural trends. By providing an economic pretext for banning Jewish vacationers, antisemitism became an "issue" in the marketing strategy of the tourist industry. The same economic logic that had once positively targeted Jews as holidaymakers with ample pocketbooks now led some businesses to meet the demand for vacation places that were guaranteed to be free of Jews. Before the Great War the number of facilities banning Jews was not high, but it was substantial enough that in 1905, the *Centralverein* noted that "in the land of poets and thinkers," a goodly number of baths and spas publicly proclaimed that they do not welcome Jewish guests.[39]

After the Great War, calls to ban Jewish holidaymakers increased, and as the 1930s approached, the number of facilities declaring themselves "free of Jews" grew.[40] There are several reasons for this development. During the Weimar years, the tourism industry greatly expanded. With many more people traveling, the relative significance of the Jewish tourists among the holidaymakers declined. But more choice for consumers meant more competition among holiday providers who found themselves under growing pressure to differentiate themselves, often by excluding Jews. The stifling economic conditions of the Weimar years and the political instability of the Republic were further factors rendering Jews "questionable" for the tourist industry. In 1922 one hotel owner reported to the banker and *Centralverein* member Oscar Schueller that he got into serious trouble with some of his regular guests because of Jewish families who spent their summer holidays in his hotel. Urging Schueller not to take his decision personally, but to look at it from a purely business perspective, he bluntly explained, "since I am obviously keen to continue welcoming my regular [non-Jewish] customers every summer, I have decided not to take Jewish guests in my hotel any

---

[39] Quoted in Frank Bajohr, "'Unser Hotel ist Judenfrei.' Alltagsantisemitismus in Bade- und Kurorten im 19. und 20. Jahrhundert," *Gesprächskreis Politik und Geschichte im Karl-Marx-Haus* 10 (2007), 5.

[40] For a detailed discussion of this period see Bajohr, "Unser Hotel," and Jacob Borut, "Antisemitism in Tourist Facilities in Weimar Germany," *Yad Vashem Studies* 28 (2000), 7–50.

longer."[41] A year later the swastika featured on the advertising material of this hotel. Cynical as this statement may be, at least this hotel owner took the time and had the courtesy to explain his choice. In many other cases the position of the hotel was not as upfront. Often, private people wrote to the *Centralverein* to inquire about a specific facility's policy toward Jewish guests. In 1930, the *Centralverein* received a complaint about a hotel in the spa city of Wiesbaden. The owner of the hotel had allegedly declined to do business with Jewish-owned companies, stating that Germans "should only buy from German businesses."[42] At the same time, the letter-writer made clear, the hotel had frequently advertised in the Jewish press, including in the *CV-Zeitung*. Furthermore, at least half of the hotel's customers were Jews. Such an ambiguous situation explains the need for more information on the hotel's policies.

For their part, Jews wanted to spend their holidays in a safe and relaxing atmosphere without being confronted by questions about their belonging.[43] In response, several Jewish organizations created a kind of a databank of places where Jews were not welcome. In addition to these lists of antisemitic hotels that had been published regularly in the Jewish press since the turn of the century, the *Centralverein* set up a special travel service in the early 1930s to offer updated information, free of charge, on tourist facilities hostile to Jews.[44]

These "blacklists" illuminated the equivocal position of Jewish consumers in Germany in the interwar years. With the growing numbers of the facilities enumerated on the blacklists, hotel owners became increasingly aware of these registers. Their dramatically differing responses are preserved in the *Centralverein* archive.[45] Taken as a whole we can discern three major responses of hotel owners to being included on these registers. The first, and most common, reaction was indignation and protest to being included on the list of antisemitic establishments. In 1922, for example, the bureau investigated the case of Herr J. Most, owner of the Sanssouci hotel in the mountain area of Saxony. Most had allegedly

---

[41] "Da mir nun selbstverständlich sehr viel daran liegt, meine alte Stammkunde hier in jedem Summer wieder begrüßen zu können, so habe ich mich entschlossen, fernerhin in meinem Hause keine israelitischen Familien aufzunehmen." CAHJP, CVA, record no. HM2/ 8760, 483.

[42] CAHJP, CVA, record no. HM2/8760, 1015–1016.

[43] For a bold account of Jewish motivations when choosing holiday destination see Gaza, "Through a Women's Eyes," *The Jewish World* (July 12, 1923), 14.

[44] "Reisedienst des Centralvereins," *CV-Zeitung* (June 6, 1932), 247.

[45] More on these lists and how they were compiled see in Borut, "Antisemitism in Tourist Facilities."

advised one of his Jewish guests "to return to Jerusalem" and told another that he no longer wanted Jewish guests in his hotel. Most admitted that he might have said these things but claimed that he had acted rashly. Arguing that his words by no means reflected his attitude to Jews, he expressed his genuine interest in having Jewish guests continue to stay in his hotel.[46]

An even more intriguing example is a letter sent to the *Centralverein* at the beginning of summer 1927 by Georg Hübner, the owner of a small hotel in Bad Salzschlirf, a spa town in a Catholic area near the city of Fulda in central Germany. Hübner vehemently protested against his hotel being included on the list of antisemitic hotels, claiming that this classification breached his rights as a business owner. He even threatened to take legal action against the *Centralverein* for the losses he suffered as a result. Hübner admitted that he had a "nationally minded" (*National eingestellt*) son but made it clear that his son's political orientation did not reflect his own and that it was he, and not the son, who ruled the roost in the business.[47]

In another interesting case, the *Centralverein* responded to a hotel owner's complaint by explaining that the hotel had been put on the list in 1927 after it was determined that it advertised itself as a "pure Christian establishment" (*Rein christliches Haus*). The hotel owner replied that Jews were equally welcome as Christians in his house and explicitly asked for the name of his establishment to be removed from the list.[48]

In some spa towns, including Bad Salzuflen in North Rhine-Westphalia, the local Jewish community protested against the blacklists, complaining that these registers generated a misleading impression of their town as hostile to Jews. In Bad Salzuflen, one letter-writer admitted, there were a few antisemitic establishments, but the majority of hotels welcomed Jews and some of them even offered Kosher food.[49] Some hotel owners made

---

[46] CAHJP, CVA, record no. HM2/8747, fr. 266.

[47] Ibid., HM2/8761, 130. The son Georg Hübner refers to in his letter was no other than the notorious Herbert Hübner. Born in 1902 in Bad Salzschlirf, Herbert Hübner was a member of radical right-wing organizations at the beginning of the 1920s. In 1923 he took part in the Hitler putsch and from 1932 was an active member of the SS. After World War II, Hübner was sentenced in the Nuremberg trials to 15 years' imprisonment for war crimes and crimes against humanity. He was released from prison in 1951 and began a new life as a salesman in Bonn. On Herbert Hübner see Isabel Heinemann, *"Rasse, Siedlung, deutsches Blut:" Das Rasse- und Siedlungshauptamt der SS und die rassenpolitische Neuordnung Europas* (Göttingen: Wallstein, 2003), 620.

[48] Ibid., HM2/8760, 787. There we also find writings attesting to the friendly attitude of the hotel to Jews.

[49] Ibid., HM2/87665, 610. Such official registration of hotels in different spa towns with the word "kosher" in Hebrew lettering can also be found in CAHJP, CVA, record no. HM2-8761.

**Berichtigung.**

Die von mir weitergegebene Behauptung, Hitler habe im Park-Hotel Kaiserhof, Frankfurt a. M., gewohnt und dort seine Wache aufgestellt, entspricht, wie ich mich zwischenzeitlich überzeugt habe, nicht den Tatsachen.

Ich bedauere diese Aeusserung und berichtige sie, um falschen, in diesem Zusammenhang mir zugetragenen Gerüchten über die politische Einstellung der Inhaber des Park-Hotels Kaiserhof entgegenzutreten.

Frankfurt a. M., den 15. November 1930.

**H. Mayer.**

FIGURE 6.1 "Correction"
From: *CV-Zeitung* vol. IX, no. 47 (November 21, 1930), 610.

their protests public. In an announcement with the title "correction" (*Berechtigung*) published in the advertising section of the *CV-Zeitung* at the end of November 1930, the Park Hotel Kaiserhof in Frankfurt counteracted claims that Hitler stayed in the hotel. These rumors, the statement asserted, were not only false but did not reflect the political attitude of the hotel owner.

Not all responses to the blacklisting of antisemitic hotels were negative. Some hotel owners approved the inclusion of their establishment on the register of antisemitic hotels, while others simply ignored these lists. Rarer still was the request to be included on the blacklists, but this happened too. In his comprehensive discussion of so-called spa antisemitism, Jacob Borut reports on a resort in the Thuringian forest that filed a complaint in 1926 to *Centralverein* officials for *not* being included on the list of the hotels hostile to Jews. Borut uses this and other similar examples as evidence of the rapid advance of antisemitism from the mid-1920s. Beyond the standard explanations for the rise of antisemitism following the Great War, focusing on economic adversity, social instability, and political radicalization, there was a strong commercial basis for the rise of anti-Jewish sentiment that has been underappreciated in the historical literature. The tendency of modern consumerist society to address and promote identities made the marketplace an arena in which the question of belonging became a contentious issue. By examining Jewish reactions to the different boycott attempts, as I will in the next section, I aim to further demonstrate how the transformation of the marketplace into a space for participation and exclusion contributed to the increasing racialization of German society.

## FROM BOYCOTT TO BUYCOTT

Jewish leaders sought initially to delegitimize boycotts by launching legal challenges within the conventional political and social process. Jewish officials were reluctant to compromise these legal attacks on boycotts against Jews by organizing counter-boycotts against antisemitic establishments.[50] A task force was set up by the *Centralverein* to fight the boycott met in December 1932. Reporting that the legal action taken against the boycotts had proved effective but insufficient, the committee planned to launch an information campaign explaining to the general public the devastating consequences of boycotting Jews.[51] By educating consumers about the importance of choice in the marketplace, the committee hoped to convince consumers that boycotting Jews ultimately harmed consumers themselves. They also planned to distribute a special catalog of Jewish-owned businesses to civil servants, with the reminder that "the German civil servant is allowed to buy where he wants" (*Der deutsche Beamte darf kaufen, wo er will*).[52]

In addition to the official focus on preemptive legal measures, Jews took affirmative action by engaging in their own consumer boycott, or buycott, by making public the names of antisemitic businesses, hotels, and holiday resorts, as outlined above. The blacklist of antisemitic hotels comprised just one aspect of how Jews organized themselves as consumers in order to create a more Jewish-friendly marketplace. The Jewish press also designated special advertising pages for hotels and accommodation that were specifically recommended for Jewish guests.

One of the most prominent organizations that endorsed this form of Jewish buycott was the *Verein zur Förderung rituelle Speisehäuser* (Association for the Promotion of Ritual Restaurants). Founded in Hamburg at the turn of the century, the association's work was inspired by Jewish rabbinic traditions calling upon Jews to be more conscious of their consuming habits, including refraining from purchasing certain products in order to regulate the market.[53] In 1929 there were approximately 380 restaurants and hotels in Germany and abroad under the supervision of this association. So pervasive was its influence that there is almost no

---

[50] "Antisemitischer Boykott und jüdischer Selbsthilfe. Ein Mahnwort an unsere Frauen," *Jüdische Frau* 1 (12) (1925), 5.
[51] CAHJP, CVA, record no. HM2/8768, fr. 581.    [52] Ibid., record no. HM2/8778, 2165.
[53] On rabbinic thinking about consumption see Jacob Neusner, *The Economics of the Mishnah* (Chicago: University of Chicago Press, 1990); Meir Tamari, *The Challenge of Wealth: A Jewish Perspective on Earning and Spending Money* (Northvale, NJ: J. Aronson, 1995).

FIGURE 6.2 "Recommendable summer and bath resort." A typical advertisement page for hotels and accommodations
From: The orthodox newspaper *Der Israelit* (June 23, 1927).

German Jewish newspaper of the period in which its logo – indicating that a hotel or restaurant was under its supervision – was not to be found (see Figure 6.2).

The association worked closely together with the association of Jewish hotel and restaurant owners (*Verein jüdischer Hotelbesitzer und Restaurateure e.V*), which had a vested interest in promoting its facilities to Jewish consumers.[54] Together, they helped to forge the notion of a consumer culture for Jews. The Jewish press helped support this trend by encouraging business owners and readers to advertise and shop "Jewish." As we saw earlier, Jewish newspapers vigorously worked to make their readers more aware of the significance of Jewishness in the marketplace, elevating consumption almost to an act of Jewish affirmation.

At the same time, the Nazis were constructing their own "Jewish-free" consumer spaces. The Nazi press published its own blacklists of "Jewish"-owned businesses and publicized establishments that expressly welcomed Nazi customers. From the late 1920s, advertisements began to appear that specifically addressed Nazi shoppers. Under headings such as *Wo kauft der Nationalsozialist?* (Where does the National Socialist go shopping?), the advertising sections of the Nazi press listed Nazi-orientated businesses calling upon consumers to shop "National Socialist." Shopping guides were created to direct consumers to Nazi-orientated businesses, and as the 1930s approached, more shops and local businesses started putting up signs indicating their political orientation. Early on, the Nazis recognized the power of consumption to mobilize both support for the party and to marginalize those groups identified as enemies of the Nazi movement, above all the Jews.[55] Consumerism thereby played a pivotal role in the alliance between Nazi ideas and middle-class ideals. It was a coalition that would shatter the once widespread assumption among German Jews that the marketplace was a civilizing force that promoted rights and tolerance.

### FROM BOYCOTT TO PERSECUTION

As late as January 19, 1933, the German Jewish press triumphantly reported that the German state had finally recognized the seriousness of the boycott situation and would now call upon the police force to act against this kind of "disturbance of peace and order."[56] According to these reports, this decision was informed by the understanding that the frequent and uncontrolled use of economic boycott, even if initially directed solely against Jews, would in time

---

[54] This association also published a Newsletter: *Jüdisches Wochenblatt: offizielles Mitteilungsblatt des Vereins Jüdischer Hotelbesitzer und Restaurateure.*

[55] Ahlheim, *"Deutsche, kauft nicht bei Juden!"*; Wiesen, *Creating the Nazi Marketplace*; Shelley Baranowski, *Strength through Joy: Consumerism and Mass Tourism in the Third Reich* (New York: Cambridge University Press, 2004).

[56] "Eine 'Große Anfrage' und eine deutliche Antwort. Reichsminister und Landesministerium gegen Boykott," *CV-Zeitung* XII (3) (1933).

become a general menace, undermining the social, economic, and "German" national cohesion.[57] Despite the optimistic tone underlining this statement, it reflected a dramatic shift in the Jewish discourse. Whereas in the past, the language of economic rationality dominated the struggle against economic discrimination, by the 1930s the language of German nationalism and national interest became more prevalent in this debate.[58] Despite this clear and inexorable trend, pockets of resistance remained in the marketplace, such as the case of Jewish cattle traders, that demonstrate that even after the Nazi takeover, economic interests could act to undermine or deflect antisemitism.[59] But by the mid-1930s, it became apparent that the marketplace had turned into a site of Jewish exclusion reflecting a new social order in which the idea of economic rationality was increasingly informed by the notion of *Volksgemeinschaft* and racial segregation.

Eleven days after the German Jewish press had announced the achievements in the struggle against the boycott, the National Socialist Party came to power. Shortly thereafter, on Saturday, April 1, 1933, the Nazis organized a general boycott against Jewish businesses, turning what until then had appeared as a haphazard and ineffective attempt to exclude Jews into state-sponsored policy.[60] Following the April boycott a series of both legislative and informal measures were instated against Jews, aiming first to isolate and eventually to force them to leave Germany. A growing number of retailers hung signs on their shop window indicating "Jews will not be served" (*Juden werden hier nicht bedient*), and the Nazi party pressured retailers to label their businesses as either "German" or "Jewish." Already at the beginning of the 1930s this trend was conceived as a tangible threat to Jewish life in Germany, mainly in small places where it became almost impossible for Jews to buy groceries as well as other basic products and services.[61] Small businesses accustomed

[57] Ibid.

[58] On this change and how it also shaped Jewish discourse more broadly see a special report on German Jewry that was published in the *Jewish Chronicle* in 1930. "German Jewry. III. The Economic Position: Communal Organization," *Jewish Chronicle*, no. 114 (June 1930).

[59] For a detailed study of Jewish cattle traders see Fischer, *Ökonomisches Vertrauen und antisemitische Gewalt*; Ibid., "Clashing Gears: Jewish Cattle Traders, Farmers, and Nazis in Conflict, 1926–1935," *Holocaust Studies: A Journal of Cultural History* 16 (1–2) (2010), 15–39.

[60] Barkai, From Boycott to Annihilation; Saul Friedländer, *Nazi Germany and the Jews: The Years of Persecution, 1933–1939* (New York: Harper Collins, 1997).

[61] See, for example, the correspondence regarding the situation of Jews in the city of Elbing in East Prussia, now Poland. In 1935 the local grocery store decided, apparently upon its own initiative, to stop selling food to Jews. CAHJP, CVA, record no. HM2/8783, fr. 1922–1927.

to advertising in the Jewish press were pressured to retract their business, while Jewish companies found it increasingly difficult to advertise in the general press.[62] A survey conducted of thirty-four small towns in the Württemberg region in South Germany reveals that in mid-1934, of the forty-nine local newspapers published in these areas (twenty-two dubbed middle-class, or *bürgerlich*, with the remainder, National Socialist), only thirteen accepted advertisements from Jewish-owned businesses.[63] These numbers shrank further during the second half of the 1930s when the so-called Aryanization process, that is, the confiscating or stripping Jews of their possessions, was well under way.[64]

Ironically, the aggrieved reactions from outside of Germany to the rise of National Socialism often conspired to make an ominous situation for the Jews even worse, as German Jewish businesses were caught up in general boycotts against German products in Europe and across the Atlantic.[65] Letters poured into the *Centralverein* from around the world, requesting firsthand information about the situation of Jews under National Socialism. Even if only 50 percent of what was written in the press about

[62] See, for example, a letter in the local Jewish newspaper of the Jewish community in Frankfurt (*Frankfurter Israelitisches Gemeindeblatt*) to the *Centralverein* in which the editor of the advertising section reports that all hairdressers that used to advertise in non-Jewish newspapers had been instructed to stop doing so. In CAHJP, CVA, record no. HM2/8804, 92.

[63] On this see the report in CAHJP, CVA, record no. HM2/8804, 281–288. It should be noted that this survey was conducted after many Jewish business owners complained about their growing difficulties to advertise in the general non-Jewish press. Many of these complaint letters could be found today in what is left from the *Centralverein* archive.

[64] In recent years a number of new studies were published on the Aryanization process in different cities. See, for example, Frank Bajohr, *"Aryanisation," in: Hamburg: The Economic Exclusion of Jews and the Confiscation of their Property in Nazi Germany* (New York: Berghahn Books, 2002); Hanno Balz, *Die "Arisierung" von jüdischem Haus- und Grundbesitz in Bremen* (Bremen: Edition Temmen, 2004); Christof Biggeleben, Beate Schreiber and Kilian J. L. Steiner (eds.), *"Arisierung" in Berlin* (Berlin: Metropol Verlag, 2007); Wolfram Selig, *"Arisierung" in München: Die Vernichtung jüdischer Existenz 1937–1939* (Berlin: Metropol Verlag, 2004).

[65] For further literature on the boycott movement against Germany and its impact on German Jews see, for example, Sharon Gewirtz, "Anglo-Jewish Responses to Nazi Germany 1933–39: The Anti-Nazi Boycott and the Board of Deputies of British Jews," *Journal of Contemporary History* 26 (2) (1991), 255–276; Richard A. Hawkins, "'Hitler's Bitterest Foe': Samuel Untermyer and the Boycott of Nazi Germany, 1933–1938," *American Jewish History* 93 (1) (2007), 21–50; Moshe Gottlieb, "The Anti-Nazi Boycott Movement in the United States: An Ideological and Sociological Approach," *Jewish Social Studies* 35 (July – October 1973), 198–227; William Orbach, "Shattering the Shackles of Powerlessness: The Debates Surrounding the Anti-Nazi Boycott of 1933–41," *Modern Judaism* 2 (1982), 149–169.

the situation of Jews in Germany was true, a South African letter-writer exclaimed, "the balance remaining is still enough to cause a man sleepless nights." The position of the Jews in Germany, the writer continued, "which after all is supposed to be a civilized country . . . is just as bad as the position of Jews in the half-wild Russia of the eighties and nineties, even if pogroms are not yet the fashion on Kürfurstendamm."[66] Both Jewish-and non-Jewish-owned German companies requested *Centralverein* support in countering the calls to boycott German goods.[67] At least at the beginning of 1933 the boycott attempts from outside the country appear to have had an impact on German businesses, especially on those operating in North America. The infamous April boycott against Jewish businesses was officially called in response to these allegedly anti-German sentiments and the calls to boycott German goods. While some prominent German Jews, for example, the writer Lion Feuchtwanger, called for open resistance in the form of economic warfare against Germany, German Jewish officials felt it a matter of "urgent duty" to fight against what in Jewish publications was referred to as anti-German atrocity propaganda (*Greuelpropaganda*) abroad.[68] The *Centralverein* published official condemnations of the calls to boycott Germany, underscoring the unequivocal loyalty of German Jews to the fatherland.[69] In addition to public proclamations, letters were sent to Nazi officials, including to Adolf Hitler, stating that the involvement of individual Jews and Jewish organizations in the attempts to boycott Germany did not reflect in any way the interests of German Jews and that the authorities should acknowledge the work of German Jewish representatives to protect German interests. These reactions conveyed the fears among Jewish officials that the calls to ban German products would fortify the Nazis' partition between Jews and other Germans and would thus exacerbate segregation. In the immediate period after the National

---

[66] In CAHJP, CVA, record no. HM2/8758, 2312.

[67] One revealing example is a letter that was sent to the *Centralverein* from the company Albert Meissner Sohn on April 18, 1933. Reporting on the decline of sales abroad, especially among Jewish customers in North America, the letter asks if the *Centralverein* could send them anti-boycott material in different languages. The company planned to send these leaflets to its clients abroad hoping to win back their trust. CAHJP, CVA, record no. HM2/8758, 2110. It should be noted that the company Albert Meissner Sohn still operates to this day in export and in the wholesale trade of tools, hardware, and machinery in the city of Wuppertal.

[68] On Lion Feuchtwanger's call to boycott Germany see, for example, in "Boycott against Germany: Jewish Campaign," *The Manchester Guardian* (December 18, 1933), 11.

[69] See, for example, the editorial of the *CV-Zeitung* 13 (March 30, 1933), 105–107, as well as in the following issue of the *CV-Zeitung* 14 (April 4, 1933), 119–121. Further on this see CAHJP, CVA, record no. HM2/8758, 2194.

Socialists came to power, German Jews found themselves in the impossible situation of fighting on two fronts: within the Third Reich they struggled to maintain their rights, while toward the outside world they strove to protect German interests as if they were not deprived of their rights in Germany.

By the mid-1930s, German Jews had no choice but to accept segregation as a new social reality, retreating to all-Jewish spaces for consumption.[70] Thus, for example, after their membership in the German automobile club *Der Deutsche Automobil-Club e.V.* (DDAC) was rescinded, Jewish car owners founded their own car club. The *Auto-Club 1927 e.V.* grew rapidly, from 1,842 members in 1934 to 3,069 the next year.[71] In November 1936, the Gestapo forced the club to change its name to the "Jewish car club" (*Jüdischer Auto-Club*). The club continued to operate under this name until it became illegal in late 1938. Almost all Jewish outlets experienced a similar membership boost in the immediate years following the Nazi takeover. The Jewish press expanded significantly, growing from a print run of 140,000 in 1934 to 350,000 by 1938.[72] This development was fortified by the economic isolation of Jews. Jewish-owned businesses were compelled to orientate themselves more than ever toward Jewish consumers. The advertising sections of the Jewish press became an obvious marketing choice in a consumer culture that was exclusively oriented to Jews.

From 1933 until the start of World War II, approximately two thousand anti-Jewish decrees were passed, such as the Law for the Restoration of the Professional Civil Service of April 7, 1933, which prevented Jews from serving the German state, as well as the infamous Nuremberg laws of 1935. Other, less well-known anti-Jewish legislation forbade public officials from purchasing from Jews and prohibited Jews from visiting the cinema and sporting competitions. Those Jews who stayed in Germany after November 1938 could do their shopping only at designated times of day. They could not possess a radio set and were denied comfort food such as chocolate. After the beginning of the war they were not permitted

---

[70] On the politics of segregation and consumption: Grace Elizabeth Hale, *Making Whiteness: The Culture of Segregation in the South, 1890–1940* (New York: Pantheon, 1998).

[71] On the initial aims of the club see "Was will der Deutsche Auto-Club?" *Monatsschrift der Berliner Logen U.O.B.B.* 8 (6) (1928), 159–160. See also CAHJP, CVA, record no. HM2/ 8778 and HM/8797; Landesarchiv Berlin A Pr. Bu. 030-04 Nr. 697, as well as in Dorothee Hochstetter, *Motorisierung und "Volksgemeinschaft": das Nationalsozialistische Kraftfahrkorps NSKK 1931–1945* (Munich: Oldenbourg, 2004), 403–420.

[72] Katrin Diehl, *Die jüdische Presse im Dritten Reich. Zwischen Selbstbehauptung und Fremdbestimmung* (Berlin: de Gruyter, 1997); Herbert Freeden, *Die jüdische Presse im Dritten Reich* (Berlin: Jüdischer Verlag, 1987).

to buy basic groceries such as milk and rice.[73] By the end of the 1930s the marketplace had become exclusively a site of exclusion, revealing the incapacity of consumer capitalism to repel political fanaticism and persecution.

The Nazi politics of Jewish exclusion did not create what some historians regard as a "renaissance" of Jewish culture in the Third Reich.[74] When it came to consumption, the Nazi program of Jewish segregation and exclusion deepened and accelerated developments that were well under way before the party came to power. In the two coming chapters I consider several examples of how commercial interests coincided with a Jewish politics of belonging.

---

[73] Moshe Zimmermann, *Deutsche gegen Deutsche. Das Schicksal der Juden 1938–1945* (Berlin: Aufbau-Verlag, 2008), 72–73; Joseph Walk, *Das Sonderrecht für die Juden im NS-Staat. Ein Sammlung der gesetzlichen Maßnahmen und Richtlinien – Inhalt und Bedeutung* (Heidelberg: C.F. Müller Juristischer Verlag, 1981).

[74] Moshe Zimmermann, *Die deutschen Juden 1914–1945* (Munich: Oldenbourg, 1997), 69.

# 7

## Advertising National Belonging

At the end of the nineteenth century, advertising companies appeared in large numbers in Europe. As mentioned earlier, Jews played a prominent role in this newly enlarged industry.[1] Jewish and non-Jewish advertisers alike sought to transform their audiences in order to shape consumers' mind-sets and behavior. At the same time, advertisers recognized that consumers were sovereign individuals who made their own choices. As Don Slater cogently noted, "to be a consumer is to make choices: to decide what you want, to consider how to spend your money."[2] This tension between the desire to shape consumer beliefs and actions, and the recognition that in a free market the consumer is at liberty to choose as he or she wishes, informs the history of Jewish experiences of advertising, both as advertisers and as a target group of advertisements.

Seeking to explain the persuasive power of marketing, sociologist Erving Goffman postulated that "advertisers do not create the ritualized expressions they employ; they seem to draw upon the same corpus of displays, the same ritual idiom, that is the resource of all of us who participate in social situations."[3] In a similar vein media scholar Irene

---

[1] There are some excellent accounts on the history of advertising in different countries, none of which, however, seriously discuss the "Jewish" aspects of this story. For such literature see, for example, Dirk Reinhardt, *Von der Reklame zum Marketing. Geschichte der Wirtschaftswerbung in Deutschland* (Berlin: Akademische Verlag, 1993); Jackson Lears, *Fables of Abundance: A Cultural History of Advertising in America* (New York: Basic Books, 1994); Timothy de Waal Malefyt and Brian Moeran (eds.), *Advertising Cultures* (Oxford: Berg, 2003).

[2] Don Slater, *Consumer Culture & Modernity* (London: Polity, 1997), 27.

[3] Erving Goffman, *Gender Advertisement* (London: Macmillan Press, 1976), 84.

Costera Meijer describes advertising "as an act of telling stories that enable a certain interaction with and management of 'reality'."[4] Following this approach, in the following two chapters I would like to consider the promotional culture that developed at the end of the nineteenth century as a public site in which different political affiliations were developed and enacted.

In generating and securing markets for their products, advertisers targeted potential customers according to different categories of belonging, such as gender, class, region, and religion. Citizenship was an additional, and pivotal, form of group membership. In this chapter I explore how commercial advertisers promoted a positive notion of citizenship among Jews. Identified simultaneously as a discrete group of consumers and as an integral part of a broader community, Jews held a contradictory position. I demonstrate in the following chapter how advertisers promulgated contrasting forms of belonging among Jews in a period when consumption went through a rapid process of politicization.

### ADVERTISING THE NATION

As we saw in Chapter 2, during the first decade of the twentieth century, most advertisements in the Jewish press were aimed at an anonymous target group and in principle could have been published in almost any newspaper. Hoping to reach as large an audience as possible, advertisers developed a broad set of images and copy calculated to appeal to as many people as possible. Advertisements in the Jewish press (as in the non-Jewish press) evoked the patriotism of consumers and strove to correlate "good" Jewish citizenship with the purchase of certain goods. In England, the Peter Walker & Son brewery advertised its products in the *Jewish Chronicle* under headings such as "British Beer sets the standards to the world and Peter Walker's is Britain's standard brewery" or "The Lager that is British is also the lager that is purest, lightest and healthiest."

In continental Europe, too, nationalism played a prominent role in the advertising sections of the Jewish press. Stamped conspicuously with the word "kosher," a 1911 advert in the orthodox Jewish newspaper *Der Israelit* simultaneously evoked gender, nationalism, and a strong sense of Jewishness in a pitch for soup, promising that "What the Zeppelin airship does for Germany, Marok products do for Germany's women!"

---

[4] Irene Costera Meijer, "Advertising Citizenship: An Essay on the Performative Power of Consumer Culture," *Media, Culture & Society*, 20 (1998), 236.

---

**Was  Zeppelin's  Luftschiff**  **sind  die  Marok-Präparate**
**für  Deutschlands  Gauen** **für  Deutschlands  Frauen!**

שרכ **Bouillon-Würfel „Marok" zur** für die Fleischküche verwendbar für ¹/₄ Liter = 1 Würfel 5 Pfg.
שרכ **Suppen-Würfel „Marok"** mischt für Fleisch und Milch verwendbar für ¹/₄ Liter — 1 Würfel 5 Pfg.
שרכ **Suppen-Würze „Marok"** mischt für Fleisch und Milch verwendbar per Flasche 50, 70 und 130 Pfg.
Zur Verbesserung von schwachen Suppen, Saucen, Gemüsen, Salate u. s. w. genügen einige Tropfen.
שרכ **Erbswurst „Marok"** ¹/₁ Pfd. — 4 Teller 15 Pfg., ¹/₁ Pfd. — 8 Teller 25 Pfg., ¹/₁ Pfd. — 16 Teller 45 Pfg.
ca. 15 Minuten aufkochen, ohne weitere Zutaten gibt eine delikate Erbsensuppe.
שרכ **Marok-Suppen** erhältlich in 13 verschiedenen Suppen-Arten.  Ein Würfel genügt für 2—3 Teller.
Zu haben sind à 15 Pfg. Mockturtle, Oxtail, Tomaten; ferner à 10 Pfg. Erbsen, Bohnen, Linsen, Gries, Reis mit Julienne, Frühlings, Kartoffel, Sago, Rumford u. Ribele.
Sämtliche Suppen sind für die Fleisch- und Milch-Küche verwendbar, mit Ausnahme der Mockturtle und Oxtail. Diese beiden Sorten sind „nur für die Fleischküche" zugelassen und tragen gelbes Etikett, während die Milmich-Suppen rot etikettiert sind.

**Adolf Zinner jr., Hamburg, Grindelallee 138.** | Hergestellt unter Aufsicht Sr. Ehr-
würden Herrn Rabb. Dr. B. Wolf in Köln am Rhein.
**Engros-Vertrieb** für Frankfurt a. M. und Umgegend:  **N. Wolf, Börneplatz 8—10.**

FIGURE 7.1  What the Zeppelin airship does for Germany, Marok products do for
Germany's women!
From: *Der Israelit* no. 49 (December 7, 1911), 13.

Furthermore, the Marok label was identified as being under the strict
kosher supervision of the orthodox rabbi Dr. Benedict Wolf from the
city of Cologne, and the word *"Marok"* itself seems to derive from the
Yiddish, or Ashkenazi pronunciation of Hebrew, and means "soup"
(*Marak* in Modern Hebrew).

These early examples of nationalism and consumerism notwithstanding, it was during the Great War that consumption became a central
feature of national life. As consumers, Jews in particular were constantly
reminded of their obligation to the nation; consumption became integral
to the idea of citizenship itself. Images of national comradeship abounded.
One advertisement, from the German chocolate manufacturer Stollwerck,
displayed an image of two soldiers sharing a bar of chocolate (Figure 7.2).
At a time when national loyalty and the war-time contributions of Jews
were being challenged, this image of solidarity among German soldiers
would have had a special resonance among Jews, indicating that at least as
consumers they were indeed conceived as part of the *Volksgemeinschaft*.

The federation of German chocolate manufacturers (Verband
Deuscher Schokolade-Fabrikanten) placed advertisements in the press,
calling on Germans to buy only German chocolate. In an ad placed in
the Jewish periodical *Ost und West* in 1915 (vol. XV, no. 1–5, 7), the
federation proclaimed that "every German who elevates German companies, fulfills therewith an important patriotic duty." As this example
makes clear, business interests were readily conflated with nationalistic
sentiments, with the consumer a vital resource for both.

Across the channel, the advertising pages of the Jewish press celebrated
British nationalism. The chocolate manufacturer J. S. Fry & Sons, for

FIGURE 7.2 Ad for Stollwerck Chocolate. The Slogan Says: "10 minutes rest – out with Stollwerck gold!"
From: *Ost und West* vol. XV, no. 1–5 (1915), 4.

instance, advertised its cocoa drink (certified kosher) on the front page of the British *Jewish Chronicle*, with an image of a boy carrying a gun alongside the caption "One of Britain's future hopes." The ad further explains "We are what we assimilate" and that "pure cocoa (like Fry's) is all goodness" (see Figure 7.3).

Another illustrative example of how advertisements rendered consumer products into political messages is a 1915 promotional campaign for the *De Reszke* cigarettes in the *Jewish Chronicle*. Although this cigarette brand was named after the renowned Polish tenor Jean De Reszke, the campaign not only proclaims *De Reszke* to be the world's best cigarette but, since *De Reszke* cigarettes are British-made, smoking them helps to maintain jobs for British workers. Calling to "smoke patriotically," the ad even suggests that since the managing director of the company is from Russia, the cigarette forms a kind of a British-Russian alliance and further supports the war effort.[5]

---

[5] By comparison, the Jewish-owned (Josef Garbáty-Rosenthal) Garbáty cigarette firm rebranded its cigarettes in an act of German patriotism. See, for example: www.museum-digital.de/berlin/index.php?t=objekt&oges=609 and http://objekte.jmber lin.de/object/jmb-obj-308540;jsessionid=53F718F0CDB6C55BB365AA70547FB37A. Likewise with Manoli cigarette products (firm owned by Jakob Mandelbaum), available at http://objekte.jmberlin.de/object/jmb-obj-308518.
See also Manoli in the Jewish press as a (Jewish) example of "deutsche(r) Tüchtigkeit"/Leistungsfähigkeit, available at http://sammlungen.ub.uni-frankfurt.de/cm/periodical/pa geview/2600606?query=Manoli.
Manoli also advertised in the German Jewish press, available at http://sammlungen.ub.uni-frankfurt.de/cm/periodical/pageview/2594601?query=Manoli.

FIGURE 7.3  Ad for Fry's Cocoa on the title page of the *Jewish Chronicle* showing a child running with a gun
From: *Jewish Chronicle* (October 15, 1915).

FIGURE 7.4 Dr. Oetker's Call to German Housewives to never buy English Products again
From: *Ost und West* vol. XIX, no. 11/12 (1919), 9.

In Germany, the food manufacturer Dr. Oetker urged German house-wives never again to buy English cornstarch and to purchase the much-improved German version instead. First published during the Great War, the Dr. Oetker advertisement continued to appear in both Jewish and non-Jewish newspapers during the postwar years.

In the turbulent years after the Great War, the politicization of the marketplace occurred more quickly in Germany than in most other European countries, as inflation and unemployment brought increased attention to public policies surrounding consumption. The automobile industry in particular made use of political issues to promote its products. A 1927 Mercedes-Benz advertisement prominently displayed the company's logo, alongside a line of Mercedes cars being driven across Germany, represented, significantly, with its pre–World War I borders (Figure 2.1). Conveying dynamism and modernity, this advertisement from the official newspaper of the central association of Jews in Germany also addresses political matters. By incorporating the lost territories in the east in its idealized map of Germany, the ad suggests that driving a Mercedes-Benz will retrieve Germany's sense of unity and lost pride. Such ads continued to appear in the Jewish press well into the 1930s, even after the rise of National Socialism, encouraging Jews to make the link between automobiles, modernity, and the *Volksgemeinschaft*.

Across the channel in 1926, the Empire Marketing Board was formed to persuade consumers to "buy Empire." It placed ads in the Jewish press, urging consumers to always "ask first for home produce" and to "ask next for the produce of the empire overseas."[6] In this case, Jews were addressed not as Jews but simply as citizens of the United Kingdom. But it is precisely the absence of any denotation of Jewish singularity in these materials that makes them so revealing of the multiple forms of consumer identity Jews could hold, more or less simultaneously.

The concept of citizenship is not solely based on the notion of belonging; it involves a strong sense of exclusion as well. Here too we can trace a strong correlation to consumption that, as Pierre Bourdieu compellingly postulated, operates according to the logic of distinction.[7] Perhaps the most extreme way to distinguish between groups of people is racial. From the 1890s, the use of racist motifs in commercial advertising became widespread. Most of these advertisements displayed people of color as subordinate to white Europeans. People of African descent were rendered ridiculous in these images, with deformed appearances. They were often frequently depicted in grotesque mimicry of their white "superiors," or in a position of extreme servitude, sometimes being enlightened by European civilization. Targeting exclusively white consumers, such advertisements rendered race their defining characteristic. Commodifying whiteness thus highlighted one basic commonality that all white consumers were able to share, regardless of their class, religion, region, or gender – their privileged position as white Europeans.

The advertising pages of the Jewish press were no exception. Here too are frequent examples of racist images and degrading depictions of colonized peoples. The Jewish recipients of these advertisements assumed the comfortably elite gaze of white Europeans. A case in point is an advertisement for a margarine called Palmin, a renowned German brand that is still found in German supermarkets today. Under the slogan "Fundamentally different in their nature and appearance! But yet when it comes to Palmin, still of one opinion!" this 1926 commercial presents the dairy-free butter as a kind of a cultural bridge between races. The use of the bridge metaphor is not accidental. By proclaiming that Palmin is used in kitchens all over the world, including in what is presented as "the homeland of the palm tree" – that is, Africa, as represented by the young

---

[6] The ad cited here is from the *Jewish Chronicle*, April 25, 1930. Further on the Empire Marketing Board and consumerism in Britain in general see: Stephen Constantine, *Buy & Build: The Advertising Posters of the Empire Marketing Board* (London: H.M.S.O., 1986), Matthew Hilton, *Consumerism in Twentieth-Century Britain: The Search for a Historical Movement* (Cambridge: Cambridge University press, 2003).

[7] Pierre Bourdieu, *Distinction: A Social Critique of the Judgment of Taste*, trans. Richard Nice (Cambridge, MA: Harvard University Press, 1984).

# Grundverschieden
## zwar in Wesen und Erscheinung! Aber, was *Palmin* betrifft, doch einer Meinung!

**Palmin in allen feinen Küchen der Welt**
.... natürlich auch im Heimatland der Palmen. — Palmin: jedem Jünger der Kochkunst als etwas vertraut, das durch nichts ersetzt werden kann.

Palmin — durch nichts zu ersetzen! — ist und bleibt nun einmal das beste Speisefett der Welt. Palmin in jeder Küche, das echte Palmin!

*Palmin* das naturreine COCOS-SPEISEFETT

FIGURE 7.5 Advertising for Palmin Margarine Containing Explicit Racial References. This ad was placed in both the religious Orthodox *Der Israelit* weekly and the liberal *CV-Zeitung* at the end of 1929. Palmin was also marketed with Hebrew letters as a kosher product
Here from: *Der Israelit* (December 5, 1929), 15.

black man – this advert nevertheless evokes an irrefutable division between two fundamentally different races.

`In the ad, a young white cook trainee points his finger at a young black man in Eastern clothing who folds his hands on his chest in what appears to be a gesture of gratitude. The two young men seem to look at each other, but despite their proximity there is an apparent distance between the two figures, alluding to the imbalance of power between them.[8] We can safely surmise that the addressees of the Palmin commercial gazed at the black figure from the standpoint of white Europeans. There is no reason to assume that this was any different for those ads that appeared in the Jewish press. Despite the intense discussions regarding the nature of Jewish difference, the use of such racist images in ads placed in the Jewish press suggests that Jews were at least sometimes encouraged to consider themselves members of the dominant white majority, rather than to see themselves as a subordinated racial group.[9] The fact that Palmin was marketed as a kosher product further supports this reading of the ad.

This reading is based on my subjective understanding of how contemporaries might have responded to such ads. There are undoubtedly other possible readings of such displays. Lacking any evidence of contemporary reactions to these commercials, we can only speculate about the potential responses to them. With this impediment in mind, I would like to move to a more document-based analysis of the interplay between modern consumerism and new forms of Jewish mass politics.

---

[8] For what is still a stimulating analysis of advertising images see Goffman, *Gender Advertisement*. Further on this see also: *Decoding Advertisements: Ideology and Meaning in Advertising* (London: Boyars, 1978); William Leiss, Stephen Kline and Sut Jhally, *Social Communication in Advertising: Persons, Products and Images of Well-Being* (Toronto: Methuen, 1986); Anne M. Cronin, *Adverting Myths: The Strange Half-Lives of Images and Commodities* (London: Routledge, 2004).

[9] On this latter discussion see, for example, Karen Brodkin, *How Jews Became White Folks: And What That Says about Race in America* (New Brunswick, NJ: Rutgers University Press, 1998); Sander L. Gilman, "Are Jews White?" in: Les Back and John Solomos (eds.), *Theories of Race and Racism: A Reader* (London: Routledge, 1999), 229–238.

# 8

## The Consumption of Jewish Politics

The pre-1933 advertising pages of the German Jewish press provide a few examples of the political awareness of advertisers as they sought to promote products to Jewish consumers. The effects are occasionally unintentionally humorous. A 1926 advertisement for a beverage designed to aid digestion urged readers to take it before the *Centralverein* general assembly (Figure 8.1). No evidence survives to indicate whether this potion did relieve the digestive problems of *Centralverein* members faced with the burgeoning antisemitism and economic travails of the late 1920s.

Even more presumptuous was a series of advertisements for a sparkling wine that challenged Jews in the increasingly desperate year of 1932, "Why don't you do anything against your pessimism? We would like to convey to you a formula that gives vibrancy, self-confidence and energy – all essential for a successful struggle against bad times. Drink a glass of champagne – a glass of Schönberger Cabinet – in its unmatched quality, maturity and digestibility an infallible remedy against the blackest pessimism!"[1] Similar claims were even more common in commercials for insurance companies (see Figure 8.3), who advertised intensively in the Jewish press during the dramatic period between the economic crash of 1929 and the rise to power of the National Socialists in January 1933.

---

[1] "Warum tun Sie nichts gegen Ihren Pessimismus? Wir wollen Ihnen ein Rezept verraten, das gibt Ihnen Beschwingtheit, Selbstbewußtsein und Energie – lauter unentbehrliche Dinge zum erfolgreichen Kampf gegen die Schlechten Zeiten. Trinken Sie einmal ein Glas Sekt – in seiner unerreichten Güte, Reife und Bekömmlichkeit ein unfehlbares Mittel gegen den schwärzesten Pessimismus!" here from *Der Schild* 11 (6) (1932), 47.

FIGURE 8.1 An Advertisement Calling Readers of the *CV-Zeitung* to Obtain
Boeson-Fruchtsaltz, before coming to the *Centralverein* General Assembly
From: *CV-Zeitung* (March 5, 1926), 149.

Advertisements that responded to current events or explicitly addressed members of certain Jewish organizations were just one of the ways in which consumerism and Jewish politics intersected. At the beginning of the 1930s, the *Centralverein* launched a campaign to create jobs for unemployed Jews. In the association's official newspaper, notices urged readers to "Fight the economic crisis! [and] Help reduce unemployment! Create work by buying!"[2] (*Kampf der Wirtschaftskrise! Hilf die Arbeitslosigkeit zuverringen! Gibt Arbeit, indem Du Kaufst!*). Such measures are another indication of the growing awareness in Jewish circles of the political and social significance of consumption.

### SELLING ZIONISM

A further, no less significant, aspect of the link between politics and consumption was the emergence of a commercialized politics at the beginning of the twentieth century. In her stimulating study *Selling Suffrage*, Margaret Finnegan demonstrates how consumerism became an integral part of the women's suffrage movement in America.[3] In the Jewish context Zionism was probably the most salient expression of this new form of politics, in which the commercial realm became a site of political discourse. As in the case of other political movements, Zionists maintained a Janus-faced relationship with the new consumer culture. Most Zionist thinkers associated consumption with both femininity and Diaspora Judaism, regarding it as an impediment for the "normalization" of Jewish society and even as a threat to Jewish endurance as a whole. As we saw earlier, Zionist denouncements of consumption as a culture of comfort and conformity that incited Jewish self-denial were consonant with mainstream cultural criticism of the first half of the twentieth century. Yet Zionism, like other political movements of the time, had to reconcile its utopian hopes for a new Jewish society that would transcend the petty materialism of Diaspora Jews with their more pragmatic need to operate in the consumer-oriented society of the present.

From the time of its inception, the Zionist movement emulated commercial marketing strategies, often turning political convictions into a product of emotional and spectacle manipulation. Promoting the Zionist project as

---

[2] Here from the *CV-Zeitung* (Beilage) (March 11, 1932), IV.

[3] Margaret Finnegan, *Selling Suffrage: Consumer Culture and Votes for Women* (New York: Columbia University Press, 1999). The following section owes many of its insights to Finnegan's stimulating study.

if it were a consumer good, Zionism sought to sway Jewish minds with the colorful techniques of advertising and merchandising.[4] This promotion effort featured iconic images of Zionist leaders such as Theodor Herzl on a variety of objects, including cigarette packs, machetes, plates, cups, carpets, flags, maps, postcards, and calendars.[5] Tapping into modern commercial aesthetics, these appeals turned on questions of display and good taste.[6] It is difficult to establish just how widespread these so-called Zionist commodities were, let alone to fully appreciate the diverse impact they had on Jews in different parts of the world. While such goods might have helped supporters to express their commitment to the Zionist cause, they could have just as easily run the risk of trivializing these ideas by displaying Zionism as nothing more than another philanthropic organization advocating for a Jewish territory merely as an asylum for persecuted Jews. From the point of view of the Zionist movement at least, such products were conceived not only as promotional lures and emblems of faith but also as a source of the revenue Zionists needed for their cause.

Beyond explicit Zionist commodities, special emphasis was also placed on goods from Palestine that, as Michael Berkowitz has suggested, "constructed a mythical Palestine homeland and national landscape in the mind of European Jewry."[7] "A buy Palestine goods" campaign is overdue, proclaimed the Anglo-Jewish weekly *The Jewish World* in 1927.[8] Suggesting the "Empire shopping campaign" as the model for promoting products from the Jewish settlement in Palestine, the article indicated that many items on the daily shopping lists of Jewish families could be

---

[4] On the use of modern marketing and advertising for Zionist propaganda see in the different issues of the *Bulletin of the Jewish National Fund Head Office* and from 1928 *Karnenu* (both in Hebrew).

[5] David Tartakover, *Herzl in Profile: Herzl's Image in the Applied Arts* (Tel Aviv: Museum of Tel Aviv, 1979). Further on the issue of Zionist nationalism and consumer goods in the context of Israeli consumer culture today see Anat First and Tamar Hermann, "Sweet Nationalism in Bitter Days: A Commercial Representation of Zionism," *Nations and Nationalism* 15 (3), 2009, 506–523.

[6] The question of display and good taste played a central role in this context, and the Zionist movement often engaged artists to design its objects. On this see, for example, "The artistic side of JNF propaganda" (in Hebrew), *Bulletin of the Jewish National Fund Head Office* 3 (1925), 34. For a more general discussion on the connections between Zionism and art see Dalia Manor, *Art in Zion: The Genesis of Modern National Art in Jewish Palestine* (London: Routledge, 2005).

[7] Michael Berkowitz, *Zionist Culture and West European Jewry before the First World War* (Chapel Hill: University of North Carolina Press, 1993), 119.

[8] Gaza, "Through a Woman's Eyes," *The Jewish World* (November 17, 1927), 6.

obtained from Palestine. All over Europe the Zionist movement organized bazaars and special exhibitions to raise awareness and display the variety of products from the Holy Land.

The Jewish National Fund (hereafter JNF) provided advice on how best to organize such events. Comparing the bazaar to a department store, one manual explained that "the longer visitors stay, the more they spend."[9] This implied that the bazaars and exhibitions not only were expected to display a variety of goods and activities but should also be aesthetically appealing so that visitors would not rush through the Zionist outlet without detection. While these events were organized according to strict commercial principles, the JNF also reminded its members to sell only Jewish-made products, thus conflating further the political and economic agenda of these events.[10] From 1929 to 1932, the JNF raised twenty thousand British pounds in this way. In some European countries, such as Germany, an effort was made to found a special chain of "Palestine shops" (*Palästina-Läden*) for marketing goods from the developing Jewish polity. Speaking at the Fifth Annual Dinner of the Harvard Menorah Society, May 5, 1913, the agronomist and Zionist activist Aaron Aaronsohn reported on Boris Schatz and his Bezalel art school in Jerusalem, who started to sell Bezalel works in different places around Europe. According to this account in Moscow all the grand dukes bought Bezalel rugs with Jewish emblems and symbols. It is further stated that the Wertheim department store in Berlin sold Bezalel rugs too and that Liberty & Co. was the exclusive seller in London.[11]

Unfortunately, the history of the Palestine shops as well as other retail outlets, such as department stores, dealing with goods from Palestine remains obscure. Almost nothing is known about their life spans, their owners or customers, and whether or not they were profitable. Given the prominence of the goods coming from Palestine in the advertising sections of the Jewish press, it appears that even if these promotional efforts did not always result in a purchase, they were important in exposing Jewish consumers to goods made in Palestine. Ranging from wine, oranges, and soap to cigarettes and carpets, the Palestine products were presented as centerpieces in the construction of modern notions of Jewishness,

---

[9] "Organizing the Bazaar," *Bulletin of the Jewish National Fund Head Office* 8 (1924), 88–90, here 89.

[10] This issue is discussed in correspondence on a planned Palestine exhibition in Berlin in 1925 between the JNF head office in Jerusalem and the Berlin branch, Central Zionist Archive (hereafter CZA), KKL 5, 96.

[11] *B'nai B'rith Messenger*, May 30, 1913, 3.

conveying a strong bond between commodity and community. To this end, the authenticity of the products became essential – as in the case of the Palwin (Palestine Wine) and Bozwin (the Beauty of Zion Wine) wines, two rival brands each claiming the honor of being the genuine product of Palestine (Figure 8.2).[12]

Occasionally, the Zionist movement placed promotional ads in Jewish newspapers that were designed to look like editorial articles. In 1927 the *Israelitische Familienblatt*, a Jewish weekly newspaper, published in its advertising pages a series of Zionist ads in the format of articles on Palestine. The *Familienblatt* was not happy with the Zionist attempt to blur the boundaries between the editorial and advertising sections of the newspapers.[13] It feared that this practice could compromise the weekly's impartial position and alienate readers. Nevertheless, the Zionist marketing experts persisted in placing such pseudoeditorial pieces in both Jewish and non-Jewish publications, which they considered to be the most effective way to reach readers who might not otherwise be exposed to Zionist publications.[14]

During the interwar period, advertisers started addressing Zionist consumers, some of which displayed consumption as a performative integral to the Zionist project. The JNF distributed children's games. A biblical doll's game costing two and a half Reichsmarks, paper cutout sheets called "Merchawiah" for seventy-five pfennig each, and "Palästina-Domino" for the same price are just a few examples of children's games that were usually marketed around the Jewish holidays.[15] A JNF advertisement urged: "Zionists! Make your children happy on the Hanukkah holiday! Give them Keren Kayemet (JNF) games!" (*Zionisten! Macht euren Kinder zu Chanukkah eine Freude! Schenkt Ihnen die Spiele des Keren Kajemeth!*).

In addition to the children's games, the JNF produced stories for children to endorse the work of the JNF and instill the habit of giving to the national cause at an early age. For this purpose, the JNF assigned the writer and educator Dov Kimchi to write a series of short stories promoting the Blue Box – the flagship of the JNF fund-raising enterprise – among

---

[12] Jonathan Fishburn, "A Mirror on History: Old Advertisements in the Jewish Chronicle," *Jewish Quarterly* (Autumn 2003), 89–92.

[13] On the dispute with the *Israelitische Familienblatt* in CZA, KH4/B/1860.

[14] On Zionist propaganda in the non-Jewish press see, for example, the report on JNF 1926 activities in Germany CZA, KKL 5, 98, page 13.

[15] For a short survey of these games see "Games as Tools," *Bulletin of the Jewish National Fund Head Office* 1 and 2 (1926), 9–10.

FIGURE 8.2 On the left Palwin an ad warning against imitations, claiming to be "the only genuine Palestine wines." On the right an ad for Bozwin promising "a thousand pounds guarantee of Palestinian purity, genuineness and Kashrut behind every bottle."
Both images are from *The Jewish Chronicle* of 1922 [September 22 p. 17, and October 20 p. 27].

children.[16] One of these tales narrates the story of "the silver coin and his little friend Annie." It begins like this:

My name is a silver coin; I glisten and glitter and I'm hot, too. A hot silver coin? Have you heard of a hot silver coin? I say again I'm a hot silver coin. Little Annie who is in the second class in the girls' school warmed me in her hands. For two whole days she warmed me.[17]

The story goes on to describe Annie's adventures with the silver coin until she finally decides to forgo all temptation to spend it on new toys or sweets and puts the coin in the Blue Box – the "redemption box," as it is referred to in the story. What I find most intriguing about this tale is that it is written from the perspective of the coin, thus providing a unique insight on the Zionist approach to money and the relationship between giving and spending. The coin is not depicted as an abstract and passive object, but as an active agent of the Zionist project. This pragmatic approach is one way the JNF attempted to respond to what could seem a substantial, and unbridgeable, distance between private and national capital in the Zionist discourse about money.[18] As a fund-raising organization, the JNF carefully, and cannily, presented itself as a vehicle through which the pursuit of personal profit could also benefit the national interest. The story ends with the coin reflecting on its life's trajectory:

Sometimes I think also of little Annie, especially when it's very hot. Then the sun pricks, and strokes but I don't run wild anymore like a fool let loose.
  I work. I work with the sweat of my brow. I force and push the shoots: Grow, Grow big![19]

In a recent book on the JNF as an agent of Zionist propaganda, Yoram Bar-Gal claimed that children were targeted in this way for purely educational and not political or fund-raising purposes.[20] I am not entirely convinced by this argument, not least because the JNF explicitly declared

---

[16] On the blue box and its significance for the Zionist movement see Yoram Bar Gal, "The Blue Box and JNF Propaganda Maps, 1930–1947," *Israel Studies* 8 (1) (2003), 1–19.

[17] This and other quotes from the story are taken from the manuscript of the English translation found in CZA, KKL5 2353, here page 1.

[18] Menachem Ussishkin, "National Capital and Private Capital" (in Hebrew), *Karnenu* (1933), 20.

[19] CZA, KKL5 2353, here page 7.

[20] Yoram Bar-Gal, *Propaganda and Zionist Education: The Jewish National Fund, 1924–1947* (Rochester: University of Rochester Press, 2003).

the latter to be one of the aims of such initiatives.[21] Rather than maintaining a clear distinction between education, propaganda, and fundraising, the intensive and somewhat aggressive targeting of children blurred the boundaries between these allegedly distinct realms. Moreover, the attempt to promote the Zionist message by approaching children coincided with contemporary marketing strategies that "discovered" children and adolescents as a consumer group in its own right.

The Zionist movement was thus fully in line with modern consumerism. But the commodification of the Zionist project was not due solely to the search for more effective persuasion methods or new ways to generate income for the movement. Having to struggle for a political voice, Zionists considered the commercial realm as an arena for recognition and endorsement. It offered new sites of enunciation and helped to neutralize fears and anxieties about the nature of the Zionist project. There was nothing subtle about this act of validation. Zionism celebrated its ties to – and recognition from – the marketplace. One fund-raising campaign was designed for the so-called golden quarter, the last three months of the year when both the Hanukah holidays and Christmas are celebrated. On an allocated day during that period, Jewish businesses were asked to donate 1 percent of their net earnings to the JNF. After successfully running a pilot trial of this fund-raising day in Poland and Galicia, the JNF published a report explaining how best to organize what was now dubbed "the Hebrew trader day."[22] Mobilizing Jewish and non-Jewish businesses to participate in this fund-raising venture was one factor in determining the success of the undertaking. Alerting consumers to just how significant their purchases were on this "trader's day" was the other. By bringing more customers to traders, the JNF also made the day more attractive to businesses. Success for the day also meant success, of course, for the JNF.

The JNF also called on contributing businesses to redecorate their display windows to reflect and promote the spirit of Zionism, with the possibility of a competition to select the best display of Zionist-inflected good taste. These fund-raising methods were not limited to the densely populated Jewish areas of Eastern Europe but were implemented in places

---

[21] See, for example, "Blue Box Stories for Children" (in Hebrew), *Bulletin of the Jewish National Fund Head Office* 3 (1926), 5.

[22] "The grand Hanukah Operation" (in Hebrew), *Bulletin of the Jewish National Fund Head Office* 1 (1926), 7–8.

such as London, New York, and Berlin.[23] In some places, including Amsterdam, local JNF branches ventured to hire display spaces in central locations of the city to exhibit Zionist information. The link between visibility in the public space and political agency cannot be overestimated in this context.

The area of tourism is another well-documented example of how Zionism harnessed commercial and political activities.[24] While tourism was considered an important source of revenue for the Zionist project, its political benefits were seen as equally, if not even more, important. The "Zionist Information Bureau for Tourists" was founded in 1925 to advance the tourist trade in Palestine. Business ties were established with all major travel companies such as Thomas Cook, Lloyd, and the German shipping company Hamburg-America-Line (HAPAG). These dealings did not only promote Palestine as a reputable tourist destination; they also provided credibility to Zionist efforts to shift the focus of Palestinian tourism from its prevailing image as a sacred Holy Land to that of a secular utopia for Jews. In the late 1920s, for example, passengers of the Lloyd Triestino shipping company could find Zionist information material aboard its vessels to Egypt and Palestine.[25] The bureau even managed to convince Thomas Cook, one of the world's biggest travel agencies, to include the Jewish settlement in Palestine alongside renowned historical and religious sights in its package tours.[26]

The advertisements, guidebooks, illustrated talks, and films on Palestine produced by the Zionist Tourist Bureau were not merely part

---

[23] Ibid., 8.

[24] Michael Berkowitz, *Western Jewry and the Zionist Project 1914–1933* (Cambridge: Cambridge University Press, 1997), 125–146; Kobi Cohen-Hattab, *Travelling the Land: Tourism in the Land of Israel during the Mandate Period, 1917 to 1948* (in Hebrew) (Jerusalem: Yad Ben-Zvi, 2006); Ibid., "Zionism, Tourism, and the Battle for Palestine: Tourism as a Political-Propaganda Tool," *Israel Studies* 9 (1) (2004), 63–85. For a contemporary perspective see Fritz Loewenstein, "Palästina-Touristik," *Palästina* 11 (3) (1928), 149–152; Julius Berger, "Die wirtschaftliche Bedeutung der Palästina-Touristik," *Palästina* 14 (7) (1931), 318–329; Björn Siegel, "*Visiting the Orient:*" *German-Speaking Jewry, Zionism and Early Forms of Tourism to the Middle East (1897–1914)*, Centre for German-Jewish Studies Research Paper No. 11, 2015.

[25] See in CZA, KH4/B/1866. Apparently with a special permit from the Zionist movement, young Jewish *Chaluzim* (pioneers) received a discount with the Lloyd Triestino ships going to Palestine. On this see the report on the changing travel tariffs on Lloyd's ships in *Palästina* 10 (3) (1927), 137.

[26] Cohen-Hattab, "Zionism, Tourism, and the Battle for Palestine," 75. A similar arrangement was also made with HAPAG in 1928, see "Erweiterung des Touristenprogramms der Hamburg-Amerika-Linie," *Palästina* 11 (11) (1928), 535.

of a well-oiled marketing campaign designed to lure tourists to the country. They also represented the Zionist approach to Palestine, which was challenged both by skeptical Diaspora Jews and by the Palestinian Arabs who claimed their right to the land. Given these contesting narratives, Zionist promotional efforts concentrate on sightseeing, not *Aliyah* (immigration). The marketing of Palestine did not aim to turn travelers into settlers, but it did aim to give voice to the Zionist claim for a Jewish state in Palestine. Informing the pragmatic objectives of the Zionist tourist program was not only *Realpolitik* but also marketplace conditions. Despite the growth in tourism to Palestine in the period before World War II, overseas travel remained a privilege of the leisure classes. The Zionist movement was thus compelled to develop imaginative new methods to make Palestine accessible to wider groups of people. A travel lottery was one option through which the Zionist movement sought to popularize the idea of visiting the land of Israel, with a tour to Palestine offered as a lucrative prize in raffles organized by the JNF.[27] Another intriguing promotional method was the board game "Travel the Land," which took players on a virtual tour of the Jewish homeland.[28] Even the insurance department of the JNF considered offering an all-inclusive twenty-five-day free tour of Palestine and Egypt as a bonus for every life insurance policyholder of $10,000 or more.[29] Insurance was another, rather unexpected, commercial activity through which the Zionist movement sought economic as well as cultural capital. Further research is needed on this topic before it will be possible to gauge the full scope of Zionist insurance activities. For now, it is sufficient to call attention to the celebrated ties between the Zionist movement and one of Europe's foremost insurance companies of the time, the Viennese *Phönix Lebensversicherung* (hereafter Phönix Life).

### INSURING ZION

Even before the Great War, Zionist leaders had earmarked the insurance business for special treatment. By setting up an insurance company, the Zionist movement sought to secure a solid source of income that would complement the fluctuating revenues from donations with which the

---

[27] A detailed plan for such a lottery in CZA, KKL 5, 97; also see in CZA, KKL 5/4874/2, and KKL 5/4874/2.

[28] "Travel the Land" (in Hebrew), *Karnenu* 4 (1929), 60, as well as in CZA, KKL 5, 2387.

[29] CZA, A130/116 Phoenix.

movement normally funded its undertakings. The idea was to use the capital accumulated by the insurance business as a kind of "venture capital fund" for developing the Jewish polity in Palestine. Furthermore, insurance schemes offered the chance to bind people to the Zionist movement who might be unmoved by abstract ideals alone. The use of insurance for marketing purposes was not uncommon at the beginning of the twentieth century. A well-documented example is the so-called insurance newspaper: these were periodicals that offered different kinds of insurance as a benefit to their subscribers.[30] For the Zionist movement, insurance wasn't only a promotional tool but a particularly suitable marketing method for Jews.

A variety of preconceptions about Jews and their special affinity for insurance informed the insurance scheme, some of which conflicted with the reformist aspirations of the Zionist movement. Perhaps more than any other commercial activity, insurance was associated with such quintessential middle-class values as security, saving, and family. It corresponded to a bourgeois lifestyle that a number of Zionist thinkers considered assimilationist and even decadent. Even more prominent was Zionist denunciation of the Jewish concentration in commerce and other professions that purportedly comprised the so-called *Luft* economy of Diaspora Jewry. Yet from a business point of view these low-risk commercial occupations were precisely what made Jews such an attractive target group for the modern insurance business.

The Zionist movement celebrated the phenomenal contribution of Jews to the evolution of the insurance industry both as entrepreneurs and as consumers.[31] The centrality of the family in Jewish life as well as the history of Jewish persecution, they suggested, had historically made Jews more receptive to the idea of insurance. "The Jew," one Zionist publication asserted, "with his circumspection (*Vorbedachtsamkeit*) and his pronounced sense of family was always anxious to protect his family against

---

[30] On this practice see Reuveni, *Reading Germany*, 117–122.

[31] We have evidence on the involvement in and the use of different kinds of insurance by Jewish merchants in particular, since the Early Middle Ages: Julius Graf, "Anteil der Juden an der Entwicklung der Versicherung: Vortrag," *Dr. Bloch's Österreichische Wochenschrift* 29 (1912), no. 50, 843–845, no. 51, 863–865, no. 52, 879–881; Menachem Slae, *Insurance in the Halachah: A Legal-Historical Study Based upon the Response Literature and other Jewish Legal Sources* (Tel Aviv: Israel Insurance Association, 1982); Nachum Gross, Salo Wittmayer Baron, and Arcadius Kahan (eds.), *Economic History of the Jews* (New York: Schocken, 1975); Gerald D. Feldman, *Allianz and the German Insurance Business, 1933–1945* (Cambridge: Cambridge University Press, 2001).

troublesome times."[32] Insurance, it was thus postulated, enabled a feeling of security in what was otherwise, and particularly for Jews, a precarious world. Another promotional publication boldly proclaimed, "experience has shown that insurance companies earn more from Jews who, due to their moderate lifestyle, live longer and are more accurate with their policy payments."[33]

All the same, without adequate capital or the administrative know-how, the plan to create a Zionist insurance company was ultimately unsuccessful and had to be abandoned. Yet the idea to use the insurance business to further the Zionist project remained alive. Instead of founding its own insurance outlet, the Zionist movement sought to forge an alliance with an established insurance company that could provide the capital, bureaucratic apparatus and the business standing required for the successful realization of such an undertaking. Negotiations were held with several companies, including the Austrian Phönix Life until eventually an agreement was signed in 1911 with the Swiss *Basler* insurance company. The Zionist movement was to receive a special commission for every Jewish customer the company insured. Expectations were high, but so too was the disappointment. Soon enough it became apparent that revenues for the Zionist movement would be much lower than those initially anticipated. Both the advent of the Great War and the fact that *Basler* insurance operated in only a few West European countries contributed to the failure of this enterprise.

Following the war, the JNF took charge of the Zionist insurance idea, seeking new partners to increase the global profile of the fundraising operation. It is not entirely clear how and when exactly talks with the Viennese Phönix Life resumed. Founded in 1882, Phönix Life was a distinguished brand with branches in over a dozen countries, many of them in densely populated Jewish areas of Central and Eastern Europe. In addition, approximately 70 percent of its employees were Jews, including the company's agile managing director Wilhelm Berliner, who, due to his mysterious walks, extraordinary talents, and short stature, came to be known as the "Napoleon of the insurance industry."

---

[32] See the manuscript: "Der jüdische Nationalfonds und die Lebensversicherung," CZA, KKl 5/1510 Phönix contract. Parts of this manuscript were published under the same title in the *Jüdische Rundschau* (July 14, 1925), 482.

[33] "The Insurance Business of the Jewish National Fund" (in Hebrew), *Karnenu*, 4 (1927), 73.

There is no reason to believe that Phönix Life was motivated by ideology, nor that its parent company, Berliner, had an interest in the Zionist movement. As a matter of fact, the company appeared equally keen to establish similar links with other Jewish organizations, some of which were forthrightly anti-Zionist, such as the Reich Federation of Jewish Front Soldiers (RJF), the orthodox Agudat Israel, and the German nationalist *Centralverein*.[34] Here we get a sense of a Jewish public sphere that transcended political animosities and fractions.

Seeking to strengthen its positions in the Jewish market, Phönix Life saw the engagement with the JNF as a business opportunity, not a political act. With this joint venture it sought to expand its activities in Europe as well as develop new markets in the Middle East. Interestingly, it was this entrepreneurial spirit and expansion course that made Phönix Life so alluring to the Zionist movement. To be sure, not all Zionists raved about the JNF insurance scheme. Some found it morally distasteful to conflate a private commercial endeavor, with an institution aiming to redeem the soil of Palestine as the inalienable property of the Jewish People. Such juxtapositions, it was argued, could create serious conflicts of interest and would undermine Zionists' claim to represent the Jewish national interest. Others argued that such an agreement would reduce the JNF to nothing more than an agent for the commercial interests of big corporations.[35] The JNF dismissed all these allegations, maintaining instead that the insurance business would not only boost the Zionist project but would lay the foundation for a worldwide Jewish insurance company with its center in Palestine, an idea promulgated by no one other than Theodor Herzl, the visionary of the Jewish state.[36]

After intensive negotiations, a four-year contract between Phönix Life and the JNF was finally sealed on January 1, 1925. According to this agreement Phönix Life guaranteed favorable terms and lower rates to every customer who signed up in association with the JNF.

---

[34] From the companies promotional material we learn that Phönix Life has exclusive agreements with the following Jewish organizations: the JNF (Zionists); the Jewish Women's Association of Germany, JFB (Jewish nationalist); and the Reich Federation of Jewish Front Soldiers, RJF (German Jewish nationalist). Beyond the organizations stated in the advertisements Phönix Life also had different kinds of agreements with the orthodox Agudat Israel, and the German nationalist *Centralverein*.

[35] For this criticism see, for example, the letter from the American JNF branch in New York from March 19, 1926 in CZA, KKL 1511.

[36] See Herzl's diaries, *Theodor Herzl Tagebücher, 1895–1904* (Berlin: Jüdischer Verlag, 1922), 94.

The JNF, for its part, undertook to promote Phönix Life products in all regions in which Phönix Life was authorized to do business.[37] For this purpose the JNF set up a special insurance department in Jerusalem with branches in all countries included in the contract at that time. In its publications, the JNF insurance department emphasized that as an insurance agency it operated according to strict commercial principles. In return, Phönix Life agreed to pay special annual commissions to the JNF of approximately 1 percent or no less than five thousand British pounds every year.[38] The contract also stipulated that Phönix Life would invest up to two-thirds of the income it earned from the agreement within Palestine.

The Zionist press celebrated the arrangement with Phönix Life as a major achievement that would increase the "national capital" and motivate more Zionists to obtain insurance, which was in itself considered to be an "act of national, as well as economic, value."[39] A major marketing campaign was launched to advance the JNF insurance program. Promotional articles in the Jewish press, advertisements, and insurance agents were sent off to persuade would-be customers, most of them Jews, to purchase JNF insurance. By 1933 about six hundred agents worked for the JNF insurance departments, administering a total of sixty-six thousand policies. This brought the Zionist movement an average of seven thousand pounds annually.[40] Although this amount comprised roughly 1 percent of the total JNF revenue, the agreement with Phönix Life was still considered a major success. Ties between the two parties further strengthened when Phönix Life helped fund the National Institutes compound in Jerusalem at the end of the 1920s, which became the official seat of the Jewish Agency for Israel, the JNF, and Keren Hayesod (the

---

[37] At the time when the contract was signed in 1925 this commitment applied to the following countries: Austria, Czechoslovakia, France, Hungary, Poland, Yugoslavia, Rumania, Italy, Germany, Belgium, Holland, Bulgaria, Greece, and former territories of the Ottoman Empire. The Baltic countries as well as Spain are further countries considered for future expansion. Explicitly excluded from the agreement are England and North America, where *Phönix Life* was not permitted to operate. "The contract with Phönix Life," CZA, KKl 5/1511.

[38] The annual commission was divided between the local branches that received one and a half percent of the total insurance sum, or no less than 3,500 English Pounds, and the head insurance office in Jerusalem that got 1 percent of the overall insurance sum, or no less than 1,500 English Pounds.

[39] Moshe Ungerfeld "A New Source of Income for the Jewish National Fund" (in Hebrew), *Davar* (December 31, 1926), 5.

[40] Some of these figures were also published in the Zionist press, for example, in the daily *Davar*, "From the Insurance World" (in Hebrew), *Davar* (October 18, 1933).

(a)

**Nach einer sachlichen Prüfung**

wird jeder Zionist seine Versicherungen

## nur dem Phönix

geben.

Nur der Phönix kann Ihnen auf Grund des
Empfehlungsvertrages mit dem Keren Kajemeth
folgende Vorteile bieten:

**Sie ersparen**
die Hälfte der sonst üblichen Zu-
schläge für Ratenzahlungen.

**Sie ersparen**
die Hälfte der Aufnahmegebühr.

**Sie ersparen**
die Zusatzprämie für Einschluß der
Vollinvalidität.

**Sie ersparen**
wesentliche Beträge, weil die Tarife
des Phönix sehr billig sind.

**Sie fördern**
die Versicherungsaktion des Keren
Kajemeth, durch die sehr erhebliche
Beträge dem Bodenkauf in Palästina
zugeflossen sind.

**Nur 50,52 Mark monatlich für 20000 Mark**
kostet die Versicherung für einen 32 jährigen,
zahlbar nach dem Tode bzw. im 60. Lebensjahre.

*Wenden Sie sich
vor jedem Versicherungsabschluß an die*

**VERSICHERUNGSABTEILUNG
DES KEREN KAJEMETH**
**BERLIN W 15, MEINEKESTRASSE 10**
Bismarck 3181-3182

(b)

FIGURE 8.3 On the left advertisement of the JNF insurance office in Germany
asserting "after substantial examination every Zionist would take insurance
coverage from *Phönix.*" The ad further lists the various advantages provided by
this agreement to Zionist costumers. It also indicates that by purchasing JNF
insurance, policyholders support the acquisition of land in Palestine
From: *Jüdische Rundschau* (February 26, 1929), 101. On the right a 1933 ad
stating "Difficult times for German Jews! Secure your future with Phönix Life
insurance." *Jüdische Rundschau* (March 3, 1933), 90.

Foundation Fund). For Phönix Life too, the relationship with the JNF
steadily grew in importance, and by the early 1930s it accounted for
nearly 20 percent of the company's total revenue. This explains why the
two parties agreed to renew their contract in 1929, on terms that were
even more favorable for the JNF.

Plans were now made to further develop the JNF insurance department. This included establishing links with other insurance companies as well as extending the work of the JNF insurance program beyond the Jewish market. But Phönix Life was not happy to learn about the JNF's expansion plans. In a letter sent to the director of Phönix Life in Germany, the JNF complained about director Wilhelm Berliner, who allegedly described the JNF in a speech at the end of 1932 and "in the presence of a partly Aryan audience" as a malignant growth (*Auswucherung*) in Phönix Life operations.[41] In another confidential account, Berliner was quoted as saying that even without the agreement with the JNF, Phönix Life would have retained its leading position in the Jewish market and that the ties with Zionism compromised the company's position among non-Jews.[42] Some Zionists were even concerned that Berliner might use the rise of National Socialism as a pretext to dissociate Phönix Life from the Zionist movement. But these fears were ungrounded. Phönix Life had no desire to terminate its affiliation with the JNF, and, in 1933, the two parties agreed to extend their relationship to the end of 1944. Later that year, the achievements of the JNF insurance program were commended with a special resolution at the eighteenth Zionist Congress in Prague. In light of the rise of National Socialism and the distressing economic situation in Palestine, Zionists were exhorted to "unconditionally support this work, and help to refine and sustain its unity."[43] By the end of 1933, the Zionist press reported triumphantly that the agreement with Phönix Life had been extended proof, it claimed, that even the economic upheavals of the last decade had not seriously affected the financial situation of the company.[44] Little did the writers realize that the end of the bond between the Zionist movement and Phönix Life was rapidly approaching.

Contrary to what was reported in the press, the economic crash of 1929, as well as the advance of fascism in Europe, hit the Viennese insurance company hard. But even specialists who were well aware of Phönix Life's financial difficulties did not anticipate its sudden and dramatic collapse. On February 18, 1936, fifty-four-year old Wilhelm Berliner passed away, under what some claimed were suspicious circumstances. Shortly after his sudden death, lists of all the organizations and individuals he illicitly funded were discovered. They revealed that Berliner had been at the center of

---

[41] See CZA, A 130/22.   [42] Ibid.
[43] Menachem Ussishkin, "Referat über KKL," *Stenographische Protokolle der Verhandlungen der Zionisten-Kongresse* (Vienna: Fiba-Verlag, 1934), 208.
[44] See, for example, "From the Insurance World" *Davar* [in Hebrew] (September 18, 1933), 4.

a huge network of corruption, which tainted some of the pillars of Austrian society.[45] The exposure of Berliner's business practices and the company's true, and disastrous, financial situation spurred a major international crisis involving many countries, banks, insurance agencies, and policyholders across and even beyond Europe. Contemporaries described the scandal as no less than "another bomb for the peace of Europe."[46] The crash of Phönix Life shook the Zionist movement to the core. It not only caused economic difficulties of serious proportions but also robbed many Jews of their trust in Zionism during a time of extreme political turbulence in Europe and in Palestine, where the emerging Jewish polity was now challenged by the Great Arab Revolt beginning in April 1936.

About what it called the "Phönix catastrophe," the JNF urged its agents not to deceive themselves. On all counts, the JNF admitted the Phönix crash "is a *grave blow* to Jewish interests" (emphasis in original).[47] In the attempt to win back the confidence of the Jewish public, the Zionist press tried to distance Zionism from the scandal. It condemned Berliner's deceptive business practices and framed the episode as an antisemitic scam, further indication, if there was such a need, of the hopeless situation of Jews in Europe.[48] For policyholders in Palestine, arrangements were made with local insurance companies to renew the policies and cover at least some of the losses caused by the liquidation of Phönix

---

[45] According to *Time* magazine "with magnificent liberality [Berliner] bribed every political group that might possibly make things difficult for him," including the Austrian Nazi party. *Time* even provided the following list of organizations allegedly sponsored over the years by Berliner: the Jewish National Fund 500,000 schillings ($93,500); the Austrian Nazis 494,000 ($92,400); the Peasants' Union 182,000 ($34,000); the Heimwehr 95,000 ($17,800); the Association of Austrian Legitimists (Monarchists) 9,000 ($1,700); the Socialist Technicians' Trade Union 3,000 ($560); Schuschnigg's Catholic Ostmarkische Sturmscharen 2,000 ($375). From "Austria: Scandalous Phönix-Wien," *Time* (May 11, 1936). On the affair see also Isabella Ackerl, "Der Phönix-Skandal," in: Ludwig Jedlicka and Rudolf Neck (eds.), *Das Juliabkommen von 1936. Vorgeschichte, Hintergründe und Folgen. Protokoll des Symposiums in Wien am 10. und 11. Juni 1976* (Vienna: Oldenbourg, 1977), 241–279; Gerald D. Feldman, "Insurance Company Collapses in the World Economic Crisis. The Interwar Depression," in: Harold James (ed.), *The Interwar Depression in an International Context* (Munich: Oldenbourg, 2002), 57–75.

[46] "Austria: Ph," *Time* magazine XXVII (16) (April 20, 1936).

[47] "An die Landesstellen des Keren Kayemet Leisrael," CZA, S53/1845.

[48] For the Zionist press response see, for example, "Phönix und die jüdischer Nationalfond," *Die Neue Welt* (May 1, 1936), 1–2; "Die Phönix und die Zionisten," *Die Stimme* (April 6, 1936), as well as *Die Stimme* (May 1, 1936); Eliyahu Monschik, "To Phönix Policyholders in Eretz Israel and the Zionist institutions" (in Hebrew), *Davar* (May 20, 1936), 3; "Der Phönix Zusammenbruch," *Jüdische Rundschau* (April 17, 1936), 4.

Life. Despite all these efforts, the JNF insurance program could not regain its pre-1936 status. In addition to the extreme political turbulence of the period, the development of an independent insurance industry in Palestine further rendered the JNF indemnity venture obsolete. Yet after the war, the insurance idea continued to play a prominent role for Zionism. In the wake of the Holocaust, the Zionist project, and, after 1948, the State of Israel, came to seem like an investment itself, akin to an insurance policy, which guaranteed safe haven for Jews seeking to escape from all kinds of upheavals, as well as to maintain their Jewish identity.

These last comments bring me back to Hannah Arendt's implied association between modern consumerism and Jewish politics, with which I commenced this exploration. From Arendt's standpoint, the propensity of Zionist leaders to conflate the political and commercial realms is an indication of how a victimized group loses the capacity to act effectively in the political sphere. Not surprisingly, recent so-called post-Zionist critiques of Jewish nationalism, which associate consumerism with a culture of escapism, are sympathetic to Arendt's critique of Zionism. But the collapse of the distinction between political and commercial longings, as revealed by the relationship between the JNF and Phönix Life described in this chapter, can engender a new kind of agency and political identity in a victimized group. Notwithstanding the obvious differences between these readings, both approaches convey the emergence of mass culture and consumerism as a new framework for discussing modern Jewish politics.

\* \* \*

PART III

# HOMO JUDAICUS CONSUMENS

As discussed in Parts I and II, between roughly 1900 and 1933 Jews began to be considered a discrete group of consumers. Three main reasons account for the creation of a specifically Jewish consumer identity. The first and most elementary was the way in which modern consumer culture began to promote different notions of belonging as a means of increasing, and targeting, consumption. Second, the rise of nationalism and modern antisemitism fomented the perception of Jews as a distinct group of consumers, making Jewishness an "issue" in the marketplace. And, finally, Jewish politics of identity provided a further inspiration for consolidating a notion of a distinct Jewish consumer culture. How did Jews themselves conceive and enact Jewishness as consumers and in what ways, if at all, could certain consumer practices be identified as "Jewish"? In Part III, I will scrutinize Jewish consumer experiences to better understand the interaction of material culture and identity, with a particular focus on how consumer choices and practices helped constitute Jewishness.

The discussion will be broken into four chapters, which juxtapose Jewish consumer culture with the ways Jews were imagined and acted as consumers. Chapter 9 will look at different consumer practices, suggesting that what distinguished Jewish consumption was not how or what goods Jews acquired but why and where they obtained them. Consumer choices, I will argue, constituted a type of "cultural positioning." Based on diaries, memories, and lists of household possessions, Chapters 10 and 11 will explore the varied meanings that belongings held for their Jewish owners. This discussion is grounded in Walter Benjamin's observations on the significance of domestic space for the modern city dweller. According to Benjamin, "[L]iving (*wohnen*) means leaving traces."[1] Although it is difficult to precisely identify a distinct Jewish taste or to establish to what extent Jewishness informed consumer choice, at least those who debated over the question of Jewish difference acknowledged a world of Jewish goods. This becomes even more evident in Chapter 12, which returns to the question of how Jews were perceived as consumers. Here I discuss the relationship between Jewishness, material culture, and gender issues, as well as anxieties over the advance of modern consumer culture and its effects on Jewish endurance and assimilation. Taken together these chapters underline the close interaction between Jewish identity and modernity. No one has formulated the nature of this relationship better than the sociologist Zygmunt Bauman, who characterizes modernity as a force making "all being contingent, and thus a 'problem,' a 'project,' and a 'task.'"[2] In the modern period, Bauman argues that identity is lifted to a level of awareness that transforms it into "an objective of self-reflexive activity, an object of, simultaneously, individual concern and specialized institutional service."[3] This description applies to the question of Jewish identity, which in modern times became a matter of personal choice, a form of cultural positioning that also determined the perception and meaning of material goods and consumer experiences. Consumption, I argue, played a vital role in constituting different notions of Jewishness. These notions were never fixed but, as Rachel Rich notes about bourgeois identities, "were constantly negotiated and interpreted in a range of situations and locations which shaped and punctuated daily life."[4]

---

[1] This is an adjusted translation from Walter Benjamin, *The Arcades Project* (Cambridge, MA: Harvard University Press, 1999), 9. The original quote is also available at www .textlog.de/benjamin-paris-hauptstadt.html.

[2] Quotation from Leora Auslander, "'Jewish Taste?' Jews and the Aesthetics of Everyday Life in Paris and Berlin, 1920–1942," in: Rudi Koshar (ed.), *History of Leisure* (Oxford: Berg Publishers, 2002), 359.

[3] Ibid. Further on this see Charles Taylor, *Sources of the Self: The Making of the Modern Identity* (Cambridge: Cambridge University Press, 1992).

[4] Rachel Rich, *Bourgeois Consumption: Food, Space and Identity in London and Paris, 1850–1916* (Manchester: Manchester University Press, 2011), 17.

# 9

## The Cost of Being Jewish

Being Jewish requires consumption. By dint of its dietary requirements, dress prescriptions, and special ritual objects, Judaism necessarily constrains and directs the consumer practices of its adherents. Even clothing can be deemed "kosher" or "nonkosher," with biblical regulations forbidding Jews from wearing fabric made of linen and wool sewn together. In the early twentieth century, advertisements for approved clothing occasionally appeared in the Orthodox Jewish press, promising kosher garments on demand (Figure 9.1).[1]

Dietary regulations are an even more obvious example of the nexus between consumption and Judaism. Pork and shellfish are *tryfa*, that is, impure, and can never be made kosher, or suitable, for Jewish consumption, while even permissible animals must be slaughtered in strictly prescribed ways. It is also prohibited to mix dairy and meat, and foods for Passover holidays generally require a special Kosher-for-Passover certification.

In the mid-nineteenth century, as modern food production became increasingly complex, the question of whether mass-produced food was suitable for Jewish consumption became ever more challenging. Efforts to standardize the kosher status of manufactured products such as margarine, olive oil, toothpaste, soap, cigarettes, and medicaments were contentious. Debates over these rulings revealed that maintaining a Jewish way of life was not merely a matter of religious confession or ethnic affiliation. It was also a matter of consumption, as Jews had to learn to actively

---

[1] For further examples see Leonard Greenspoon (ed.), *Fashioning Jews: Clothing, Culture, and Commerce* (Ashland: Purdue University Press, 2013).

FIGURE 9.1 "Men, boys and Bar Mitzvah Cloths in strict Kosher-fashioning."
An Advert of the Frankfurt Branch of the Carsch Department Store
From: *Der Israelit* (April 8, 1925), 7.

choose, or shun, particular goods. Being Jewish meant becoming a newly aware consumer.[2]

Jews who followed dietary and dress codes relied on an infrastructure of merchants who could supply them with what they needed. They also needed sufficient money to purchase the goods required to live according to Jewish tradition. Given the deep connections between Jewish identity and expenditure, it should come as no surprise that general economic

[2] For an overview of some of these debates in Eastern Europe see Roni Be'er Marx, *Between Seclusion and Adaptation: The Newspaper HaLevanon and East European Orthodox Society's Facing up to Modern Challenges*, PhD. Diss. Hebrew University of Jerusalem, 2011, 87–91. On the margarine question, see Michael Cahn and Butter Verfälschung, *Eine Warnung für jeden jüdischen Haushalt* (Frankfurt a.M.: J. Kauffmann, 1891); for lists of permissible medicaments during the Passover holiday see the publications of the Vereinigung traditionell-gesetzes treuer Rabbiner Deutschlands, *Arzeinverordnungsvorschläge für Pessach* (Berlin: Lebensmittel-Kommission, 1927/1928).

trends bore heavily on the choice to maintain a Jewish life.[3] Especially in periods of economic crisis, serious doubts were often raised about whether individual Jews could maintain their Jewish identity or even whether Jewish institutions would be able to endure. This was certainly the case both in America during the Great Depression and in Europe between the two world wars.[4] In the period before the Great War, the notion of the declining German Jews was fiercely debated, and by the mid-1920s, there were widespread fears that the Jewish middle class would dissolve as a result of the economic fallout of the Great War. Among other things, the war and its economic ramifications were seen as a Jewish catastrophe. In the Jewish press at the time it was bluntly stated that "no other people have suffered from the war and its consequences more than the Jews."[5] In particular, inflation was considered to have delivered an especially hard blow to Jews, since its ill effects were felt most severely in commerce and the free professions. "Being Jewish has never been easy, least of all in times of economic adversity," admitted Ludwig Hollandär (1877–1936), president of the *Centralverein* and chief editor of the *CV-Zeitung*.[6]

Across the Atlantic, anxieties about the economic viability of Jewish life sometimes took violent forms. The so-called kosher meat riots erupted in May 1902 when butchers in New York City closed their shops in protest after packers raised the price of kosher meat from 12 to 18 cents per pound. It was mainly Jewish women who took to the streets in spontaneous outrage at the high prices. The protest started on the Lower East Side before spreading among Jews further uptown. It passed

---

[3] Martin Liepach, *Das Wahlverhalten der jüdischen Bevölkerung: zur politischen Orientierung in der Weimarer Republik* (Tübingen: J.C.B. Mohr, 1996), 73–95.

[4] Beth S. Wenger, *New York Jews and the Great Depression: Uncertain Promise* (New Haven: Yale University Press, 1996). For the central European case see Jacob Lestschinsky, *Der wirtschaftliche Zusammenbruch der Juden in Deutschlnad und Polen* (Paris: Exekutive-Komitee für den jüdischen Weltkongress, 1936); Felix A. Theilhaber, *Der Untergang der deutschen Juden: Eine volkswirtschaftliche Studie* (Berlin: Jüdische Verlag, 1911); Jillius Hirsch, "Die Wirtschaftliche Zukunft der Ostjuden," *Neue Juedische Monatshefte* 3 (16) (1919), 330–340.

[5] On the debate around Theilhaben study see John Efron, *Defenders of the Race: Jewish Doctors and Race Science in Fin-de-Siècle Europe* (New Haven: Yale University Press, 1994), 154. The quotation is from Kurt Zielenziger, "Der Untergang der jüdischen Mittelstandes," *CV-Zeitung* (November 13, 1925), 729–730. This article was mentioned in other Jewish newspapers of the time, for example, *Die Jüdische Frau* 1 (14) (1925), 9.

[6] Ludwig Hollandär, "Warum sind und bleiben wir Juden?" *CV-Zeitung* (December 16, 1932), 513. This article was reprinted in several local community newspapers in Germany too.

from there to Brooklyn and Newark and even reached Boston.[7] In several places crowds of up to a thousand people assembled, calling "Down with the butchers!" "We'll have our rights!," and "Don't buy from them!"[8]

On the Lower East Side, Jews demanded lower prices. Some even called for a rabbi to fix for the price of meat for the entire New York Jewish community.[9] The press reported that women were seen attacking store-owners and those who dared to shop at the kosher butchers during the protest. In some cases, women seized meat that had been purchased and threw it into the street. Depicting the protesters as a "dangerous class" of "very ignorant" women who "mostly speak a foreign language," a *New York Times* editorial called for a swift and resolute police repression of the protest. The article explained that harsh measures were required since rioters "do not understand the duties or the rights of Americans. They have no inbred or acquired respect for law and order as the basis of the life of the society into which they have come ... The instant they take the law into their own hands ... they should be handled in a way that they can understand and cannot forget. Let the blows fall instantly and effectively."[10]

It is a testament to the strong emotion behind the protests that nearly four hundred policemen were needed to quell the riots, which lasted over a week.

The scale and intensity of these protests, which continued sporadically until the end of the 1930s, indicates just how sensitive eastern European Jews in America were to the price of kosher meat. The historian Paula Hyman uses these riots to offer a revised history of immigrant culture, arguing that Orthodox, socialist, anarchist, and Zionists should no longer be seen as antagonists but as fellow immigrants joined by a common set of cultural practices.[11] Hyman sees the demand for kosher meat as evidence of the ties between different Jewish groups and an expression of Jewish resilience despite ideological divides. Historian Herbert Gutman, on the

---

[7] On the Boston riots see Jack Tager, *Boston Riots: Three Centuries of Social Violence* (Boston: Northeastern University Press, 2001), 146–147.

[8] *New York Times* (May 18, 1902).

[9] Calls to regulate prices for "Jewish products" were not uncommon. One case in point is the struggle around the prices of the *Ethrog* (Citron) at the end of the nineteenth century in Eastern Europe. On this debate see Be'er Marx, *Between Seclusion and Adaptation*, 95–99.

[10] Quoted in Herbert G. Gutman, "Work, Culture, and Society in Industrializing America, 1815–1919," *American Historical Review* 78 (3) (1973), 576.

[11] Paula E. Hyman, "Immigrant Women and Consumer Protest: The New York Kosher Meat Boycott of 1902," *American Jewish History* 70 (1) (1980), 102.

other hand, considers the kosher meat riots as a late manifestation of a preindustrial antipathy to modernization and sensitivity to traditional values. He cites the demands made by some protesters that rabbis fix the price of kosher meat, as they had in the *shtetls* of the old world, as evidence that premodern notions of a "just price" economy fueled the food riots.[12]

But there is more to be said here. In modern times when being Jewish gradually became a matter of personal choice, growing numbers of Jews appeared to fail to see either the attraction or economic rationale of living a fully Jewish life. Jewish community leaders thus felt called to take action in order to uphold a Jewish sense of belonging. This involved the creation of varied networks of Jewish societies – from welfare organizations, education, to clubs and recreation activities – with the aim of reengaging Jews who had forsaken an active Jewish life. Just how much it cost in economic terms to participate in Jewish life played a crucial role in this endeavor. Widespread concerns about the benefits of community membership in Bremen at the end of the 1920s, for example, led the Jewish community to issue a list of over thirty different amenities available to members in return for their fees.[13] Price was not always an obstacle, to be sure, but one cannot overestimate the significance of the economic costs of Jewish living for both Jewish communities and individual Jews seeking to practice in one form or another their Jewishness.

Jewish families have always been expected to pay a premium in order to purchase kosher food. According to a 2002 survey prepared for the *American Jewish Committee*, for example, American Jewish families require $25,000 to $35,000 a year of discretionary income to be able to participate in a Jewish way of life, including membership of synagogues and Jewish centers, sending their children to Jewish schools, making federation donations as well as trips to Israel, and eating kosher.[14] Such capital is often beyond the reach of even upper-middle-class Jewish families. No wonder that so many families in America, and elsewhere, find it difficult to afford to live a traditional Jewish life today. Community leaders express concerns that the high cost of Jewish living might

---

[12] Gutman, "Work, Culture, and Society," 576–577.

[13] "Was leistet die Gemeinde für mienen Beitrag," *Jüdisches Gemeindeblatt Bremen* 3 (19) (1931). On German Jewish community life more generally, see "German Jewry. III. The Economic Position: Communal Organization," *Jewish Chronicle*, no. 114 (June 1930).

[14] Gerald Bubis, *The Costs of Jewish Living* (New York: American Jewish Committee, 2002).

accelerate "checkout" rates among Jews, turning organized Jewish life into a status symbol of the privileged J/few.

But why did Jewish life become so expensive? Sociologist Barry Kosmin suggests that the problem is more than just economic. According to him, it reflects a fundamental shift in Jewish values, which he terms "embourgeoisement." Kosmin notes that many things that are today perceived as being Jewish, such as lavish synagogues and community centers, and ostentatious bar and bat mitzvah celebrations, are simply manifestations of materialistic behavior and have no intrinsic affiliation with Judaism.[15] He posits instead a negative correlation between material comfort and Jewish living and argues that although in earlier periods Jews were much poorer, they lived a full Jewish life regardless of the costs.

As indicated earlier, neither the notion that the cost of a Jewish way of life is excessive nor the critique of conspicuous Jewish consumption is new. Nor, indeed, do such notions apply only to Jews living in the consumerist societies of the West. At the beginning of the twentieth century, the Zionist sociologist Arthur Ruppin observed that unlike their fellow Christian Europeans, Jews never seem to be satisfied with the best that money could buy. Relating this idiosyncrasy of Jewish life to the allegedly classless or in-between position of Jews as a minority group, Ruppin explained that unlike the Christian who is usually "content when he has arrived at the standard of his class," Jews never develop fixed standards of living and "therefore [are] always in a state of uncertain equilibrium, always pushing forward, never satisfied."[16]

Based on a similar reading of the Jewish experience, in her 1913 book on the "modern Jewess," Else Croner underscored Jewish emphasis on domesticity, which is commonly perceived as the quintessential women's realm. Croner claimed that since Jews were inclined to conceive the outside world as a hazardous domain, the Jewish home was perceived as a sanctuary in which one could simply be a human being without having the fear of exclusion or a struggle for recognition. This is also why, according to Croner, Jews place more value on interior design than non-Jews, making the aesthetics of their homes a signifier of Jewishness. Moreover, she even suggested that Jews shopped differently from non-Jews. According to Croner, a non-Jew who could afford to buy a house would purchase a family home, while a Jew with the same income would

---

[15] Quoted in: Aryeh Meir and Lisa Hostein, *The High Cost of Jewish Living* (New York: American Jewish Committee, 2002, 1992), 11.

[16] Arthur Rupin, *The Jews of Today* (New York: Henry Holt and Company, 1913), 52.

be inclined to rent an elegant apartment in a sought-after neighborhood in the city rather than building his own family house in the residential areas of the suburbs.[17] At the same time, Croner noted that many Jewish families were living beyond their means, a tendency she describes using the Jewish concept of *Kavod* (literally translated as "honor" or "respect"), akin to the bourgeois idea of respectability. According to Croner the Jewish urge for *Kavod* dates to the times when Jews were confined to ghettos. Closely huddled together in small spaces isolated from the rest of the world, Jews formed a kind of closed society in which respectability became an important mechanism for regulating social life. Croner added that material status symbols such as clothing, housing, charity, and gift duties were an integral part of this way of life.[18] In a similar manner the British Jewish weekly *The Jewish World* ascribed the Jewish preoccupation with respectability and the keeping "of good appearance" to the Talmudic injunction that one should spend less on his food than on his clothes.[19]

Despite such speculations, Jews had a good reason to complain about the costs of being Jewish. In the early modern period, for example, Jews were required to pay special taxes for securing the tolerance of the authorities. These levies took different forms. One particularly notorious method of taxing was to force Jews to purchase certain goods in order to obtain certain certificates and permits. A well-known case is the so-called *Judenporzellan* (literally "Jewish porcelain"). In order to boost the production of his newly founded porcelain factory, Frederick the Great issued a decree in 1769 binding Jews under his rule to purchase the king's porcelain.[20] In this way he not only secured a consumer market for his goods in Prussia but also compelled Jews, as merchants, to trade his products beyond the borders of his kingdom. According to some accounts, Moses Mendelssohn was among those required to purchase the king's goods in order to obtain permits. It is said that over the course of his life,

---

[17] Else Croner, *Die moderne Jüdin* (Berlin: Juncker, 1913), 56–58.   [18] Ibid., 55–56.
[19] Gaza, "Through a Woman's Eyes," *The Jewish World* (March 29, 1923), 10; as well as (August 9, 1927), 4.
[20] See Raymond Wolff, "Das Judenporzellan," "Der Bär von Berlin," *Jahrbuch des Vereins für die Geschichte Berlins* 230 (1983), 67–84; Tobias Schenk, "Das Juden Porzellan" der Königlichen Porzellan-Manufaktur Berlin. Ein Beitrag zur Problematik preußischer Judenpolitik im 18. Jahrhundert," University of Münster, MA thesis, 2003; Tobias Schenk, "Das 'Judenporzellan' Eine kommentierte Tabellenpräsentation zur Rechts- und Sozialgeschichte der Juden im friderizianischen Preußen (1769–1788)," available at www.perspectivia.net/content/publikationen/friedrich300-quellen/schenk_judenporzellan/einfuehrung.

he came to own some twenty monkey figures of the alleged *Judenporzellan*.²¹ Up until Fredrick II's death in 1786, Prussian Jews were forced to spend approximately 275 taler on porcelain from the royal *Berliner Porzelanmanufacture*. Some of it remained in circulation long after the notorious decree was put out of force in December 1787.

Writing in 1907, the poet Thekla Skorra recalls how fascinated she was as a child with an old porcelain cup that stood in her great-grandmother's living room cabinet. She describes the cup as an elegant white object featuring colorful flowers and the figure of a woman floating over the caption *Humanité*, which was written in golden letters. When she asked why the family never drank out of this cup, her grandmother hesitantly replied, "[D]on't touch it, my child, it tastes salty, too many tears have been poured in it."²² In Skorra's depiction this alleged piece of *Judenporzellan* did not merely epitomize Jewish suffering and subordination during times when Jews were not considered part of *Humanité*; it also underscored the improvement of the Jewish position from the end of the eighteenth century. Leaving Germany in 1935, Hannah Salomon-Janovski, a daughter of the sociologist Albert Salomon, reported that the coffee set her family used at their New York residence was also dubbed *Judenporzellan*.²³ While Skorra situated the *Judenporzellan* within a narrative of progress with emancipation at its apogee, for the Salomons the porcelain set brought by the family from Berlin symbolized the forced exodus from the old *Heimat* and the dissolution of Jewish emancipation in Germany.

It is, nevertheless, doubtful whether the Salomon's coffee set, or for that matter most other porcelain dubbed at the beginning of the last century *Judenporzellan*, was indeed original. In fact there was much confusion as to what constituted *Judenporzellan*. Some applied this term to designate

---

²¹ It is quite certain that the monkeys owned by Mendelssohn were not, strictly speaking, *Judenporzellan*. Not only did the king's porcelain factory never manufacture monkey figures, but Mendelssohn's name does not appear in any of the lists recording the recipients of the factory's products. Moreover, according to this legend Mendelssohn acquired the figures in order to get his marriage permit, yet he was married in 1762, seven years before the king's decree was implemented. It is, however, likely that Mendelssohn was forced to buy the monkeys that were brought to Berlin from Saxony during the seven years' war. On this, see Wolff, "Das Judenporzellan", 80–82.

²² Lass stehen, mein Kind, es schmeckt salzig draußen, sind zu viel Tränennen drin gewesen, "Thekla Skorra, 'Judenporzellan'," *Ost und West* 7 (4) (1907), 248.

²³ Peter Gostmann, Gerhard Wagner and Albert Salomon, *Werke: Biographische Materialien und Schriften 1921–1933* (Wiesbaden: Sozialwissenschaften Verlag, 2008), 51.

any kind of low-quality porcelain, while others believed that *Judenporzellan* were porcelain objects principally designed for Jews, some of which even featured Jewish motifs. Notwithstanding the varied understanding of the term, it appears that by the beginning of the twentieth century *Judenporzellan* became a desirable object, the ownership of which became a status symbol that indicated membership in a select circle of Jewish families from the old Berlin. This inversion of meaning – from the sign of cultural subordination to emblem of cultural prestige – helps explain the debates regarding the meaning and authenticity of the *Judenporzellan*.[24]

For my purpose, I would like to highlight the linkage suggested in this discourse between goods and identity. The following sections will expound on this conjunction in order to gain a better understanding of the interplay between Jews and their belongings. This raises two major sets of interrelated challenges. The first is the fundamental issue of how to determine the nature of the relationship between people and their things. The second is the more practical, nonetheless difficult, question of what types of historical sources can document the material world of people who did not leave behind much evidence, either of their interaction with objects or of their consumer experiences more generally.

Over the past few decades, some inspiring scholarship has improved our understanding of the significance of materiality in the social process.[25] Yet the challenge remains. Although for most of us it is difficult to imagine human society without goods, we still have difficulty grasping the means by which things acquire their meaning, not to mention how commodities shape the ways we perceive the world. In the context of Jewish history this becomes an even greater challenge, given the limited sources available for research. Currently, the scholarship on Jewish consumer practices is very limited, let alone studies on the diverse ways in which Jews have allocated meaning to their belongings. The following pages offer at least a partial glimpse into the world of Jews as consumers and users of things.

[24] Olga Bloch, "Altes und Neues Berliner Porzellan," *Blätter des Jüdischen Frauenbundes für Frauenarbeit und für Frauenbewegung* VII (1) (1931), 3–5. For a more contemporary discussion see Jenna Weissman Joselit, "Mendelssohn's Tea Pot: How Artists Reinvent the Past, and the Jewish Future," *ZEEK* (December 18, 2013), available at http://zeek .forward.com/articles/117960/.

[25] In particular I am indebted to the work of Leora Auslander on the topic. See, for example, her "Beyond Words," *American Historical Review* 110 (4) (October 2005), 1015–1045; Ibid., "Historians and the Study of Material Culture," *American Historical Review* (December 2009): 1354–1404; Ibid., "The Boundaries of Jewishness or When Is a Cultural Practice Jewish?" *Journal of Modern Jewish Studies* 8 (1) (2009), 47–64.

## GETTING AND SPENDING

Since the end of the nineteenth century, efforts have been made to document certain aspects of everyday Jewish life. Thanks to such undertakings there is now a significant scholarship on many aspects of the social and economic activities of European Jews from the Middle Ages to the beginning of the twentieth century. Interestingly most of this research is focused on getting – that is, on how Jews earned money – almost entirely eschewing the no-less important question of how they spent their earnings. As a result, we know much about Jewish professional life, but very little on their behavior as consumers.

Three main reasons might account for this scholarly preoccupation with getting rather than spending. To begin with, anxieties regarding Jewish pauperism motivated research on Jewish livelihoods. Second, concerns over Jewish overrepresentation in certain vocations, particularly commerce and finance, have kept the focus on work rather than consumerism.[26] And finally, the absence of scholarship on Jewish expenditure could be connected to what some consider the "ghettoization" of Jews as moneymakers. According to this view, Jews stood out in their role as moneymakers but not as moneyspenders, and scholars followed suit. If initially interest in the question of Jewish livelihoods was informed by the attempt to "normalize" Jewish social and economical structure, in the realm of spending, a more pressing question, perhaps, became how to generate and maintain Jewish difference.

A 1911 survey of working-class households in the United States and Great Britain is probably the only official set of data we have that contains information on Jewish household expenses at the beginning of the last century.[27] The British Board of Trade initiated the study in order to gain a better understanding of the living conditions of low-wage workers in

---

[26] For a more detailed discussion of the question of fears about Jewish pauperism see Derek Penslar, *Shylock's Children: Economics and Jewish Identity in Modern Europe* (Berkeley: University of California Press, 2001), 11–50; as well as Stefi Jersch-Wenzel (ed.), *Juden und Armut in Mittel- und Osteuropa* (Cologne: Böhlau, 2000). On the ideological origins of Jewish statistics see Mitchell B. Hart, *Social Science and the Politics of Modern Jewish Identity* (Stanford: Stanford University Press, 2000). It should be noted that even Hart's important study overlooks this imbalance and does not reflect upon the topic of consumption at all.

[27] George Ranken Askwith, *Cost of living in American Towns: Report of an Enquiry by the Board of Trade into working-class rents, housing, and retail prices, together with the rates of wages in certain occupations in the principal industrial towns of the United States* (London: H.M. Stationery, 1911). I would like to thank Ian Gazeley for calling my attention to this survey.

different countries and cultural settings. While the survey mainly defined class by income and occupation, it recognized "the composite nationality" of America and distinguished between income groups according to their place of origin and ethnicity.[28] Within this framework the survey collected information on 758 Jewish families, most of which had immigrated to the United States from Russia. The survey found some sizable differences between groups of immigrants. For example, it pointed out that Jews tended to arrive in America as families, while most other immigrant groups frequently sent unaccompanied men in advance. Jews lacked an attachment to their place of origin, explained the surveyors, and therefore decided early on to make the United States their home country.

Not surprisingly, the most noticeable peculiarity of the Jewish households was their food consumption. Beyond total abstinence from pork, Jews spent less than other groups on flour, potatoes, and sausages, and bought almost no lard, suet, dripping, or condensed milk. At the same time, Jews consumed larger quantities of poultry, fish, fresh milk, eggs, and rye bread.[29] Although the survey notes that the quantity of rye bread tended to fall as incomes rose, Jewish dietary regulations determined the food consumption of these families more than any other factor, including income. Since the survey focused on expenses for food, it is difficult to establish how Jewishness informed other areas of spending. This applies to similar data collected at the end of the 1920s on the household expenses of Jewish emigrants to Palestine. With the advance of National Socialism such information played an important role in Zionist efforts to encourage migration to Palestine.[30] Though a cost-of-living index for the *Yishuv* (Jewish settlement in Palestine) was published regularly from the beginning of 1930s, at this stage it is difficult to discern anything specifically Jewish from these data.[31] Further research on patterns of expenditure could be carried out on Jewish family household account books, a unique set of documents that await systematic historical investigation.

---

[28] Ibid., lxviii.

[29] Ibid., lxxxviii. For further observations on Jewish eating habits at the beginning of the last century in America, see Mary L. Schapiro, "Jewish Dietary Problems," *Journal of Home Economics* 11 (2) (1919), 47–59; Michael M. Davis Jr. and Bertha M. Wood, "The Food of the Immigrant in Relation to Health," *Journal of Home Economics* 13 (1) (1921), 19–25.

[30] See, for example, "Wieviel kostet ein Haushalt in Palästina?" *Jüdische Rundschau* 14 (April 28, 1933), 169.

[31] For this information see *Palästina: Zeitschrift für den Aufbau Palästinas* that was published in Vienna from 1902 to 1938.

Keeping careful records of personal and household expenses became an integral part of middle-class decorum in the second half of the nineteenth century. Jewish families were no exception. They too sought to follow the advice given in the literature of the developing science of home economics by keeping close record of their expenses. Typically maintained by women, the expense books are a valuable source of information on how middle-class Jews sought to create efficient and thrifty households. Record books were typically divided into three main areas of spending: necessities such as food and accommodation; more flexible expenses such as clothing, education, and health; and finally lifestyle products and leisure activities. These documents demonstrate how middle-class ideals of organization and compartmentalization as well as modesty and moderation were translated into practice.[32]

As a rule, the account books of Jewish families did not separately list the costs associated with Jewish living. Put together, however, these sources reveal similarities that can be explained by shared Jewish traditions and practices, as well as by the status of Jews as a minority group in an overwhelmingly Christian society. Indeed, the expense books reveal the ways in which Jews sought to integrate into a "typical" middle-class way of life, a strong feature of Jewish assimilation. As Marion Kaplan has compellingly demonstrated, Jews linked their claims for belonging to their embourgeoisement. They accepted the Enlightenment idea of *Bildung* connecting the improvement of their status within the larger culture and their own self-betterment with their integration.[33] This emphasis on *Bildung* was by no means atypical for Jews in Germany. Reports from the British Isles convey similar inclination indicating "the heaviest load of [Jewish] family expenditure is devoted to such excellent causes as education and the development, mental, moral, spiritual and cultural of their offspring."[34]

According to some scholars, this desire for more integration is a form of mimicry.[35] I find this approach problematic for two main reasons.

---

[32] Rich, *Bourgeois Consumption*, 25.

[33] See especially her seminal study, Marion Kaplan, *The Making of the Jewish Middle Class: Women, Family, and Identity in Imperial Germany* (New York: Oxford University Press, 1991), 54.

[34] Gaza, "Through a Woman's Eyes" (September 11, 1930), 9.

[35] The first use I found for the concept of mimicry in the Jewish context goes back to Joseph Jacobs, *Studies in Jewish Statistics: Social, Vital, Anthropometric* (London: D. Nutt, 1891), 34. Writing about what he depicts as a recent fashion among English Jews to make their surname sound more British, Jacobs explains that mimicry is a technical term used in natural science to express the devices by which insects and small animals adopt colours and forms reassembling their surroundings so as to escape the notice of their enemies.

To begin with, Jews were just one of many groups intent upon attaining rights and recognition in the nineteenth century. All over Europe we find examples of social, ethnic, and religious groups campaigning for emancipation and integration, including, most prominently, laborers and women. Other examples include Protestants in France, Catholics in Germany or England, and different ethnic and religious groups living in central and Eastern Europe. Any attempt to scrutinize a specifically Jewish longing for more belonging should be placed within this broader framework, taking into account the complex relationships between the desire for homogeneity and the reality of diversity in European cultures.[36]

With this last point in mind I come to my second concern regarding the depiction of Jews as a subaltern people residing in Europe. It appears to me that this interpretation presupposes a fixed and hegemonic culture, which by definition is other to Jewish culture so that the mere attempt to belong to it can only underscore Jewish difference. This I believe is based on a misleading representation of European bourgeois culture. Moreover, this approach is further based on a crude, undifferentiated representation of how Jews actually lived in European societies. Despite their minority position and the long and undisputed history of Jewish maltreatment, Jews were also active agents of European culture. One of the ways in which they actively shaped the culture around them was by how they ran their households. By making their homes repositories of good taste and cultivation, Jews were centrally engaged in constructing a bourgeois way of life that extended into the culture at large. This was a way of life in which "respectability was almost entirely based on appearance, and behavior was assumed to be a clear indicator of moral worth."[37]

The emphasis on family planning and homemaking, the prominence of learning, and the investment in education, as well as relatively high spending on lifestyle products such as design objects, spa holidays, theater, and different cultural goods, such as books and art, typified Jewish household expenditures long before becoming emblematic middle-class

---

[36] For a general discussion of this issue see Matthew Festenstein, *Negotiating Diversity: Culture, Deliberation, Trust* (Cambridge: Polity Press, 2005).

[37] Rich, *Bourgeois Consumption*, 139. For more on the Jewish role in the making of the bourgeois lifestyle, Victor Karady, *The Jews of Europe in the Modern Era: A Socio-Historical Outline* (Budapest: Central European University Press, 2004), 1–75; Simone Lässig, *Jüdische Wege ins Bürgertum: Kulturelles Kapital und sozialer Aufstieg im 19 Jahrhundert* (Göttingen: Vandenhoeck and Ruprecht, 2004).

signifiers.[38] In fact, the association of Jews with upscale lifestyle goes back to premodern periods when Jewish traders played a prominent role as suppliers of fashion and luxury goods to European court societies. This position, requiring knowledge of and sensitivity to changing tastes, illuminates how information about what was *en vogue* among upper-class Europeans could have made its way into the Jewish society, and perhaps also vice versa. Indeed, early modern sources allude to a supposedly Jewish propensity to live stylishly, in elegance and comfort.[39]

Moreover, what are commonly considered the typical bourgeois values of respectability, prudence, and frugality were also familiar parts of Jewish tradition. So, too, was the bourgeois emphasis on the home as the quintessential woman's realm compatible with the often strongly gendered lines of Judaism. According to the Talmud, housework comprises one of the obligations of women toward her husband. Beyond the physical upkeep of the household, a woman's most important task was to provide the religious base for her children and the proper religious environment for all members of the family. By making the home an important site of religious socialization and ritual practice, homemaking in Judaism achieved an almost spiritual dimension.[40] Bourgeois culture more generally may be seen to have empowered women by fixing their position in the home. Even Jewish writer and pioneering campaigner for women's emancipation Fanny Lewald (1811–1889) made her motto the words *"Ordnung und Sparsamkeit"* (order and frugality).[41] A wealthy woman like Alice Scherk, wife of Ludwig Scherk who was the founder and general director of the Scherk perfume and cosmetics company, noted in her diary that "our home is most sacred to us; it is even more precious to us than our beautiful business and the beautiful factory."[42]

---

[38] For an early discussion of these trends see appendix A to Jacobs, *Studies in Jewish Statistics*.

[39] Schnapper-Arndt, "Mittheilungen über Jüdische Interieurs zu Ende des siebzehnten Jahrhunderts," *Zeitschrift für die Geschichte der Juden in Deutschland* 2 (2) (1888), 182–193.

[40] *Henry Berkowitz, Kiddush or Sabbath Sentiment in the Home* (Philadelphia: The Jewish Chautauqau Society, 1898); Nahida Ruth Lazarus, *Das Jüdische Haus* (Berlin: Duncker, 1898); Max Dienemann, "Lebensgestaltung der jüdischen Frau," *Der Morgen* 5 (1930), 420–430; Moshe Meiselman, *Jewish Woman in Jewish Law* (Jersey City: Ktav Publishing, 1978), 17.

[41] Quoted in Selma Strern, "Die Entwicklung des jüdischen Frauentypus seit dem Mittelalter," *Der Morgen* 6 (1926), 650; further on this, Ernst Simon, "Drei jüdische Frauentypen," "Jüdische Haushatungsschulen in Deutschalnd," *Blätter des jüdischen Frauenbundes für Frauenarbeit und für Frauenbewegung* XI (4) (1935), 3–6.

[42] Alice Scherk, *Diary Entry* (November 1, 1919), Jewish Museum Berlin.

In her study of the "modern Jewess," Else Croner described the position of Jewish women in this way: "In the Jewish home, even in the Jewish palace, the status of the spouse always remains the same because the woman is the soul of domesticity."[43] This is also why Martin Buber ascribed such an important role to women in his call for the renewal of Jewish life. "For a people without a country, for a people in the Diaspora," he proclaimed in 1902, "the home is the moving force of life. In the *galut* [diaspora] the Jewish home is the Jewish nation."[44] Chapter 11 will return to this discussion about the significance of the home and the role of women.

Looking at middle-class Jewish homes it is thus difficult to distinguish between bourgeois ideals and Jewish traditions. Equally difficult is to establish how Jewishness informed consumer's choices. The household expense books alone cannot offer an adequate answer to this question. Beyond issues of representation, an even more fundamental problem is the lopsidedness of such sources. While these records provide valuable information on the expenditure structure of Jewish households, it is not likely that such accounts books could be identified as specifically Jewish. Non-Jewish households may have generated very similar accounts and expenditures. This does not imply that "being Jewish" did not matter for how Jews behaved as consumers. It merely suggests that in order to decode household expenditures as a form of Jewishness, we should look at how Jews positioned themselves in the world of goods. Such an expedition will not only require a more qualitative approach to the study of Jewish expenditures but also involve a discussion of the no-less challenging question of the geography of Jewish spending.

---

[43] "Im jüdischen Haus, auch im jüdischen Palast, ist die Stellung der Ehefrau immer gleich geblieben, weil sie die Seele der Häuslichkeit ist," Croner, *Die moderne Jüdin*, 54.

[44] Martin Buber, "The Jewish Woman's Zion," in: Gilya Gerda Schmidt (ed.), *The First Buber: Youthful Zionist Writings of Martin Buber* (Syracuse: Syracuse University Press, 1999), 116. See also Bertha Badt-Strauss, "Jüdische Familien," *Der Morgen* 8 (3) (1932), 225–231; Meta Samson, "Das möbilierte Zimmer," *Der Morgen* 10 (2) (1934), 58–62. For a broader discussion on the Jewish home see Sharon Gillerman, *Germans into Jews: Remaking the Jewish Social Body in the Weimar Republic* (Stanford: Stanford University Press, 2009); Simon J. Bronner (ed.), *Jews at Home: The Domestication of Identity* (Oxford: The Littman Library of Jewish Civilization, 2010).

# Place and Space of Jewish Consumption

Like other consumers, Jews had to learn the language of things in order to take their place within modern society. Such proficiency, as Pierre Bourdieu argues, was a powerful mechanism for the construction of social identities. According to Bourdieu, social differences are most readily captured in the concept of class, which both determines the likes and interests of people and is defined by their taste. But class is just one form of social distinction. In his analysis, Bourdieu did not give much significance to religion or ethnicity as variables that have much impact on taste or consumer choices.[1] The example of Jewish consumption serves to extend Bourdieu's approach beyond the notion of class.

Jews always had a strong identity in the marketplace. Max Daniel, born in 1891 in the small Pomeranian district town of Bublitz, recalled in his memoir that the situation of Jews in his hometown was good and that "it did not matter where one made his shopping."[2] He noted that the peasants who brought their products to the town's weekly market preferred Jewish customers since they received better prices from them for certain unusual goods, like tropical fruit. As this testimony suggests, even when Jews were free to purchase wherever they desired, being Jewish was not a neutral matter. Being Jewish conditioned how consumers were approached and which special products (and sometime special prices) were made available. Jews were sometimes considered more open to exploring so-called exotic

[1] For this critic of Bourdieu's approach see, for example, Roger Silverstone, *Television and Everyday Life* (London: Routledge, 1994), 104–132.

[2] Monika Richarz, *Jüdische Leben in Deutschland. Selbstzeugnisse zur Sozialgeschichte im Kaiserreich* (Stuttgart: Deutsche Verlag-Anstalt, 1979), 214.

tastes and more willing to spend on new products. Jewish cookbooks and
personal recipe collections also suggest that Jews incorporated ingredients
such as bananas, pineapples, and oranges into their cuisine, at a time when
those items were still highly unusual in Europe.[3]

Rudi Bach, a trainee in the Landauer Brothers department store, provides a different, and perhaps more common, illustration of the prominence of Jewishness on the marketplace at the beginning of the 1920s.
Founded in 1884, the Landauer department store specialized in textiles.
By the beginning of the century the company had branches in different
cities in South Germany, making the Landauers one of the foremost
Jewish families in Stuttgart.[4] In his memoir, Bach evokes the lighthearted
and prankish working atmosphere of the men's wear department in
Stuttgart's main store. He recalls that if "some dour peasant proved to
be a tough customer, a salesman would call a colleague, who looked, but
wasn't Jewish, and say: 'Mr. Landauer, may I ask you to take care of this
gentleman.' Being honored by 'Mr. Landauer' waiting on him in person,"
Bach playfully notes, "the good man could, of course, no longer resist."[5]
Across the Channel in the woman's column of *The Jewish World*, we find
another no less intriguing anecdote of "an elegantly attired Jewess, seated
majestically in a large West End store, and deliberately seeking to convince the sales-people who attended her that there was nothing whatsoever Jewish about her."[6] Responding to the newspaper's inquiry about
this incident, the salesman claimed that such behavior was normal,
explaining that "by his experience, just as he and all who beheld her [the
Jewish shopper] knew that externally the lady was typically an Israelite."[7]

Deploring such posturing, for *The Jewish World* this witty anecdote
was designed to illustrate that it was impossible for the Jewish woman to
pass as non-Jewish. For our purposes, it is more important to underline
the basic fact that a "Jewish look" was a trope both when selling and

---

[3] For more information on the lure of exotic food see Ruth Abusch-Magder, "Eating 'Out':
Food and the Boundaries of Jewish Community and Home in Germany and the United
States," *Nashim: A Journal of Jewish Women's Studies & Gender Issues* 5 (2002), 66.

[4] More on this company and the Jewish textile industry in South Germany see Jacob Toury,
Eva Ch. Toury and Peter Zimmermann, *Jüdische Textilunternehmer in Baden-
Württemberg, 1683–1938* (Tübingen: J.C.B. Mohr, 1984); Roberta S. Kremer (ed.),
*Broken Threads: The Destruction of the Jewish Fashion Industry in Germany and
Austria* (Oxford: Berg, 2007).

[5] Rudi Bach, *Multa Multum*, 27, available online at the Leo Baeck Institute Memoirs
Archives http://digital.cjh.org/R/QDG536IJ8DUUY8X5FBX7U54DUK5BFFCJINP7IC
H92EYLQHIYLK-01360.

[6] Gaza, "Through a Woman's Eyes," *The Jewish World* (March 1, 1928), 9.    [7] Ibid.

buying things and that Jews and non-Jews alike were involved in this kind of "Jewish guessing game." Growing up in the Netherlands in an assimilated Jewish family with strong connections to Germany, Gerda Laqueur recorded in her diary several references to what she describes as a typically Jewish appearance. During a visit to one of Berslau's finest shopping streets, for example, she noted that almost every seventh face on that street looked Jewish.[8] Such examples illustrate how being Jewish was woven into the very texture of the marketplace. Shopping always had some kind of Jewish meaning.[9]

From diaries and memoirs we also learn how Jews experienced the marketplace. Victor Klemperer's childhood recollection contains a striking illustration of the strong connection between Jewishness and consumption. In a dairy entry from August 1927, Klemperer records the first time he went with his mother to buy a piece of bacon, which of course is *tryfa* (i.e., strictly not kosher) in a Christian shop.[10] Klemperer depicted this act as a defining moment of his life as a German and a Jew. As the son of a rabbi, Klemperer experienced the consumption of nonkosher food as a transgressive act that freed him from the grips of Judaism and initiated his lifelong quest for self-knowledge. In a rare confession, Klemperer explained that ever since that purchase it had always been his utmost desire to "come over" (*herüberzukommen*) to a feeling of Germanness (*Deutschtum*). Forty years after that event took place, he noted, "[E]verything in Germany pushes me back to [being] the Jew." But still, he then continues,

If I became a Zionist I would be even more laughable than if I became a Catholic. I am always suspended like an airplane over all these things and myself. That is incidentally the most Jewish thing about me. And perhaps the most German. But the German nevertheless finds somewhere a unity of feeling [or perhaps a feeling of unity]. The Jew remains also above his feelings.[11]

Klemperer's reflections call to mind Arthur Ruppin's depiction of the classless or in-between position of Jews, discussed in Chapter 9. According to Ruppin, this Jewish state of suspense also determines

---

[8] Gerda Margarethe Oestreicher-Laqueur, *Gerdas Tagebücher. Deutsch-jüdisch-niederländische Familiengeschichte, 1918–1939* (Konstanz: Hartung-Gorre Verlag, 2010), 116.

[9] For further examples see Kerry M. Wallach, *Jewish Women and the Jewish Press in Weimar Germany*, University of Pennsylvania, PhD. Diss., 2011.

[10] Steven Aschheim reads this entry as a manifestation of Klemperer's identity crisis, see Steven Aschheim, *Scholem, Arendt, Klemperer: Intimate Chronicles in Turbulent Times* (Bloomington: Indiana University Press, 2001), 83.

[11] Klemperer, *Daries*, entry August 1927.

Jewish consumer choices. Most fascinating in both of these accounts is the juxtaposition between the nature of Jewish identity and Jewish consumer experiences.

Although not always as dramatic as Klemperer's, other Jewish testimonies convey similar feelings about the lasting impression made by consuming nonkosher food, especially for Jews from traditional households. Betty Lipton, for example, who left Berlin for Melbourne in 1939, recalls that the first time she ate in a nonkosher restaurant she "thought the roof would fall in or the building would collapse." But, as she quietly professes, "[I]t didn't."[12] Interestingly, she recalls that the chicken she tasted was not so different from the kosher chicken she was accustomed to. Unlike Klemperer, Betty Lipton continued to keep a kosher household while eating nonkosher food outside her home. This appears also to have been the case for many other Jews for whom the act of consumption enabled a kind of suspension, to borrow Klemperer's phrase, which allowed them to hover over and explore different notions of belongings and, in so doing, retain their sense of Jewishness. Evidence from the 1911 survey on Jewish immigrants to America suggests that Jews spent more than other consumers on meals away from home.[13] Like a dinner party, a restaurant meal afforded an opportunity to display cultural capital as well as to demonstrate belonging to a certain social group. In the Jewish context, an appetite for eating out can be understood in relation to the distinction between outside and inside food. According to Ruth Abusch-Madger, eating outside home might have meant abandoning traditional Jewish food ways, but in fact it seems to have contributed to a renewed sense of Jewish identity.[14]

Historically, Jewish dietary laws set Jews apart from the society surrounding them. Maintaining such strict separation always presented a challenge for Jews.[15] With the onset of modernity the difficulty of meeting strict dietary laws became more acute, and correspondingly

---

[12] Quoted in John Foster (ed.), *Community of Fate: Memoirs of German Jews in Melbourne* (Sydney: Allen & Unwin, 1986), 28.

[13] George Ranken Askwith, *Cost of living in American Towns: Report of an Enquiry by the Board of Trade* (London: H.M. Stationery, 1911), ixxxviii. For further evidence and reflections on eating out see Gaza, "Meals Out," *The Jewish World* (May 11, 1933), 6–7.

[14] Ruth Abusch-Magder, "Eating 'Out': Food and the Boundaries of Jewish Community and Home in Germany and the United States," *Nashim: A Journal of Jewish Women's Studies & Gender Issues*, 5 (2002), 53–82.

[15] Hannah McK. Lyons, "The Kosher Kitchen," *Journal of Home Economics* 20 (6) (1928), 389–393.

more calls for leniency with respect to food emerged. Yet, while the demand to relax or even eliminate Jewish dietary restrictions was motivated by the desire to blur the boundaries between Jews and other groups, it ironically brought renewed attention to eating practices as signifiers of Jewishness. As David Kraemer explains in his stimulating book on Jewish eating and identity, "[T]hose who erected strong fences at the boundaries also allowed for openings, even when they did not recognize them. And those who destroyed inherited fences erected new signposts of Jewishness, even when they were unaware of them."[16]

For the sociologist Margarete Sallis-Freudenthal, it was already common for Jews to cross the boundary between kosher and nonkosher food worlds in the period before the Great War. She recalls that while her parents' families no longer kept kosher by 1900, both her grandmothers continued to purchase meat from Jewish butchers.[17] For other Jews, some nonkosher food was acceptable. Pork remained prohibited often more out of disgust than a desire to follow Jewish dietary law.[18] These examples reveal not only how taste is culturally bound but also how traditional foodways informed Jewish consumer choices.

Jewish cookbooks helped forge a sense of distinct Jewish taste. One of the first was Josef Stolz's *Kochbuch für Israeliten* (Cookbook for Israelites), published in 1815. In Germany alone, ten more Jewish cookbooks were published during the nineteenth century. Several of them, like Rebekka Wolf's 1856 *Kochbuch für Israeliten Frauen*, went through several editions.[19] At the turn of the century, Jewish newspapers started publishing recipes and other advice for the Jewish cook, including entire menus for Jewish festivities.[20] With the help of such documents, historians can estimate the resources and efforts needed to prepare Jewish meals. The hierarches of foods and dishes also provide insight into cultural

[16] Kraemer, *Jewish Eating and Identity Through the Ages* (New York: Routledge, 2007), 145. See also Seymour E. Freedman, *The Book of Kashruth: A Treasury of Kosher Facts and Frauds* (New York: Bloch Pub. Co., 1970).

[17] Margarete Sallis-Freudenthal, *Ich habe mein Land gefunden. Autobiographischer Rückblick* (Frankfurt a.M.: Verlag Josef Knecht, 1977), 11.

[18] Marion Kaplan, *The Making of the Jewish Middle Class: Women, Family, and Identity in Imperial Germany* (New York: Oxford University Press, 1991), 72.

[19] Ibid., as well as Gil Marks, *Encyclopedia of Jewish Food* (Hoboken: John Wiley & Sons, 2010), 139–142; Ruth Abusch-Magder, "Kulinarische Bildung: Jüdische Kochbücher als Medien der Verbürgerlichung," in: Kirsten Heinsohn and Stefanie Schüler-Springorum (eds.), *Deutsch-Jüdische Geschichte als Geschlechtergeschichte* (Göttingen: Wallstein, 2006), 159–177.

[20] Margarete Turnowsky-Pinner, "Die jüdische Frau die Presse," *Menorah*, no. 6–7 (1928), 375–377.

assumptions of the time.[21] On a more basic level, these meals shaped Jewish sociability. Almost every Jewish celebration involved an elaborate feast that brought together family and friends. Special dishes – like *challah* bread on Friday evening or the special food for Passover Seder – were an essential part of the ritual.[22]

Dinner parties were another way that bourgeois and Jewish identities were consolidated. One striking example is the dinner parties organized by the Hartog family from Berlin. Carl Hartog (1877–1931) was born in Goch, a small town on the border between Germany and the Netherlands. After finishing his training as a gynecologist, he moved to Berlin in 1907 where he opened his own private clinic. In 1914 he married Henrietta Mayer (1891–1979), and during the Great War their daughter Ursula was born. Typical of upper-middle-class Jewish family, the Hartogs held dinner parties.[23] The family kept a close record of these social events. These accounts, preserved in the Jewish Museum in Berlin, contain guest lists, seating plans, menus, and, in some cases, detailed accounts of the costs for over fifty-five dinner parties held at the family home between 1914 and 1931, the year of Carl Hartog's death.

The dinner party provided middle-class families, such as the Hartogs, an opportunity to display good taste, manners, and palate. Keeping up with this bourgeois practice, the Hartogs, for example, used a mixed-gender seating plan. On some occasions, the guests played bridge, which, at the time, was a game played more at higher levels of the social hierarchy, most frequently among members of the professions.[24] The costs of such dinner parties varied according to the number of guests and type of menu. Either way, the economic situation of the 1920s made a dinner party an expensive undertaking and, as the decade drew to a close, the Hartog family correspondingly tightened its budget for the dinners. For example, a dinner for twenty-three people on December 8, 1926, cost the Hartogs approximately 207 German Reichsmarks, a handsome amount in a period when the monthly average salaried income of a white-collar

---

[21] Rachel Rich, *Bourgeois Consumption: Food, Space and Identity in London and Paris, 1850–1916* (Manchester: Manchester University Press, 2011), 15.

[22] For an overview of such food see Marks, *Encyclopedia of Jewish Food*.

[23] The Hartog family papers are housed in the Jewish Museum Berlin 2001/212/61–70 Mappe 7, Sammlung Carl and Henriette Hartog. For an interesting comparison with a broader account on so-called German hospitality, see Mrs. Alfred Sidgwick, *Home Life in Germany* (New York: MacMillan Company, 1912), 196–204.

[24] Pierre Bourdieu, *Distinction: A Social Critique of the Judgment of Taste* (Cambridge, MA: Harvard University Press, 1984), 217.

employee was less than 200 Reichsmarks.[25] Expenses included flowers, table decoration, drinks, and of course food. Meat and fish were the most expensive items on the lists.[26] In comparison, alcoholic beverages were relatively inexpensive. For an evening with approximately twenty guests the family used to buy three bottles of red wine, four of white, five bottles of sparkling wine, and on some occasions a few bottles of beer. The beverages offered at these dinners thus seem to reflect the general inclination of the upper middle classes of the period to favor wine and champagne over beer and other brews.

Compared with the multicourse meals of the prewar period, during the 1920s, menus gradually become shorter and simpler. Dinner at the Hartogs consisted of three courses, usually a soup followed by the main course (typically meat and/or fish with sides) and an elaborate desert consisting of cakes, fruit, and ice-cream. The menu for one dinner party in 1928 attended by twenty-one guests included bouillon soup; zander fish with crab tails and champignon; filled turkey with mixed salad; and Charlotte cake, apple strudel, nut ice-cream with chocolate dressing, and fruit salad. The overall cost of the evening was just over 220 Reichsmarks.

For some gatherings the family hired extra help to assist with the cooking and probably the serving of the food. Most of the parties took place during the colder months of the year and were not held to celebrate Jewish holidays or lifecycle events. Looking at the lists of guests we see that many of the male invitees held academic titles and were probably Carl Hartog's colleagues; others appear to be family friends or relatives. The full names of female guests are listed only if they are invited on their own or are close enough to the family to be identified by their first name alone. Otherwise, women are recorded only as escort, that is wife, of a certain *Herr Professor Dr.* It is difficult to establish from these lists which of the guests were Jewish. Many of the names on the lists "sound" Jewish, and given the high representation of Jews in the medical profession in Berlin at the time, it is likely that a number of Professor Hartog's

---

[25] Hilde Walter, "The Misery of the New Mittelstand," in: Anton Kaes, Martin Jay and Edward Dimendberg (eds.), *The Weimar Republic Sourcebook* (Berkeley: University of California Press, 1994), 188. For a more elaborative study of the issue of spending during the Weimar years see Claudius Torp, *Konsum und Politik in der Weimarer Republik* (Göttingen: Vandenhoeck & Ruprecht, 2011).

[26] On this specific occasion it was turkey (44.50RM) and fish (25.40RM) – salmon, zander, or forel. All information is from "Sammlung l Hartog," Jewish Museum Berlin, Inv.Nr.: 2001/212/1–145; BIB/12, 1896–1952.

colleagues were Jewish as well. The Hartog family might not have been religious, but they took part in organized Jewish life, for instance, as members of the B'nai B'rith Yehuda Halevi Lodge in Berlin.[27] Although it is not clear whether the family kept kosher, no pork seems to have been served at these dinner parties – the main course was usually turkey or fish.

Cooking is a typical means of expressing bourgeois values, and the meals offered at the Hartogs certainly reflect an upper-middle-class lifestyle. Although there is no reason to assume that the food served at these dinner parties was kosher, it is most likely that mainly Jews were catered to on these occasions. The Hartog's dinner parties reveal what contemporaries already referred to as the "individualism of the Jew's observance." As one commentator explained, "[T]here are Jews who keep nothing else but insist on eating kosher food; and there are Jews who, while scrupulously observing the Holy Days and Festivals, bother not about what kind of food they eat."[28]

Some consider this kind of flexibility a sign of Jewish inauthenticity. The Zionist author Eugen Hoeflich, for one, questioned the propensity of big city Jews to continue dining in kosher restaurants even after they had lost their religious faith. According to him it was merely the force of habit and the associated fear of change that induced these Jews, which he depicted as *Bastardtypus* (bastard types) of German national Jewry, to eat kosher. For members of the so-called Jewish renaissance movement like Hoeflich, the consumption of kosher food was not an authentic expression of Jewishness, but a shallow Jewish automatism.[29] Either way, in a period when the consumption of kosher food was generally declining, producers and distributors of kosher products appreciated the higher price they generally received for their products. Ironically, the rise of antisemitism and of calls to boycott Jews helped to sustain a small but voracious market for kosher products in the period since the end of the nineteenth century.

Antisemitism was an important stimulus for the creation of designated spaces for Jewish consumption and a distinct sense of Jewish consumer

---

[27] On B'nai B'rith in Germany see Cornelia Wilhelm, *The Independent Orders of B'nai B'rith and True Sisters: Pioneers of a New Jewish Identity, 1843–1914* (Detroit: Wayne State University Press, 2011); Andreas Reinke, "Between Ethnic Solidarity and National Allegiance – the German Order of the B'nai B'rith," *Jahrbuch des Simon-Dubnow-Instituts* 1 (2002), 321–342.

[28] Gaza, "Through a Woman's Eyes," *The Jewish World* (September 4, 1930), 6.

[29] Armin A. Wallas (ed.), *Eugen Hoeflich (Moshe Ya'akov Ben-Gavriel) Tagebücher 1915 bis 1927* (Vienna: Böhlau, 1999), 177.

consciousness. The Jewish press was another driving force, urging Jews to be more cognizant about where and from whom they do their shopping. As we saw in Chapter 2, through special promotional campaigns the Jewish press urged readers to favor businesses that marketed specifically to Jewish costumers. Informing such efforts were not only fears of Jewish exclusion, or new notions about Jewish identity, but also palpable economic interest. Especially after World War I, the Jewish press increasingly depended on revenues from advertising. But the Jewish press was not the only venue invoking a sense of distinctiveness among Jews as consumers. In the next section, I consider how Jewish directories, or published address books, contributed to the demarcation of a Jewish space of consumption.

## MAPPING THE JEWISH MARKETPLACE

Even before the Great War, Jewish organizations like *B'nai B'rith* and the *Kartel Jüdische Verbindungen* (Federation of Jewish Fraternities) had started publishing directories that contained lists of businesses owned by their members. Founded in 1900, the *Verein zur Förderung rituelle Speisehäuser* (the Association for the Promotion of Ritual Restaurants), to name here another example, sought to encourage Jews to keep kosher by disseminating lists of restaurants and hotels that catered to the dietary prescriptions. In 1927, a register of Jewish book dealers was published to promote the Jewish publishing industry in Europe. An even more prominent example is *The Jewish Year Book*, which first came out in London in 1896 and is still published to this day. Presenting itself as "an annual record of matters Jewish," the year book listed all kinds of Jewish organizations, provided useful information on Jewish life in the British Empire, and contained a business section representing commercial interests of and for Jews.[30] Similar directories appeared from the mid-1920s in other European countries like Switzerland, Austria, and Germany. The most renowned of these was the *Jüdisches Adressbuch für Gross-Berlin* (Jewish Address Book for Greater Berlin). In addition to mapping all kinds of Jewish activities in the city, the Berlin address book featured a comprehensive business section with advertisements for a wide range of products and services, as well as the names and addresses of community members. By juxtaposing this diverse information, the Berlin directory

---

[30] *The Jewish Year Book: An Annual Record of Matters Jewish* (London: Greenberg & Co., 1897).

made visible – and helped to forge – a Jewish urban topography. Shopping was an integral part of this Jewish landscape.

Despite the evidence contained in these directories, it remains difficult to establish how much of an impact they had on how, and whether, Jews and other consumers perceived a specifically Jewish space of consumption. One indisputable source of evidence for such a space is the advertising section and the list of resorts and hotels recommended for Jews, previously discussed in the section on the so-called Jewish buycott. These registers of "Jewish-friendly" establishments had appeared in the Jewish press since before the Great War, but as the demand for information on the "Jewish" orientation of holiday facilities grew in the 1930s, the lists became more comprehensive and their use became more common. These records did not reveal whether the owner of a specific business was Jewish or not; such information was officially considered irrelevant. More importantly, the lists of hotels and resorts that welcomed Jews facilitated a sense of place in which Jewish holidaymakers would be able to relax and feel comfortable without being confronted by their Jewishness.

Jews did not incline to confine themselves to confessional affiliation, ethnic ties, or even political sympathies when going shopping. Instead, they often shopped where and when they liked, as they sought desirable goods at desirable prices. Critics of this sort of "shopping around" called upon Jews to demonstrate more restraint and refinement when going shopping. The advertising sections of the Jewish press were subject to similar scolding. While the editorial pages were highly responsive to any hint of antisemitism, the commercial sections did not always display similar fastidiousness about what and who advertised in the newspaper. Readers wrote letters to the editor lamenting that the local Jewish press published advertisements from companies associated with anti-Jewish policies or beliefs. Thus, for example, Jewish newspapers featured advertisements for Ford cars despite the infamous antisemitic views of the company's founding father, Henry Ford.[31] There is no reason to assume that Jewish consumers were unaware of such discrepancies. Moreover, as argued in Chapter 2, it is precisely this sense of ambivalence that

---

[31] Neil Baldwin, *Henry Ford and the Jews: The Mass Production of Hate* (New York: Public Affairs, 2002). Ford's outspoken antisemitism did not preclude doing business with Jews. A well-known example is the business relationship between Arnold Bernstein shipping company and Ford. On Bernstein see Björn Siegel, "Arnold Bernstein," in: Daniel R. Wadhwani (ed.), *Immigrant Entrepreneurship: German-American Business Biographies, 1720 to the Present*, vol. 5. Available at: www.immigrantentrepreneurship .org/entry.php?rec=242

earmarked how Jews conceived themselves as consumers in the pre-1933 period. By retaining their freedom of choice, Jews made a statement about the kinds of consumers they were that was also a statement of how they viewed themselves more broadly in the social sphere. Having the freedom to move between multiple registers – socially and in terms of consumption – was part of what it meant to be Jewish.

## THE COFFEE HOUSE AND COMFORT FOOD

Despite their propensity to patronize many businesses, Jews did find ways to share certain spaces and practices as consumers. Take the case of Hirsch Hildesheimer, a Berlin newspaper editor and passionate coffeehouse goer in the city of Berlin at the end of the nineteenth century.[32] Every morning he went to the famous Café Bauer on the corner of Friedrichstrs and Unter den Linden, which boasted a vast collection of over 300 different newspapers. For Hirsch Hildesheimer, this particular coffeehouse provided an excellent working place. He sat at his regular table surrounded by a huge mountain of all the newspapers that appeared in Germany, collecting information for *Die jüdische Presse*, the small but influential weekly representing Orthodox Jews in Berlin that he had edited since 1883. Everyone knew him, and he was often surrounded by groups of people who came to talk to him at his regular table. The fact that Café Bauer did not keep kosher was not a matter that appeared to disturb the otherwise orthodox Hildesheimer. Even on Shabbat he kept going to the coffeehouse. Only during the Passover holiday did he abstain. For Hildesheimer the coffeehouse was much more than just a convenient workplace where he could enjoy a cup of coffee and meet colleagues and friends, most of them Jews as well. Located at the heart of imperial Berlin, Café Bauer was a space that was both cosmopolitan and bourgeois. Hildesheimer's devotion to the coffeehouse might seem excessive, but it was by no means uncommon among Jews of the time. In all major central European cities, coffeehouses became regular meeting places for Jews. As Sarah Wobick-Segev compellingly demonstrates in her work on Jewish coffeehouse

---

[32]  This section is based on Henriette Hirsch (b. 1884), daughter of Hirsch Hildesheimer and granddaughter of Esriel Hildesheimer – the rabbi of the Orthodox community in Berlin and founder of Berlin Orthodox Rabbinical Seminar. These memories are now available online at the Leo Baeck digital collection www.lbi.org/. For an English translation of selected sections of the text see Monika Richarz (ed.), *Jewish Life in Germany: Memoirs from Three Centuries*. Translated by Paula P. Rosenfeld and Sidney Rosenfeld (Bloomington: Indiana University Press, 1991), 173–179.

culture, such consuming spaces provided Jews a venue where they could buy a sense of belonging to a culturally heterogeneous milieu that was, nevertheless, socially and economically much more homogeneous, that is, bourgeois.[33]

Though many coffeehouses reflected a Jewish longing to belong to a wider, heterogeneous community, such consuming spaces also became places of Jewish difference. Conrad Rosenstein, a Berlin dentist, described Café Leu – located next to the administrative center of the Jewish community – as the foyer of the "Jewish parliament." It provided a meeting place for a range of Jewish groups, where "one could hear the heartbeat of Berlin Jewry."[34] While coffeehouses predominated in the northern cities of Germany, in southern cities beer gardens served the same function. Even pious Jews living in the countryside did not always abstain from the beer garden on the Shabbat.[35]

From the testimony of Adolph Asch, a Jewish attorney from the city of Posen (now in Poland), we also learn how consumption reflected social distinctions among Jews. In prewar Posen, Asch recalls, better-off Jews used to enjoy a glass of wine at the restaurant Kaatz, while less privileged Jewish businessmen usually drank beer at the Jewish-owned beerhouse Falk. Asch also notes that Jewish families with children favored the bakery of Beely and Manske at the city park, where they could enjoy an apple pie with whipped cream for fifteen pfennig or without cream for only ten pfennig.[36]

Indeed, the taste for confectionery appears to have been another Jewish particularity. Jewish cookbooks dedicated ample space to recipes for cakes, cookies, desserts, and sweets, and German Jews were almost religious in their observation of the *Kaffee und Kuchen* (coffee and cake) hour.[37] Even according to the 1911 survey of Jewish working-

---

[33] Sarah Wobick-Segev, "Buying, Selling, Being, Drinking: Jewish Coffeehouse Consumption in the Long Nineteenth Century," in: Gideon Reuveni and Sarah Wobick-Segev (eds.), *The Economy in Jewish History: New Perspectives on the Interrelationship between Ethnicity and Economic Life* (New York: Berghahn Books, 2011), 127. More generally see Robert Liberles, *Jews Welcome Coffee: Tradition and Innovation in Early Modern Germany* (Lebanon: Brandies University Press, 2012).

[34] Quoted in Richarz, *Jüdische Leben in Deutschland*, 74.

[35] Heike Specht, *Die Feuchtwangers: Familie, Tradition und jüdisches Selbstverständnis* (Göttingen: Wallstein Verlag, 2006), 132; as well as the testimony of Willi Wertheimer, quoted in Richarz, *Jüdische Leben in Deutschland*, 184.

[36] Quoted in Richarz, *Jüdisches Leben in Deutschland*, 228.

[37] In one such award-winning book that was popular in central Europe at the beginning of the last century (and is still available on Amazon today), almost half the recipes are for sweet food: Marie Kauders, *Witwe Marie Kauders' erste israelitische Kochshule:*

class families in New York City, the quantity of cakes, rolls, and biscuits consumed by Jews was very large – the average quantity per family per week amounting to 7.5lb, as compared with 4.4lb in American British Northern groups.[38] Food companies quickly recognized the Jewish appetite for sweet food. From the turn of the century, the German company Dr. Oetker placed advertisements for its cakes and cookies in the Jewish press across central and Eastern Europe.[39]

All major bean-to-bar chocolate makers promoted their products in Jewish newspapers across and beyond Europe. Some of them even made their chocolate kosher. Even Arthur Ruppin, who otherwise took much pride in his frugality, records in his memoirs that when he started working for money as a teenager, he kept just enough money for himself to buy chocolate almost every day, before he gave the rest to his parents.[40] More research is required to determine the scope and nature of what appears as a Jewish appetite for comfort food.

---

*vollständiges Kochbuch unter Berücksichtigung der böhmischen, ungarischen, englischen und französischen Küche* (Prag: Pascheles, 1901). Kaplan, *The Making of the Jewish Middle Class*, 74.

[38] Askwith, *Cost of Living in American Towns*, ixxxviii.

[39] See, for example, the Jewish monthly *Ost und West* of 1911. In the 1920s Dr. Oetker intensely advertised in Yiddish daily newspapers in Polen.

[40] Alex Bein (ed.), *Arthur Ruppin: Memoirs, Diaries, Letters* (New York: Weidenfeld and Nicolson, 1972), 30.

# The World of Jewish Goods

Objects help to make us comfortable, but they also shape and give meaning to our lives. Despite a recent "material" turn in much historical writing, there is still some way to go before the importance of material culture is fully recognized.[1] Marcel Proust suggests that to gain a true historical understanding, we must push past analysis to things themselves: "the past is hidden somewhere beyond the reach of the intellect – in some material object."[2] Perhaps the significance of things – as opposed to ideas – is best captured by how people make sense of their own life histories. In their reconstruction of things past, anthropologist Barbara Kirshenblatt-Gimblett explains, "some individuals create *memory objects* as a way to materialize internal images, and through them to recapture earlier experiences."[3] By transforming the intangible into a tangible object, Kirshenblatt-Gimblett suggests, people become creators and curators of their memory. Jewish memories of the period before the Holocaust support this idea. Long after he had left his childhood home, one Hamburg physician recalled in his testimony two grand copper engravings (*Kupferstiche*) that hung on the walls of his parents' house. One depicted the dramatic encounter between David and King Saul just as the latter reached for his lance with the intention of eliminating his young

---

[1] Further on this see Leora Auslander, "Beyond Words," *The American Historical Review* 110 (2005), 1015–1045.

[2] Maecel Proust, *Remembrance of Things Past*, vol. 1 (New York: Random House, 1981), 47–48.

[3] Barbara Kirshenblatt-Gimblett, "Objects of Memory: Material Culture as Life Review," in: Elliott Oring (ed.), *Folk Groups and Folklore Genres: A Reader* (Logan: Utah State University Press, 1989), 331.

contender. The other captured the tragic figure of Judith as she was preparing to assassinate Holofernes. Of all the artifacts on display in his parent's house, it was these two engravings – representing not only dramatic moments in Jewish history but intensely felt personal tragedies – that left a profound and lasting impression on Goldschmidt. In writing his memoirs soon after his escape from Germany in 1939, Goldschmidt expressed his own astonishment that after so many years he was still able to vividly recall the engravings' cataclysmic scenes.[4]

Henriette Hirsch's memoirs, which we already cited in Chapter 10, provide another example of the centrality of objects in individual and collective Jewish memory.[5] Born in 1884 in the building of the Berlin Orthodox Rabbinical Seminar, her memories provide a glimpse into the household of one of Germany's most prominent orthodox Jewish families – the Hildesheimer family. At the start of her account, Hirsch explains that it is not her intention to write a work of literature or to provide a "strictly ordered" report of the history of the Hildesheimer family in Berlin. She sees her testimony as an eclectic collection of childhood reminiscences, aimed at presenting an intimate picture of life in a Jewish family at the turn of the century. Within this framework, objects mediate between present and past, fixing and making accessible what is, both for her and for her readers, a vanished world. Hirsch begins her account with a detailed description of her childhood home, which she notes "left an unforgettable impression on each person who knew it." What was so impressive about the house was not so much its alluring aesthetics or exceptional architecture. Visiting the house many years later, Hirsch notes that she was struck by the building's extreme simplicity (*Primitivität*) and small size. "It seemed to me that I was not myself," she confesses, "when I saw everything before with such different eyes."[6] By calling attention to the discrepancy between her childhood and adult perceptions of the building, Hirsch underscores the importance of the interaction between the house and the people living in it. In her narrative it was the people and their belongings that made the house a meaningful and memorable place. Her dramatic perceptual shift doesn't merely reflect the difference between a child's view of the world and an adult's perspective. Writing after the Holocaust from her new home in the state of Israel, Hirsch also draws attention to the impossibility of ever again revisiting her

---

[4] Moses Goldschmidt, *Mein Leben als Jude in Deutschland 1873–1939* (Hamburg: Ellert & Richter Verlag, 2004), 43.
[5] See footnote 32 in Chapter 10.   [6] Ibid.

childhood home, and all that surrounded it. That life, and that Germany, is gone forever.

The Hildesheimer family home was part of a dual-use building, with the family residence at the front and a synagogue in the backyard. This arrangement was common in many central European cities because local authorities required Jews to keep their houses of worship from being visible from the street.[7] Even when not required to do so, Jewish communities often preferred to locate their synagogues away from the public eye, partly because of the higher rental costs of building on the street, but also to avoid drawing too much attention. All this meant that while central European Jews had generally secured the right to worship freely by the end of the nineteenth century, they were still limited in how publicly they could display it. As a result, the architecture of Jewish life – synagogues and community buildings – often stood at odds with its surrounding non-Jewish environment. Whereas non-Jewish community institutions occupied the foreground of public space, Jewish institutions were usually located away from the public domain until the end of the nineteenth century. In this respect, the *Haskalah* dictum to "be a man in the outside world and a *Jew* at *home*" reinforced the Christian domination of the public sphere: Jewish spaces were opaque, even invisible, to the non-Jewish gaze. Looking at Jewish homes, however, it almost seems that the *Haskalah* desire for a public sphere that will repeal religious differences, confining any form of Jewish distinction to private life turned on its head.

As we reach the twentieth century, Jewish homes became more like non-Jewish homes, but the position of Jews' public life remained a sensitive issue. Well aware of this development, Jewish communities sought a variety of solutions to the perceived problem of Jewish visibility in the public domain. They hired professional architects to design synagogues and other large buildings and chose to locate many of them in prominent public locations. Distinctive designs were sought to distinguish Jewish houses of worship, and in the latter half of the nineteenth century, a series of imposing new synagogues appeared in the major European cities.[8] These conflicting trends allude to the innate tensions and ambivalence of "being Jewish" in the period before the Holocaust.

---

[7] Harold Hammer-Schenk, *Synagogen in Deutschland. Geschichte einer Baugattung im 19. und 20. Jahrhundert, 1780–1933* (Hamburg: H. Christians, 1981); Carol Herselle Krinsky, *Synagogues of Europe: Architecture, History, Meaning* (New York: Dover Publications, 1996).

[8] Ernst Hiller, "Betrachtung über den modernen Synagogebau," *Ost und West* 6 (1) (1906), 29–36.

## A JEWISH HOME?

Returning to Hirsch's memories, it is interesting to note that one of the first things she recalls about her childhood house is the big clock that hung over the door leading to the synagogue. In addition to the big clock, there were two other pendulum clocks in the house, one standing by Hirsch's grandfather's apartment and the other in her father's study room, both of whom were very important public figures. Maintaining the clocks was a costly, and serious, endeavor – Hirsch notes that no one dared to intervene with the clocks.[9] Timekeeping dominated life in the household and mediated the flow between public and private spheres, helping to coordinate the multiple identities – father, scholar, rabbi – of the members of the family.

In her memoir, Hirsch showcases her home, a characteristic bourgeois household in the turn-of-the-century Berlin. Aesthetics, and, in particular, modern style, was of the utmost importance. Every room had its own style that reflected its different function. The first floor was dominated by the rooms belonging to Hirsch's grandfather, Rabbi Hildesheimer: the great study that housed his impressive library of books (mostly in Hebrew), to which was attached a small and simply furnished bedroom. On the same floor was the family dining room, a lounge with a grand comfortable sofa, a table, and some chairs. Next to the lounge was the *Gute stube*, or the drawing room, with a red plush sofa in front of an oval wooden table with several red plush chairs standing around it. All, Hirsch annotates, were very comfortable, and the atmosphere was relaxed and *gemütlich*, or cozy. During the weekdays the furniture in the *Gute stube* was covered. Only on Sabbath, the high holidays, and for special guests was the room unveiled. In the same room stood a piano, another typical signifier of bourgeois households at the time, on which the children of the house used to play with, as Hirsch remarks, "moderate" talent. As in many other middle-class homes, the living area of the Hirsch's house was intended to be not only a comfortable space but a space that encouraged family harmony, and enabled the display of the family's good taste and financial success. The Hirsch's house also followed the gendered lines of most middle-class houses of the time, with a cozy, feminine drawing room contrasting with sober and masculine dining and study areas.

---

[9] On the importance of punctuality (*Pünktlichkeit*) for Hildesheimer see Sammy Gronemann, *Schalet: Beiträge zur Philosophie des "Wenn schon"* (Berlin: Philo Verlag, 1927), 257.

While the living area was a stage for the family to display itself to outsiders, the kitchen was a private place, removed from visitors' eyes. Equipped with a coal stove, a wall closet, and a washbasin with running water, the kitchen was designed to cater to the dining area while maintaining a typical middle-class separation between a public dining space and a private food preparation space. The division between backstage and display areas also meant that food did not have to be moved through areas where it did not belong.[10] Domestic employees were crucial to maintaining this distinction between public and private. A housemaid lived in a small room off the kitchen. Other domestic personal staff included a nanny, a maid, and a cook, normally an orthodox woman who could be trusted to keep a strict kosher kitchen. Finally, there was the house backer, a laundress, and additional help for special occasions. Every day, Hirsch reports, a hairdresser came to the house to do her mother's hair, who wore a wig according to orthodox Jewish tradition. Except for the cook, most of the domestic personal staff were not Jewish, a common arrangement in Jewish households of similar social position.

Hirsch's parents' bedroom, on the second floor of the house, was furnished with a big wooden bed and a wardrobe. Next to the main bedroom was Hirsch Hildesheimer's study, with an extremely large desk, a leather sofa, a few chairs, and a table where he hosted friends and colleagues. Next to the study was the children's playroom that featured a horizontal bar and a swing, which the children were allowed to use only when their father was out. The room also contained small desks on which the children used to prepare their school homework as well as a small sofa, a coffee table, and a few small chairs. In this miniature bourgeois salon, the children were served hot chocolate and sandwiches, emulating bourgeois rituals and table manners. The sleeping area was divided between the four girls and two boys of the family.

The Hildesheimers were an orthodox Jewish family, living according to Jewish law. Yet it is difficult to delineate what was specifically "Jewish" about their living style, aesthetic taste, or consumer choices. One indicator of Jewishness were the books in Hebrew as well as the Jewish newspapers, both kept in the study rooms of the house, along with ritual objects like Sabbath candles, menorah, *kiddush* wine cup, *havdalah* set, and of course the *mezuzah* (doorpost) further signifying Jewishness – though it is unclear whether these objects were publicly displayed within the house.

---

[10] Rachel Rich, *Bourgeois Consumption: Food, Space and Identity in London and Paris, 1850–1916* (Manchester: Manchester University Press, 2011), 46.

Otherwise, it is hard to say what was specifically Jewish about the home. Based on Hirsch's testimony it is even difficult to establish to what extent keeping kosher affected the architecture of the household. The family kept separate dishes for milk and meat and had extra kitchenware that was used only during the Passover festival. But the extent to which living in accordance to Jewish law informed, for example, their choice of chinaware, furniture, or even their clothes, is not clear. The design of the house, the possessions within it, and the family's lifestyle are all difficult to distinguish from non-Jewish homes of similar social status.

The sense of conformity with a wider culture is further enhanced by Hirsch's comments on her family's leisure activities, such as weekend excursions; summer vacations; and visits to museums, the theater, and dancing halls, all of which were typical signifiers of upper-middle-class life at the time. In an interesting passage Hirsch evokes what she calls her mother's "generosity" (*Großzügigkeit*). According to Hirsch, her mother never spent large sums of money on herself or displayed her spending ostentatiously. "It was her greatest pleasure," she recalls, "to make other people gifts, and bring them joy."[11] The main beneficiaries of her practices of consumption were family members and domestic personnel; attending to their well-being was a central pillar of her bourgeois responsibilities as mother and lady of the house.

Taking into account all of the ways in which the Hildesheimers were typical of middle-class families, what does Hirsch's memoir reveal about what it was that made a house Jewish? This is a difficult historical question to answer and remains difficult to answer in contemporary terms. In a recent survey on Jewish American material culture, many respondents rejected the suggestion that their homes constituted a Jewish space, explaining that their homes were not "Jewish enough" or even not "real Jewish."[12] Going back to the beginning of the last century in western and central Europe, it seems that in almost all respects, even pious Jews lived a private life remarkably similar to that of their non-Jewish peers.[13] In one

---

[11] Hirsch, memories (available online at the Leo Baeck digital collection) www.lbi.org/. For an English translation of selected sections of the text see Monika Richarz (ed.), *Jewish Life in Germany: Memoirs from Three Centuries*. Translated by Paula P. Rosenfeld and Sidney Rosenfeld (Bloomington: Indiana University Press, 1991), 173–179.

[12] Vanessa L. Ochs, "What Makes a Jewish Home Jewish?" *Cross Currents* 49 (4) (1999/2000), 491–510.

[13] On this point see especially Leora Auslander, Jewish Taste, comparative studies on Jews in Berlin and Paris where she compellingly demonstrates how "Jewish taste" was embedded in local cultures rather than a transnational Jewish signifier.

reading, this is another manifestation of the Jewish longing to fit into the surrounding culture. But the example of the Hildesheimer's household suggests that in the absence of intrinsic tension between Jewish traditions and a modern middle-class lifestyle, the two were easily amalgamated, even in orthodox homes.

Combining traditional Jewish teachings or the study of the "Torah with the way of the land" (תורה עם דרך ארץ) was part of an explicit project to modernize Jewish orthodoxy proposed by rabbinic authorities such as Samson Raphael Hirsch and Asriel Hildesheimer.[14] Moritz Daniel Oppenheim's well-known paintings of Jewish family life are a further illustration of how popular the image of a harmonious coexistence between Jewish tradition and bourgeois way of life was in the second half of the nineteenth century.[15]

### MAKING A DIFFERENCE

As bourgeois culture came increasingly to dominate modern urban life, tastes, and habits of citizens became more standardized. Yet this very process also provided the premise for a new set of social and cultural distinctions whereby Jewishness could be defined not as a matter of faith or ethnicity but in terms of aesthetic taste and consumer choice. Interestingly, Jewish taste in western Europe at this time was often described as pretentious and bland. This assessment was associated part of a critique of the so-called Jewish parvenu who came to epitomize a range of social misgivings for Jews and non-Jews alike. If Jews in western Europe were condemned for bad taste, their brethren in Eastern Europe were often portrayed as having no taste whatsoever. Traveling in the eastern parts of Galicia at the beginning of the 1890s, the American author and illustrator Joseph Pennell noted that

all through this part of the country a window-curtain in a Jew's house is almost unknown, and privacy is unsought. On the other hand, there is nothing to see in his house. Its interior is the barest, most forlorn, most uninteresting imaginable, and it is not, as far as I could discover, until after the Jew is dead that he has the slightest pride in his look.[16]

[14] Mordechai Breuer, *Modernity within Tradition: The Social History of Orthodox Jewry in Imperial Germany* (New York: Columbia University Press, 1992).
[15] Richard I. Cohen, *Emergence of Jewish Artists in 19th-Century Europe* (Abingdon: Merrell Publishers, 2001).
[16] Joseph Pennell, *The Jew at Home* (New York: D. Appleton and Company, 1892), 51.

Such assessments notwithstanding, it is improbable that Jewish consumers exhibited uniformly bad taste. Ample evidence attests to Jewish refinement; Jews were frequently considered trendsetters.[17] "I believe it is a fact which no-one will gainsay that Jewish women on an average dress far better, more elaborately, and more stylishly than do, say, English women of parallel class," observed one British commentator.[18] What distinguished Jews as consumers was less the presence or, for that matter, the absence of a manifestly Jewish aesthetics, but rather the cultural positioning of their consumer choices as Jews. That is to say that Jewishness was not evinced in the style or the goods themselves, but in the symbolic meaning of consumer choices and in the varied ways things were placed, used, and conceived as "Jewish."

As noted before, those with antisemitic views often assigned Jewish meanings to consumer choices, a revealing expression of which can be found in *Home Life in Germany*, published by Cicely Sidgwick. Sidgwick, herself a German Jew, observed that Jewish women responded to antisemitism at the turn of the century by dressing exceptionally well. In German cities, she wrote, "when you see a woman who is 'exquisitely' slim, graceful, dainty from head to foot, and finely clad, then you may vow by all the gods that she has Jewish blood in her."[19]

Gift-giving around Jewish life cycle events provide a further example of the reciprocal relations between Jews and things, in particular at Bar Mitzvah, weddings, and Chanukah, which for a growing number of families was celebrated in tandem with Christmas.[20] As indicated in Chapter 2, even if there was nothing explicitly Jewish about the gifts themselves, the fact that they were given on Jewish occasions made them into "Jewish things." In other words, the process by which goods are made "Jewish" takes place when meaning is allocated to objects by telling their story within an established Jewish narrative. In this way, even things that have no overt relation to Judaism could be conceived as "Jewish" when evoking certain sentiments and images. Thus, for example, one of

---

[17] For a fascinating discussion of different perceptions of mainly Jewish women that also deals with the issue of taste, see Elvira Grözinger, *Die schöne Jüdin: Klischees, Mythen und Vorurteile über Juden in der Literatur* (Berlin: Philo Verlag, 2003).

[18] Gaza, "Through a Woman's Eyes," *The Jewish World* (March 29, 1923), 10. On this see also Gaza, "The Smart Jewess and Her Silly Critics," *The Jewish World* (June 15, 1933), 5–6.

[19] Mrs. Alfred Sidgwick, *Home Life in Germany* (New York: MacMillan Company, 1912), 321.

[20] Gaza, "Through a Woman's Eyes" (December 15, 1927); Sammy Gronemann, *Schalent: Beiträge zur Philosophie des "Wenn Schon!"* (Berlin: Philo Verlag, 1927), 35–42.

the respondents in the survey on "what makes a Jewish home Jewish," stated that for her, "a Jewish home is books." This woman further explained that the books "don't have to be Jewish. [But] if I don't see books, I don't think it is a Jewish home."[21] This notion of Jews as educated people neatly corresponds to the bourgeois idea of *Bildung*. By the end of the twentieth century in the United States, *Bildung* had come to be seen as a signifier of Jewishness.

## JEWISH STYLE

Examining everyday Jewish life in the early modern period in Germanic lands, Herman Pollack calls attention to the strong influence of the non-Jewish environment on what he calls Jewish folkways. He notes that even food that came to represent central European Jewish traditions had no distinct Jewish origin, including *Kugel* (usually a sweet pie baked out of noodles or potatoes commonly served for Shabbat and other celebrations), *tsimmes* (a sweet dish made from roots, chickpeas, and dried fruits traditionally served for the Jewish New Year dinner of Rosh Hashanah), or *kneydalach* (matzah balls or dumpling made from matzah meal usually severed in a soup at the Pessach dinner).[22] Even the celebrated bagel was widespread in Eastern Europe long before becoming the poster food of American Jewry.[23] As Pollack convincingly shows, there was no innate tension between Jewish culture, religious heritage, and the lifeways of the non-Jewish environment.[24] The integration of the tradition of the past with the culture of the present to become part of everyday life was not an exclusive feature of the early modern period. Yet unlike premodern times, during which the Jews were firmly fixed in place in society regardless of their folkways, in the modern era choice became central to Jewish difference and even the smallest everyday choices could turn into meaningful acts.

As Jews became more integrated into mainstream culture, the world of things became more rather than less important as a means of expressing difference or asserting belonging to a wider culture. Efforts to craft a so-called *Judenstill*, or Jewish style, arose in response, with the aim of rendering material a distinctive sense of Jewish belonging, with all the

[21] Ochs, "What makes a Jewish home Jewish," 495.

[22] Hermann Pollack, *Jewish Folkways in Germanic Lands from 1648 to 1809* (Cambridge, MA: MIT Press, 1971).

[23] Maria Balinska, *The Bagel: The Surprising History of a Modest Bread* (New Haven: Yale University Press, 2008).

[24] Pollack, *Jewish Folkways*.

contradictions inherent in it. The new synagogue architecture mentioned earlier was one significant manifestation of this drive to find a Jewish style. The search for Jewish authenticity also inspired artists to seek typically Jewish forms of expression.[25] In a 1930 exhibition in the Berlin Museum of Decorative Arts on *Kult und Form*, Jewish artists displayed their new designs for traditional Jewish ritual objects, such as Sabbath candles, menorah, and *kiddush* wine cup, stating that "in accordance with [Jewish] tradition we reject the use of eclectic forms in art and strive to retain intimate relationship between cult and life by using plain forms of expression."[26] The return to elementary form and the emphasis on the function of objects epitomized modernist developments in the arts after the Great War, a movement in art and design also known as the New Objectivity.[27] Some Jewish commentators celebrated this new aesthetic trend as particularly suited to the design of Jewish objects, claiming that by underlining the function of the objects, a deeper link to an historical tradition was manifest.[28] The monthly magazine *Menorah*, which sought to unite often-divergent Jewish subgroups, went even further. It called on readers to wonder why a Jewish journal should contain so many images of modern urban buildings and suburban family houses, as well as photos of stylish living rooms, furniture, and all kinds of household goods. Although these new designs did not appear to have much to do with Judaism, explained the art historian Max Eisler, many prominent figures in modern

[25] Olga Bloch, "Moderne Silberareiten der Berliner Silberschmiedin Emmy Roth," "Jüdische Haushatungsschulen in Deutschalnd," *Blätter des jüdischen Frauenbundes für Frauenarbeit und für Frauenbewegung* VI (7) (1930), 2–3; Michael Brenner, *The Renaissance of Jewish Culture in Weimar Germany* (New Haven: Yale University Press, 1996), 153–185.

[26] Quoted in: Max Osborn, "Moderns Kultgerät," *Jüdisches Gemeindeblatt Berlin* 21 (1) (1931), 10. On this exhibition see also Lotte Pulvermacher, "Kult und Form: Ausstellung von modernem jüdischen Kultgerät im Kunstgewerbemuseum, Berlin," *Bayerische Israelitische Gemeindezeitung*, 7 (1) (1931), 4–5; Will Pelß, "Neuzeitliche jüdische Kulturgeräte," *Menorah* 9 (3) (1931), 149–150. For a historical overview of such exhibitions see Jens Hoppe, *Jüdische Geschichte und Kulture in Museen. Zur nichtjüdischen Museologie des jüdischen in Deutschland* (Mümster: Waxmann, 2002); for an inspiring discussion of Jewish ritual objects as commodities see Michal S. Friedlander, "Tradition as Commodity: The Production of Jewish Ceremonial Objects in Hanau am Main," in: Julie-Marthe Cohen (ed.), *Jewish Ceremonial Objects in Transcultural Context* (Leuven: Peeters, 2004), 163–191.

[27] Sergiusz Michalski, *New Objectivity: Painting, Graphic Art and Photography in Weimar Germany* (Cologne: Taschen America, 2003).

[28] Pulvermacher, "Kult und Form," 4. "Der Zusammenhang mit Tradition wird nicht im Äußerlich Formaleren gesucht, sondern im Erfassen des geistigen Gehalts des Ritus, für den das Kultgäret die Funktion trägt."

design were of Jewish origin, and it is the "Jewish spirit," he proclaimed, that is producing a new aesthetic form: "free from any atavism – and thus more vibrant. Not imposing (*proklamatorisch*) – and therefore more pure."[29] In a series of articles published in *Menorah* in 1926, Eisler advocated modern design as a Jewish gestalt serving Jewish goals that would ultimately help to raise "the Jewish soul in the spirit of religious solemnity."[30]

Research already took heed to what appears as a strong Jewish attraction to modernism. Given the frequency with which Jews were perceived to be pioneers and agents of change, it should come as no surprise that Victor Klemperer chooses the image of an airplane to describe his Jewishness. From his diaries we learn that he was passionate about all modern technology: driving as well as flying along with the new media of film and radio.[31] Moses Goldschmidt shared Klemperer's enthusiasm for automobiles. Being the registered medic for a number of prominent hotels in Hamburg, Goldschmidt needed to travel frequently in the city. In his memoir, he describes in great detail the two electric cars he successively owned in the mid-1920s. After the Hannoversche Waggonfabrik (HaWa) stopped manufacturing its city electric car in 1927, and despite his obvious penchant for the HaWa electric vehicle, Goldschmidt decided to switch over to a petrol-driven automobile. In 1928 he procured a four-seat convertible Adler automobile that he used until the Nazis disowned his driving permit at the end of 1938.[32] Reflecting on why he felt so comfortable in functionalist style, historian Herbert Strauss recalled the first time he encountered a fully Bauhaus interior at the house of his school mate Günter, son of the only Jews of Sephardic origin in his home town of Würzburg in south Germany. His memories of the warmth, open-mindness, and, presumably, also the Jewishness, of his family friends gave him the "feeling of being at home in New Functionalism ever since."[33]

---

[29] Max Eisler, "Vom neuen Geist der jüdischen Baukunst," *Menorah* 4 (9) (1926), 519–527, here 527.

[30] Ibid., 520. In this context it is interesting to note that at the beginning of the 1950s Ruth Glazer still lamented on the lack of or poor aesthetics in Jewish life in America and called for the beatification and revivification of the Jewish tradition, Ruth Glazer, "The Jewish Object," *Commentary* 12 (1951), 63–67.

[31] On these aspects of the Klemperer dairies see also Claudia Buhles, *... nur wahr will ich schreiben – Victor Klemperer in der Weimarer Republik – Alltag und Selbstverständnis eines deutsch-jüdischen Professors* (Saarbrücken: Conte, 2003).

[32] Goldschmidt, *Mein Leben*, 170–171.

[33] Herbert Arthur Strauss, *In the Eye of the Storm: Growing Up Jewish in Germany, 1918–1943: A Memoir* (New York: Fordham University Press, 1999), 40.

The household of the renowned pathologist János Plesch provides another glimpse into a somewhat more eclectic, but nonetheless cosmopolitan interior. Coming to Berlin from Budapest in 1903, Plesch took active part in the cultural life of the Weimar period. He hosted prominent figures at his spacious house on Budapester Str. 22 in Charlottenburg, a sought-after part of the city where many well-to-do Jews resided.[34] The house contained both antique and modern furniture from many countries and in many styles: a cabinet from Japan; a Louis XVI bed, pots, and pictures from France and China; a clock from the Netherlands; an Italian armchair; a table from Spain; as well as a refrigerator and other electric devices from Germany. It also held an impressive collection of paintings, most notably a Rembrandt, as well as works by Camille Pissarro, Eugène Delacroix, and Max Liebermann. Most of these were exhibited in the music salon of Plesch's grand home. For insurance purposes, Plesch's house was estimated at the end of the 1920s to be worth 3.25 million RM, equivalent to approximately one million dollars today.[35]

It is difficult to establish how and to what extent being Jewish informed such extravagant lifestyle. Most Jews lived in rather modest circumstances, to say the least. Moreover, as Leora Auslander reminds us, one should be careful not to overstate the argument about the link between Jews and modernism. Not only did the majority of Jews not reside in modernist interiors, but there was also vocal discontent among Jews with the new aesthetic trend. "I say! Away with the modern nonsense, let's stick to the good old German style interior," wrote one reader to the Jewish monthly *Menorah* in response to its support of the New Objectivity movement.[36] Interestingly, the letter-writer found no contradiction between feeling at home in a "German interior" and being Jewish. For many, German *Gemütlichkeit* was part of a Jewish tradition. Calling

---

[34] On Plesch, see his autobiography János Plesch, *The Story of a Doctor* (London: Victor Gollancz Ltd., 1947).

[35] Jewish Museum Berlin, Dok 86/25/88/-95, 100–112 (Professor Dr. Jonos Plesch). Shortly after the Nazi takeover the Plesch family left for England. After the war Prof. and Mrs. Plesch decided for reasons of health and age (73 & 67) to leave England for Switzerland. Taking their most personal belongings that had been in their possession for 30 years, they estimated the value of their household in 1947 at £1,425, which is over $70,000 in today's value. However, they left the Rembrandt painting with their daughter in London.

[36] Max Eisler, "Von der neuen Baukunst," *Menorah* 9 (1–2) (1931), 35–42, here 42. The quoted reader's response appeared in the following article Max Eisler, "Aus dem Kunstleben: Bauen und Wohnen," *Menorah* 9 (3–4) (1931), 125–134, here 126.

attention to the profound difference between the lives of Jewish women in the Restoration era (ca. from 1815 to 1848) and the emancipation period, historian Selma Stern noted that while "The soul of Jewish women in the age of emancipation vibrates in a thousand shades. The Jewess of the Restoration period, in contrast, had something of the clear, unchanging shapes of the buildings and furniture of its time."[37] Others feared that the pace of modern life would make the memory of the warmth of the traditional Jewish home dwindle in an ever more distant past.[38] This was the message of an exhibition on the Jewish home organized by Marta Coblenz and the B'nai B'rith sisterhood in 1927. In contrast to modern styles that emphasized functionality and the rational use of space, the exhibition displayed the home as site for religious practice, reiterating once more the importance of *gemütlichkeit* for upholding Jewish tradition.[39]

Other modern trends came in for similar criticism. The women's weekly *Die Jüdische Frau* deplored the *Bubikopf*, or pageboy, hairstyle that became fashionable during the 1920s, claiming that antisemites associated it with Jews and calling on Jewish women to eschew the haircut and instead the grow their hair in the traditional longer styles.[40] The Union of Traditional Torah-Faithful Rabbis (*Die Vereinigung traditionell gesetzestreuer Rabbiner*), one of the most prominent organizations of German Orthodox Jews, was much more overt with its condemnation of the modern look. In a public statement from 1926, the Union asserted its "holy duty" (*heilige Pflicht*) to call upon the entire Jewish public to unite in the struggle against the degenerative trends in fashion. Juxtaposing the degrading influence of modern fashion (*Kleidersitten*) with the traditional values of modesty set forth in the Torah, the rabbis urged Jewish women to make chastity and decorum the hallmarks of their appearance.[41]

Discussions of Jewish modernism were thus part of a broader debate on the nature of Jewishness. But there is more to be said here. While some Jews

---

[37] Selma Stern, "Die Entwicklung des jüdischen Frauentypus seit dem Mittelalter," *Der Morgen* 6 (1926), 650.

[38] Joseph Freimark, "Die jüdische Frau und das jüdische Haus. Ausstellung des Schwesterbundes der U.O.B.B. Logen in Köln a.Rh," *Menorah* 5 (7) (1927), 489.

[39] Ibid.; as well as in Kerry M. Wallach, *Jewish Women and the Jewish Press in Weimar Germany*, University of Pennsylvania, PhD. Diss., 2011, 244.

[40] Susi Würzburg, "Bubikopf," *Die Jüdische Frau* 2 (9/10) (June 15, 1926), 8. See also "Die jüdische Frau im Spiegel der nationalsozialistischen Presse," *CV-Zeitung (Monatsausgabe)* 11 (November 1931), 73. For further examples of this discussion on Jewish hair see Wallach, *Jewish Women and the Jewish Press*, 249–252.

[41] On this statement, see Doris Wittner, "Frauenmode," *CV-Zeitung* 28 (June 9, 1926), 373–374; "Gegen Entartungen der Mode," *Die Jüdische Frau* 2 (9/10) (June 15, 1926), 8.

sought to employ new forms of expressions to underscore Jewish difference, others used explicitly Jewish venues to emphasize similarity with the
surrounding society. Beyond its function as a place of Jewish worship, the
synagogue was often used as a space in which Jews could display "how far"
they have made it, socially and financially, in the "outside" [non-Jewish]
world. In a similar manner, Jewish celebrations like Brith (circumcision),
Bar Mitzvahs, and weddings became lavish banquets full of high-society
style.[42] Even funerals and memorials were occasions to show-off opulence
and success. In the American context, Jenna Weissman Joselit documented
how funeral rites that had been communal undertakings in Europe became
the exclusive affair of private funeral homes "serving Jewish tradition in
a modern manner," as one funeral home claimed in its advertising brochure
at the beginning of the last century.[43] At that time, she reports, hotels close
to Jewish cemeteries started offering funeral parties, and the traditional,
somewhat doleful, *Shivah* (week-long mourning period) slowly transformed into an exercise in conviviality.[44]

In his memoir, Conrad Rosenstein recalls the Bar Mitzvah party of one
of his schoolmates. He playfully depicts the limousines rolling up the quiet
streets of Berlin, the young maidservants in black and white helping the
ladies out of their fur coats, some of them, he indelibly remembered,
"deeply décolleté" and "fragrant with a variety of choice perfumes."[45]
Rosenstein felt completely out of place amongst what he described as
a Jewish leisured class. He noted that the only person in the party who
took an interest in him was his friend's grandmother, from whom, he
added, originated the family fortune in the first place.

Condemnation of inordinate expenditures by Jews has a long and
illustrious history. In early modern periods, Jewish communities enacted
so-called sumptuary regulations to restrain and control habits of consumption. Decadent celebrations on the occasion of Brith, Bar Mitzvahs,
and weddings were by no means limited to the twentieth century.[46]
The communal book of the Jewish community of Pentras in southeastern

---

[42] At the end of the 1920 some wedding ceremonies were even filmed. See the editorial of
*The Jewish World* (August 23, 1928).
[43] Jenna Weissman Joselit, *The Wonders of America* (New York: Hill and Wang, 1994), 278.
[44] When it comes to mourning we still know very little about how modern lifestyle trends
refashioned Jewish funeral ceremonies in Europe.
[45] Rosenstein in: Richarz, *Jewish Life in Germany*, 172.
[46] Salo Wittmayer Baron, *The Jewish Community*, vol. II (Westport: Greenwood Press,
1942), 301–319; Aryeh Spero, "Conspicuous Consumption at Jewish Functions,"
*Judaism* 1 (37) (1988), 103–110; Victor Karady, *The Jews of Europe in the Modern
Era* (Budapest: Central European University Press, 2004), 55–57.

France reveals that at the beginning of the eighteenth century "when occasion arises for any religious festival ... such as a circumcision or wedding, they [community members] indulge in expenditure greater than they can afford, so that there is trembling in place of joy as they see the drain of their money, making them limit their household expenditure and their payments for (communal) taxation."[47]

Many Jewish communities were riven by destructive disagreements about resentment created by the extravagant spending of some members. Such anxieties impelled the North German communities of Hamburg, Altona, and Wandsbek to limit the number of people that could be invited to festivities, and to abolish what appears the fashionable late eighteenth-century trend for decorating banquet tables with confectionery.[48] The communal legislation also stipulated that party-givers make charitable donations that were proportional to the number of invitees. Such documents offer unique insight into the everyday life of Jews in different periods, revealing the enduring tension between how Jews actually lived and what community leaders wished to promote as a Jewish "inner worldly asceticism," to use Max Weber's phrase. The next chapter will address how consumption became a form of negotiation about the boundaries of Jewishness.[49]

---

[47] Ceci Roth, "Sumptuary Laws of the Community of Pentras," *The Jewish Quarterly Review* 18 (4) (1928), 362–363.

[48] M. Kayserling, "Luxusverbote," *Mitteilungen für der Gesellschaft für jüdische Volkskunde* 1 (1904), 40–43; Max Grunwald, "Luxusverbot der Dreigemeinden (Hamburg – Altona – Wandsbek) a. d. Jahre 1715," *Jahrbuch für Jüdische Volkskunde* 25 (1923), 227–232. Moshe Kaplan and Davis Wiskott published a series of sumptuary regulations from different communities in Europe and North Africa, which are available on the Jewish Legal Heritage Society website www.mishpativri.org.il/new/motarot.php.

[49] This formulation draws upon David Kraemer, *Jewish Eating and Identity Through the Ages* (New York: Routledge, 2012), 5.

# I 2

## Spending Power and Its Discontents

Attempts to regulate consumption in the form of sumptuary laws date to ancient times. In the early modern period the numbers of such regulations increased rapidly as the upper classes tried fruitlessly to control the manner of living of the steadily rising lower classes.[1] As earnings rose in all echelons of society, new social groups sought to emulate the lifestyle of the wealthy and to defy their sumptuary laws. Formally designed to prevent people from spending beyond their means, the presence of sumptuary regulations indicates a culture in which material display is important. As much as these regulations were part of the attempt to restrain consumption, in other words, they also publicized the fact of social ascent.

To be sure, social mobility was either generated or repressed by sumptuary legislation. Instead, such laws were part of a paternalistic worldview in which the wellbeing of subjects was seen as purview of the authorities.[2] The sphere of fashion was particularly subject to this sort of paternalistic control. As historian Quentin Bell observed in his seminal study *Of Human Finery*, a "society which produces changing fashions must itself be a society which is changing."[3] This basic perception of ongoing change typically produced means to cope and control fluctuations. For our purposes here it is, however, important to call attention to the special significance of emulation within this process. In the context of the sumptuary regulations, fashion was condemned as a deviation from the social norm.

[1] Millia Davenport, *The Book of Costume* (New York: Crown, 1948), 190.
[2] Reinhold August Dorwart, *The Prussian Welfare State before 1740* (Cambridge, MA: Harvard University Press, 1971), 25–50.
[3] Quentin Bell, *On Human Finery* (London: The Hogarth Press, 1947), 70.

It was conceived as inappropriate mimicry that promotes people to spend beyond their means. This very reaction delineates how emulation became a demonstrative act divulging the ambition and effort of different groups and individuals to gain recognition and improve their social status. Jews were part of this development both as producers and as addressees of sumptuary enactments.

Scrutinizing Jewish sumptuary regulations, the British historian Cecil Roth noted that it was natural for Jewish communities to have imitated their neighbors in this, as in so many other respects.[4] In many cases sumptuary laws were imposed upon Jews by secular authorities, "scandalized," as Roth insinuate, "at the ostentation permitted themselves by these social pariahs."[5] Jewish extravagance, in other words, was sometimes construed as a form of Jewish assertion and efforts to constrain Jewish spending therefore could be read as an indication of anxiety over increasing Jewish power and status.

But this is only one way to read the regulations against luxury and ostentation. Research also underscores the interconnectivity between sumptuary laws and questions of belonging. In his work on the city of Bern, historian Simon Teuscher demonstrates how kinship was used as an organizing principle for legal and administrative regulations, *inter alia*, sumptuary laws. Referring to regulations that limited the number of people who could be invited to baptisms and weddings, Teuscher argues that this legislation aimed ever more at converting festivities that had used to bring together a broad range of acquaintances into family celebrations.[6] Limiting the size of banquets held at Jewish celebrations coincided with a more general tendency to accentuate the nuclear family. Jewish sumptuary regulations sharply limited the display of wealth in public. For Jews and non-Jews alike, efforts to regulate consumption indicate anxiety about the devious effects of overspending on moral standing, social relations, and community cohesion. By implementing their own sumptuary laws, Jews made the discussions on spending and luxury a specifically Jewish matter, part of the attempts to define the boundaries of Jewishness.

---

[4] Ceci Roth, "Sumptuary Laws of the Community of Pentras," *The Jewish Quarterly Review* 18 (4) (1928), 357.

[5] Ibid.

[6] Simon Teuscher, "Politics of Kinship in the City of Bern at the End of the Middle Ages," in: David Warren Sabean, Jon Mathieu and Simon Teuscher (eds.), *Kinship in Europe: Approaches to Long-Term Developments 1300–1900* (New York: Berghahn, 2007), 86.

Jewish sumptuary legislation used traditional sources to call for restraint and discretion, reminding Jews that the Torah compels Jews to demonstrate mindfulness.[7] Often casting the pursuit of luxury and fashion among Jews as a result of contamination with foreign ways, sumptuary regulations were enacted all over the Jewish world from Eastern Europe to North Africa and Yemen. These bans on the public display of wealth were often driven by a desire to preempt anti-Jewish sentiment. At the same time, sanctions against the wearing of so-called Christian dress were designed to champion Jewish distinctiveness. Leisure activities that involved close contact with non-Jews such as dances, local celebrations, theater, or coffee house visits were strictly regulated or even forbidden in some communities. The question of appearance in the public sphere was pivotal to the Haskalah movement, which called among other things for Jews to abandon distinctive attire and, in so doing turned traditional Jewish dress into a symbol of resistance to modernization.[8]

More significant, however, is the connection made by Jewish sumptuary regulations between giving and spending. As indicated above, banquet size was linked to the host's wealth and fiscal contribution to the community. By giving more in the form of what amounted to a banquet tax, one could essentially buy permission to hold a bigger and more ostentatious function. In this way community authorities sought to reconcile the unrelenting demand for grand celebrations with anxiety over the response by less fortunate members of the community. Tolerating spending so long it was coupled with giving helped to ratify community cohesion.[9] Even so, it did not eliminate the innate tension between spending and giving, or the ever-present concern about the allegedly Jewish propensity for excessive expenditure. Well into the modern period, Jews were urged to demonstrate moderation and self-discipline as consumers. Especially in times of economic hardship, when anti-Jewish sentiments were on the rise, discussions on the "problem" of Jewish spending intensified. This was most definitely the case in the period after World War I in Weimar Germany, during the years of hyperinflation and unemployment. As antisemitism became more virulent, the German Jewish press in particular urged their

---

[7] For a useful collection of such regulations see the Bezalel Landau, *Regulations against Luxsurys* (Hebrew), available at www.daat.ac.il/daat/kitveyet/niv/landoy2-1.htm; as well as Jacob Neusner, *The Economics of the Mishnah* (Chicago: University of Chicago Press, 1990).

[8] Eric Silverman, *A Cultural History of Jewish Dress* (Oxford: Berg, 2010).

[9] James D. Faubion and Jennifer A. Hamilton, "Sumptuary Kinship," *Anthropological Quarterly* 80 (2) (2007), 533–559.

readers to exercise restraint and avoid attention-seeking through consumption.[10]

Depicting Jews as war profiteers and immoral sybarites was one of the most common antisemitic slurs of the period. It was an accusation all the more painful, wrote a member of the *Centralverein*, "because such sins are committed in Jewish circles."[11] In a 1922 booklet entitled *Luxus und Not* (luxury and distress), the *Centralverein* depicted luxury as a social evil that deepened the gap between the rich and the poor and as an antireligious phenomenon that generated vanity and arrogance. Since "the Jews are the most social and most religious element in history," the pamphlet postulated, "the insane luxury was alien to them" until very recently.[12] Such polemics also made the point that Christians were not much better in this regard than Jews but this was scant consolation since the leisure class was commonly perceived to be predominantly Jewish.

The efforts to urge Jews to exercise more prudence as consumers became so excessive that Ludwig Hollandär wondered "which respectable family is washing its dirty laundry in public?"[13] Rather than focusing on what he called Jewish *innere Mission* (home missionary), Holländer proposed that German Jews should improve their sense of *Slebstwürde* (self-respect). Strengthening Jewish dignity, Holländer maintained, would augment their sense of responsibility and eventually help to significantly reduce the number of reckless *Prahlsüchtigen* (those addicted to showing off) who discredited German Jewry.[14]

While liberal Jews were primarily concerned that Jewish conspicuous consumption would hinder integration, Orthodox and nationalist Jews feared the opposite: that luxury – especially the alleged Jewish obsession with fashion – would lead to excessive assimilation. They all sought to shed the taint of Jewish *materialism* by calling attention to the alleged menaces of overspending on Jewish community survival. Although calls for Jews to renounce material goods were addressed to both men and

---

[10] "Uebt Zurückhaltung! Ein Mahnwort gegen Putzsucht und Schlemmerei," *Israelitische Familienblatt* (August 9, 1923).

[11] No author stated, *Luxus und Not* (Berlin: Philo Verlag, 1922), 3.

[12] Ibid., 3, 4. Cf. Alfred Sidgwick, *Home Life in Germany* (New York: MacMillan Company, 1912), 177.

[13] Ludwig Holländer, "Selbstwürde," *CV-Zeitung* (August 8, 1922), 173.

[14] "Mit dem Gefühl solcher Würde aber wird die Verantwortung wachsen und die Zahl jener Leichten Prahlsüchtigen, Verantwortungslosen abnehmen, die das deutsche Judentum durch Bestimmung und Handeln stündlich beschmutzen." Ibid., 174.

women, the latter were considered the Achilles heel of efforts to tame the so-called Jewish propensity for overconsumption.

### RIVAL VIEWS OF THE FEMININUS JUDAICUS CONSUMENS

Prejudice against female consumers has a long and illustrious history. Both Jewish and non-Jewish commentators have long associated men with the sphere of production and the spiritual world, while women have commonly been linked with materialism and consumerism. Even liberal intellectuals such as the Jewish industrialist and politician Walter Rathenau observed the growing importance of female consumers in modern times with great apprehension. In his 1917 book "In Days to Come," Rathenau noted that in the modern economic structure, the man was meant to earn and the woman to spend. "Today," he wrote, "the wife is the purchaser, almost exclusively and unremittingly. The shops, the streets, and public vehicles of our towns are filled with women; it is they who order goods and keep accounts, they who furnish and provide, they who construct."[15] According to Rathenau, one of the unfortunate outcomes of the growing importance of female consumers was the decline of handicrafts. The woman, he propounded,

lacks appreciative insight for craftsmanship; for the good, the useful, and the genuine; above all for the proportion and artistry. Furthermore, she fails as regards a steadfast will for the essential ... She is influenced by casual stimuli, by a specious appearance of solidity, by bargains, glitter, false reckoning, and by the glib tongue of the salesman. All the worst customs of retail trade are the outcome of the qualities of women purchasers.[16]

Typically, Rathenau does not simply display women as the motor of modern consumerism, but also as victims of modernization. Modern consumer capitalism, he claimed, forced women to take over new duties and responsibilities as consumer. Driven from the seclusion of the home, women were left unprepared to cope with new challenges in the outside world. "The motherly strength of woman's nature," Rathenau further proclaimed, "has not been enhanced by her activities as purchaser, by the life of the streets, by self-determination."[17] As a result, women started developing "meretricious tendencies, previously kept in check by man," thus given rise to a new type of women that Rathenau describes as "masculinized female."[18]

[15] Walther Rathenau, *In Days to Come* (New York: Alfred A. Knopf, 1921), 153.
[16] Ibid.    [17] Ibid., 154.
[18] Ibid. Further to this discourse Mila Ganeva, *Women in Weimar Fashion: Discourses and Displays in German Culture, 1918–1933* (Rochester: Camden House, 2008); Vibeke

Rathenau, whose views were by no means uncommon at the time, does not make special reference to Jewish women. Even when discussing what he describes as "an unedifying product of our civilization," the "woman of luxury" whom he clearly associates with the social life of the newly enriched, he does not make any explicit reference to Jews or Jewish women. Interestingly, these sections of Rathenau's book were reprinted in the Jewish women's journal *Die Jüdische Frau*, turning Rathenau's portrayal of the lust of female shopper into a Jewish matter.[19]

As indicated in previous sections, the pejorative serotype of the female consumer was sometimes seen to challenge the very fabric of the Jewish community. More often than not, women were held responsible for radical assimilation and blamed for the disintegration of tradition. With the growth of modern consumerism and its emphasis on the individual's pursuit of happiness, these debates acquired new relevance in Jewish circles. Long before the introduction of notions like the JAP (Jewish American/Austrian Princess), Jewish women were rebuked for being materialistic, superficial, idle, and, above all, assimilationist. "Luxury animals" (*Luxustierchen*) was what the German Jewish Zionist Hans Goslar called Jewish women. Sholem Aleichem depicted shopping-addicted Jewish mothers and their daughters to mock the Jewish female addiction to consumption in his satirical novel *Marienbad* (first published as a book in 1917).[20] A report in the Warsaw-based Jewish newspaper *Ha-Tsefirah* denounced so-called materialistic and self-centered daughters of Israel for their taste in luxurious clothing and expensive accessories, taste that threatened not only to impoverish their parents but to bring destruction (*shoah*) to the whole Jewish people. Such ostentatious consumption only served to confirm the preconception that "Jews are loaded with gold and money" gained at the expense of the gentiles.[21] In a review

Rützou Petersen, *Women and Modernity in Weimar Germany: Reality and Its Reflection in Popular Fiction* (New York: Berghahn Books, 2001).

[19] "Walther Rathenau über die Frau," *Die Jüdische Frau* 1 (2) (1925), 6.

[20] On the history of the JAP see Riv-Ellen Prell, *Fighting to Become Americans: Assimilation and the Trouble between Jewish Women and Jewish Men* (Boston: Beacon Press, 1999); for an overview of such criticism in the German-speaking context see Kerry M. Wallach, *Jewish Women and the Jewish Press in Weimar Germany*, University of Pennsylvania, PhD. Diss., 2011, 266–271; Susanne Omran, *Frauenbewegung und "Judenfrage:" Diskurse um Rasse und Geschlecht nach 1900* (Frankfurt a.M.: Campus Verlag, 2000), for a broader discussion, David Biale, "Jewish Consumer Culture in Historical and Contemporary Perspective," in: Gideon Reuveni and Nils Römer (eds.), *Longings and Jewish Belongings: The Making of Jewish Consumer Culture* (Leiden: Brill Publications, 2010), 23–38.

[21] "Letters from Gelicia" (in Hebrew), *Ha-Tsefirah* (May 5, 1890), 2.

of representations of Aryan and Jewish women in modern literature, journalist Karl Pinn noted that if Jewish men are rebuked, "not unjustly," as "unscrupulous businessmen," their dance around the golden calf is often depicted as nothing more than an effect of their wives' indulgences in luxuries and external status symbols.[22]

In the British weekly newspaper *The Jewish World*, an author writing under the pseudonym "Gaza" penned a section titled "Through a Woman's Eyes." The writer reproached women who yearned to accumulate wealth under the false premise that money could provide security. "Jewish Women are notorious sinners in this respect," Gaza warned, "I know ever so many young Jewish women who start out ... with the idea that so long as they have plenty of money they can buy everything necessary in life."[23] In her study of the modern Jewess, Else Croner also referred to the relentless "tapping on the purse" (*Pochen auf den Geldsack*) of the modern Jewish woman. This image of the Jewish woman of leisure was commonly constructed as the inversion of the preemancipation Jewess, who was *Gemütlich* and pragmatic.[24] According to Croner "in the soul of the modern Jewess came haste and feverish unrest ... she wants to enjoy ... to be seen and to impress, through the luxury of the accommodation, the lifestyle, the toilet, the pageantry of her celebrations and society."[25] Across the Channel, Gaza made similar observations. "One has but to glance at the female population of the East End to know how Jewesses love conventionality," she wrote in 1926, stating, "I am sure that before a Jewish woman adopts a certain mode of dress, decoration, furnishing, or style, she first makes sure that it is fashionable in the general world."[26]

Although her article acknowledges the social function of fashion as a vehicle of integration, Gaza fears that Jewish women had become "abject slaves of their get-ups," absorbed in a materialistic quest.

---

[22] Karl Pinn, "Arierin und Jüdin in der Modernen Literatur," *Die jüdische Frau* 1 (13) (1925), 14.

[23] Gaza, "Through a Woman's Eyes," *The Jewish World* (April 8, 1926), 8.

[24] Further on this view see Biale, "Jewish Consumer Culture," 23–25.

[25] "In die Seele der moderner Jüdin ist eine Hast und fiebernde Unruhe gekommen ... Sie will genießen ... auffallen, imponieren, durch Luxus der Wohnung, der Lebensweise, der Toilette, Prunk in Festlichkeit und Gesellschaft, im Auftreten und Benehmen ... die jüdinnen von heute sind häufig in dem Irrtum befangen, durch Wichtigtuerei zu imponieren und zu gefallen." Else Croner, *Die Moderne Jüdin* (Berlin: Juncker, 1913), 17–18. For a similar position Emil Bernhard Cohn, "Die jüdische Frau und der Luxus," "Jüdische Haushatungsschulen in Deutschalnd," *Blätter des jüdischen Frauenbundes für Frauenarbeit und für Frauenbewegung* VII (8) (1932), 1–2.

[26] Gaza, "Through a Woman's Eyes" (July 1, 1926), 8.

According to this reading, the excessive, even questionable taste of Jewish women indicates that even if Jewish families made it economically, they would never manage to fully integrate into non-Jewish society. Moreover, Gaza goes on to claim that the materialism of Jewish women poses a palpable threat to the survival of the Jewish race, proclaiming:

I know in my own mind that it is true that Jewish men are spiritual, and that Judaism has an ennobling and uplifting effect on its male adherent. I must candidly confess that, speaking in broad terms, Jewish women are far more materialistic than English women ... I believe the materialism of Jewish women is responsible for large number of exter-marriages, for, as I said before, Jewish men are frequently far more spiritual inclined than are their women folk, and they often find in non-Jewish women those characteristics which attract them just because they do not repel them with their blatancy and coarseness ... That is one of the evils of the materialism of Jewish women ... if the cessation of persecution, reacting primarily upon women, renders them idle voluptuaries lounging amid the ease and comfort of their elegant homes, if their interest can only be exerted by the bedecking of themselves with costly raiment and fine jewellery, if even the care and upbringing of their own children is too much for them ... then I fear that the sons of such mothers will indeed lower the standard of the Jewish race and that we ... will sink to a lower level altogether.[27]

These scolding words echo Martin Buber's famous 1901 speech "The Jewish Woman's Zion," in which responsibility was laid for the decline of her people at the feet of Jewish women. Yet, while Gaza ascribed the materialism of Jewish women to the social position of Jews as a minority group, for Buber it was a matter of the "assimilatory nature" of the Jewish woman: her disposition to adapt to every given situation, notwithstanding the consequences. According to him the dissolution of the Jewish people was greatly augmented by the legal emancipation of Jews. "The drive for self-preservation" of the Jewish woman, he then concluded,

adapted itself to the new life conditions in the same extreme manner as their segregation had previously. Women, who adapt themselves most easily to their environment and its ways, participated in a most lively manner in the evolving fanaticism of assimilation. And because everyone wanted the latest, the internal development of Judaism was paralyzed, all internal drive was stifled, the family destroyed, general solidarity suspended, [and] autonomous culture destroyed.[28]

---

[27] Gaza, "Through a Woman's Eyes" (March 29, 1923), 10–11.
[28] Martin Buber, "The Jewish Woman's Zion," in: Gilya Gerda Schmidt (ed.), *The First Buber: Youthful Zionist Writings of Martin Buber* (Syracuse: Syracuse University Press, 1999), 114.

Like other critics of Jewish women, Buber hoped his harsh words would provoke a more empowering approach to the so-called Jewess question.[29] While Corner regarded the modern situation of Jewish women as a kind of "illness of childhood" which had set in after Emancipation and would be overcome in time, Buber and many of his Zionist followers assigned the modern Jewish woman a key role in the renewal project of Jewish life. Buber's vision of the so-called Jewish renaissance was clearly gender-based. In accordance with his view about the Jewish home as a Jewish national site, Buber suggested that while Jewish men should work on the idea of national unity, Jewish women should restore the living *Volkstum* (tradition) by making their homes more Jewish.[30] This involved decorating their houses with Jewish objects and upholding Jewish customs and rituals. For Buber, the return of Jewish women to the home had the potential to transform the house into a place of distinctive aesthetic style and Jewish practice. This wasn't only a matter of women being the quintessential homemakers, but was based on the idea that "the woman possesses the gift of economic intuition and economic activity to much greater degree than the man."[31] This propensity, according to Buber, made the Jewish woman a more skilled consumer with the talent to make her home a place of Jewish "strength and beauty."[32] In this way, Buber granted shopping a Jewish meaning.

### LEARNING TO SHOP JEWISH

By the beginning of the twentieth century, shopping had become an almost exclusively feminine activity.[33] A rich literature of guidebooks for good housewifery as well as training programs had developed to equip women to be good shoppers and homemakers. In the Jewish context the growing significance of consumption was strongly linked to the forms of Jewish living. "Good shopping" meant meticulous consumption, which was itself a form of income conservation. Thrift was a way of easing the

---

[29] Gustas Löffler, "Geschlechtlichkeit und Sitlichkeit," *Der Morgen* 1 (April 1925), 84–100.
[30] Sharon Gillerman, *Germans into Jews: Remaking the Jewish Social Body in the Weimar Republic* (Stanford: Stanford University Press, 2009), 17–53.
[31] Ibid., 116. On this see also Croner, *Die Moderne Jüdin*, 113–125.
[32] Buber, "Jewish Woman's Zion," 117.
[33] Alice Salomon, *Einführung in die Volkswirtschaftslehre. Eine Lehrbuch für Frauenschulen* (Leipzig: Verlag von B. G. Teubner, 1909), 103–113; Rosa Bodenheimer, "Die Frau als Konsumentin," unpublished manuscript found in Zionist Central Archive A15/1145.

tension between social aspiration and financial pragmatism. According to Marion Kaplan, since Jews were disproportionally involved in commerce, careful domestic money management could compensate for the vagaries of the broader economy and moderate the impact of fluctuating business revenue.[34] Wise spending was in this way seen as a core Jewish value and a prerequisite for stable family life.

As indicated earlier, the women's section of various Jewish newspapers gave advice on how to forge a lifestyle that was simultaneously bourgeois and Jewish.[35] Training programs for young women as well as special home economic schools for Jewish girls were set up in major German cities. Their aim was to teach young women how to run a modern household and to inculcate "an awareness of the special responsibilities of the Jewish woman."[36] The Jewish *Frauenbund* (League of Jewish Woman), in particular, strongly advocated Jewish household education and established training programs even in the countryside, such as the well-known case of the Jewish girls school for home economics in Wolfratshausen (upper Bavaria).[37]

Beyond courses in cooking, cleaning, and sewing, these programs offered training in economics, accounting, and civil and Jewish law, all of which were designed to help women run a more efficient, and a more

---

[34] Marion Kaplan, *The Making of the Jewish Middle Cass: Women, Family, and Identity in Imperial Germany* (New York: Oxford University Press, 1991), 168.

[35] Today we still find in many German Jewish family collections cookbooks as well as advice literature, for example, Elisabeth Freund's booklet *Hausfrau Hilf dir Selbst!* (Stuttgart: K. Thienmamms Verlag, 1930), all of which give an indication of the popularity of the household library among Jews.

[36] Emma Mainz, "Aus der Arbeit der jüdischen Haushaltungsschule," *Gemeindeblatt der israelitischen Gemeinde Frankfurt a.M.*, 2 (5) (January, 1924), 2; "Haudwirtschaftliche Kurse des Jugendamt der Gemeinde," *Gemeindeblatt der deutsch-israelitischen Gemeinde zu Hamburg* 4 (12) (1928), 2; see also "Israelitische Gartenbauschule in Ahlem," *Neuen Jüdischen Monatshefte. Zeitschrift für Politik, Wirtschaft und Literatur in Ost und West* (January 10, 1920), 177–178.

[37] For an overview of their work see "Jüdische Haushatungsschulen in Deutschalnd," *Blätter des jüdischen Frauenbundes für Frauenarbeit und für Frauenbewegung* IX (2) (1933), 9–10, as well as in no. 3 page 7, more generally on the *Frauenbund*, Marion A. Kaplan, *The Jewish Feminist Movement in Germany: The Campaigns of the Jüdischer Frauenbund, 1904–1938* (Westport: Greenwood Press, 1979). On the work of the *Frauenbund* on the land see Ludwig Stern, "Zur Gründung einer jüdischer Haushaltungsschule auf dem Land," *Bayerische Israelitische Gemeindeblatt Nr 11/12* (1925), 216; Kirsten Jörgensen and Sybille Krafft, "Wir lebten in einer Oase des Friedens...," in: *Die Geschichte einer jüdischen Mädchenschule 1926–1938* (Munich: Dölling und Galitz Verlags, 2009).

Jewish, household.[38] Some of these schools even received official recognition as a fully fledged vocational facility, on par with other non-Jewish schools of similar status.[39] In 1925 one school took part in the International Exhibition of Culinary Art in Frankfurt and won a medal and honorary prize for both its "Jewish national dishes" and the festively decorated Friday evening table.[40]

For the Zionist movement, the consumer education of women was an activity with national implications. Beyond their crackdown on all types of *sumptuousness*, Zionists worked hard to persuade consumers in and outside of Palestine to buy the goods of the developing Jewish polity in the Holy Land.[41] Jewish women were not merely called on to run a frugal household bound by Jewish tradition and tasty kosher cooking. They were also expected to express their Jewishness when going shopping. For the pro-Zionist weekly newspaper *The Jewish World*, for example, "the economic duty of every Jewess ... [is] to make every purchase incident on the daily life a brick in the great and wonderful edifice of our nationhood."[42] This exhortation was based on the recognition that consuming was critical in modern times. If the pen, so the article goes, is mightier than the sword, "now we know that the shopping-basket is actually mightier than either of them."[43] In Jewish terms this meant that Jewish women were now seen as holding in their hands a potent and valuable weapon, so that when they purchased Palestine products they

---

[38] Helene Meyer-Stargard, "Zur Rationalisirung der Hauswirtschaft," "Jüdische Haushatungsschulen in Deutschalnd," *Blätter des jüdischen Frauenbundes für Frauenarbeit und für Frauenbewegung* V (4) (1929), 8–9; Otto Driesen, "Die Frauenschule des Phlanthropins," *Gemeindeblatt der israelitischen Gemeinde Frankfurt a.M.* 1 (3) (December 1922), 2.

[39] "Jüdische Haushaltungsschule," *Gemeindeblatt der israelitischen Gemeinde Frankfurt a.M.* 4 (4) (December 1925), 10; Further on the legal status and history of this facility, "Der Beruf der technischen Lehrerin und Gewerbelehrerin," *Gemeindeblatt der israelitischen Gemeinde Frankfurt a.M.* 6 (3) (December 1927), 63, "40 Jahre jüdische Haushaltungsschulr in Frankfurt a.M." 16 (2) (November 1937), 17–18.

[40] "Jüdische Haushaltungsschule," 10.

[41] Ludwig Grünbaum, "Die Frage der Lebenshaltung als Problem der Konsumentenerziehung," *Palästina. Zeitschrift für den Aufbau Palästinas* 19 (10) (1936), 491–497; for more recent work on this topic Anat First and Tamar Hermann, "Sweet Nationalism in Bitter Days: A Commercial Representation of Zionism," *Nations and Nationalism* 15 (3) (2009), 506–523; Hizky Shaham, "'Buy Local' or 'Buy Jewish'? Separatist Consumption in Interwar Palestine," *International Journal of Middle East Studies* 45 (3) (2013), 469–489.

[42] Gaza, "Through a Woman's Eyes" (November 17, 1927), 6.

[43] Gaza, "The Strength of the Shopping-Basket," *The Jewish World* (June 8, 1933), 4.

helped to safeguard the national effort to build a Jewish homeland in Palestine.

But Jewish nationalism was just one reason Jewish women were urged to think about their Jewishness when going shopping. In addition to efforts by the Jewish press to forge a specifically Jewish taste, the rise of antisemitism after World War I significantly shaped Jewish habits of consumption. With the growing number of calls to boycott business owned by Jews, Jewish women necessarily became more conscious of their shopping. The journal *Die Jüdische Frau*, for example, lamented in 1925 that out of indifference, forgetfulness, or simply by accident some Jewish women still did their shopping at businesses known to be antisemitic.[44]

Six years later, the *Centralverein* organized a special action day (*Kulturtag*) on what it depicted as a timely discussion of "fashion, society, and antisemitism."[45] The event took place shortly after the September 12 Kurfürstendamm riots, in which on the Jewish New Year's Day of Rosh Hashanah in 1931 members of the notorious Nazi Stormtroopers (*Sturm Abteilung* – SA) stormed one of Berlin's most elegant shopping streets, smashing the windows of Jewish-owned shops, and attacking passersby who looked Jewish.[46] Leading the discussion were journalist Margarete Edelheim, and the feminist author Ilse Reicke, both of whom addressed the misguided stereotype of the "Kurfürstendamm Jew," arguing that after so many years of economic adversity, by the early 1930s the notion of the Jewish leisure class was nothing but an antisemitic fantasy. Moving to broader questions about the relationship between fashion and modernity, Ilse Reicke deplored the National Socialist's submissive idea of women. As opposed to the Nazi model of the woman as "maid and servant" (*Magd und Dienerin*), Reicke strongly advocated for a modern ideal of an independent, creative, and "in-life-standing" woman. For Riecke, true womanhood (*wahre Frauentum*) depended not merely on good taste and conscious consumption but required a demonstrative act of female emancipation and self-assertion.[47] In Germany at the beginning of

---

[44] Spectator, "Antisemitischer Boykott und jüdische Selbsthilfe: Ein Mahnwort and unsere Frauen," *Die Jüdische Frau* 1 (12) (1925), 4–6.

[45] Dr. E.R.J., "Mode, Gesellschaft und Antisemitismus," *CV-Zeitung* (December 4, 1931), 561.

[46] Hecht Cornelia, *Deutsche Juden und Antisemitismus in der Weimarer Republik* (Bonn: Dietz, 2003), 253.

[47] Margaret Mary Finnegan, *Selling Suffrage: Consumer Culture and Votes for Women* (New York: Columbia University Press, 1999).

the 1930s, such a position rendered consumerism a forceful site for potential female resistance against National Socialism.


### PURCHASING EMPOWERMENT

With the Nazi takeover and the segregation of Jews in Germany, the question of Jewish consumption became increasingly irrelevant. Jewish women and men found themselves forced to do their shopping in a marketplace designated for and run by Jews. While in Nazi Germany the notion of a distinct Jewish consumption became everyday reality, outside of the Third Reich many Jews still grappled with the question of how best to address the persecution of their brethren in Germany. In many places boycott campaigns against German products were organized. Informing such initiatives was the premise that economic pragmatism could suppress ideological convictions. In one of her weekly columns in *The Jewish World*, Gaza reported in July 1933 that Hitler himself had made the illuminating announcement that the bread of the German people must take precedence over ideas, policies, and theories. Gaza commented that "if he had not already banished every intelligent woman into the hinterland of a kitchen where she must be 'tasted and not heard' this very elementary piece of practical politics might have escaped from German lips before now."[48]

Musing over the effectiveness of "economic warfare" against Nazi Germany, Gaza then suggested that a league should be formed of Jewish women who refused to buy German goods. Her motion came in response to what she considered the male dominance of the official boycott movement, which focused its embargo efforts on suppliers rather than consumers. Leading the British boycott campaign at the time was the "Captain Webber's Organization for ending Hostilities to German Jews." In mid-1933, Webber's Organization issued five thousand certificates to shop owners in London and the province, by the signing of which the traders publically declared to "neither buy or sell German goods ... until the Hitler Government renounced its policy of antisemitic persecution."[49]

---

[48] Gaza, "Jewish Women Shoppers League," *The Jewish World* (July 20, 1933), 6–7. Sections of this article were reprinted that next day in The *Jewish Chronicle* (July 21, 1933), 31.

[49] In mid-1935 the organization declared bankruptcy. On the anti-Nazi boycott movement in England see Sharon Gewirtz, "Anglo-Jewish Responses to Nazi Germany 1933–39: The Anti-Nazi Boycott and the Board of Deputies of British Jews," *Journal of Contemporary History* 26 (2) (1991), 255–276.

FIGURE 12.1 Captain Webber's Organization Boycott Campaign Certificates
From: *The Jewish World* (June 1, 1933).

Complementing this initiative, Gaza sought to accentuate the power of
the female consumer by mobilizing Jewish women as a force in the anti-
Nazi campaign. By being conscious about their shopping, demanding
information on the origin of the products on sale, and refusing to buy
German products, Jewish women could reveal to the world their special
character as well as act as a valuable weapon on behalf of the persecuted

FIGURE 12.2  The sign on the car reads: "Stop Persecution. Boycott German Goods. Buy British" The caption to the picture explains "protests by world Jewry against the persecution of their co-religionists in Germany continue unabated. Above shows part of last Sunday's motor-procession which toured London with effective posters."
From: *The Jewish world* (April 27, 1933).

Jews of central Europe.[50] Calling the Jewish boycott, a "holy war," Gaza claimed that "every Jewish woman shopper is a front line soldier in the cause of her brutally attacked and martyred brethren within the German Reich."[51] Through a simple but highly organized and discriminating method of making purchases, she thus hoped that Jewish women would be able to make the struggle against Nazi Germany more effective. By shunning German goods, Jewish shoppers were also patriotically endorsing British products and making a visibly Jewish contribution to the British economy and loyalty to their country. For this reason, slogans that urged consumers to shun German goods were often coupled with an appeal to buy British (Figure 12.2).

The plan for a league of Jewish women shoppers met with almost unanimous support. At the end of 1933, the league was finally founded, with Nellie Maude Guedalla as its president.[52] The league issued graphic materials such as stamps and badges that Jewish shoppers could wear to

[50]  Gaza, "The Strength of the Shopping-Basket," 5.
[51]  Gaza, "Jewish Women Shoppers League," 6; ibid., "Woman of Israel, Strike a Blow for Justice!" *The Jewish World* (July 27, 1933), 6–7.
[52]  Gaza, "A Call We Dare Not Refuse," *The Jewish World* (September 28, 1933), 4. Reports on the imitative could also be found in the "Jewish Boycott of German Goods: Machinery Set Up," *The Manchester Guardian* (November 18, 1933), 15; "Ill-Treatment of Jews in Germany," *Times* (March 22, 1934), 9. On the involvement of the writer Philip Guedalla in the work of the league see Gaza, "Women Declare Holy War," *The Jewish World* (October 19, 1933), 4. See also ibid., "Jewish Women and a Boycott," *The Manchester Guardian* (December 30, 1933), 10.

identify themselves and organized public meetings and special boycott events, to further promote the boycott as a modern weapon in the struggle against National Socialism.[53] All of these activities were regularly reported on by the press.

The women shoppers' league remained active in different forms until the end of the 1930s. Despite its achievements, it never managed to embrace all Jewish women in Britain, or, for that matter, to effectively mobilize the Jewish shopping basket to alleviate the suffering of the Jews under National Socialism. Similar initiatives in Britain and elsewhere also met with limited success. If the idea informing the work of such leagues was that shopping was a "new Amazonian force [that] may yet alter the entire history of our time,"[54] such initiatives faced almost inevitable failure in the face of extraordinary historical and political forces.

Nevertheless, in the 1930s these initiatives offered Jews in Europe a way to express their feelings of fear and indignation in response to an increasingly dire situation. "People must express their feeling or they will burst," proclaimed a prominent member of the Board of Deputies of British Jews shortly after the Nazi takeover at the beginning of 1933.[55] But the boycott of German goods and services not only helped to transform feelings of powerlessness and anger through directed action; it was also conceived as a gesture of self-respect and pride aimed at showing that "the Jew still remains staunch and unshaken against the ravages of his remorseless enemies."[56] In this sense, the consumer struggle against National Socialism helped transform consumption into an activity that was expressive and self-reflexive, a venue in which multiple ways of belonging could be imagined and performed. Being Jewish was, and still is, an integral part of this array of modern identities.

\* \* \*

---

[53] On these activities see, for example, the *Boycott Bulletin* issued by the Jewish representative council for the boycott of German goods and services.

[54] Gaza, "Jewish Women Shoppers Again," *The Jewish World* (August 24, 1933), 5.

[55] Quoted in Gewirtz, "Anglo-Jewish Responses to Nazi Germany," 261.     [56] Ibid.

# 13

# Beyond Consumerism: The Bridge, the Door, and the Cultural Economy Approach to Jewish History

> The Jew has emancipated himself in a Jewish fashion, not only by acquiring money power (*Geldmacht*), but because through him and apart from him money has become a world power and the practical Jewish spirit has become the practical spirit of the Christian nations. The Jews have emancipated themselves insofar as the Christians have become Jews
>
> (Karl Marx, *The Jewish Question*, first published 1844).[1]

Karl Marx approached the "Jewish question" on the basis of the deep realization that even full political emancipation does not entail human emancipation. In Jewish terms, Marx's essay is a challenging and perplexing analysis that could be equally read as a defense for Jewish rights as much as an expression of anti-Jewish bigotry and a vehicle for antisemitic tropes about Jews and money. Seeking to break away from a religious approach to the Jewish question, Marx distinguished between the "Sabbath Jew" and the "everyday Jew," depicting the latter as a modern Shylock driven by the forces of practical need, self-interest, and, above all, money. In a way this book has followed Marx's suggestion to focus on the "worldly Jew," with the important difference that while Marx and his followers have typically been concerned with the accumulation of wealth, this study has looked instead at how Jews spend their money.

Exploring the question of Jewish spending, the twelve chapters of this book offered an initial account of the ways by which consumerism generated and reinforced Jewish notions of belonging, making Jewish consumer culture a decisive factor in the Jewish experience of modern times.

---

[1] This is a slightly amended translation to the one available at www.marxists.org/archive/marx/works/1844/jewish-question/.

The aim of this study, however, was not merely to fill a gap by alluding to the crucial and somewhat neglected axis of consumption, identity, and Jewish history. Instead, by taking a consumerist approach to the history of European Jews, this book has placed the Jewish desire for more belonging in a broader framework: the emergence of modern consumer culture with its manifest tendency to endorse and generate multiple identities. In shifting focus from getting to spending, this study helps to provide a more nuanced understanding of ways in which Jews simultaneously integrated into their surrounding culture and developed their own sense of being different in the tumultuous first half of the twentieth century. Too often, the question of Jewish difference has been reduced to a simple opposition between inclusion and exclusion from the surrounding culture. As I have shown, the tension between simultaneously belonging and being apart is an underappreciated feature of Jewish experience and a critical piece of the puzzle of Jewish difference.

In a wider sense, this approach is part of a broader movement to understand culture on the basis of economic activities. The study of Jewish consumer culture is part of an ongoing attempt to introduce the "economic turn" to Jewish studies.[2] In this final chapter, I explore the conjunction of history, culture, and the economy, beginning with a brief overview of different conceptualizations of the nature of this relationship. By treating the economy as a culture in its own right, I argue, we gain new ways of reading history in general, and Jewish history in particular.

## CULTURE VS. THE ECONOMY

My own interest in the relationship between culture and the economy goes back to my work on reading culture in Germany in the years before the National Socialist takeover in 1933.[3] The standard approach to studying the culture of reading has been to treat it as a formative activity that shaped how people conceived reality and made sense of their lives.

---

[2] Jonathan Karp, "An 'Economic Turn' in Jewish Studies," *AJS Perspectives: The Magazine of the Association for Jewish Studies* (Fall 2009), 8–13; Gideon Reuveni, "Prolegomena to an 'Economic Turn' in Jewish History," in: Gideon Reuveni and Sarah Wobick-Segev (eds.), *The Economy in Jewish History: New Perspectives on the Interrelationship between Ethnicity and Economic Life* (New York: Berghahn Books, 2011), 2–25; as well as, "New Perspectives on the Economy in German-Jewish History," *Transversal: Zeitschrift für Jüdische Studien* 14 (1) (2013), 29–41.

[3] Gideon Reuveni, *Reading Germany: Literature and Consumer Culture in Germany before 1933* (New York: Berghahn Books, 2006).

In the course of my research, I realized that a framework was needed that considered reading as a social activity located in the nexus between intellectual and material culture, between culture and the economy. Situating reading in the space between culture and the economy demonstrated how common thinking about book reading, in particular, is embedded in this process of semantic determinism, presupposing that reading had a unique status as "culture" and a formative activity. Consequently, I began questioning notions of culture and the economy and was particularly intrigued by the nature of their relationship.

Considering books as commodities rather than as vessels of meaning enabled me to explore changing attitudes to the relationship between culture and the economy. While some stressed the cultural value of books and reading, positing that books lay outside material interests, others viewed books as a commodity to be traded on the basis of supply and demand like any other product. Interestingly, both approaches assume that the economy and culture are separate, if not antithetical, realms. Seeing themselves as trapped between the two worlds of economy and culture, book traders and publishers sought to come to terms with the hybrid position of their vocations. By adopting a conceptual framework that viewed books as both cultural and economic capital, they hoped to refute criticism of the book trade from either realm and turn their ambiguous position into an advantage.

Gerhard Menz, head of the School for Book Trade Studies (*Seminar für Buchhandelsbetriebslehre an der Handelshochschule*) in Leipzig, provides the most comprehensive and meticulous such conceptual framework. In an inaugural lecture of 1925, Menz asserted that books were not merely materializations of ideas but were also economic products.[4] The "book economy" (*Buchwirtschaft*), argued Menz, simultaneously constituted a "cultural policy" (*Kulturpolitik*). This special situation also provided the background to Menz's attempt to develop a unique view of the link between the economy and culture – a view that he called *Kulturwirtschaft* or "cultural economy."[5]

Menz took a pragmatic approach to the relationship between culture and the economy. Supply and demand drives the production and

---

[4] A version of the speech was published as Gerhard Menz, "Das Buch als Ware und Wirtschaftsfaktor," *Archiv für Buchgewerbe und Gebrauchsgraphik* 67 (1930), 445–459. See also Friedrich Uhlig, "Zehn Jahre Seminar für Buchhandelsbetriebslehre an der Handels-Hochschule zu Leipzig," *Börsenblatt für den deutschen Buchhandel* 102 (1935), 1053–1057.

[5] Gerhard Menz, *Kulturwirtschaft* (Leipzig: Linder Verlag, 1933).

consumption of cultural goods just like any other goods, and those activities constituted an industry that could be analyzed accordingly. Yet viewing "culture" as an economic activity does not need to imply the removal of the distinction between economic and cultural realms or, for that matter, the diminution of the status accorded to culture. On the contrary, according to Menz's theory of cultural economy, increased production and consumption of cultural goods should bolster the special status of culture. Menz seems to recognize that it is "cultural capital," in the Bourdieuian sense of this term, that determines the status of consumer goods. Hence one of the culture producer's main tasks is to create demand for their goods as cultural capital, which thereby increases their economic capital as well. According to this approach, culture and the economy are treated as interrelated yet distinct domains.

Analyzing this early twentieth-century debate regarding the nature of books brought out the normative dimensions of the relationship between culture and the economy. Not only is it difficult to establish the ontological status of "culture" and "the economy," but more significantly it is important to recognize how the various meanings assigned to these terms inform our perception of the nexus between "culture" and "the economy." In my "reading of reading," culture and the economy emerged as two powerful ideas whose continued use has significant consequences for how we organize and understand the social process.

### CULTURAL ECONOMY

At the time when I was first coming to terms with Menz's concept of *Kulturwirtschaft*, I was unaware that a group of some of the leading commentators on the relationship between culture and the economy had gathered for a special workshop at the Open University in the UK. These researchers, from disciplines such as anthropology, sociology, media studies, and geography, discussed what at first struck me as a very similar notion to Menz's "cultural economy."[6]

Both approaches reject a simplistic "binary opposition" between economy and culture, seeking a third way. However, there are some significant differences between Menz's concept of *Kulturwirtschaft* and the notion of

---

[6] See especially Paul du Gay and Michael Pryke (eds.), *Cultural Economy. Cultural Analysis and Commercial Life* (London: Sage, 2002); Helmut K. Anheier and Yudhishthir Raj Isar (eds.), *The Cultural Economy* (London: Sage, 2008); and, of course, the *Journal of Cultural Economy*, published since 2008.

cultural economy at the beginning of the new millennium. To begin with, Menz's concept is much narrower than the current one. It deals with economic aspects of what scholars and policy-makers today refer to as a "creative economy," "copyright industry," or "cultural industries" (not to be confused with the Frankfurt School notion of "culture industry") – an occupational sector that includes individual artists and self-employed creative professionals, as well as the activities of nonprofit cultural organizations and commercial enterprises engaged in the applied arts.[7] Moreover, Menz's concept hoped to establish a positive relationship between culture and the economy. While he viewed culture and the economy as two distinct yet related domains, he sought to establish a hierarchical relationship between them, granting culture primacy over the economy.

The twenty-first-century notion of "cultural economy" is much broader in scope and challenging in its theoretical sophistication than Menz's. It emerged from what Paul du Gay and Michael Pryke describe as the "cultural turn" in social sciences. This refers both to increasing interest in the production of meaning – as represented by the growing importance of culture, creativity, and knowledge in the economy since the end of the twentieth century – and to the growing awareness of the constitutive role of discourses.[8] Instead of viewing the economy as an ontological "other" to culture, existing prior to and independent of it, the turn to culture suggests that the subjects and the objects of the world are constituted through the discourses used to describe them and to act upon them. Consequently for the British school, "doing 'culture economy' means acting on the premise that economics are performed and enacted by the very discourses of which they are supposedly the cause."[9]

Exposing the discursive nature of the culture/economy dichotomy at first appears to reverse the Marxist model of the superstructure in which the economic domain remains autonomous from and dominant to culture. Yet, in my view, it would be misleading to read the concept of cultural economy simply as a return to the quasi-Hegelian view that culture dominates the economy. For du Gay, Pryke, and others, "cultural economy" is an analytical concept and not another normative conceptualization of the nature of

---

[7] For a detailed bibliography of these areas see Alan Schussman and Kieran Healy, *Culture, Creativity and the Economy: Annotated Bibliography of Selected Sources (2002)*, available at www.kieranhealy.org/files/drafts/creative-economy-bib.pdf (November 15, 2014).

[8] On this see the introductory chapter of du Gay and Pryke, *Cultural Economy*.

[9] Ibid., 6.

the relationship between culture and the economy. Thus, the "cultural economy" approach is much more radical than earlier attempts to determine and fix the relationship between culture and the economy. It calls for the dismissal of this distinction altogether, a distinction that has dominated social scientific thought for the last two hundred years or so.[10]

## THE EMERGENCE OF THE ECONOMY

To fully appreciate this shift toward a discursive understanding of the relationship between culture and the economy, we ought briefly to look back at the history of this disjuncture. In his seminal work *Keywords: A Vocabulary of Culture and Society*, Raymond Williams explores the changing meanings of a set of pivotal term or keywords we use when we wish to discuss central processes of our common lives.[11] There is no need to elaborate here on the shifting meanings and multifaceted uses of the term "culture," which, according to Williams, is one of the two or three most complicated words in the English language. For Williams, it is precisely the polysemism of such terms as "culture" that makes them such powerful ideas.

Interestingly, the term "economy" does not appear as a keyword in Williams's book. It is unclear why until recently the economy escaped the kind of critique to which so many other so-called keywords of modern social discourse have been subjected. Today, however, the central importance of the term "economy" is beyond question. Yet the use of the term to signify the creation and management of wealth, and/or as the totality of the relation of production, distribution, and consumption, is relatively new. As recently as the 1920s, the second edition of Palgrave's *Dictionary of Political Economy* contained no special entry for the term "economy." It used the word only to mean "the principle of seeking to attain, or the method of attaining, a desired end with the least possible expenditure of means."[12]

---

[10] For an illuminating overview of some of the debates over the nature of the economy up to the beginning of the twentieth century see Siegfried Landshut, "Historisch-systematische Analyse des Begriffs des Ökonomischen," in: *Politik. Grundbegriffe und Analysen. Eine Auswahl aus dem Gesamtwerk*, vol. 1 (Berlin: Verlag für Berlin-Brandenburg, 2004), 182–291.

[11] Raymond Williams, *Keywords: A Vocabulary of Culture and Society* (London: Fontana, 1976), 12.

[12] Quoted in: Timothy Mitchell, "Fixing the Economy," *Cultural Studies* 12 (1) (1998), 85.

Historians trace the emergence of the economy as a category in public discourse to eighteenth-century Europe when new concepts of human conduct and the foundations of the social body developed. Based on Albert Hirschman's seminal discussion of the opposition between passion and interest,[13] Susan Buck-Morss, for example, argues that a new understanding of the primacy of economic activity within a polity necessitated the discovery that "such a thing as an 'economy' exists."[14] The translation of a new language and imagery of nature into a vocabulary and set of metaphors for imagining the social body implies that "the discovery of the economy was also its invention."[15] The "economy" emerged as a new discursive object at the same time as did the nation-state and the development of a new understanding of the relationship between people and nature.

The development of economics as a science that aimed to establish certain laws regulating market behavior enhanced the perception of the economy as a self-governing realm for which self-interest and the profit motive provided the ordering force.[16] The economy was more and more perceived as a piece of "nature" in the midst of social life. In the words of Austrian economist Carl Menger, "economic theory is related to the practical activities of economizing men in much the same way that chemistry is related to the operations of the practical chemist."[17] According to Menger, although human beings did exhibit free will, the market could be observed as operating according to "definite laws of phenomena that condition the outcome of the economic activity of men and are entirely independent of the human will."[18]

During the nineteenth century, the age of the bourgeoisie, culture played a constitutive role in the emergence of a distinct economic realm. Culture and the economy came to denote separate if not contending realms. This led

---

[13] Albert Hirschman, *The Passions and the Interests: Political Arguments for Capitalism before Its Triumph* (Princeton: Princeton University Press, 1977); Ibid., *Rival Views of Market Society and Other Recent Essays* (New York: Viking, 1986).

[14] Susan Buck-Morss, "Envisioning Capital. Political Economy on Display," *Critical Theory* 21 (1995), 439.

[15] Ibid. See also Stephen Gudeman, *Economics as Culture. Models and Metaphors of Livelihood* (London: Routledge & K. Paul, 1986); and Thomas L. Haskell and Richard F. Teichgraeber (eds.), *The Culture of the Market: Historical Essays* (Cambridge: Cambridge University Press, 1993).

[16] On this line of thought see especially Jerry Z. Muller, *The Mind and the Market: Capitalism in Modern European Thought* (New York: Alfred A. Knopf, 2002).

[17] Carl Menger, *Principles of Economics*, originally published in 1871, available at http://mises.org/library/principles-economics, 48.

[18] Ibid.

to different attempts to determine and regulate the relations between these realms. Karl Marx's superstructure model that explained the relationship between culture and economy was a salient expression of the ongoing attempt to resolve what was already perceived as a clear division by the mid-nineteenth century. Even Max Weber, who proposed examining economic developments as an offshoot of cultural practices, retains the vocabulary of "culture" and the "economy." In the concluding section of his famous study on *The Protestant Ethic and the Spirit of Capitalism* Weber states that the modern economy, that is, capitalism, had been stripped of its original religious and ethical meaning. In what is by now one of the most quoted lines from his work, he notes that the pursuit of wealth changed from a light cloak that could be thrown aside at any moment to an iron cage from which it was impossible to escape.[19]

This notion of the modern economy as an iron cage became even more prominent in the period between the two world wars. In his famous lecture delivered at the meeting marking the fiftieth anniversary of the Association for Social Policy (*Verein für Sozialpolitik*), Alfred Weber (brother of Max) expressed his concern over what he called the proletarianization of intellectual life. He described the disappearance of benefactors, or patrons, for intellectuals (*Rentenintellektuelle*) and the emergence of the working intellectuals (*Arbeitsintellektuelle*) who were forced to adapt to the forces of the marketplace.[20] No longer was culture able to remain separate from all economic and commercial considerations. Instead, the economy seemed to govern everything.

This so-called economization of culture took many forms. For example, economic vocabulary penetrated everyday discourse in almost all major European languages.[21] Terms like division of labor, interest rates, inflation, or capital suddenly became relevant to the daily lives of millions of people. The stock exchange turned into the barometer of social life, as the "state of the economy" became the pictogram for the modern human condition.[22] Paradoxically, the failure and in some instances even the

---

[19] Max Weber, *The Protestant Ethic and the Spirit of Capitalism*, trans. Talcott Parsons (London: Allen & Unwin, 1976).

[20] Alfred Weber, *Die Not der geistigen Arbeit* (Munich: Duncker & Homblot, 1923).

[21] See, for example, Catherine Gallagher, *The Body Economic: Life, Death, and Sensation in Political Economy and the Victorian Novel* (Princeton: Princeton University Press, 2006); Joseph Vogl, *Kalkül und Leidenschaft. Poetik des ökonomischen Menschen* (Zürich: Diaphanes, 2004).

[22] For example, Bernd Widdig, *Culture and Inflation in Weimar Germany* (Berkeley: University of California Press, 2001).

collapse of economic arrangements facilitated the creation of the economy as a new discursive object governing social life.

This process was sustained and enhanced by the emergence of the ideological states during the period between the wars. Liberal democracy, fascism, and communism made the economy a central interpretive category of human conduct and a vehicle for the reform and management of society. In this period Frederick Winslow Taylor's ideas of scientific management took hold, and John Maynard Keynes developed his work *The General Theory of Employment, Interest and Money* advocating interventionist government policy to mitigate the adverse effects of economic development.[23] In the interwar period, econometrics was developed, that is, the attempt to create a mathematical representation of economic processes as a self-contained and dynamic mechanism.[24] But it was only after World War II that the economy became the principal category of social life and economics the most attractive, most "scientific" discipline, outside the exact sciences. The Cold War contributed significantly to this development. Economic expansion became synonymous not only with the national interest, but with a whole way of life on both sides of the Iron Curtain.

Intellectuals of different political affiliations shared an uneasiness concerning the growing significance of the economy. Assuming the normative dualistic approach to the relationship between culture and the economy, many pointed to the devastating effects of the economy on culture. Perhaps the most well-known critique was launched by members of the Frankfurt school of critical theory. In their seminal work *Dialectic of Enlightenment*, Max Horkheimer and Theodor W. Adorno introduced the idea of a "culture industry" which rendered the masses into conformity by means of mass production and consumption of popular culture. According to Adorno and Horkheimer, modern consumer society is part of the economic system that refuses to utilize available resources to abolish hunger, and instead fully exploit them for mass consumption.[25]

A more refined and for that matter more radical assault on the economization process can be found in the more recent work of the late French philosopher and social critic Jean Baudrillard. Today, Baudrillard

---

[23] Brendan Sheehan, *Understanding Keynes' General Theory* (Basingstoke: Palgrave, 2009).

[24] On this process of the scientification of economies see Philip Mirowski, *Against Mechanism: Protecting Economics from Science* (Totowa, NJ: Rowman & Littlefield, 1988).

[25] Max Horkheimer and Theodor W. Adorno, *Dialectic of Enlightenment* (New York: Herder and Herder, 1972), 113.

observes, capital does not only have to produce goods: "it is [also] necessary to produce consumers ... [and] demand."[26] According to Baudrillard, the breakdown of the seemingly logical relationship between production and consumption created a new order "which is no longer that of either production, or consumption, but that of the simulation of both."[27] For Baudrillard, this shift towards the production of demand represented the beginning of a new postmodern era in which "the principle of simulation, and not of reality" regulates social life.[28]

This sense that the boundaries between culture and the economy were being blurred gave rise to a more novel claim that economic life was becoming "culturalized." Best articulated in Lash and Urry's 1994 *Economics of Signs and Space*, the culturalization thesis suggests that economic and symbolic processes are more than ever interlaced and interarticulated.[29] Lash and Urry point to the growing significance of aesthetics, lifestyle, and postmaterialistic values (e.g., environmentalism or the organic and health food movements) as economic drivers; the increasing importance of nonquantifiable elements such as emotions and morality in business management; and the ongoing growth of so-called copyright and knowledge industries as indications of the growing culturalization of the economy. Based on this analysis, theorist Georg Franck introduced the notion of "mental capitalism" or the "idea-economy." He wrote:

Imagine how the old [Marxist] warriors would rub their eyes if they saw what has happened to the old relationship between basis and superstructure! According to materialist doctrine, the mental superstructure is only a dependent reflex of the material production conditions. This doctrine claimed to have put the idealist worldview, which had been standing on its head, back on its feet. But what are those conditions doing now? They are standing on their head out of their own accord. Idea-economy has taken the lead.[30]

Proponents of the culturalization thesis refrain from making normative judgments on the relations between culture and the economy. Yet by

---

[26] Jean Baudrillard, *In the Shadow of the Silent Majorities* (New York: Semiotex(e), 1983), 27.

[27] Ibid., 52.

[28] Jean Baudrillard, *Selected Writings* (Stanford: Stanford University Press, 2001), 123.

[29] Scott Lash and John Urry, *Economies of Signs and Space* (London: Sage, 1994), 64.

[30] Georg Franck, *Mentaler Kapitalismus: Eine politische Ökonomie des Geistes* (Munich: Hanser, 2005); ibid., *Ökonomie der Aufmerksamkeit. Ein Entwurf* (Munich: dtv, 2007). The quotation is from Georg Franck, *The Economy of Attention*, available at www.to.or .at/franck/gfeconom.htm (November 15, 2014).

asserting the increasing importance of culture in economic life, they uphold the dualism between culture and the economy. This is precisely where the cultural economy approach departs from this version of the culturalization thesis. As explained above, cultural economy is enacted as a poststructuralist form of analysis displaying the economy as a cultural site, and thus refuting the culture-economy dichotomy altogether.

Despite their differences, theorists of the economization of culture and those positing a culturalization of the economy both claim that things are radically different now than in the past. For historians, however, the notion that economic activities are embedded in normative institutional frameworks and cultural practices cannot be a novel claim.[31] It has been more than four decades since historians like E.P. Thompson and Fernand Braudel noted that the economy becomes a historical force only as in so far as it is encoded in culture and interpreted in experience.[32]

### THE BRIDGE AND THE DOOR

Attractive as this notion of cultural economy may be, at this stage it still seems abstract and elusive. Even more problematic is the attempt to eliminate altogether the division between culture and the economy. By abolishing this distinction we are risking a foundational principle of our knowledge, which has helped to organize and exert a sense of control over our world since the Enlightenment.[33] This last point finally points to the title of this chapter, which is based on Georg Simmel's essay *Brücke und Tür* (Bridge and Door).[34]

According to Simmel, part of what human beings do is separate what is related and relate what is separate. The bridge and the door are metaphors for this human predisposition. The bridge connects what is otherwise separate while the door separates what is otherwise joined. By so doing, Simmel noted, a space is unified in itself though separated from the rest of

---

[31] Karl Polanyi, *The Great Transformation* (New York: Octagon Books, 1944).

[32] On this see Richard Bieranacki, "Method and Metaphor after the New Cultural History," in: Victoria E. Bonnell and Lynn Hunt (eds.), *Beyond the Cultural Turn* (Berkeley: University of California Press, 1999), 62–92, here 65f. See also Peter Temin, "Is it Kosher to talk about Culture?" *The Journal of Economic History* 57 (2) (1997), 267–287.

[33] Gavin Jack, "After Cultural Economy," *Ephemera* 2 (3) (2002), 263–275.

[34] Georg Simmel, "Brücke und Tür," *Der Tag. Moderne illustrierte Zeitung*, no. 683, Morgenblatt (September 15, 1909).

the world. Yet the essence of the door is its capacity to open and thereby create a link between the human space and everything that is outside.[35]

With these observations Simmel provides us a useful way to think about different conceptualizations of the interplay between culture and the economy, which can be seen to operate as bridges and as doors – that is, connecting what otherwise seems separate, and separating what is otherwise unified. Yet the bridge and the door are more than merely descriptive of our cognitive styles. According to Simmel things must be separated in order to be together.[36] Instead of imposing general analytical distinctions or dismissing binary oppositions – as differing theorists of the economy and culture have done – we might as well acknowledge that by thinking about culture and the economy, we cannot escape building bridges and placing doors. This does not imply that these notions are mere constructions detached from the "real world," but rather that we should be more receptive as to how these distinctions operate and constantly negotiate the boundaries between these realms.[37] History offers an excellent venue for such an endeavor. This can be illustrated by the following brief discussion of the conjunction between culture, the economy and Jewish history as they relate to four key concepts – trust, risk, circulation, and identity.

## CULTURAL ECONOMY APPROACH TO JEWISH HISTORY

The general image of the Jews is overloaded with tropes and motifs taken from the sphere of economics. Yet, despite the centrality of economics to Jewish life and to the image of Jews and Judaism in modern times, Jewish historiography has generally tended to highlight the religious, cultural, and political aspects of the Jewish past rather than its economic features. In recent years, there has been a slow but steady change in the approach to the economy in Jewish studies. This new interest in Jewish economic history relates to the more general developments discussed above. Our understanding of Jewish history stands to benefit from a cultural approach to the economy. Not merely new areas of research, but new kinds of

---

[35] Michael Kaern, "George Simmel's the Bridge and the Door," *Qualitative Sociology* 17 (4) (1994), 397–412.

[36] Ibid., 408.

[37] Noel Castree, "Economy and Culture Are Dead! Long Live Economy and Culture!" *Progress in Human Geography* 28 (2) (2004), 204–226; as well as the introduction to Hartmut Berghoff and Jacob Vogel (eds.), *Wirtschaftsgeschichte als Kulturgeschichte. Dimensionen eines Perspektivenwechsels* (Frankfurt a.M.: Campus, 2004).

questions will become possible once we place the economy at the center of the Jewish experience.

Take the example of trust, no doubt one of the basic forms of social life and a vital basis for any economic activity.[38] What enabled people to trust each other in historic economic interactions? On what basis did people of differing faiths and ethnic backgrounds come to trust each other enough to do business together? This question is to a large degree still unaddressed by historians of Jewish history. Within this context, the problem of access to credit is a source of exciting questions. The availability of credit in the towns of the early modern period was tied to membership in particular corporations. Central to the honor of the merchants in the central European estate society was the concept of the "merchant's credit." This concept reflected not just the modern sense of creditworthiness, but also depended on an estate-based reputation. A person's creditworthiness was closely identified with his trustworthiness as a member of a certain guild. Since Jews were prohibited from belonging to guilds, what effect did this have on their ability to participate in economic networks of trust and confidence? It appears that since the Jews were bound into the estate system as a quasi-independent guild, their creditworthiness, as well as their economic transactions in general were tied to their identity as Jews. This does not seem to be a peculiarity of the premodern period. Evidence suggests that even in the nineteenth century, Jewish business people were compelled to remain Jewish to access inheritances.

Closely associated with the complex of issues surrounding trust is the matter of economic risk-taking. Jews were commonly regarded as particularly willing to take economic risks even in uncertain businesses. Max Weber's idea of "adventure" or "pariah capitalism" is perhaps the most profound expression of this view regarding the allegedly special Jewish inclination to take risks. Weber developed this idea as a rejoinder to Werner Sombart's work on Jews and modern capitalism.[39] First published in 1911, Sombart presented his so-called *Judenbuch* as a direct

---

[38] On the notion of trust in the economy: Tanja Ripperger, *Ökonomik des Vertrauens* (Tübingen: Mohr Siebeck Verlag, 1998); Ute Frevert (ed.), *Vertrauen: Historische Annäherungen* (Göttingen: Vandenhoeck & Ruprecht, 2003).

[39] On Sombart and Max Weber see Arthur Mitzman, *Sociology and Estrangement. Three Sociologists of Imperial Germany* (New York: Knopf, 1973); Freddy Raphael, *Judaïsme et capitalisme. Essai sur la controverse entre Max Weber et Werner Sombart* (Paris: Presses Univ. de France, 1982); Avraham Barkai, "Judentum, Juden und Kapitalismus. Ökonomische Vorstellungen von Max Weber und Werner Sombart," *Menora* 5 (1994), 25–38; Colin Loader, "Puritans and Jews: Weber, Sombart and the Transvaluators of Modern Society," *Canadian Journal of Sociology* 26 (4) (2001), 635–653.

response to Weber's earlier study *The Protestant Ethic and the Spirit of Capitalism*. Yet while Sombart essentially accepted Weber's approach to the religious sources of modern capitalism, he claimed that everything Weber had ascribed to Puritanism was actually rooted in and more intensively practiced by the Jews. Sombart identified the Jews themselves, as opposed to Jewish culture or religion, as the originators and power-house of modern capitalism because of their alleged racial and physiolo-gical dispositions.[40] Interestingly, Weber set out to defend his thesis not by refuting Sombart's stereotypical depiction of the Jewish economic nature, which he conspicuously accepted as a given, but by reproaching Sombart's concept of capitalism. According to Weber, what distinguishes modern capitalism from its earlier forms is the shift from the mere pursuit of profit to a system that seeks to increase investment by a disciplined organization of labor and rationalization of production.[41] Thus, based on Sombart's characterization of the special "Jewish" form of capitalism, Weber pro-pounded: "The Jews stood on the side of the politically and speculatively oriented adventurous capitalism."[42] Unlike Puritanism, which, according to his analysis, carried the ethos of the rational organization of capital and labor, Jewish economic ethos, Weber argued, was motivated by purely acquisitive instincts, and thus was traditional and not modern.[43]

For Weber, the special nature of Jewish economic activities was a result of their status as a "guest" or "pariah people." Their inferior position in society, he argued, compelled Jews to take more risks in business. As interesting as these observations are, they are not grounded in histor-ical research. In fact we still know very little about Jewish business ventures or about their perceptions of risk. Moreover, according to Mary Douglas and Aaron Wildavsky's classic study *Risk and Culture*, the willingness to take on risk and the fear of risk are aspects of what they regard as a continuing dialog on how best to organize social relations.[44] From this perspective, risk is understood as "a joint product of knowledge

---

[40] Moshe Zimmermann, "The Man Who Preceded Sombart – Ludolf Holst," in: Nachum Gross (ed.), *Jews in Economic Life* (Jerusalem: Shazar, 1985), 245–256.

[41] Gary A. Abraham, *Max Weber and the Jewish Question: A Study of the Social Outlook of His Sociology* (Urbana: University of Illinois Press, 1992), especially ch. 8. For a different view, see Jack Barbalet, "Max Weber on Judaism: An Insight into the Methodology of the Protestant Ethic and the Spirit of Capitalism," *Max Weber Studies*, 6 (1) (2006), 51–67.

[42] Weber, *The Protestant Ethic*, 165.    [43] Ibid.

[44] Mary Douglas and Aaron Wildavsky, *Risk and Culture: An Essay on the Selection of Technological and Environmental Dangers* (Berkeley: University of California Press, 1983), 68.

about the future and consent about the most desired prospects."[45] This implies that if indeed Jews were more inclined to take economic risk and that they were aware of the hazards of these ventures, they were much more embedded in the economic and social system than previously assumed by scholars like Max Weber and many others.

This last point brings us to another instrumental concept in the analysis of culture, the economy, and Jewish history: circulation. The idea of circulation extends beyond the mere exchange or flow of goods and money. Michel Foucault's renowned *Archaeology of Knowledge* has already established evidence of circulation as a fundamental category of early modern science.[46] Foucault's focus was the interdisciplinary discourse on the interchangeable relationship between medicine and economics. Stephen Greenblatt sought to broaden the field of investigation to include social relationships and processes. He formulated the concept of the "circulation of social energy" to expand this analysis beyond the archaeology of western knowledge.[47] This methodical approach is based on the idea that the breakdown of culture and society occurs in different subsections between which a continuous "negotiation" and "exchange" takes place. Through the application of such methods, one is able to create new perspectives on social interconnections, the formation of identities, as well as the relationships between economics and culture. Beyond the question of to what extent Jews participated in this circulation of so-called social energy, another equally fascinating question is the degree to which such theories of circulation correlate with the images of the Jewish intermediator and the wandering Jew.[48]

The somewhat rudimentary discussion above of trust, risk, and circulation suggests that the question of group identity is closely associated with the issues surrounding culture, the economy, and Jewish history. Based on

---

[45] Ibid., 69.
[46] Further on this see Harald Schmidt and Marcus Sandl (eds.), *Gedächtnis und Zirkulation. Der Diskurs des Kreislaufs im 18. und frühen 19. Jahrhundert* (Göttingen: Vandenhoeck & Ruprecht, 2002).
[47] Stephen Greenblatt and Shakespearean Negotiations, *The Circulation of Social Energy in Renaissance England* (Berkeley: University of California Press, 1988).
[48] For an illuminating discussion, see Kirill Postoutenko, "Wandering as Circulation: Dostoevsky and Marx on the 'Jewish Question'," in: Gideon Reuveni and Sarah Wobick-Segev (eds.), *The Economy in Jewish History: New Perspectives on the Interrelationship between Ethnicity and Economic Life* (New York: Berghahn Books, 2011), 43–61; Galit Hasan-Rokem, "Contemporary Perspectives of Tradition: Moving on with the Wandering Jew," in: Nicolas Berg and Omar Kamil (eds.), *Konstellationen. Über Geschichte, Erfahrung und Erkenntnis. Festschrift für Dan Diner zum 65. Geburtstag* (Göttingen: Vandenhoeck & Ruprecht, 2011), 309–331.

Marx's remark that "Judaism continues to exist not in spite of history, but owing to history,"[49] it was initially Marxist scholars who pointed to the connection between economic activity and Jewish identity. In an essay from 1890, the Marxist theoretician Karl Kautsky noted that in the premodern period to be a Jew meant not only to be a member of a particular nation, but also of a particular profession.[50] This notion of a "people-class" was enhanced and further developed by scholars such as Ber Borochov and later Abram Leon in his famous study on the Jewish question written in 1940.[51] The significance of this theory does not lie merely in the association between Jews and certain professions but in the suggestion that Jewish identity and survival is embedded in the economic and social system.

The most prevalent approach today continues to explain the multi-faceted interaction between the economy and Jewish identity in terms of the minority status of the Jews. In his influential study *Economic Structure and Life of the Jews*, the prominent economist Simon Kuznets explains Jewish economic distinctiveness in such terms.[52] "If the economic structure of an entire people is considered to be 'normal,' " Kuznets explained, "then the economic structure of a small and permanent minority must, by definition, be abnormal. If not, a minority would soon lose its identity as a specific group."[53] Kuznets's groundbreaking work put the question of the "normalization" of Jewish economic life, which had played a central role in the history of European Jewry since the eighteenth century, in a new light and emphasized the importance of economics as fundamental to the development and perpetuation of group identity. More recently, Derek Penslar has taken up and further developed this idea.[54] For him, the connection between group identity and economics is beyond question. This relationship applies to all minorities, but especially to the Jews, whose concentration in particular economic sectors provided a structural firewall against the loss of collective identity in the face of rampant modernization and secularization beginning in the eighteenth

[49] Karl Marx, *The Jewish Question*.

[50] Cited in Nathan Weinstock's introduction to Abram Leon, *The Jewish Question: A Marxist Interpretation* (New York: Pathfinder Press, 1970), 38.

[51] Leon, *The Jewish Question*.

[52] Simon Kuznet, "Economic Structure and Life of the Jews," in: Louis Finkelstein (ed.), *The Jews: Their History, Culture and Religion* (New York: Schocken, 1960), 1597–1666.

[53] Ibid., 1601.

[54] Derek J. Penslar, *Shylock's Children: Economics and Jewish Identity in Modern Europe* (Berkeley: University of California Press, 2001).

century. Penslar considers the blurring of contemporary North American Jewry's economic distinctiveness as one of the major challenges facing modern Jewish identity, echoing similar fears about the fate of German Jews in the Weimar years.[55] In the late 1920s, some prominent Jewish social scientists had already expressed serious doubt about whether German Jewry could retain its sense of communal identity after inflation and depression practically destroyed its distinctive social and economic fabric.[56]

Given that the economy has played such a defining role in upholding Jewish distinctiveness and a sense of belonging, can "Jewish economy" illuminate economic life in general? This is another exciting question that future research will need to consider. It is clear that the conjunction between culture, the economy, and Jewish history opens significant new territory for historical study, which I hope this book has helped to illuminate.

* * *

[55] In this context Penslar cites Edna Bonacich and John Modell's study on the economic basis of ethnic solidarity, claiming that "when minorities become like a majority economically, it is difficult to preserve their distinctiveness." Penslar, *Shylock's Children*, 261.

[56] See Alfred Marcus, *Die wirtschaftliche Krise des deutschen Juden. Eine soziologische Untersuchung* (Berlin: Georg Stilke, 1931); Jacob Lestschinsky, *Das wirtschaftliche Schicksal des deutschen Judentums. Aufstieg, Wandlung, Krise, Ausblick* (Berlin: Zentralwohlfahrtsstelle der Deutschen Juden, 1932). More generally on this discourse see Donald L. Niewyk, "The Impact of Inflation and Depression on German Jews," *Leo Baeck Institute Yearbook* 28 (1983), 19–36; Martin Liepach, "Das Krisenbewusstsein des jüdischen Bürgertums in den Goldenen Zwanzigern," in: Andreas Gotzmann, Rainer Liedtke and Till van Rahden (eds.), *Juden, Bürger, Deutsche. Zur Geschichte von Vielfalt und Differenz 1800–1933* (Tübingen: Mohr, 2001), 395–418; Moshe Zimmermann, *Die deutschen Juden 1914–1945* (Munich: Oldenbourg, 1997).

# Index

Abusch-Madger, Ruth, 193
Addison, Joseph, 111
Adorno, Theodor W., 26, 242
Advertisements, xiv, xv, 30, 31, 32,
    35, 44, 147, 150, 167, 199
  American companies, 72
  and consumer culture, 29
  and nationalism, 145–152
  for cooking, 39
  for Jews, 29, 72
  for kosher, 27, 175, 197
  for sparkling wine, 153
  holidays, 63
  marketing campaign, 26
  newspapers, 27, 29,
      30, 50
  religious, 62–65
  target group, 144
  vs editorial pages, 32
  with Star of David, 42–55
Advertising agencies
  Jac. Strenlicht, 58
  Joseph Jacobs Organization, 74
  Rudolf Mosse, 59
Agudat Israel, 166
Alcohol, 18, 23, 196
  war on, 11–14
Alliance Israélite Universelle, 118
Altona, 217
American Jewish Committee,
    179
Americanization, 71
Amsterdam, 162

Antisemitism, xvi, 7, 17, 20, 23, 55, 92, 153,
    173, 199, 210, See also boycott
  and consumer culture, 197
  and the marketplace, xvi, 103, 122–123
  and the social question, 7
  as a cultural code, 4, 22
  in the USA, 71
  pre-1933, 40, 135
  rise of, 197
  World War I, 229
Arendt, Hannah, 23, 26, 27, 88, 97–102,
    171
Aristotle, 82
Aryanization, xiii, 140
Asch, Adolph, 201
Assimilation, 14, 36, 70, 72–74, 92, 164,
    174, 186, 221, 223
Auslander, Leora, xii, 32, 214
Australia, 66
Auto-Club 1927, 142

B'nai B'rith order in Berlin, 56–59, 197,
    198, 215
Bach, Rudi, 191
Bad Salzuflen, 134
Baer, Abraham, 12, 13
Bagel, 79
Bahya ibn Paquda, 88
Bar/Bat Mitzvah, 76, 130, 210, 216
Bar-Gal, Yoram, 160
Baudrillard, Jean, xiv, 242
Bauhaus, 213
Bauman, Zygmunt, 26, 75, 174

Beauty of Zion Wine, 158
Bell, Quentin, 218
Ben Israel, Menasseh, 108–110, 112
Benjamin, Walter, 174
Bentham, Jeremy, 108
Berkowitz, Michael, 156
Berlin, xii, 7, 40, 46, 57, 59, 124, 182, 193, 195, 200, 206
Berliner, Wilhelm, 165, 169
Bern, 219
Bernstein, Elizabeth, 76
Berslau, 192
Biale, David, 78, 101
*Bildung*, 6, 86, 186
  as signifier of Jewishness, 186, 211
Blue Box, 158
Blum, Max, 57
Board of Deputies of British Jews, 233
Borden Company, 72
Borochov, Ber, 79, 112, 249
Borut, Jacob, 135
Boston, 178
Bourdieu, Pierre, xiii, xiv, 26, 106, 130, 131, 150, 190, 195
Boycott, 22, 120
  counter, 136
  economic, 121
  German goods, 141, 230–233
  Jewish-owned businesses, 103
  movement, 230
  strategy, 129
Braudel, Fernand, 244
Breitbart, Siegmund, 44
Bremen, 38, 40
Brenner, Michael, 28
Brewer star. *See* Star of David
British Board of Trade, 184
Brooklyn, 178
Buber, Martin, 189, 225–226
Bublitz, 190
Buck-Morss, Susan, 240
Budapest, 214
Bulgaria cigarette factory, 48–55

Capitalism debate, 8
Captain Webber's Organization, 230
Carlebach, Josef, 36
Carmel wine, xi
Central Association of German Citizens of Jewish Faith. *See Centralverein*

*Centralverein*, viii, 11, 59, 60, 61, 62, 119, 120, 128, 132, 133, 134, 135, 136, 140, 153, 154, 155, 166, 177, 221, 229
Chamberlain, Houston Stewart, 38
Chanukah, 63, 64, 158, 210
Child, Josiah, 110
China, 214
Chlorodont toothpaste, 39
Christmas, 210
Coblenz, Marta, 215
*Coburger Nationalzeitung*, 125
Coffee, 37–39, *See also Kaffee Hag*
  houses, 220
  Café Bauer, 200
  Café Leu, 201
Cohen, Andy, 72
Cohen, Lizabeth, 105
Cologne, 146
Conspicuous consumption, 221
Consumer culture
  ambivalence, 32
  and civil rights, 102
  and identity, 68
  and Jewish history, 29
  and religion, 29
  and the Great War, 55
  capitalism, xiv, 26, 66, 85, 143, 222
  definition, 29
Consumer education, 226–230
Cookbooks, 191, 194
Costera Meijer, Irene, 145
Costs of Jewish living, xvii, 175–183
Croner, Else, 180, 224, 226
Crowell, Oliver, 109
Cultural economy, xvii, 236, 237–239

Daniel, Max, 190
Daunton, Martin, 114
Davies, Christie, 94
de Grazia, Victoria, 105
Delacroix, Eugène, 214
Department stores, xiii, 18–22, 23
  boycott, 22
  Landauer Brothers, 191
  Liberty & Co., 157
  Tietz, 6, 33
  Wertheim, 157
*Der Deutsche Automobil-Club e.V.* (DDAC), 142
Dessler, Eliyahu Eliezer, 86

*Deutscher Verein gegen den Mißbrauch geistiger Getränke* E.V., 12
Dewey, John, 70
*Die Vereinigung traditionell gesetzestreuer Rabbiner*, 215
Dinner parties, 195–197
Dirt and Trash writings, 4–7
Dohm, Christian Wilhelm, 112, 115
Douglas, Mary, 94, 247
Dr. Oetker, xi, 149, 202
Dresden, 17, 48, 49, 52, 53, 58
du Gay, Paul, 238
Duisburg, 36
Düsseldorf, 6

Economic warfare, 230
Edelheim, Margarete, 229
Efron, John, 16
Egypt, 162, 163
Eher, Franz, 53
Elazar, Daniel J., 101
Empire Marketing Board, 149
England, xiv, 109
Erich Hamann (chocolate manufacture), 40

Feuchtwanger, Leon, 141
Fine, Leonard, 78
Finnegan, Margaret, 155
Fischer, Samuel, 10
Fontane, Theodor, 131
Food riots, 179
Ford, Henry, 199
Förster, Paul, 17
Foucault, Michel, 248
France, 33, 187, 214
Franck, Georg, 243
*Frauenbund* (League of Jewish Woman), 227
Frederick the Great, 181
Freud, Sigmund, 89, 93
Fromm, Erich, 88

Galicia, 209
Gaus, Günter, 98, 99
Gaza (journalist), 224, 230
Gellately, Robert, 20
German Social Democratic Party, 13
Germany, xiv
    animal protection, 14
    antisemitism, 3
    book culture, 10

consumers, 31
Enlightenment, 86
First World War, 11
*Gemütlichkeit*, 214, 215
    holiday in, 131
    national interest, 139
    Nazi, 230
    pre-1933, xv
Gestapo, 142
Gift-giving, 210
Gitelman, Zvi, 101
Goffman, Erving, 144
Gold Medal Flour, 72
*Goldene Medinah* ('land of Gold' or 'golden land'), 69
Goldschmidt, Moses, 213
Google Jew, 76
Göring, Hermann, 17, 53
Goslar, Hans, 223
Gotha, 16
Graetz, Heinrich, 95
Great Arab Revolt, 170
Great Depression, 177
Greenblatt, Stephen, 248
Gutman, Herbert, 178

Halter, Marilyn, xii
Hamburg, 49, 99, 203, 213, 217
Happiness, xv, 74
    and the marketplace, 84
    definition, 82
    Jewish concepts of, 85–89
    material wealth, 87
    World Database, 83
Hartog, Carl, 195–197
*Haskalah*, 205
Heidegger, Martin, 97
Heine, Heinrich, 43
Heinze, Andrew R., xii, 71
Helgoland, 131
Herzl, Theodor, 156, 166
Hexagram. *See* Star of David
Hildesheimer, Hirsch, 200
Hilton, Matthew, 114
Hirsch, Henriette, 200, 203–205, 206–209
Hirsch, Samson Raphael, 86, 209
Hirschfeld, Isidor, 131
Hirschman, Albert, 83, 107, 110, 240
Hitler, Adolf, 37, 135, 141, 230
Hoeflich, Eugen, 197
Holland, 114

Hollandär, Ludwig, 177, 221
Holocaust, xvi, 78, 171, 203
Home economic schools, 227
Horkheimer, Max, 242
Household expenses, 184–186
Hyman, Paula, 178

Insurance, 60, 64, 164
  businesses, 153, 164
    Allianz, xii
    Phönix Life, xii, 163–171
    Swiss *Basler*, 165
  department of the JNF, 163
Israel, xiv, 67, 171
  consumer culture, 79

J. S. Fry & Sons chocolate company, xi
Japan, 214
Jewgle. *See* Google Jew
Jewish Museum Berlin, 77, 195
Jewish National Fund (JNF), 157, 158, 165,
    166, 167
  insurance, 167, 169, 171
Jewish press. *See* Newspapers
Jews, ix
  "real", 208
  alcohol consumption, 13
  ambivalence, 32
  and business practices, ix
  and capitalism, x, 246–247
  and family life, 164
  and holidays, 63, 161
  and money, ix
  and non-Jews, 76, 88, 169, 189, 192, 209,
    211, 219, 220
  and objects, 210
  and taste, 187, 209
  and the economy, 108–111
  as cattle traders, 139
  as holidaymakers, 129–135, 199
  *as homo economicus*, 110
  as modernizers, 111
  as moneymakers, x, 184
  belonging, 29, 66, 179, 201, 234
  boycott, 121, 124–129
  boycotts by, 136–138
  city, 197
  comfort food, 200–202
  consumer choices, 210
  cookbooks, 35, 72
  costs of Jewish living, 175–183

Diaspora, 164
  economic history, 248–250
  economic rationale, 179
  economic sensibilities, xvi
  emancipation, xv, 4, 29, 69, 80, 102,
    105–107, 112, 116, 118, 130, 182,
    215, 225, 226
  Germany, 192
  home, 206–209
  humor, 91–96
  identity, 23, 27, 78, 171, 174
  in America, 68–71
  in the publishing world, 6
  integration, 186, 211, 225
  Jewish consumers, xiv, xviii, 27, 35, 39,
    72, 173–174, 190
  Jewish Question, 67, 78
  liberal, 221, 222
  marketplace, 62
  music, 39
  non-Jewish, 28, 109
  Orthodox, xi
  privileged, 100
  Sephardic, 213
  spending, 184–189, 218, 220, 227
  style, 211–216
  taxes, 181
  under National Socialist, 138–143
  virtual, 77
  Yiddish-speakers, 69
JNF. *See* Jewish National Fund
*Judenporzellan (Jewish porcelain)*, 181–183

Kaffee Hag, xi, 37–39, 40
Kallen, Horace, 70
Kant, Immanuel, 83
Kaplan, Marion, 186, 227
Karp, Jonathan, 111, 114
*Kartel Jüdische Verbindungen* (Federation
    of Jewish Fraternities), 198
Katzenstein, Simon, 13
Kautsky, Karl, 249
Keren Hayesod (the Foundation Fund), 168
Keynes, Maynard, 242
Kimchi, Dov, 158
Kirshenblatt-Gimblett, Barbara, 203
Klemperer, Victor, 192–193, 213
Kosher, xi, 33
  certificate, 33, 175
  cheesecake, 75
  chocolate, 36, 147

coffee, 37, *See also* coffee
consumption of, 197
cooking, 228
costs, 177, 179
household, 193
market, 75
meat riots, 179
non-kosher, 194
supervision, 75
Kosmin, Barry, 180
Kraemer, David, 194
Krenter, Salomon, 48
*Kunerol Werke* (margarine
manufactures), 44
Kurfürstendamm riots, 229
Kuznets, Simon, 249

Lagerfeld, Ilse, 48
Laissez faire economy, 117, 119
Laqueur, Gerda, 192
Lash, Scott, 243
League of Jewish women shoppers, 232
Leon, Abram, 249
Levy's Rye Bread, 76
Lewald, Fanny, 188
Liebermann, Max, 214
Lipton, Betty, 193
London, 107, 157, 198
Luxury, 218–222
women, 223
Luzzatto, Simone, 109

Maisel beer, 45
Margarine, 42, 44, 150, 175
Hadassah, 36
Tomor, xi, 33–36
Marketplace, 27, 32, 42, 44, 117, 173
ambivalence, 42
and civility, 107–108
antisemitism, xvi, 122
citizenship, 112–117
free, 116
identity, 190
Jewish, 62, 117–121
moderation, x
multiculturalism, 78
tolerance, 138
Zionism, xvii
Marx, Karl, 234, 241, 249
Mason, Jackie, 75
Maxwell House Coffee Haggadah, 72, 74

May, Karl, 5
Mayer, Henrietta, 195
Meat riots, 177–179
Melbourne, 193
Mendelssohn, Moses, 106, 112–117
Menger, Carl, 240
Menz, Gerhard, 236–237, 238
Mercedes-Benz, 31, 149
Mill, John Stuart, 82
Miller, Michael, 22
Minz, Leo, 61
Montefiore, Charlotte, 100
Montesquieu, Charles de, 110
Moscow, 157
Multiculturalism, 25, 78
Munich, 54, 124

Napoleonic era, 68
National Socialism, 44
advertisements, 149
and the marketplace, 123
rise of, 121, 140
struggle against, 233
women, 229
Nelson, Benjamin, 108
Nestlé, xi
Netherlands, 214
New Objectivity, 212, 214
New York, 37, 46, 68, 73, 177, 182, 202
New York Giants, 72
New York Times, 178
New York Yankees, 72
Newspapers, 7, 33, 194, 202, 227
and advertisements, 30
editorial, 30
in coffee houses, 200
insurance, 164
Nazi, 53
titles
*Allgemeine Zeitung des Judentums*, 117
*Augsburger Allgemeine Zeitung*, 43
*Berliner Tageblatt*, 60
*CV-Zeitung*, 59, 60, 61, 62, 133,
135, 177
*Der Israelit*, 39, 56, 60, 145
*Der Stürmer*, 54
*Die Jüdische Frau*, 215, 229
*Die jüdische Presse*, 200
*Die Neuzeit*, 117
*Die Tat*, 9
*Die Welt*, 124

Newspapers (cont.)
  Forverts (Forward), 74
  Gemeindeblatt der jüdischen
    Gemeinde zu Berlin, 61
  Ha-Tsefirah, 223
  Im deutschen Reich, 59
  Israelitische Familienblatt, 158
  Jewish Chronicle, 145, 147
  Jüdische Rundschau, 60
  Jüdisches Adressbuch für Gross-Berlin
    (Jewish Address Book for Greater
    Berlin), 198
  Menorah, 212
  Ost und West, 61
  The Jewish World, 156, 181, 191,
    224, 228
  The Jewish Year Book, 198
  Völkischer Beobachter, 50
  Westdeutscher Beobachter, 6
  Yiddish, 72
Nord, Philip, 20
Norderney, 131

Oppenheim, Moritz Daniel, 35, 209

Palestine, 118, 162, 164, 166, 170, 228
Palestine products, 228
Palestine shops, 157
Palestine Wine, 158
Paris, xii, 43
Pennell, Joseph, 209
Penslar, Derek, 120, 249
Peter Walker & Son brewery, 145
Philippson, Ludwig, 117–119
Pinn, Karl, 224
Pissarro, Camille, 214
Pleckon, Elizabeth H., xii
Plesch, János, 214
Poland, 161
Pollack, Herman, 211
Porcelain, 45, 181, See also Judenporzellan
Portland, 74
Posen, 12, 201
Prinz, Joachim, xvii
Proust, Marcel, 203
Pryke, Michael, 238
Pschorr brewery, 53

Rahden, Till van, 56
Rathenau, Walter, 222–223
Reemtsma Company, 49

Reemtsma, Phillipp F., 50, 53
Reich Federation of Jewish Front Soldiers
    (RJF), 166
Reicke, Ilse, 229
Rembrandt, 214
Rich, Rachel, 174
Riesser, Gabriel, 116, 117
Risk, 246–247, 248
  commercial, 164
Roselius, Ludwig, 37, 39
Rosenstein, Conrad, 201, 216
Roth, Cecil, 219
Rudhart, Ignaz von, 116
Ruppin, Arthur, 14, 180, 192, 202
Russia, 13, 185

S. Fry & Sons, 146
Sabbath, 95, 206
  candles, 207
  Jew, 234
  oneg, 96
Sacramento, 74
Sallis-Freudenthal, Margarete, 194
Salomon, Albert, 182
Schatz, Boris, 157
Scherk, Ludwig and Alice, 46–48, 188
Schipper, Yitzhak (Ignaz), 94, 95
Schnur, Harry Carl, 53
Schöck, Stephan, 13
Scholem, Gershom, 42
Seminar für Buchhandelsbetriebslehre an
    der Handelshochschule, 236
Shakespeare, ix
Shehitah (Jewish ritual slaughter), 16
Shipping companies
  Hamburg-Amerika-Linie (HAPAG), 40,
    162
  Lloyd Triestino, 162
  North German Lloyd, 40
Shlain, Tiffany, 78
Sholem Aleichem, 92, 95, 223
Sidgwick, Cicely, 210
Simmel, Georg, 23, 24, 66, 244–245
Skorra, Thekla, 182
Slater, Don, 144
Smith, Adam, 114, 123
Sombart, Werner, 8, 246, 247
South African, 141
Star of David, 42–55, 77
Stern, Selma, 215
Stolz, Josef, 194

Storm-trooper (SA), 52, 229
Straus, Raphael, 120
Strauss, Herbert, 213
Stuttgart, 191
Sumptuary regulations, 216, 218–221
Switzerland, 198
Sznaider, Nathan, 80

Talmud, 188
Taylor, Fredericj Winslow, 242
Teuscher, Simon, 219
Thomas, Hans, 9
Thompson, E.P., 244
Tietz, George, 59
Tietz, Leonhard, 6
Tirosh-Samuelson, Hava, 85
Trust, 245–246
*Tryfa* (strictly not kosher), 192

Urry, John, 243
Usury, 108

Vajda, Béla, 43
Van den Bergh, Simon, 33
Van den Bergh(food manufactures), xi, 35
Venice, 109
*Verband Deuscher Schokolade-
    Fabrikanten*, 146
*Verein für Sozialpolitik*, 241
*Verein jüdischer Hotelbesitzer und
    Restaurateure e.V*, 137
*Verein zur Förderung rituelle Speisehäuser*,
    136, 198
Vienna, 46
Volkov, Shulamit, 3, 4, 18, 21, 28, 87, 123
Voltaire, 107

Wagner, Richard, 15, 38
Wandsbek, 217
Warsaw, 223
Weber, Alfred, 241
Weber, Max, 217, 241, 246–247, 248
Weber, von Ernst, 15

Weissman Joselit, Jenna, xii, 74, 216
Weizmann, Chaim, 79
*Westdeutsche Nahrungsmittelwerke
    mbH*, 36
Wex, Michael, 88, 92
Wiener, Alfred, 120
Wieser, Max, 10
Wildavsky, Aaron, 247
Williams, Raymond, 239
Williams, Rosalind, 19
Wobick-Segev, Sarah, 200
Wolf, Benedict, 146
Wolf, Rebekka, 194
Wolfratshausen, 227
Women, 8, 13, 19, 62, 87, 178, 188, 210
    and assimilation, 223, 225
    and boycott, 127, 129, 230–233
    and the meat riots, 178
    as consumers, 127, 180, 222–226, 233
    as homekeepers, 186–189, 226
    as initiators of consumer culture, 9
    emancipation, 188, 229
    hairstyle, 215
    in the restoration era, 215
    masculinized, 222
    National Socialism, 21
    spending, 186
    suffrage movement, 155
Württemberg, 140
Würzburg, 45, 213

Yemen, 220
*Yishuv* (Jewish settlement in Palestine), 185

Zangwill, Israel, 69, 70, 92
Zionism, 60, 79, 80
    and consumer culture, 80, 155–163
    and normalization, 81, 112
Zionist movement, xvi, 43
    congress, 169
    consumer education, 228
    insurance, 163–171
    leaders, 163, 171